BUSHVILLE WINS!

ALSO BY JOHN KLIMA

Willie's Boys: The 1948 Birmingham Black Barons, the Last Negro League

World Series, and the Making of a Baseball Legend

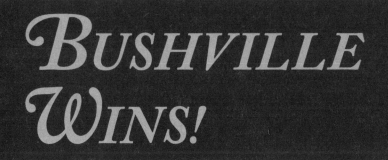

BUSHVILLE WINS!

The Wild Saga of the 1957 Milwaukee Braves and the Screwballs,

Sluggers, and Beer Swiggers Who Canned the New York Yankees

and Changed Baseball

John Klima

Thomas Dunne Books
St. Martin's Press 🏛 New York

THOMAS DUNNE BOOKS.
An imprint of St. Martin's Press.

BUSHVILLE WINS! Copyright © 2012 by John Klima. All rights reserved. Printed in the United States of America. For information, address St. Martin's Press, 175 Fifth Avenue, New York, N.Y. 10010.

www.thomasdunnebooks.com
www.stmartins.com

Design by Omar Chapa

ISBN 978-1-250-00607-3 (hardcover)
ISBN 978-1-250-01514-3 (e-book)

First Edition: July 2012

10 9 8 7 6 5 4 3 2 1

To underdogs everywhere

CONTENTS

We played in a city like Milwaukee, who each night had 40–45,000 people at the ballpark, and they went out for one thing—to see the ball club be successful.

—HENRY AARON, 2011

PART I

THE SHIFT

1

DAVID VERSUS GOLIATH

Lou Perini's secret weighed on him like the water pails he once hauled on his father's work crew. He had a plan so extraordinary he dared tell nobody, not breathing a word to his wife, his seven children, or the Jesuit priest who routinely passed him while he whispered his daily rosary. But on the morning of March 14, 1953, when Perini emerged in the lobby of the Dixie Grande Hotel after an exhaustive all-night planning session, his tousled hair and crooked collar were barely a shade better kept than the Boston sportswriters. Perini had a blueprint for the future so bold that it was going to change baseball forever.

Perini was a forty-nine-year-old bulldozer of a man, the firm son of Italian immigrants and American prayers and dreams, born and raised on Boston baseball. He had an eighth-grade education but possessed a natural ability for engineering and an obsession with efficiency and productivity. The game was his passion but being president of his family's construction company was his profession. He inherited the business from the father who taught him humility, equality, and togetherness by requiring him to haul water pails for workers on steaming hot summer days. His father, Bonfiglio Perini, had arrived in America with nothing, scratched his name into the Ellis Island registry, and clawed his way to the top. He insisted his sons speak English and he taught them to appreciate all people and to believe that wealth should never equal tyranny. After Bonfiglio died, Louis built the local family construction business into an international corporation, with savvy befitting a tycoon and the humble gratitude of a man of God.

For all the highways and bridges, and subways and runways that Perini built, almost nothing meant as much to him as building his baseball team, the Boston Braves. He saw baseball as a bridge to a better world. There were two teams in Boston then—the Red Sox and the Braves. The wealthy Red Sox were never for sale; the impoverished Braves were. So in 1944, Perini and two of his construction pals bought into the dream. Perini's first significant move was to fire manager Casey Stengel. Fast with a quip and slow with a win, Casey lived in sixth place. Perini wanted to die in first.

Perini and his partners were nicknamed the "Three Shovels," and even though the Braves made it to the 1948 World Series, there wasn't enough money in Boston to dig the Braves out of obscurity. They went from bad to worse, their ballpark was a plywood dump in the wrong part of town, and their players weren't much better. Their fan base was going strong on the nostalgia of the 1914 World Series champ "Miracle" Braves. Memories were plentiful but ticket sales were poor. Perini used to bring his family to the ballgames just to help fill the stands. The fans were few and dying, so Perini bought out his partners and began plotting the path to save the Braves.

He was never happy unless he was building, but he wasn't happy building from the boardroom. He abhorred silk suits in favor of heavy wool and wore the same cheap necktie until it was so worn that his wife made him throw it out. But when it was time to do business, Perini became a bulldozer. He moved ideas and men and he plowed them over if they stood in his way. But Perini never saw himself as a bully. He invested heavily in a charity he created called the Jimmy Fund. He was a former sandlot catcher who wrote large checks for football stadiums and donated large sums of money to amateur sports programs. Sports were for dreamers and offered paths to new lives. Perini understood that nobody wanted to be on the bottom forever. Baseball offered a wondrous opportunity for equality and a fertile proving ground for the underdog.

When Perini barreled into the lobby of the Dixie Grande that spring training morning in Florida, he was the underdog. The Boston sportswriters thought Perini must have made a big trade. They were right in one sense—Perini was making a trade, but not for a player. He was about to let the world in on his secret and blow up tradition.

"This was a difficult decision to make," Perini announced. "But we've made up our minds to take the team into Milwaukee."

Perini was furiously trying to keep control of a plan he devised in 1950 and hoped to execute in 1954. But time and circumstances were working against him. If Perini was going to save his dying franchise, the time had come to plow the earth. The dumbfounded Boston sportswriters peppered Perini with questions. He avoided the details because he didn't have time, and the transaction was complicated. Baseball writers knew how to handle big news about ballplayers, but this was something else. They were exploring factors none of them had experience with. Instinctively, they resented that an outsider like Perini defied the baseball establishment. They felt entitled to the scoop and were furious and insulted that he hadn't warned them the day before, when he had denied the rumors of the Braves leaving Boston. "When I said it I meant it," Perini shot back. "I was sincere but things came up that make it necessary for us to move."

The world sighed in unison: why Wisconsin? The Milwaukee Brewers had been a minor league team since 1902, one stop below the big leagues in classification, and a few dozen steps lower in national respect. They had a short stint as a National League team seventy-five years ago, but that was before the modern majors existed. In 1950, a dozen American cities were larger. Milwaukee's population of 600,000 was less than one-tenth of New York City's seven million. Why would Perini betray the proud Boston baseball tradition in favor of the Germanic Midwestern city they knew only by stereotype? For many across the country, Milwaukee was the train station on the way to Chicago—a fine place for a trip to the restroom, a bratwurst at a minor league game, and a cheese wheel. Old European prejudices prevailed and archaic images of gruff German and Polish working sloths who could barely say "Ticket, please" in proper English came to mind.

As an Italian in an Irish town, Perini had grown up around that sort of ethnic discrimination. It motivated and guided his conscience. He was a man for the people, especially when it made good business sense. But Perini also believed this was about more than money. For months, he had saturated himself with Milwaukee research. He collected maps and studied its civic planning. He understood its economy and grasped the huge financial component. And he invited a special guest over to the family home in Boston for dinner. "I remember coming home from school a few times and Fred Miller was at the house," Lou's son, David, remembered. "My dad just introduced him as Mr. Miller from the Miller Brewing Company of Milwaukee, Wisconsin. I wasn't sure who he was or why he was there."

Perini wasn't surprised that the Boston writers were crushing him. They used to call him Lovable Lou, but not this time. Perini knew the writers hated his decision, but he wasn't afraid to fight. The Boston Braves were losing $30,000 a week and losses exceeded one million dollars in both 1951 and 1952. The Boston Braves had been established in 1876, but couldn't compete emotionally or economically with the Red Sox. On mantels from Connecticut to Maine were framed images of Jesus Christ and Ted Williams, though which one walked on water first was debatable. The Braves' most popular player was Warren Spahn, a young left-handed pitcher, whose box-office draw was limited to once every four games, and then only at home, where Braves Field's finest delicacy, fried clams, wasn't enough to compete with storied Fenway Park. Perini felt the pinch when Braves attendance bottomed out at 281,000 in 1952, his ball club so pathetically dismal and lacking energy that the home plate umpire jumped a train home before the end of the last game of the season.

That morning at the Dixie Grande, nobody saw Perini as a visionary. Always gregarious and warm to the press with a drink and a sandwich, Perini found himself on the defensive. "Maybe Milwaukee isn't a major league city now," he said. "But I feel it will become one." He broke up the news conference and hustled for the elevator. The Boston writers rushed to the pay phones to call their news desks, quickly dictating breaking news copy. The elevator couldn't arrive fast enough for Perini, who hadn't slept, and had no time to rest. Imploding baseball history was no small project, and at that moment he could have used his favorite hard hat and a cool drink of water. But this announcement was only the first shovel in the dirt on the way to building a much larger vision of what baseball was going to look like in the twentieth century and beyond.

Perini's plan bridged the game between the Victorian era and the modern age, between wooden ballparks and steel stadiums, between tradition and geography and between mom-and-pop ownership and corporate entities. He had sparked a seismic shift that within a decade caused relocation to Los Angeles and San Francisco, expansion beyond the original sixteen teams, and the increased influences of television, technology, travel, and commerce. He dreamed of a baseball team with Blacks, Latinos, and hard-edged, American country good old boys working together for the common good.

Perini believed that baseball could help him achieve what his father believed in—an equal society. A corporation could make a killing and simultaneously benefit the middle class to achieve harmony between the wealthy and the workers. He refused to take away who they were and strove to enhance them. Perini loved the utopian idea of balance between race, class, economics, occupation, and education. Baseball was his concrete and Wisconsin was his land.

Over the next five days, Perini had much work to do. He sifted through telegrams from the mayor of Boston and the governor of Massachusetts begging him to keep the Braves in Boston, but he refused to cave to civic pressure. "Somebody has to tell me why this isn't a good move," he said. "I'm sick of pounding my head against a stone wall. This is no sudden thing. I've known for two years that it was inevitable. Boston is simply not a two-club city."

But moving to Milwaukee was not a one-man job, either. Perini needed a business partner to get this done. He found one in Fred Miller who, like Perini, was an immigrant's son who had grown his father's local company to national levels. Miller loved the thrill of competition and yearned to bring big league baseball to Milwaukee. He played nose tackle at Notre Dame, where legendary football coach Knute Rockne inspired Miller's leadership style. Miller emerged as a chairman who believed in people as well as profits. But he also knew he needed to make Milwaukee more economically influential if he wanted to make the cash flow like the beer. So he dreamed big, spent bigger, and held pep rallies. He initiated a corporate expansion program in 1947 with sports as the centerpiece, launching company softball and baseball teams, organizing group outings to baseball games, and plastering the Miller name inside taverns from one end of Wisconsin to the other. He was determined to bring major league baseball to Milwaukee and to forever connect the Miller brand with the strong civic pride that would assuredly arrive with a major league team. To prove Milwaukee was a major league town, he was influential in the construction of County Stadium. Miller's blueprint between beer and baseball would be emulated around the country, but he had to entice a team to move to Milwaukee first.

Miller had two choices: the National League's Braves or the American League's St. Louis Browns, the worst team in each division. He was also picking which owner's personality fit his plans best. His preference was Perini, who owned territory rights in Milwaukee because he had wisely purchased the Brewers in 1946 and stationed the Braves top Triple-A team there. Ownership of the Brewers gave Perini the right of first refusal to move into Milwaukee's new stadium or to block anyone else from moving in.

Miller's other option, Bill Veeck, never dreamed that the tidy profit he turned on the sale of the minor league Brewers in 1945 would come back to haunt him when the next owner sold the team to Perini a few months later. Veeck desperately wanted back into Milwaukee, where he had owned the Brewers in the 1940s, especially when Milwaukee County began building the ballpark in 1950, spending millions to fund the project. Perini helped Milwaukee work around the steel shortage caused by the Korean War to build the country's first postwar ballpark. Miller saw the excitement that building the new ballpark caused and believed the city was ready for major league baseball.

The citizens sensed the big leagues coming. Along with the rest of the city, Bobby Uecker, then eighteen and an aspiring big league catcher, watched the new stadium rise above the downtown skyline, a modern marvel amid the smokestacks, and thought there was no way this palace could possibly be for the Brewers. "This couldn't be a Triple-A park," Uecker said. "People used to drive past the ballpark as it was being built, just to say, 'Holy Jesus, look at this place!'"

When Milwaukee County Stadium was ready to open in time for the 1953 season, Miller wanted the Boston Braves immediately but Perini thought it was a year too soon. That wasn't good enough for Miller. Anxious to never have a minor league team play in Milwaukee's new stadium, Miller invited Veeck's St. Louis Browns to move in for the 1953 season instead, but because Perini controlled the territory rights, he exercised his power to block the move. That infuriated Wisconsin.

Miller let the people scream for him, and the implication was clear: he would never forgive Perini for blocking the Browns. For the first time, Perini felt the ire of the Wisconsin people, who turned on him for depriving them of a major league team. Perini never forgot the note from the twelve-year-old Milwaukee girl who closed her letter by writing "I hate you!" In their anger, Perini saw their passion and pride, and he decided he would rather be with the people of Wisconsin than against them. Unwilling to jeopardize his relationship with Miller and alarmed that he had so antagonized the Wisconsin people, Perini decided on that March morning that the Braves would speed up their plans and move now.

The Wisconsin people were jubilant when they heard the news. Their anger turned to love, and Perini was happy to have the support of Miller and to be on the right side of Wisconsin's fierce independence. The city threw a big party, "like World War II was over," said Uecker.

But one major obstacle remained. Perini needed the approval of National League president Warren Giles and the seven other team owners. He knew he couldn't win the vote without Miller backing him. He asked Miller to call Giles and voice his support for the new Milwaukee Braves. Miller appealed to the Milwaukee public and the next morning Giles had 116 telegrams waiting for him, including one from the statehouse in Madison, where Gov. Walter Koehler urged:

A MATTER OF TREMENDOUS IMPORTANCE TO THE STATE OF WISCONSIN
AND THE CITY OF MILWAUKEE. I SINCERELY HOPE THAT THE INTEREST
OF THE PUBLIC WILL NOT BE OVERLOOKED.

Perini needed all the muscle he could get, because he was seeking permission to do the unprecedented. Though comparatively new to baseball politics, Perini understood how old boys operated. If he was going to ask them to change the way the game had always been structured, he had better have a lot of money ready to come into the league. Perini could build all the highways he wanted, but he knew that nothing whetted the appetites of owners like cash.

On March 18, 1953, Perini's pitch lasted an hour. Behind closed doors, he argued that baseball could not survive in its present state. That the Red Sox were squeezing the Braves out of Boston was only a symptom of the gross inequity Perini believed existed. He argued that too much power and money was in New York City, and that too much of it belonged to the Yankees, which was not only to the detriment of the Braves, but to the New York Giants, the Brooklyn Dodgers, and the National League as a whole. Perini geared his arguments to sway Giants owner Horace Stoneham and Dodgers owner Walter O'Malley, predicting that within a decade, New York would no longer be a three-team town. Either some teams were going to have to find new cities with new stadiums, or they would be buried under the rotting wood of their ancient ballparks. Perini, with his fist on the table and his eyes on Stoneham and O'Malley, said the Braves would go first and, in the process, prove that baseball was growing bigger than the original sixteen teams that had founded the modern major leagues in 1903.

Stoneham could smell the money. He had the best young player in baseball, but even if Willie Mays returned from the army in time for the 1954 season, he was not optimistic about ticket sales. His ballpark, the Polo Grounds, was a horse-and-buggy trapped in the atomic age. He was tired of playing in the shadow of the Yankees and embraced Perini's desire to escape the Red Sox. He dreamed along with Perini and wanted his own territory far away from the Northeast. Stoneham wiped the lenses of his thick glasses and saw the new frontiers Perini was seeing. He threw him his support, and now Perini was one vote away.

O'Malley was the most stubborn and most powerful owner in the National League. His best players were in their best years and he didn't want to break up a good thing, but he also knew that they wouldn't play forever, and when it was over, Ebbets Field was as good as dust. Though O'Malley hated tampering with tradition, he hated the termites in his ballpark more.

When he agreed with Stoneham, Perini had New York cornered. The other five owners waved their cigars and voted yes, giving Perini the unanimous decision he needed and Giles the power to ratify. Lou Perini owed Horace Stoneham the first case of Miller High Life. The Boston Braves were now officially the Milwaukee Braves.

Perini emerged from the meeting drenched with sweat, fatigued but victorious. Fred G. Fleig, Giles's assistant, marveled at Perini's abilities. "I have listened to a lot of good sales talks in my time, but none better than Perini's," Fleig said. "He's baseball's greatest salesman." David Perini described his father as a man whose energy allowed him to "stand and talk to people until they were exhausted."

The bulldozer dislodged a team that had been in Boston for seventy-five years and made the National League's first move in fifty years. No team had ever moved so far west. He held his head high and remembered his father. Now it was his turn to take the wagon. When a reporter asked him how he was able to win the other owners, he noted, "All I can say is that I'm glad Veeck isn't in our league."

Perini was jubilant but nostalgic. He still had the heart of a Boston Braves fan, but his business sense prevailed. "I feel certain that Milwaukee will make a very fine representative in the National League," he said. "It is a major league city in every sense of the word . . . manufacturing, the people, the surroundings, everything about it. They had the fortitude to go out and build facilities for a major league club. Other large cities can take a page from Milwaukee's book."

Much of the country couldn't see Perini's vision yet, starting with the sportswriters, who were the first to rip Milwaukee. The baseball writers were a rigid and archaic New York–based establishment who demanded East Coast supremacy. The departure of the Boston Braves endangered every storyline they built their daily game reports upon, which, taken after decades, constructed a historical narrative they felt Perini jeopardized in favor of a hick town. They believed baseball lore needed the Dodgers against the Giants, each striving to beat the Yankees in the World Series. What would happen if one of those teams left New York? The Yankees needed the Red Sox to bully and the Red Sox needed the Boston Braves to feel better about life. Perini refused to buy into the storylines. This endeared him to Milwaukee fans and made their city a target for the East Coast, which could be every bit as hostile as a hard-throwing headhunter.

Prejudices permeated baseball on and off the field. It was easy to detect subtle traces of ethnic bias, from the "deeply tanned construction magnate" Perini, a nod to his Italian blood, to the working-class German Milwaukee population only eight years removed from World War II. The East Coast, as seen through the eyes of the press, simply could not view Milwaukee as an equal. They were somehow a lesser form of life, working stiffs in a factory town, the little people who deserved little respect. *Washington Post* columnist Shirley Povich was a vocal critic. "A big league park doesn't make a big league town," he wrote, insisting that Milwaukee was not a "lush new territory," that "Milwaukee fans are not noted for being fast with a buck," and that the "strongly German-American town, the last outpost of the 10-cent bottle of beer," should never be confused with Baltimore, where Veeck planned to move the Browns instead, "who take a team to their hearts."

In New York, where Casey Stengel's Yankees were in the midst of winning the World Series in five consecutive seasons, the skeptical response was expected. No members of the 1950s media were more powerful than the big-city sports columnists, whose words swayed the city, and whose circulation figures gave them the impression that small-town America thought big city America did all the thinking for them. "Good or bad, Milwaukee will support the Braves until the novelty wears off," New York *Daily News* columnist Dan Parker predicted. "They'd better be good or else it will be off to Buffalo or maybe Cedar Rapids."

Writers and fans in Los Angeles and San Francisco dreamed of becoming the next cities to get a big league team. Both cities had been vital towns to the Triple-A Pacific Coast League for fifty years, the top minor league in the country, where most teams had loose affiliations with major league teams. They called themselves the Third Major League, but since World War II, Los Angeles and San Francisco had started to wonder when the actual major leagues would come to the coast. In New York and Boston, this was a far-flung notion, and if expansion to San Francisco and Los

Angeles depended on the woebegone Braves succeeding in Milwaukee, the writers would take that bet every time.

"Milwaukee's fans are like no other in the majors," Povich concluded. "In the first place, they're the newest. In the second place, they don't know as much baseball. A bit more than half a century ago, Milwaukee was in the majors for a spell, but the city has been bush ever since."

Bush league. Nothing poked a stick in the eye of Milwaukee more than the idea that they were "Bushers," the ancient baseball term for a minor leaguer, a player who was not talented enough to compete with the best. Busher was code—it meant you weren't good enough to be here, you don't belong, you should stay away from the big time. In the eyes of New York, Milwaukee was strictly Bushville. The term was derogatory and condescending. It implied that even though Milwaukee had the Braves, they were not major league people.

Proud Wisconsin fans were infuriated and invigorated. In the next few years they would join together in a common cause, not unlike the war effort of a decade before. Milwaukee would lead the charge for all of the Midwest, all of those working-class families like the ones Lou Perini had once fetched water for, like the ones who drank Fred Miller's beer. They would take on Wall Street from Main Street to prove that Milwaukee and the Midwest were every bit as American as the big cities back east. Now they had the Braves, their darlings, who would help show the rest of the country what working people were made of.

When news that the move had been approved reached the spring training baseball field in Bradenton, Florida on March 18th, the Braves were in the fifth inning and winning, 3–0.

The next few days were a whirlwind. "Our family didn't even find out the team was moving until the stuff was on the bus," David Perini said. Players who had come up in the minors in Milwaukee were thrilled to be returning, calling the fans there the best they had ever known. Meanwhile, Perini penned a personal letter profusely apologizing to and refunding the 420 Boston Braves season-ticket holders. He also visited Red Sox owner Tom Yawkey and asked him to continue the Jimmy Fund. Players needed housing and apartments, chores that fell on the wives. Single young players made plans to sleep on the couches of veteran players once the team made it north. Pitcher Warren Spahn reluctantly abandoned the restaurant he had recently opened in Boston.

Equipment had to be re-routed to Milwaukee. Travel arrangements had to be hastily made and clubhouse boys opened a can of white paint, crossed out BOSTON on the team's steamer trunks and painted MILWAUKEE in its place, misspelling it on the first try. Roland Hemond, a young front-office clerk who got his start with the Braves because he was willing to sweep bleachers after minor league games in Hartford, was assigned to ship the team's scouting reports to Milwaukee before he was dispatched there to help open the ticket office.

Days before the tickets were finished printing, Hemond got a glimpse of what was in store for the new Milwaukee Braves: fans were waiting for tickets in long lines in the snow. The Boston Braves had to beg for cash; now, money was arriving in the mail for the Milwaukee Braves before the tickets were printed. From Milwaukee, Michigan, and Minnesota, the Heartland was coming in droves. Hemond and his friends felt so inspired and guilty that the tickets weren't ready yet that they walked the lines, handing out free cups of hot coffee. The city's two newspapers—the morning coffee, white-collar, and erudite *Milwaukee Journal* (the *Journal*) and its scrappy blue-collar competitor, the afternoon beer and lunch pail *Milwaukee Sentinel* (the *Sentinel*)—covered the story with competitive fervor their New York journalism contemporaries scarcely believed they possessed.

When the Braves posed for the 1953 team picture a few days later, half of the players were still wearing their Boston Braves caps instead of the new Milwaukee Braves hats with the bold white capital *M* threaded over a dark-blue canopy atop a red bill. Red, white and blue, they were Milwaukee's All-American boys. Perini's baseball man, General Manager John Quinn, had been wisely breaking in a core of young players as well as scouting and developing minor leaguers that the team would bring to Milwaukee. Over the next couple of weeks, the *Sentinel* ran "Know Your Milwaukee Braves" vignettes, and soon, young players from the Boston Braves like third baseman Eddie Mathews, shortstop Johnny Logan, catcher Del Crandall, pitcher Lew Burdette and veteran lefty Warren Spahn were Wisconsin superstars.

The rest of the country wasn't so sure that any of this adulation would last. The Braves didn't exactly have the reputation for winning. The fans were going to have to prove they could support a team and the players were going to have to prove they could win in an era when the World Series was the exclusive domain of New York City. On the day they heard the news, the Braves blew the game and lost 5–3 to none other than the New York Yankees, whose manager, Casey Stengel, was never one to forgive and forget a team and an owner that had once fired him.

Milwaukee, however, was waiting for its team with open arms. Mayor Frank Zeidler played cheerleader, capitalizing as the local politician who made Milwaukee major league. He was arm in arm with Fred Miller, who urged fans to come out in full force. Zeidler saw a potent public platform. "The team satisfies the ego of our population," the mayor explained. "We have long felt we are a capable people, but because of our peculiar geography, tucked away as we are behind Lake Michigan, our voice has not been heard in the land."

You could practically hear Zeidler bending the red brim of his fresh new Braves cap. "This is a means of letting people know we exist," he said. "A whole reservoir of interest has been dammed up and here is the release for it. Here, a man's world is his church, his tavern and his lodge. This is an expression of the underdog."

The New York Times couldn't resist the mayor's emotional call, reporting that Zeidler's "voice took on a faint lyrical pitch" before "he wiped his glasses with a triumphantly weary flourish." Then he spoke the words that summarized his town, his team, and his time. Speaking for the people of Milwaukee, who dreamed that one day they would be seen as big league and get a shot at the mighty New York Yankees and the New York baseball dynasty, to be seen as equals in the eyes of baseball and America, "This," he said, "is David versus Goliath."

2

THE HIGH LIFE

On the train ride to Milwaukee at the end of spring training, some of the Braves ballplayers who had not played minor league ball in Milwaukee were not sold that this was a good move. But Johnny Logan, a shortstop who had played parts of four seasons there, told his teammates not to worry. "That town was ready," Logan said. "They were happy to be major league because now they didn't have to go ninety miles to see the Cubbies."

Livelihoods did not leave much room for optimism. Players worked on year-to-year contracts with no job security or extraordinary protection, no agents and no union, cutthroat performers in a rugged life where jobs were scarce and survival was foremost. None of them understood how much moving to Milwaukee was about to change their lives and careers. They only knew that they were the lucky few—big leaguers in a time when there were only sixteen teams and the minors were flooded with guys who could steal their jobs in a heartbeat. They drank beer and played cards to pass time and ease their worries, and though they were groomed to be cold and hard in the face of adversity, they wondered what was next.

Charlie Grimm wasn't worried at all. The Braves manager was fifty-three, with wrinkles that made him look eighty-five and a personality that was twelve. Born in St. Louis with a beer bottle in his hand, he broke into the big leagues at seventeen and played until he was thirty-seven. He chirped the whole time and for this boyish banter earned the nickname Jolly Cholly. He played for the cursed Cubs, where he adored Chicago fans and became player-manager (hired and fired twice) at Wrigley Field, reading the hops by day and drinking them by night. Jolly Cholly never had a care in the world—you couldn't tell if he was in first or in last, and you couldn't tell if he was a player or a manager. Forever one of the boys, he sat in on card games and nightcaps, and reassured his players they would love Milwaukee. It was a ballplayer's town because it was a beer-drinking town. He was an icon there, who had managed the minor league Brewers to two American Association pennants. Grimm assured his players they had it made. "Last season I brought the Braves home from a road trip with a record of 10-3 and we drew only 4,500 fans," he said. "A week later the Red Sox returned home after going 1-14 and still drew 30,000 with the Philly A's. Boston is simply an American League town."

More fans than he ever imagined were waiting for the Braves as the train steamed north. When the train finally arrived, the players could hear the noise. When the doors opened, Jolly Cholly led the way. He loved the adulation and knew how to work the crowd. He opened his arms and blew them big kisses, Marilyn Monroe style. Grimm was born for fanfare and invited attention with his bright smile and enthusiasm. The roaring applause was louder than any of the players had ever heard. It was as if they had won the World Series, but all they had done was step off a train. The fans were instantly insanely crazy about them. It was love at first sight, and as Johnny Logan remembered, "pandemonium."

The players loved the attention but struggled to understand why the fans loved them just for showing up. They hadn't proven anything, but they were the toast of the town, simply because they were big leaguers with Milwaukee next to their names. "The city opened wide its heart to the major league baseball newcomers and throbbed with a rollicking, wild welcome Charlie Grimm and his Braves will remember the rest of their lives," the *Sentinel* reported. Milwaukee cops estimated between 60,000 and 80,000 fans partied at the train station and on the parade route, blowing noisemakers, clanging cowbells, and throwing confetti and scraps of paper. "This was the new home of the Milwaukee Braves," the *Sentinel* reported. "And this was Milwaukee's way of showing the visitors they were now part of the family."

Comparisons to the parties at the end of World War II weren't far off. Suddenly, the Braves were sitting in the front row. Locals compared the crowds to the ones that had arrived to welcome Wisconsin native and fired

General Douglas McArthur. He may have been kicked out of Korea, but he could sleep wherever he wanted in Kenosha . . . and so could the Braves. Hardened veteran ballplayers were dazed and touched by the love. The players rode in open convertibles down Wisconsin Avenue, waving to the crowds, who poured confetti and applause on them as if they were war heroes, presidents, heavyweight champs, Olympic heroes, or ace test pilots. When the procession passed the Gimbels flagship department store, business halted and clerks ran to the windows and onto the streets to catch a glimpse. Some employees poured the contents of wastebaskets out the window.

Along the parade route, newsreel crews filmed the event and the *Meet Your Milwaukee Braves* short movie played to thousands. Lou Perini curiously studied the audience reaction reports, pleased to see comments ranging from "Wonderful—this film was liked by all!" to "Excellent reaction from crowd!"

Newspapermen from around the country weren't so sure. They watched in amusement, wondering how long the honeymoon would last. The New York guys were dying of laughter—they knew Perini needed to draw at least one million fans in 1953 just to break even. They'd take that bet any day of the week. Riding in the lead convertible next to Fred Miller, Perini was overwhelmed with emotion and imagination. "I don't know how we could want any more enthusiasm than Milwaukee has shown," he said. "This is way beyond anything we had anticipated. There was no way we could sense that such enthusiasm would develop. The reception has been marvelous."

He said he wished the other baseball owners could witness Milwaukee's "out of this world" reception, but with this love came responsibility to give the city a champion. He believed in the power of a city getting behind its team, and he was already dreaming that one day there would be another procession down Wisconsin Avenue, when the Braves won the World Series. "This could lead to anything," he said.

When the parade reached the Schroeder Hotel in downtown Milwaukee, Perini pointed to the cameras and said, "When the newsreels are displayed around the country, people will see that Milwaukee's deeds speak louder than words." The rally continued on to the Civic Center, where thirty models in tight white sweaters carried hatboxes spelling out, "Welcome Braves." The ballplayers took a look at the girls in the white sweaters and thought maybe Milwaukee wasn't going to be so bad after all.

After the hot girls, the players got a taste of the cold weather. Rain and hail fell, but the fans wouldn't leave. They pulled on their winter gear and kept on screaming. They were thrilled—it was like Packers season in April! Jolly Cholly marched to the podium, received a peace pipe, a tomahawk, and a ceremonial headdress, made an Indian war cry, and introduced each player to the crowd. He danced a jig, but he only had to stand there to make them happy. Wisconsin governor Walter Koehler was itching to speak to the crowd, but Mayor Zeidler waved him off. He knew the people didn't want to see the politicians, just the players. The beer bosses from Schlitz and Pabst yearned for the microphone, but the only man Milwaukee wanted to hear from was Fred Miller, who employed many of them and inebriated all of them. Milwaukee Braves baseball was the body, Miller beer was the blood, and Fred Miller was Christ, the savior who brought them the big leagues, and helped Perini get a sweetheart $1,000 annual lease on County Stadium. Miller was take-charge when he had an audience. "You're the hottest fans in the country tonight!" he bellowed. "We're with the Braves—win, lose, or draw!"

The following day, the Braves came to cold County Stadium for the first time and discovered the nameplates over their locker stalls were red and white and in the shape of the Miller High Life logo. Every ballplayer had a case of High Life waiting for him in his locker. Beer was everywhere. Who needed hot coffee when a cold one was always nearby? The company called its stuff "The Champagne of Bottled Beer."

Pitcher Warren Spahn walked past the throngs of fans, signed more autographs in five minutes than he had in the last five years in Boston, and before he cracked his first High Life, he made a beeline for his new office—the pitching mound. He walked up the hill in his street clothes, thinking nothing of the diamond dust on his wingtip shoes. He told the groundskeeper to raise the mound by five inches. It was entirely legal, but unwritten rules stated that only ace pitchers could modify the home-field mound.

Everything with Spahn had a purpose—he was cunning, sharp, and extremely competitive. He didn't just want to own hitters, he wanted to confuse and torment them. The fans waiting in long lines circling the stadium would soon learn everything about him—if they could get tickets.

Front-office jack-of-all-trades Roland Hemond didn't know how to say no, but he had to learn fast. Some fans sent blank checks that had to be returned when season tickets sold out. Fans prayed for a cancellation and begged the front office to take deposits for $200 season mezzanine seats, $150 season box seats, or $110 grandstand reserved season boxes. The weather was miserable in April, but it didn't stop the fans. "They would slop through the slush to get tickets for the games they wanted," Hemond said. "The cold never bothered them and it wasn't just the Milwaukee people. We had a lot of people coming in from Northern Wisconsin, Minnesota, Iowa, and Illinois. A lot of fans from Chicago came up. Let's just say that a lot of beer was consumed in those ticket lines and by the time they got to the window, they were ready to talk business. We had to turn down a lot of people who deserved season tickets. It was really pandemonium. You'd show up early in the morning and go to bed late at night. Sometimes you had to battle angry fans to make them happy, but in time, we took good care of them." So many fans came to visit their new stadium that traffic jams formed, but not one argument ever broke out as one fan after another waited for their turn to drive past the Promised Land.

Anticipation grew as the April 14 home opener against the St. Louis Cardinals approached. The Braves' own tickets began to arrive in the mail even as they shipped Brewers tickets back to the printers. The city began construction of a pedestrian bridge for access to the stadium and arranged for special bus lines during games. Every aspect of Milwaukee commerce and Wisconsin civic life intertwined around the Braves. Big corporations and mom-and-pop stores rallied around the team and understood that all the money was in the same pot and all their hearts were in the same place.

"Tomorrow's the big day!" the full-page ad announced. "Big league baseball makes its official bow in Milwaukee's magnificent new County Stadium. We hope you'll be on hand to see history in the making—and we hope too that you'll watch your battling Braves in action often! Remember—

they're your major league team! Back your Braves! Buy the beer that brings you big league baseball broadcasts! BUY MILLER HIGH LIFE! When you're out at the new stadium—ask for, insist on MILLER HIGH LIFE and make MILLER HIGH LIFE your favorite when buying beer at your friendly tavern, restaurant, beer depot or beverage store."

The Braves were important to small business and big business alike. Every line of work in Milwaukee—dry cleaners, grocery stores, newspapers, liquor stores, drugstores, dairies, tire stores, gas stations, department stores, radio and TV stations, farm suppliers, sporting goods stores, bookstores, butcher shops—all tied themselves to the Braves. If you weren't a fan, you couldn't talk to your customers, and if your customers weren't fans, chances are you had no customers. Such was the case for the used-car lot on South 71st Street at West National, where their tiny ad promised BIG LEAGUE BUYS for the "lowest prices of the year, selling cars from '46 to '52." The dealership was named Knippel-Selig, and one of the co-owner's sons, Allan H. "Buddy" Selig, already loved baseball. When the Braves came to town, he watched the big new ballpark rise into the sky, wanted nothing more to do with selling used cars, and dreamed of the day he might have an office somewhere inside the baseball business.

There's no doubt that some of the 7,500 cars at County Stadium, parked for twenty-five cents each (exact change, please), came from old man Selig's used-car lot. The beer cooler was in the backseat and the portable grill and groceries were in the trunk. By the time the Miller High Life ad ran in the paper, the greatest tailgating party in the history of mankind was rocking and rolling. The Braves brought the big leagues to Milwaukee, but nobody needed to teach Wisconsin how to party before a ballgame. The plumes of smoke visible for miles around County Stadium rose not only from the brick smokestacks dotting the city's rugged skyline, nor were they Indian smoke signals as cartoonists often portrayed. They were from the many parking-lot cookouts. You couldn't escape the scent of smoke, burning charcoal, matches and lighter fluid, and red meat cooking on the grill, and you couldn't walk two feet without kicking an empty beer bottle or crushing a beer can.

Tailgate parties had always been a part of American fan culture but this was a new extreme. Legend had it that the practice dated back to the Battle of Bull Run during the Civil War, when fans gathered atop a bluff to watch the carnage as if it were a college football game, but it was the Milwaukee Braves fans of the 1950s and, in particular, Wisconsin sports fans who really taught America how to party.

Car radios played in the parking lot while teenagers flirted and danced in the aisles. Kids and dads brought balls and gloves and played catch, making sure not to break car windows. Some fans brought tennis balls and impromptu stickball games broke out among strangers. Your shortstop might be from Racine and your second baseman might be from Skokie. There were three major Wisconsin Indian tribes, but in April 1953, there were four when the Braves Nation united the Midwest. The dynamic camaraderie was special and transcended traditional borders. During pro football season, Green Bay Packers fans would have nothing to do with Chicago Bears or Detroit Lions fans, but in the County Stadium parking lot, the Braves and the High Life brought them all together. During college football season, the Wisconsin Badgers, Michigan Wolverines, Iowa Hawkeyes, Illinois Fighting Illini, and Minnesota Golden Gophers were sworn enemies. But from the first tailgate party on the first opening day, the Milwaukee County Stadium parking lot became the Midwest Assembly of the United Nations, representing with a beer and bratwurst celebration all that the Heartland yearned to be. The fans didn't dispute that they were small-town humble folks, but they hated being looked down on for respecting where they came from. They wanted to be seen as a proud pillar of American society, apart but not separate from the big cities of Boston and New York.

More than one hundred Wisconsin legislators bused to the tailgate party that day, united in the idea that Wisconsin's government should get behind the people. They believed in big business because they enhanced the little guy and did not take his rights, his paycheck, and his pride to fatten their coffers. Three convoys of state senators and assemblymen came from Madison and met legislators from other parts of the state in a picnic lunch where Democrats and Republicans cut out of work early to break bread, have a High Life, and pray for the Braves.

The eating and drinking didn't stop once the turnstiles finally opened at 11:30, two hours before the first pitch. The Braves were ready for their hungry fans: they ordered 15,000 pounds of hot dogs and buns, 15,000 pounds of peanuts, 2,000 cases of beer, 1,000 cases of soda, 12,000 ice cream bars, and 200 pounds of coffee. Five thousand fans streamed through the gates to watch batting practice, which started promptly at 11:35, according to the big clock atop the scoreboard. The Braves took their practice cuts in their correct batting order: Bruton CF, Logan SS, Mathews 3B, Gordon LF, Pafko RF, Adcock 1B, Crandall C, Dittmer 2B, Spahn P. "There was never music playing like there is today," then grade-school-aged fan Rick Schroeder said. He wasn't from the Schroeder family that owned the famously wealthy downtown hotel. He was from the less-known, less-famous, less-wealthy Schroeder family who operated the Sportsman Lodge, a run-of-the-mill tavern in upstate Wisconsin, where the beer was on tap downstairs and the family lived upstairs. The owner, Schroeder's father, was a Cubs fan. The son was a Braves fan, whose early experiences at County Stadium shaped his baseball career as a scout. "All you could hear was the murmur of the players and the crowd and the crack of the bat," Schroeder said. Each hitter went through three rounds, first laying bunts down and then hitting to the opposite field, then rounding the bases as the next guy hit. When it was their time to hit again, they focused on hitting the ball to center, where the ball vanished over a chain-link fence where pine trees would be planted the following opening day and dubbed "Perini's Forest." In their third and final round, each man got to turn and burn, pulling the ball for power. Eddie Mathews, the left-handed hitting slugger and matinee idol, began planting baseballs onto the hill in right field, where veterans at the local Veteran's Administration hospital scrambled for the souvenirs. When the right-handed Joe Adcock began launching balls to left field, the army of ushers clad in fire-truck red sports coats urged adult fans to either give the balls to a kid or give them back to the team.

When rookie center fielder Billy Bruton took his swings, the fans knew he wouldn't hit many home runs. He played center field for the 1952 Milwaukee Brewers, where fans knew him for his bright smile and brisk speed. He was a wispy left-handed slap hitter making his major league debut, and he became the first black outfielder from Alabama to become a meaningful member of the Milwaukee Braves. Gifted with instincts beyond the years of someone supposedly in his mid twenties, nobody knew that GM John Quinn had cleverly manipulated Bruton's age. "John Quinn cheated," Roland Hemond admitted. "He knew he couldn't get a guy who was twenty-seven or twenty-eight just getting into pro ball, so he made him a little younger."

Bruton had played ball in the army before he signed in 1950, but nobody knew anything about his baseball past. The best guess was that Bruton had played Industrial League ball in Alabama and probably in the Negro Leagues under an assumed name before surfacing in what black players called "White Folks Ball." Most Milwaukee fans were not used to seeing black players. The Green Bay Packers signed their first black player in 1950, and there were no black college football players. The sight of a black ballplayer wasn't rejected, but for small town Wisconsin, it was a new discovery. "I never saw a black person, never talked to a black person, and if it weren't for the black baseball players I wouldn't have known black people existed," Schroeder remembered.

By 1 P.M., the ballpark was packed. Bankers, doctors, and lawyers dressed in business attire clutched $3.50 box seat ticket stubs. Middle-class factory workers and outdoorsmen in plaid hunting gear spent $1.50 to sit in the grandstands. The *Sentinel* expensed a reporter seventy-five cents to buy an outfield bleacher seat, where he observed leather-faced old-timers from Green Bay, Eau Claire, Oshkosh, and Wausau chastising freckle-faced boys chewing bubble gum and eating cotton candy.

Batting practice ended for the Braves and the St. Louis Cardinals, and early-bird fans had their first look at the great Stan Musial. A band played as the batting cage was rolled off the field and the grounds crew dragged the infield, chalked the batter's box and the lines. Every one of the 34,357 seats was taken, with the standing-room crowd swelling the attendance to 45,000. Fans parked in the hills behind the stadium and crowded atop the hills in right field to watch the game. The Braves' wives were thankful for the borrowed blankets after they were stunned to discover that East Coast chic spring attire in Wisconsin didn't do them much good when the wind-chill was 40 degrees, yet the local press eagerly conveyed the details of their outfits and accessories to the housewives reading at home who, coincidentally, suddenly found such styles on sale at Gimbels. The ice cream bars weren't selling, but the hot coffee was flowing and the cold High Life was keeping fans warm. Alcohol, caffeine, excitement, civic pride, and real big league players in a real big league stadium—the big time had finally come. "There's a combination of World Series and All-Star buzzing on the field as the 1:30 starting time draws closer," the *Sentinel* reported. Newspaper tycoon William Randolph Hearst Jr. sat with *Sentinel* publisher Frank Taylor, saw the enormous crowds, and wondered how many thousands of extra copies they would sell tomorrow. Gene Ronzani, coach of the Packers, presented a symbolic welcoming gift to Lou Perini, followed by speeches, the first pitch, and a flag-raising ceremony, which brought down the house, and brought tears to the eyes of the Heartland.

The out-of-towners in the press box were not impressed. Boston columnist Dave Egan, still fuming at Perini for moving the Braves, tore into the locals. He looked down from his perch, typing with disdain and bitterness about this "group of masked marvels who masqueraded as big leaguers" in this "picturesque slice of Germany." *Sentinel* sports editor Lloyd Larson noted the divide. He was a charming guy nicknamed "Swede," but he didn't like being big leagued in his hometown. "There is evidence that it goes beyond a challenge—almost to the point of undisguised hope that Milwaukee and Wisconsin can't make it," he wrote.

By the time the first national anthem was played at County Stadium, most of the fans had so much to drink that the flag wasn't the only thing fluttering in the wind. Perini had made a wise agreement with Miller—he would allow Braves fans to bring their own beer into the park, leading third baseman Eddie Mathews to joke that Braves fans bought "a seat for the wife, a seat for the kid, and a seat for the cooler." The fans who couldn't get a ticket were listening to the radio play by play on WEMP and WTMJ radio, with Earl Gillespie and Blaine Walsh on the call, waving a Miller High Life flag from their booth and frequently reminding listeners that Milwaukee Braves baseball had been made possible by Miller High Life. The Braves took the field to a thunderous ovation from fans getting their first look at Warren Spahn, who finished the first inning when he fooled

Cardinals slugger Steve Bilko with a screwball for the first strikeout in stadium history. An inning later, Joe Adcock got the first hit and Del Crandall knocked in the first run. But after nine innings, 28,000 cups coffee, 14,000 bottles of beer sold, and Bruton's artfully athletic catch of Musial's deep drive in the eighth, the Braves and Cardinals were tied up, 2–2.

Bruton came to bat in the bottom of the 10th inning with one out. Cardinals pitcher Gerry Staley, a right-handed sinkerballer, had masterfully dueled Spahn, but his soft slop hadn't fooled Bruton, whose run-scoring triple had given the Braves a short-lived 2–1 lead in the eighth. Never one to back down, Staley went right after Bruton, a free-swinger who refused to be cheated. He dropped the good part of his barrel on a Staley sinker and lofted it high into the cold Milwaukee air, where Cardinals center fielder Enos Slaughter tracked the ball. Bruton was off and running, thinking triple, he knew he got the ball good. But Slaughter was a bloodhound. He felt the outfield grass give way to warning-track gravel beneath his feet, extended his arm, and prepared to time his leap. All of Milwaukee stood as Slaughter jumped and got his glove on the ball, but the angles weren't with him, and the ball slipped off the side of his glove and landed behind the fence for a game-winning home run. Welcome to Milwaukee! The Braves were 3–2 winners over the Cardinals, and Billy Bruton never hit another home run in 1953.

The fans cried. Every day couldn't be like the end of World War II, but Milwaukee was going to try. Spahn would always do his best for them. He pitched all ten innings and scattered six hits, considering coming out of the game in favor of a relief pitcher equal parts insulting the fans, failing his team, and embarrassing himself. "I was so anxious to make good before those people that if the tension were any more terrific I'd have blown my top," he said. "If these people can't make a guy win, I don't know what will."

At a banquet after the game, Perini told his followers, "You Milwaukee fans made it possible and desirable to move. You and you alone." Fred Miller took the podium to thunderous applause. "The Braves are now part of our community, let's prove we deserve them," he said. "I know we will."

Members of the St. Louis Cardinals were invited to the banquet, but only two players, Slaughter and Peanuts Lowrey, had the courtesy to come.

Manager Eddie Stanky sneered at Wisconsin fans earlier in the day. Milwaukee was insulted when visitors did not accept the invitations of their hosts. The city had a long memory and they established their expectations from the start—anyone who dismissed their courtesy would be considered an enemy.

The party had just begun, but in the press box, Larson already knew that the passion Milwaukee fans felt at this moment would one day turn to impatience and even anger if the Braves couldn't one day become World Champions. It seemed like a distant dream in the days of New York dynasty, when the Yankees were in the midst of winning the World Series every year and the postseason had become almost the birthright of the Bronx, with crumbs shared by the Brooklyn Dodgers and New York Giants. "We won't be judged by what happens today, tomorrow, next week, next month, or three months from now," Larson cautioned. "Not by the crowds turning out for the first appearances of the Dodgers, Giants, Phillies, and Cubs. What we do over the long haul will tell the story."

3

ASSHOLE BUDDIES

Every February before he went to spring training, Warren Spahn visited Lou Perini's Boston office to settle his contract for the coming season. Spahn laughed at the idea that he needed to give some agent 3 percent to do the talking for him. He was the best left-hander in baseball and he knew it, and he was going to make sure Perini paid him accordingly. He demanded a $30,000 salary for the 1953 season and not a dime less.

"Mr. Perini, do you know why I had such a good season last year?" Spahn asked.

"Well, Warren," Perini said. "I suppose you had such a good year because you have exceptional talents."

"Maybe I have," Spahn said. "But the principal reason is that I was happy. I had no contract or money problems. Therefore I was able to concentrate on pitching."

But the bulldozer buried him. Why should he pay Spahn $30,000 when he won 14 games and lost 19? Spahn countered that he led the National League in strikeouts for the fourth consecutive season, which people would know about if anybody actually came to Boston Braves games. Perini had a solution for that problem, too, but he wasn't letting on. He asked Spahn why he should pay so much for a pitcher with a losing record—even though Spahn had won 20 games in a season four times prior to 1952. Spahn said Perini was paying for the track record and he wasn't interested in taking the financial penalty for the hopeless Braves. "I want exactly $30,000 and unless I get it I won't be happy," he insisted.

Perini wasn't going to pay Spahn just because he liked him. When he offered $25,000, a five-thousand-dollar pay cut, Spahn was incensed. He argued that if the Braves actually had anyone who could play, he would have won 25 games instead of 14 and pushed the bulldozer for thirty-five grand instead of thirty.

Perini compromised with creativity. He offered Spahn a special arrangement. Would Spahn be interested in taking a salary of ten cents per paying customer for the 1953 season?

Perini noted Spahn's reaction, which undoubtedly reflected the following notion: Nobody gives a shit about the Boston Braves. Perini made it simple: he would pay either $25,000 flat for the 1953 season or ten cents a head. Lou was charitable, but he wasn't stupid. Spahn knew there was no way the Boston Braves would draw 300,000 fans in 1953. They had only drawn 281,000 fans in 1952. So Spahn reluctantly took Perini's $25,000, without an inkling that the team might be moving.

When Spahn got to Milwaukee and saw 35,000 fans a night, the reality sank in. Perini hadn't tried to cheat him. He offered him the chance of a lifetime, but Spahn was too stubborn to accept it. He had always been young and cocky; now he was just cocky. He could look into the packed stands at County Stadium and whisper to himself, well, shit, did I ever screw up.

On the whole, the Braves could not screw up in the eyes of the Milwaukee public. Miller Time was all the time. The city and the sticks flocked to County Stadium. The Braves were the only baseball team in the country where every single game was like a Saturday afternoon college football game. If you didn't drink, you weren't trying. It wasn't uncommon to see the ballplayers mingling with the fans on their way to work. The kids might get an autograph. The dads loved it if a ballplayer took one of their beers from one of their coolers. The common theme was acceptance, a yearning to belong to the big picture, with a staunch reluctance to abandon their roots. The city found their identity with the Braves, a bunch of hard-working guys who loved the High Life, and the players found fuel in the city, which, like them, wanted to prove they were more than bushers.

The Braves hung around the pennant race for the first half of the 1953 season, and a keen observer would have noted that the Braves were a younger team nipping at the heels of the aging Brooklyn Dodgers. When the Braves moved, Dodgers owner Walter O'Malley sent a Western Union telegram published in the *Sentinel*, promising, "We are anxious to play in your new stadium. Except for 11 games in Milwaukee, we promise to be peaceful tourists." Perini chuckled and replied to O'Malley. "We are going to welcome you as sterling competition; however, I fondly believe and expect that [we] will not be the all too generous hosts we were in Boston last season."

But the Dodgers were a veteran bunch not easily scared by the High Life, and as the season continued, Milwaukee began hearing the label that burned them: bushers. Bush was a flexible insult and allowed for creativity in any number of linguistic cocktails, such as bush league, bush town, or the worst of them all—Bushville. The fans hated it. "We'd get Bushville all the time," Rick Schroeder said. "We were blue collar and we got a lot of jokes about that. We always heard lots of stuff that we were bush leaguers, small-town hicks—and really, we were—but we didn't like to hear it from other people." The ground rules were set: Milwaukee could call itself small town, but nobody else could. They wanted the dual identity. Milwaukee wanted to be the smallest big shot in America.

Busher applied to the players in a slightly different way. Calling a big league ballplayer a busher was the highest insult. The Big Leagues, capital *B* and *L,* were tops and everyone else was a busher. In baseball lore, a busher was an untalented moron who didn't belong with the big boys and had to be told he was no good because he was too stupid to understand it himself. The premise made Ring Lardner a wealthy writer, thanks to his 1914 *Busher's Letters Home* series and his fictional protagonist, pitcher Jack Keefe, a Midwestern rube who could barely read, write, or throw a strike. The phrases bush league, bush leaguer, busher, and bush town were a part of baseball terminology for as long as anybody could remember, a vital part of the game, like beer, bats, balls and the protective cup. The linguistic mass migration from the locker room to the press box occurred during World War I, and by the time the Milwaukee Braves were living the High Life, every bush league description seemed to fit, including the passage found in the April 1915 *Sporting Life,* calling a busher "a most unsophisticated youngster."

Most of baseball looked at Milwaukee third baseman Eddie Mathews and thought exactly that. Nobody disputed Eddie could hit. Nobody disputed Eddie could drink. But he was so stubbornly flip about not caring how he acted that he agitated the clean-cut generic image of what an All-American superhero ballplayer was supposed to portray. In 1953, you could flip a coin and ask who was the best ballplayer in America—Eddie Mathews or Mickey Mantle. In Milwaukee, if you said Mantle, you might get the crap kicked out of you. "I used to stick the Mantle baseball cards in the spokes of my bike so I could see Mickey getting whacked in the face," Schroeder said. But like many Milwaukee boys, his adulation for Eddie was unmatched. When he ripped open his nickel wax packs of Topps trading cards and destroyed his tooth enamel by chewing the stale pink bubble gum, he wanted the power-hitting, High Life–loving third baseman who could run like a bull and drink like a horse. "I used to get so pissed off when I would get doubles," Schroeder said. "But I would always give a guy two cards of his choice for a Mathews. One time I got doubles of Mathews. That was the happiest day of my life."

Little boys and old men were in love with Eddie. "He's young, rugged, and clean living and I'll rate him over Mickey Mantle," said former Boston Braves manager Tommy Holmes, though he lied through his teeth. Mathews was young and ruggedly handsome, but everyone who played with Eddie knew he learned to drink hard from his daddy. There was nothing clean, polished, or perfect about Eddie except his swing, a natural left-handed groove that produced unusual power at a young age. His mouth was as loud as his bat and he loved the thrill of making someone so mad that they wanted to fight him. Eddie loved to fight because he loved to fight and if he won, he won, and if he lost, he lost. He didn't care if anyone thought he was unsophisticated or crass. Eddie knew from an early age he could hit the crap out of the ball, knew he was going to play in the big leagues, and if that didn't work, then what the hell, he would try boxing.

Eddie couldn't be clean living if he tried. He cursed profusely and didn't give a fuck what you thought. He was already drinking when he played high school ball in Santa Barbara, blasting home runs that carried beyond fences and into lore. In 1948, when he was a high school junior, Mathews played a game at Oxnard High School. There was no outfield fence around the sandlot carved out of strawberry patches and celery fields.

A trash incinerator burned deep in center field. Mathews was a school-yard legend when schoolboy catcher Buster Staniland went out with his buddies to see the Santa Barbara bomber, who was playing in front of Mexican cowboys and white ranchers.

"He hit that sonofabitch out over and past that incinerator," said Staniland, who went on to hit 150 minor league home runs. "Nobody, I mean, nobody, had ever done that. It was like the fire swallowed the goddamn ball. Nobody had ever seen that. I stood there with my mouth wide open in awe. I mean he could crush balls, with a wood bat, no batting gloves—just young, strong hands. When he got one, you knew it, you heard it, and you saw it. And then you said, 'Holy shit, I'm never going to see that again.'"

When Eddie hit home runs, he didn't take the slow trot. He rounded the bases in such a hurry that you'd think he had a fistfight waiting for him at home plate. Eddie didn't understand how to play slow. He only knew fast, hard, and aggressive. But he was also fiercely loyal to his friends, as scout Johnny Moore discovered in 1949, when he found him playing American Legion ball and fell in love with Eddie's power, profanity, and potential.

Johnny knew what he was looking for. He had an eye for left-handed hitters because he had been one, as an outfielder with a lifetime big league average of .307 in the 1930s and as a star outfielder for the Pacific Coast League's Los Angeles Angels in the 1940s. When Johnny first saw Eddie, he was in his first full year as a scout after a long playing career and a couple of short stints as a player-manager in the bush leagues. He wore out the road from his home in Sherman Oaks to Eddie's house in Santa Barbara, long dusty hauls on two-lane highways before the big freeways were built in Southern California, because he loved the way Eddie wore opponents out. Johnny loved Eddie's talent, but he also loved the way he played. He was hard and ruthless. Johnny didn't just want kids with talent. He wanted kids with balls. He accepted imperfections in favor of that which he could not give the boy. He vowed he would never let Eddie get away, and the rookie scout would never be so lucky with another ballplayer ever again.

Eddie couldn't field if you glued the ball to his glove, but Johnny didn't care. He spent the spring stalking Eddie, who blasted mammoth home runs in Ventura and Long Beach to help Santa Barbara make it to the title game in San Diego, where he hit another at Lane Field, a Triple-A park. Scouts from all sixteen teams were chasing Eddie.

But Johnny Moore knew how to talk to the old man and the kid. He told them the Boston Braves were poor and cheap, but they were also bad. Eddie could sign with the Yankees for more money, but he would get buried behind good players. He could take less from the Braves and become a more important player in a timely fashion. Eddie thought he could be in the big leagues by the time he was twenty-one, so Johnny fed Eddie's ego and told him he could make the dream a reality. He also said the Yankees would screw him at every turn. Johnny played in the big leagues and knew Casey Stengel might hate Eddie's guts for his brazen love of acting like he didn't give a shit.

The Pirates were lurking, too. Scout Tom Downey kept a liquor cabinet in the trunk of his Cadillac to make dirty deals and drink dads under the table. The Dodgers supposedly floated a $40,000 offer from Branch Rickey. But Eddie didn't give a shit. You couldn't buy his loyalty. He liked Johnny Moore and decided he wanted to be a Brave, so on the day of his high school graduation, Eddie took his diploma and dodged the scouts trying to get a piece of him. He went to the Carrillo Hotel for his senior dance with his girlfriend, his dad, and Johnny Moore. The competing scouts tailed them and lingered around the hotel lobby searching for Eddie, who unbeknownst to the Ivory Hunters, pulled home-field advantage and slipped upstairs to sign his contract with the Braves. The deal was for $6,000, just short of making him a bonus player. Evading the bonus rule granted Eddie as much time in the minors as he would need. Bonus players were rushed to the majors before they were ready and often ruined their careers. Johnny Moore had permission from Lou Perini to write the contract creatively and cover his tracks. Nobody ever learned how the extra money and perks were delivered to the Mathews family. Eddie shook Johnny's hand with that firm grip of his and escorted his girl downstairs. When they reached the lobby, he told her to wait a second. Then he walked over to the other scouts to tell them he was a Brave, and to get the hell out of here before he beat the crap out of them.

A temper like Eddie had, you had to be born with. He was the only ballplayer who could be a nasty drunk even when he was sober. When he was playing for the Atlanta Crackers in New Orleans one night in 1950, he ran into left-hander Paul Pettit, the famous $100,000 bonus baby from the Pittsburgh Pirates, who struck him out with a high-and-tight fastball. Eddie stormed back to the dugout, slammed his bat, and hopped onto the top step of the dugout, pointed at Pettit, and screamed "You bonus baby son of a bitch!" In the tenth inning, when Pettit tried to sneak another fastball past Eddie, he hit it 420 feet to straightaway center field over the big Coca-Cola sign at Pelican Stadium.

Eddie was born into bad baseball blood. He made his big league debut at age twenty on April 15, 1952, batting seventh and playing third against the Brooklyn Dodgers. They were the best team in the league and fiercely defended their territory. On his first day in the big leagues, the slender lefty Preacher Roe taught Eddie that veteran big league pitchers could make him look silly and stupid. Eddie went hitless and got on base in the second inning when Roe walked him. With two outs, Eddie tried to score from second on a single to left field. He charged hard around third. It was a ballsy, gusty, hard-nosed move. The leftfielder was Andy Pafko. Eddie dared Pafko to throw him out, but when he saw the flight of the ball carry in front of him and into the waiting hands of catcher Roy Campanella, he realized he had screwed up.

In those days, there were two towering personalities of Dodger dominance. One was Jackie Robinson and the other was Campanella. They were opposites in many ways, but just like in life and the pennant race, Campy and the Dodgers had the ball in front of the Braves. Eddie had a decision to make: he could try to hook slide around Campy or plow right into him and try to knock him over. There was no time to think about how heavy Campy really was. He was listed at 190, but that was like a pickup truck with the engine stripped out. He was the 1951 National League Most Valuable Player. Who the hell was Eddie Mathews? Some shit-nosed white-boy bush punk who tore up the minors, who the fuck do you think you are? Eddie was a Brave, so he was an underdog. He was a fullback in high school so he dropped his shoulder into Campy. Back in the day, those middle linebackers at Ventura and Oxnard High snapped like twigs. Campy was a different story. Brooklyn's bridge planted his feet over the plate, didn't budge, and knocked Eddie down. With the ball in his bare hand, he punched Eddie in the kidneys to make the tag. Eddie was gone. The Dodgers won 3–2. Eddie never forgot that play. From here on out, the Brooklyn Dodgers had made an enemy out of him.

Of course, almost nobody was at Braves Field to see that play. The game drew only 4,694 fans, a "tragic lack of fan interest," in the words of the *Christian Science Monitor*, and none of those fans realized how important Eddie was to the franchise's future. A few days later, he hit his first big league home run, a game-winner against Philadelphia. Old-timers vowed to kill anyone who messed with his swing. Rogers Hornsby loved his hitting and hated his fielding. "He might hit .500 and field .500," he said. Comparisons ranged from Shoeless Joe Jackson to Pie Traynor to Joe DiMaggio. Paul Waner, the Braves hitting coach and a lifetime .333 hitter with 3,152 hits and a 1927 NL MVP award, marveled at the young slugger. "There's nothing I can teach that boy," Waner said. "He's a natural."

Eddie was an all-or-nothing rookie but he always saved his best for the Dodgers. Eddie struck out in the first inning on September 27, 1952 at Ebbets Field. Then he hit home runs in the third, sixth, and eighth innings to become the first National League rookie to hit three homers in a game. He swung hard for a fourth in the ninth, taking a ferocious cut at a 3-0 pitch and grounding out. The Boston Braves were brutal, but 11-3 wins over the Dodgers eased the pain. Eddie hit 25 home runs and led the league in strikeouts. His power was here to stay. He proved he could hit home runs in New York, Philadelphia, and Chicago as well as he had in Santa Barbara, Oxnard, and Ventura.

When the 1953 season began, Eddie was in paradise. He didn't really like Charlie Grimm because he thought he was a horseshit manager, but at least Grimm drank with his players, players drank with the fans, and Fred Miller had a built-in incentive system that Billy Bruton discovered upon returning to his locker following his opening day game-winning homer. The hero of the day could expect a case of the High Life waiting for him. It was a great life of babes, beer, and baseball. In those glorious first few months in Milwaukee, when the weather thawed and the Braves could do no wrong, Eddie found the cases of High Life stacking up alongside the home runs and fan mail. He got hundred letters a day on perfumed stationary asking for autographs, locks of his hair, dates, his address, and his phone number. He was twenty-one and Hollywood handsome, nicknamed the Ty Power of baseball after the day's leading heartthrob, the California boy with the big-time power, so popular that the PR department ordered postcards of him by the thousands.

He was such a hero that he could get away with anything on or off the field. Like the rest of the Braves, Eddie signed autographs for free and learned he didn't have to pay for anything in town. Once he got pulled over for speeding. When the cop knocked on the window with his nightstick and realized he pulled over Eddie Mathews, he was as joyous as the boy who pulled two Eddies out of the same pack. Eddie could walk into a bar and pick his brew—Miller, Pabst, Schlitz, whatever he wanted—and pick his babes. The single life lived the High Life.

The Milwaukee Braves were having a surprisingly good season on the field and a remarkable season at the box office, thanks in no small part to Eddie, who was hitting home runs at a ridiculous pace and chasing Babe Ruth's 60 home run season record. He was two homers off Ruth's pace through August and five homers off the pace by September. He was so frequently compared to Mickey Mantle that some might have jested that Mantle and Mathews were long-lost brothers. They were born a week apart in 1931, Mathews in Texarkana, Texas, and Mantle in Commerce, Oklahoma. Both had ferocious speed, power, and appetites. Eddie's power was no fluke. He hit three home runs in one game again, this time against the Pirates in Milwaukee on September 16, and finished 1953 with 47 home runs, 135 runs batted in, and hit .302, but Eddie was never the kind of ballplayer infatuated by his statistics. He wanted to win and he needed drinking buddies to make it happen.

His best friend and road roommate was pitcher Bob Buhl, a surly, snarly former paratrooper who was airborne mean, with "wooly eyebrows invariably knitted into a scowl," the *Sentinel* wrote. Buhl never looked happy and might kick the shit out of anyone who tried to get him to smile for the camera. Buhl loved beer, but he had a dry personality. Very few guys understood anything about him. The only guy who could make him laugh was Eddie, but only Buhl would show his love by taking a swing at him. They spent many a night over many years drinking and chasing, speeding down the highway on the High Life, recklessly stupid guys who loved being ball-players and adhered to the old code of the redneck ballplayer—nobody gives a shit what we do off the field as long as we do what we need to on it.

Buhl was a beauty—a hard-throwing right-hander who didn't try to trick anyone. He handled the baseball like it was a bayonet. Fastballs inside—get your ass off the plate—or he would knock you down. Buhl's headhunting reputation was so legendary that when he knocked batters down, Warren Spahn would be the lead judge among Braves pitchers, grading the hitters like they were Olympic divers hitting the dirt when Buhl bayoneted them. If a guy landed flat on his tummy, it was a perfect 10 tumble. The batter would get up, shake the dirt out, edge off the plate, and Buhl would throw a hard sweeping slider on the outer half. The batter would look bad and Buhl would snort, count the strikeouts, and sneer at the world. Buhl would scare the hell out of sportswriters who asked him annoying questions, then in December would smile and warm up children back home in Michigan when he worked a mail route during Christmas-time to keep his legs in shape.

Lew Burdette thought Buhl was the funniest guy he had ever met. Normally, Buhl wouldn't have liked that, but it took one nut job to love another. The mark of Burdette's madness was that Buhl's crabby mood cracked him up. Burdette was too slaphappy and puckish to be pissed off. He liked to sneak up on guys reading the newspaper and light the paper on fire. He was a master at the hot foot and wouldn't hesitate to torch a guy's dress shoes or his favorite cleats. He found a fast friend and road room-mate in Spahn, and their antics became legendary. Spahn and Burdette would go to the zoo just to throw popcorn at gorillas. They went to the department store to make Spahn try on different hats because he looked awful in them. They would haze rookies by nailing their shoes to the floor, cutting up their neckties, and burning their hats. They were practically married. They could finish each other's sentences and order each other's meals. They screwed around so much when they weren't pitching that they antagonized their teammates. "The two biggest pain in the asses were Spahn and Burdette when they weren't pitching," said first baseman Frank Torre, who joined the team in 1956. "They were always screwing around on the bench and a lot of guys used to get annoyed as hell."

Burdette had a rubber arm and a twisted brain. He was strong but he never threw very hard, so he compensated with quirkiness. He was the only guy who tried to intimidate batters while he was laughing. He sniffed for thin skin, reveled in riling the easily rankled, then sank in his sarcastic teeth. He had a special gift for irritating and infuriating Jackie Robinson and Roy Campanella, two of his favorite targets. When Burdette first barked at Robinson in 1952, he called it bench-jockeying, but Robinson thought Burdette's riding was racist. From that moment on, the Milwaukee Braves made enemies out of Robinson and Campanella. During the 1950s, the Dodgers and Braves would fight for the National League. The baseball was always good and the battles were always rough. It wasn't all about race, but racial tension was there. There would be brawls, headhunting, home runs, trash-talk, and intimidation. The Milwaukee Braves already knew it—if they ever wanted to play in the World Series, they were going to have to win a street fight against the Brooklyn Dodgers. The Braves couldn't wait for the fight. But the thing was, neither could the Dodgers.

Burdette would do anything to win, so much so that many thought cheating came naturally to him. His favorite psychological weapon was the spitball—"My best pitch is the one I don't even throw," he often quipped—an illegal offering which Burdette could make sink, dive, and tail. Many umpires checked him and he always came up clean. Opponents tried to use accusatory rhetoric to get inside his head, but as the National League might ask, what head? The fact was that Burdette was a joker and a jerk, a craftsman and a cheater, but he was also a guy who wanted the ball when the heat was on.

He was one of the rare few to make it out of Nitro, West Virginia, a rugged chunk of Appalachia where dynamite chewed off mountain chunks like teeth marks from an apple and dead-end jobs, company scrip, and toxic fumes smelled up the joint. Burdette grew up around guys who thought death was around the corner, so you'd better have fun while you're here.

He pitched his way off the company team to the University of Richmond where a Yankees scout named Bill McCorry gave him a $4,000 contract in 1947.

Burdette broke into the big leagues with the Yankees long enough to grab a can of beer at the end of the 1950 season, but it was obvious Casey Stengel thought this guy was a strange brew with fringy stuff. If Casey loved you, you could drink, fuck, and smoke all you wanted, as long as you used your above-average ability to make him look like a genius. But the way Casey used Burdette at the end of the 1950 season made it clear that he didn't think Burdette could help him. He used him for one stinking inning against the pathetic Washington Senators, and after spring training 1951, sent him packing to the bush leagues. Casey didn't appreciate the man he had pissed off. Some players felt Casey didn't just hurt them. They felt he tried to ruin them. Burdette was one of those guys. The only thing he loved more than rankling was revenge. Burdette, his language filthy as a coal miner, vowed that if he ever got the chance, he would make Casey Stengel look like a fuckin' idiot for farmin' him out.

So Burdette went back to the bushes and won 14 games for the San Francisco Seals in 1951. The Seals were the dregs, but he pitched so well that Braves scout Johnny Moore fell in love with him. When Braves general manager John Quinn came to Los Angeles on August 1, 1951, to discuss potential relocation sites for the Braves, he was also on a special assignment. Moore picked his boss up at the airport and on August 2, Burdette pitched against the Hollywood Stars at Gilmore Field. "Watch this guy," Moore told Quinn. "He gets better the deeper he goes." Burdette pitched a complete game and won 5–3. He was the best pitcher on the worst team in the Pacific Coast League. Casey thought he was sending him off to Alcatraz, where "Saliva Lew" could rot and vanish in the bushes. But Johnny Moore saw a guy whose fastball moved like a bar hopper.

Hollywood Stars shortstop and leadoff hitter George Genovese went 1-for-4 with a double that night, and years later, he could remember telling his manager, "This guy don't throw hard, but he has the best goddamn spitball I've ever seen." The manager of the Hollywood Stars was Fred Haney, who winked up to John Quinn when he saw him in the stands, and had known Quinn since he was a teenage gopher for the Boston Red Sox.

The Yankees always turned the other fifteen teams into their personal farm system every September when they geared up for another World Series. They went shopping for whatever parts they needed, buying veterans from poor teams. The rich got richer and the poor got a few bucks. The Yankees wanted Johnny Sain from the Boston Braves at the end of the 1951 season. Once a formidable pitching tandem with Warren Spahn, the days of "Spahn and Sain and pray for rain," were long gone. Lou Perini wanted $50,000 from the Yankees. Money was no object, but before the deal could be completed, Quinn told Yankees general manager George Weiss that the Braves required a replacement pitcher included in the deal. Weiss submitted a list of roster-fillers, trailer-trash non-prospects in his estimation, but he told Quinn they were all gorgeous winners from the best farm system on earth. Quinn didn't miss. He listened to Johnny Moore and circled Saliva Lew's name, and as Moore predicted, Weiss thought he gypped the stupid Braves all over again.

Burdette found his stride with the Milwaukee Braves. He won 15 games in 1953 and Milwaukee loved him for all the reasons Casey hated him. Burdette was no longer a freak but a phenomenon. Burdette was jittery when he pitched, always bouncing up and down, talking to the baseball, talking to himself, talking to the hitters, barking at them down the line, talking to the sky. You could hear him grunt when he pitched even though he didn't throw hard enough to break a beer bottle. Fans loved him and hitters hated him. Maybe he had inhaled too many fumes back home, maybe he was a little broken upstairs, maybe he had too much of the High Life, but nobody thought there was anything wrong with him, and that was the wonderful part about playing in Milwaukee.

Among the screwballs, Warren Spahn had seniority. He arrived in Milwaukee as the most famous, most successful, and highest-paid player on the team. Spahn was a five-time all-star who was cunning on the mound and goofy and intentionally obnoxious off of it. Spahn was two different guys. On the days he pitched, he would rather die than lose. On the days he didn't pitch, he would rather die laughing. He used to say, "Pressure?

What pressure?" He had been in the Army Corps of Engineers during World War II. When he met his future wife during training, a Cherokee Indian named Lo Rene, he decided they should not get married until after he got home from the war, because he wasn't sure if he was coming home.

All that stood between him getting his guts blown off a bridge during the war was taking a piss break at the exact moment the bridge collapsed. Spahn vowed that if he ever got out of Remagen alive, he would live for the guys who died behind him. He played and pitched without fear. He almost never talked about the Purple Heart or the combat citations he had received, but he had damn near joined the clouds.

Spahn used to kick a hole in those clouds with his high leg kick, one of the most enduring symbols of his pitching style and an iconic athletic action that belongs to him alone. The tip of his spikes scraped the sky before his leg lunged forward and planted in the dirt. Spahn drove from there, over-the-top; as a young man he threw much harder than he did in later years. He hid the ball behind his back, so all the batters could see until the last moment were his eyes, nose, ears, and the tiny little head that wore a cap sized 6⅞. Spahn's limbs were as loose as his personality—quirky, combative, and downright dangly. Spahn's pitches behaved like greasers and juvenile delinquents, running and swerving and generally pissing people off. Spahn only got hit when his little bastard breaking balls, kooky knucklers, and slacking sliders went on the straight and narrow.

Life in Milwaukee was a cold can of beer, pitching a big game, having fun, and screwing around. Money was part of the full life coming his way, the ride he was determined to enjoy after a close call that changed him. He found his baseball soul brother in Burdette, the same way Eddie Mathews and Bob Buhl connected. The four of them were inseparable in the after-hours, especially on the road, where they were the most notorious night owls in the National League. Taken together, they were the heart of Milwaukee's misfits, the High Life offenders of the highest degree, or as Eddie lovingly called them, "My Asshole Buddies."

The Buddies had friends. Maybe the two guys with the hardest jobs in Milwaukee were Del Crandall and Johnny Logan. Crandall, the catcher, had to keep his pitchers in line, though catching Spahnie was easy as driving a Cadillac. Crandall was a no-nonsense, genial guy—a milk drinker, a pro's pro who never used profanity. He was a solid professional twenty-four hours a day, seven days a week. Crandall was born in his catcher's crouch. When he was three, his daddy put a glove on his hand and dared him to catch in the majors. Johnny Moore discovered him playing American Legion ball, scouted him at Fullerton High, and wanted him from the start. Moore was right when he said he would never find another catcher like this and by 1950, Crandall was rushed to the big leagues as a nineteen-year-old rookie. After a two-year army hitch, he was Milwaukee's everyday catcher in 1953, earning fifteen cases of the High Life and giving away fifteen cases of the High Life, one for each of his home runs. But Crandall's greatest talent was his defense. He was an excellent athlete who developed into a catcher who won four Gold Glove awards with a powerful throwing arm, leading the National League in assists six times in his career.

Crandall had the unique perspective of sharing a locker between Spahn and Burdette for years. "Spahn would win a game, the press would come around, and I would get my clothes off, shower, shave, and come back and Spahnie's still talking," Crandall said. "I'd get dressed and I'd leave and Spahn's still holding court. Burdette would win and sit down, the press would come and they'd say 'nice game' and all that stuff and Lew would say, 'Well, don't talk to me, talk to Del, he's the one that called the game.' And then he'd leave. See, the difference in the two was dramatic."

Logan, the hard-nosed and wisecracking shortstop, was a folk hero for Milwaukee kids who related to his hardscrabble upbringing. He signed out of high school in upstate New York with a Braves scout named Dewey Griggs, a hunchbacked postman who gave Logan five bucks a day to play on his semipro team. Logan needed five solid years to prove his worth as an everyday big league shortstop. He was never the most flashy or athletic guy, but he was rangy, his soft hands swallowed ground balls with ease, and he could throw from deep in the hole. He was gritty and vocal, and the more he played, the more confident he became. But no matter what he did, Logan was never the biggest or strongest guy on the field so he turned to his third baseman, Eddie Mathews, to look after him. "He was my protector, you understand," Logan said. And in return, Logan looked after Mathews, who frequently brought hangovers to the ballpark. "If he say to me, 'Eh, I don't feel too good,' that means he went out drinking with the boys, so now I would maybe cover a little more at third base. And meantime, if he said, 'Eh, everything's great,' I go play my regular thing," Logan said. By 1953, Logan was a key part of the High Life, and Milwaukee could never win without him. He never stopped playing like he had something to prove.

The same could be said for first baseman Joe Adcock. He was a rugged right-handed hitting first baseman who had been acquired in a 1953 trade with the Cincinnati Reds. Tall and handsome and from Louisiana stock, he was a good-natured country gentleman, until you got on his bad side or ran afoul of his Southern Democratic sensibilities. Once, in 1956, when New York Giants pitcher Ruben Gomez threw at his head, Adcock dropped his bat and chased Gomez all the way across the field and into the locker room, where Gomez pulled a gun, or a knife, or an ice pick, depending on who tells the story. Adcock backed off and made nice with Gomez. Adcock got himself nineteen cases of the High Life in 1953 and made himself invaluable lineup protection for Eddie—though it was obvious that a hitter of Eddie's caliber needed an equally special right-handed bat to bring out his best. Nobody ever said Joe was the guy for that—least of all, Joe himself.

They were characters and cronies in a unique time and place. "That clubhouse was alive," Del Crandall said. "There was always something going on. Mathews was usually in the middle of it. Burdette was usually in the middle of it. And Spahn! And it was just so much fun to go to the ballpark."

In the years when the barren plot of Milwaukee land was transformed from weeds and dust into County Stadium, the Milwaukee Braves were being similarly assembled. Perini's roster construction should have told Boston that change was coming—Spahn, Mathews, Burdette, Crandall, and Logan all made the trip from Boston to Milwaukee. Perini's baseball company was building for the future, with young players who became pillars and the right blend of veterans who ran like kids and fought like pros. The *Hartford*

Courant predicted in February 1953 that "if owner Lou Perini is patient, maybe Charlie Grimm will deliver another winning pennant to fly at Braves Field around 1955."

The *Courant* was close, but not quite right. The 1953 Milwaukee Braves were better than anyone imagined—tougher, younger, better fed, and watered than their Boston incarnation—but they had no idea how to beat the Dodgers. The fans were so thrilled to have the Braves that they were never booed, and if they botched a play, the fans still loved them. The Braves stayed in first place until the Dodgers caught them on June 27. The Braves kept it close but faded a month later when they lost three out of four in Brooklyn, including a doubleheader sweep on July 26 when tension between the teams simmered again.

Lew Burdette faced Jackie Robinson with runners at first and third and one out in the bottom of the first. Hitting cleanup, Robinson threaded a perfectly placed bunt back to Burdette. Robinson raced down the line, arms flailing and his fists clenched, his legs pumping and kicking dust. He streaked across the bag in front of Burdette's throw. The run scored, and boy, was Burdette pissed. When he got the ball back, he stood on the infield grass between first and the mound. Burdette's blue eyes locked with Jackie's brown eyes. Burdette was furious that Robinson bunted in that situation, but Jackie didn't mind. Breaking the rules made him who he was. Jackie thought Burdette ought to appreciate that, even calling him "the type of player who hates to lose, I'm that kind myself," but as Jackie stood calmly, Burdette burned. When he opened his mouth, it wasn't for compliments on a nice bunt. "He came back with that racial slur," Robinson said.

Burdette knew that if he wanted to get under the Dodgers skin, all he had to do was name the color of it. A week later, in the second inning of a game on August 3 at County Stadium, Burdette decided Roy Campanella was going down. He threw at his head and knocked him down once. Warren Spahn graded Campy's swan dive a nine. Campy got up and yelled at Burdette, so Burdette knocked him down twice. Spahn awarded Campy a perfect ten, and Campy was so shaken that he struck out. Burdette shouted at Campy, who said, "I started to walk away when I heard myself called a name never before uttered in my direction during the time I have been in baseball." Or, as Jackie Robinson put it, "He called Campy a nigger."

Campy exploded. He started toward the mound with the bat in his hand, wielding it like a war club. He yelled at Burdette, who wasn't scared to throw at anyone, because his Asshole Buddy, Eddie Mathews, would always drop his glove and run in from third base. There was no fight this time, but both teams knew that someday these two teams were going to throw punches. Robinson didn't mind that. What he hated most was that Burdette could call him a name and turn around and ask a black ballplayer on his own team to make a play for him. "I don't see how he can face those fellows," Robinson said.

Burdette denied he used racial slurs as readily as he denied throwing the spitball, but racial undertones were a regular part of the Braves-Dodgers rivalry. In Brooklyn on September 4, Eddie hit his 44th home run and then a double on which Burdette tried to score from second. Once again, Roy Campanella, Brooklyn's bridge, had the ball and saddled his feet around the plate. Burdette stayed on his feet and put both arms out and his fists together to pop Campy, who reeled, but never lost his footing, pushed back, and held onto the ball. Both fighters stayed on their feet and Burdette was called out. They didn't party, but they weren't about to share a High Life.

Burdette once boasted proudly that, "I was the meanest player in the National League," which Robinson actually respected. It was the fact that Robinson thought that the Asshole Buddies did not act like they put enough effort into separating the pennant race from matters of race. Robinson, baseball's social watchdog, never had complaints with Spahn, whose control was so precise that he didn't feel the need to throw at batters. He thought Mathews egged Burdette on. "If Burdette says it's his bread and butter to pitch tight, that's all right with me," Robinson said. "But when he goes beyond that, he's stretching it too far."

The 1953 Milwaukee Braves went 92-62, but finished 13 games behind the Dodgers, who had the last laugh when they clinched the pennant in Milwaukee on September 12. The Dodgers had their best team in years, but lost the World Series in six games to the Yankees, who won their fifth consecutive title. The Braves-Dodgers rivalry was great for ticket sales and helped Lou Perini surpass his wildest expectations. The Braves drew a major league record 1.8 million fans with no end in sight. Suddenly, moving an established team to a new market wasn't such a bad idea. Other owners were starting to get in line.

"In Milwaukee, big league baseball is regarded as the outstanding type of entertainment which fits well with the thinking of the people," Perini wrote. He had the cash to prove it, but his players needed to prove they could beat the Dodgers at more than drinking and fighting. He was pleased with his team's progress, but nervous. He did not like how the team faded and he sensed Charlie Grimm might be more soused than the players. The National League was getting stronger and would become tougher when Willie Mays returned to the New York Giants from the Army in 1954. The Yankees were still rolling and the New York baseball dynasty seemed stronger than ever.

The Braves were good, but they were a few players away. One of those missing parts was a big right-handed hitter like Mays. Joe Adcock was a good complementary player, but not a cornerstone bat. Perini tried to make a trade for Roy Campanella in 1948, dangling Warren Spahn as the bait, but had been turned down. He tried to buy slugger Ralph Kiner from the Pirates, but Pittsburgh General Manager Branch Rickey, regarded as the cheapest man in America, loved Kiner so much that he turned down Perini's $200,000 cash offer. Flustered, Perini found hope in the minor league reports about a player having a spectacular season in Jacksonville.

As for Warren Spahn, he was a twenty-three-game winner in 1953 and the biggest loser in the deal. He had nobody to blame but himself. Here he had the owner with the biggest heart in baseball and he had all but told him off. He cried in his beer and the Asshole Buddies consoled him. Probably told him something compassionate, like, "Spahnie, you are a stupid son of a bitch." If he had taken the deal Perini had offered before the move, he would have made $182,000 instead of $25,000. When Spahn visited Perini before spring training in 1954, he politely asked if he could still have ten cents for every ticket sold. Lou Perini declined. He was still a sweetheart, but this deal was off the table.

The foundation of the Braves was solidly in place with personality and profit. The Braves were a good team in any era, but they weren't a great team yet. The buddies needed a balance, somebody with more right-handed firepower than they could possibly imagine, a hitter who could help give Spahn and the pitchers all the runs they would ever need, a batter who could challenge Eddie Mathews to be his best, a slugger who could make Lou Perini's turnstiles click. The player who could help the Milwaukee Braves become a complete and dominant major league franchise was already in the cupboard, but to understand how Henry Aaron was a Milwaukee Brave, you had to understand why Willie Mays wasn't.

4

"GOD SENT ME A MIRACLE"

"The transfer of the Braves to the great city of Milwaukee was just the first move made in accordance with the new era which I believe can best be explained as a baseball-community partnership," Lou Perini wrote in 1953. But he wasn't just talking about shifting teams around the National League or from New York to California. Perini envisioned a worldwide baseball community decades before Major League Baseball considered globalization a reality. He traveled to Europe to promote and explore possibilities for baseball expansion and envisioned a worldwide baseball tournament. "I want to see sports (become) a really international affair," he said. Perini correctly predicted baseball would expand to Canada, naming Toronto specifically twenty-five years before it happened. "Just think," Perini said. "What if the World Series really was the *World* Series?"

Before Perini could fulfill his prophecy and make the Braves global, his team needed to become culturally diverse. He always admired Branch Rickey, and as soon as Rickey initiated a program to scout and sign Negro League players for the Dodgers in 1945, Perini did the same. When Perini couldn't achieve immediate results, he turned to Rickey's never-ending supply of former Negro League talent. In 1949, he purchased center fielder Sam Jethroe from the Dodgers for $100,000. Jethroe was an older player who possessed modest power and could run like the wind, but he wasn't the answer. Perini was looking for a home run hitter who could change the dynamic of his team and dominate the league.

Scout Bill Maughn lived in Cullman, Alabama, and covered the South for the Braves. He forever remembered the night when he stopped at

Rickwood Field while the Birmingham Black Barons were playing. He saw a young center fielder doing unusual things: a child throwing a ball harder and farther than men, a child with athletic movements that were so fast they were violent but so natural they were easy.

When he asked around, Maughn was shocked to learn that this was a high school kid playing in the black big leagues, and that this wasn't his rookie year, he was already an old pro who broke in with the '48 Black Barons. If you wanted to believe the neighborhood scuttlebutt, he had actually been playing here for years under assumed names. He had a protector and mentor, a sage second baseman named Piper Davis who hit Alabama-stride style—balanced, then out off the front foot, hands back, quick wrists, fast to the ball, sharp with his wit—and toughened the kid so White Folks Ball wouldn't have to. When the kid came up to bat, Maughn hustled over to the first-base side so he could watch the right-handed hitter's swing and time his running speed with his stopwatch. He desperately wanted to love the kid, so he needed to know that the boy could hit. He prayed the prayer of the scout: *Dear sweet Jesus, please don't let this guy be horseshit,* but Piper could have told him he didn't need to pray. Here was Lou Perini's dream player: a seventeen-year-old center fielder named Willie Mays.

But if Maughn truly was discovering Mays for the first time, then he was late, operating very discreetly, or completely in the dark. Perini said he already knew about Willie Mays. "We first scouted him when he was fourteen years old," Perini said in 1957, which meant the Braves identified Mays in 1945, almost immediately after launching their Negro American League scouting mission. "From then until he was eighteen, when his high school graduated, we watched him closely. We had an agreement to sign him for $7,000. We also had the right of first refusal if anyone else offered more. Somebody did offer more and at the last minute, we decided not to give the additional $2,500 needed to claim him. So we lost him."

That somebody was the New York Giants and their savvy and creative agent, Alex Pompez, who ran the New York Cubans of the Negro American League and had the best relationship in baseball with Black Barons owner Tom Hayes. The deal was completed in June 1950 for $15,000 total, more than had ever been paid for a player directly out of the Negro

Leagues. Bill Maughn cried, and when Perini saw Mays playing center field for the 1951 Giants, so did he.

Perini vowed this would never happen again. In 1951, he replaced farm director Harry Jenkins with John Mullen and his young assistant, Roland Hemond. The Braves continued signing lower-tier black players, including infielders Preacher Williams and Sherwood Brewer from the Indianapolis Clowns, establishing a relationship with their owner Syd Pollock. Mullen and Hemond had cordial communications with the Clowns in spring 1952 when Pollock first heard the name Henry Aaron. The tip came from a Mobile baseball man named Ed Scott, who was to Aaron what Piper Davis had been to Willie Mays. The first time Scott worked out Henry, he saw what everyone saw first: the loose and explosive hands. Aaron rattled the first pitch Scott threw him up against a corrugated tin fence deep in center field. The ball sounded like a gunshot coming off Aaron's bat, resonating blocks around. Aaron was quiet, shy, scared, nearly malnourished, cross-handed and trained on fast-pitch softball, which black boys played because little leagues and high school ball were segregated. Scott's advice to Henry was, "Major league teams are not signing just ordinary rookies out of high school. They're signing guys who got experience playing with a Negro League team." He called Pollock in Tarrytown, in upstate New York, the actual home of the so-called Indianapolis Clowns. Before Aaron arrived, Pollock noted in a letter to Mullen, "P.S. We've got an eighteen-year-old shortstop."

A few days later, Scott drove Henry to meet the rest of the world. "I carried Henry down to the train station with his little old grip," he said. "Took his picture outside the train station. Still have it in my scrapbook. He had his grip with his clothes, whatever Syd said to have, and two sandwiches. I waved at him from the platform as the train pulled out for Winston-Salem. He waved back from the window with that shy smile of his."

Clowns catcher and player-manager Buster Haywood was loud and boisterous, but he was silenced the first time he watched Aaron hit. Haywood had seen them all, from Josh Gibson to Mays, and he nearly cried when he watched the skinny shortstop from the Mobile Black Bears hittin' Alabama stride style. "God done sent me a miracle," he whispered.

Henry got a two-month taste of the life Mays lived for the two sum-mers he spent traveling with the Black Barons. His older teammates taught him everything except how to hit. "He didn't even know how to cuss," pitcher Jim Tugerson remembered. The Clowns toured the Carolinas through April, living out of the bus and eating out of paper bags, the common life of the vagabond black ballplayer. The Clowns played the Philadelphia Stars, where old man Oscar Charleston, the Stars manager and once the greatest outfielder in the Negro Leagues, tried to teach Henry to hit without cross-ing his hands. The story went that Henry tried it once and went back to hitting the same way he always had. It didn't matter how he held the bat. He held it how he felt like holding it. Didn't matter to him. Aaron's gun-shots attracted scouts wherever he went. Pollock relentlessly promoted him, admiring his level swing and even keel, writing to Scott that "he is not the type who will let publicity go to his head." Henry was leading the league in hitting and Pollock sent the newspaper clips to Mullen, who assigned upstate New York scout Dewey Griggs to be in attendance at the May 25 doubleheader against the Memphis Red Sox at Buffalo's Riverside Grounds ballpark.

But Griggs wasn't immediately impressed. He saw a scrawny black in-fielder lacking basic skills. He was frustrated that Henry wouldn't run hard. When Griggs asked why he wouldn't run, Henry told him his daddy told him to push it only when he needed it most. The impatient scout informed Henry that now was one of those times. Henry did it all in the second game, and though Griggs's initial confidential report expressed hesitation about his work ethic and questioned his intellect because of his color, he, too, heeded the music of Alabama stride style.

Griggs immediately understood that Aaron could be Perini's prize. Missing Mays had created a philosophical shift. If you found a black ball-player who could change the Braves, you better not bury him, or the Bull-dozer would bury you. So Griggs offered Pollock $5,000, a very healthy bid for a Negro League player. A thin, knowing smile crossed Pollock's face. "Turn around, just turn around, and look up behind you," he said. "Those three guys are from the Giants and they're going to be coming down here talking."

Griggs tried again.

"Ten thousand dollars," he said.

That was more like it. Pollock took the deal and Griggs ran to the nearest telephone to call John Mullen. But in his haste, he had made a vital mistake and failed to get the Clowns' travel schedule. Weeks passed and still Mullen and Pollock did not communicate. When they finally did speak, they confirmed the arrangement for a $10,000 purchase: it would be $2,500 up front and $7,500 if Aaron remained with the Braves organization. But Mullen almost made his own fatal mistake when he failed to immediately send a confirmation cable to Pollock. When the Braves didn't hear back from Pollock after a few weeks, General Manager John Quinn, Mullen's boss, demanded a progress report. "That's when we heard that the Giants were sending a telegram and were in on Aaron, too," Hemond said.

The Braves had good reason to be worried. Though Pollock initially agreed to sell Aaron to the Braves, the Giants kept on coming. They submitted bids through Alex Pompez, who was trying to help the Giants steal Aaron the way they had stolen Mays. Pollock became confused and worried. He didn't know which team he should sell Aaron to. He dreaded antagonizing major league teams because he needed their money to keep his team in business. But Pollock's most trusted confidant was Kansas City Monarchs owner Tom Baird, who hated Pompez and the Giants for the way they got Mays out of Birmingham. In hindsight, Baird was prophetic. He understood that a team that marched Henry Aaron and Willie Mays together would be invincible. "It would have been catastrophic for us to face Aaron and Mays on the Giants, in the same outfield," Hemond said. "The Milwaukee Braves would have been also-rans."

Desperate to contact Pollock, Mullen phoned the Morrison Hotel in Chicago, where the Negro American League was holding meetings. Tom Baird intercepted the phone call and went out of his way to make sure Pollock and Mullen communicated. He did everything in his power to assure that Aaron would not join Mays with the Giants, writing to a major league executive in 1959 that, "Hank Aaron would be with the New York Giants if it hadn't been for the help I gave John Mullen in the Aaron purchase."

Tom Baird saved the Milwaukee Braves and helped fulfill Perini's prophecy for nothing more than the sheer self-satisfaction of sticking it to Alex Pompez and the New York Giants. A klansman of regional stature, he took pleasure in depriving Mays, the most famous player from the Kansas City Monarchs' great rival, the Birmingham Black Barons, of playing with Aaron. "We got lucky," Hemond said. "John was relieved when Pollock told him, 'You were first, John. We're going with you.'"

The Clowns were playing in Benton Harbor, Michigan, on June 9, 1952, when news that he had been sold to the Braves reached Henry. He received a standing ovation from 1,500 fans at Edgewater Park when the announcer told the crowd that the eighteen-year-old shortstop was on his way to join the Boston Braves. Henry got two hits—a hard single and a cheap double— and meekly told a local reporter, "I ain't no long ball hitter." Buster Haywood was sad, but he hugged Henry and made sure he packed. He could see his way of life walking out the door. "The majors never give us time now to develop players," he lamented. Henry signed autographs for little leaguers who didn't know his name, then got on a train headed for Class C minor league ball on a $300-per-month contract in Eau Claire, his first taste of Wisconsin. Henry was the last of Alabama's stride style sons, descended from men like Piper Davis, Ed Scott, and a thousand other forgotten ballplayers, and God done sent the Milwaukee Braves a Miracle.

Henry roomed that summer at the YMCA, hitting rockets around the Northern League with fellow black outfielder Wes Covington. Henry's throwing arm was so strong and erratic that he almost killed a man trying to leg out a ground ball, and his first manager, Bill Adair, noted in his reports that the boy was not a true infielder, but damn, he sure could hit. Like many white baseball men, Adair could grade Aaron's bat but lacked the social experience to understand what made him tick. "No one can guess his IQ because he gives you nothing to go on," Adair reported. After the 1952 season, Henry went home to Alabama and toured with the Clowns, passing through Rickwood Field, where Bill Maughn had spied on Willie Mays four years earlier.

Next stop was Class A Jacksonville for 1953, and while the new Milwaukee Braves were living the High Life, Henry was treated like a lowlife.

He was the first black ballplayer in the South Atlantic League and he paid the price for it. Segregated motels, filthy-mouthed racist fans, and head-hunting opponents toughened young Henry's exterior like the calluses on his hands. But damn, he could hit. He led the league in everything that mattered, including pride. You could call Henry the worst name in the book and he would still hit the cover off it.

"I would be catching and he would hit the ball right out of my glove," Savannah catcher Harry Minor recalled. "His hands were so fast, he could start the bat and speed it up almost without effort, and he did this while he had people calling him the worst names you can imagine. But he was unflappable. You never saw it affect his performance."

When Jacksonville played in Macon, an elderly spectator with the internal suffering of an ancient ballplayer watched Henry hit. Ty Cobb, sixty-seven, was grouchy and too old for the heat, but watching Henry hit made him feel young again. Cobb remembered Henry's name, and when he heard in January 1954 that Henry had won the Puerto Rican Winter League batting championship, he knew his instincts were right. This boy was ready for the big leagues.

Charlie Grimm did not share Cobb's enthusiasm. On February 1, 1954, the Braves made a blockbuster seven-player, $50,000 trade with the New York Giants to acquire Bobby Thomson, a strong right-handed hitting outfielder whose "Shot Heard 'Round the World" home run captured the 1951 pennant and captivated a generation. Grimm planned to farm Aaron to Triple-A Toledo for 1954 because he had Thomson, one of the shimmering symbols of New York City's baseball dynasty. Thomson, not Aaron, was considered the heavy-hitting outfielder the High Life lacked. The veteran All-Star had 189 career home runs and four 100-RBI seasons. But a few days into spring training, Thomson fractured his ankle sliding into second base. It was a devastating injury for the Braves, who suddenly needed a new left fielder and another right-handed hitter to protect the protector, Eddie Mathews.

Ben Geraghty, who was Aaron's manager at Jacksonville, suggested Aaron was the guy to replace Thomson. Geraghty was Aaron's strongest advocate in the minors. It was his suggestion for Aaron to play winter ball in Puerto Rico in 1953–1954. According to Roland Hemond, Geraghty told John Quinn that, "If he goes to the outfield, he'll be ready to hit for you (in 1954)."

Hemond remembered typing the first scouting report the upper levels of the Braves organization had read about Aaron. "Henry Louis Aaron," Hemond recalled. "We graded by using the terms 'Fair,' 'Good,' or 'Very Good.' Aaron: Hit: very good. Run: good. Power: very good. Arm: good. Field: Very good, as an outfielder, not an infielder."

Grimm ignored the organization's enthusiasm. He knew almost nothing about Aaron and said the Braves needed a left fielder, not a second baseman, the position Henry had played for Jacksonville. Geraghty agreed that Henry wasn't a major league infielder. But Geraghty countered that Henry's arm and speed would translate well to the outfield. All he needed was a defensive tutor. He was certain Aaron would hit.

Geraghty thought Grimm's hesitation was short-sighted. Geraghty always knew Henry's glove wasn't going to get him to the big leagues. It was his bat, stupid. Though Geraghty never hit a single home run in almost a decade as a professional ballplayer, he saw lift in Henry's swing. He was adamant that Henry was ready to hit in the big leagues right now, so certain of the kid's ability that he willingly risked his reputation and probably his job. Geraghty predicted Henry would hit from the start, but you'd have to wait a few years for the real power. Geraghty also believed there was something different about this kid, an intangible that allowed him to perform at a high level no matter the social indignities that would surely accompany his success. "A Negro ballplayer must be a good ballplayer and not just a curiosity," Geraghty said. Aaron loved playing for Geraghty because he put baseball above all else.

But Grimm was different. He was not eager to give Aaron a look. He thought Aaron was too young, too green, too black, too raw, or just too quiet. A loud, obnoxious baseball man from years past, Grimm's official reasoning was that Henry wasn't ready, but nearly everyone felt Grimm was stonewalling. Perini, the Bulldozer, took notice. He was very quietly telling the Milwaukee writers to pay attention to Henry and to not pick on him because he was a defenseless black kid. Grimm naturally liked his players to be brazenly loose and loud, as ball-swaggering and beer-swigging as he was. Henry was none of those. Hell, he wasn't even white, and Grimm would never say in public what his indifference showed—that racial equality should not mean asking an established big league manager to replace a major league All-Star with a Negro League busher. Grimm didn't know anything about Aaron, knew nothing about who he was or where he came from, and had bigger players to worry about.

Ty Cobb chastised Grimm for being stupid. Though Cobb was reputed to be a racist, Henry's swing carried more clout than whatever was in his heart. Cobb was a son of the Confederacy, and all he could think was, damn, this Aaron kid sure can hit. When Cobb lunched with Grimm, he told him he would be an idiot if he didn't bring Henry to Milwaukee. "What I like about Aaron is his hitting," explained Cobb, a lifetime .367 hitter. "His mannerisms at the plate really impressed me."

All the noise Henry made was with his bat. Most people couldn't understand how someone so talented could be so humble. Eventually, Charlie Grimm realized that if he was going to be the only guy in baseball who thought the rookie wasn't ready, he was going to look awfully antiquated. There were greater hitting minds than his in complete agreement. Ted Williams was thirty-seven years old and nearing the end of the line when he saw a virtual right-handed version of himself, infused with hitting genetics and colossal pride. The only difference was in the octave of the voice and opinion, not in the balance and rhythm of the swing. "There was this crack of the bat," Williams said. "Someone hit that one on the nose. There was this skinny kid I had never seen before in the batter's box. It was my introduction to Henry Aaron."

Henry's calm mannerisms were perplexing to some of the older players. Rookies were stepped on like beer cans and routinely intimidated by older players who resented bushers threatening their careers. But there was nothing so daunting as being a black rookie. Milwaukee's major league camp in Bradenton and minor league camp in Waycross were both segregated, but Henry acted like discrimination was the least of his problems. Most white players didn't understand what black players had to go through. This, too, never seeped into Henry's performance. Henry was no different than Ted Williams had been as a rookie. He was there to hit. He was there to prove himself. He was single-minded in his obsession to prove that there was not a single damn pitcher who could throw a ball past him. He was there to be a ballplayer.

Ballplayers were not sociologists, but they were forced to confront social issues. Suspicion came out in the form of baseball questions. Joe Adcock openly wondered if the kid would hit. Then he saw a few line drives and decided Henry might kill a pitcher one day. Eddie Mathews wanted to see Henry against good pitching. "I'll admit that Aaron is a fine prospect but I want to see how he goes against Dodgers pitchers before I pass judgment," he said. Bob Buhl, who had witnessed Aaron hitting seasoned major league pitchers in the Puerto Rican Winter League, thought some of his buddies were being assholes. He scowled, "Aaron is a terrific line-drive hitter, good enough to win a regular job." He wanted this kid's bat in the lineup when he was pitching and he'd fight anyone who disagreed. When Warren Spahn watched Aaron hit, he was amazed at his serene presence. Very few rookies had ever been so focused on playing the game that outside inertia did not touch them. Then he watched him hit and made up his mind. He told the rest of his team to shut up. The kid was going to help them win. "Let the Dodgers find his blind spot," he said. "If he has one."

When the Braves and Dodgers played a Southern spring training series in Birmingham in 1954 amid concerns of police intervention prohibiting the mixing of races at a public park, Aaron went 3-for-4 in Rickwood Field, Alabama stride style, against Dodgers front-line pitchers Carl Erskine and Joe Black. Impressed, Clem Labine, another Dodger starting pitcher from the 105-victory 1953 team, said Aaron was already one of the toughest outs in baseball—and he had yet to play an official game. "He's harder to pitch to than Mantle," Labine said. "Even if you fool him, he snaps those wrists and goes to right field."

Upon watching Henry Aaron play, Jackie Robinson was moved. This baby boy was exactly the kind of young player for which he had sacrificed and suffered. Henry was the fruit of Jackie's labor. Jackie hoped other young black ballplayers would never forget those who came before them. He watched Henry hit and knew God done sent a miracle. Then he agreed with Ty Cobb for probably the first and only time in his life. When asked what he thought about Aaron, the normally talkative Jackie became annoyed and terse. Why did anyone need to ask such an obvious question? "He's ready," Robinson snapped.

On Opening Day, 1954, Henry Aaron, wearing number 5, joined the High Life, batting fifth and playing left field. He knew very little about Milwaukee, except perhaps that the National Baptist Conference had been held there in 1950. Mobile clergy had attended, reporting in the local congregational newspaper, *The Advocate,* that "Milwaukee had not seen so many colored people as were assembled before the congress. My! What a multitude!"

A new era had begun, but the 1954 Braves were no closer to winning it all. Eddie hit 40 home runs, Spahn won 20 games, Burdette won 14 and rookie pitcher Gene Conley, who moonlighted as a basketball player for the Boston Celtics, won 14. Center fielder Billy Bruton took Henry under his wing personally and professionally. "He was like a father to me," Henry said. "He was a little bit older than I was. I looked upon him as someone I could get information from. He was a very intelligent player. I talked to him quite a bit. I got to know his family, his wife, you know, I knew him pretty well."

Henry flashed his future, hitting .280 with 13 home runs before he broke his ankle at the end of the season. He was only twenty and he finished second in the National League Rookie of the Year voting.

Lou Perini kept an eye on him. He had a genuine concern for his young rookie. He didn't want Henry to feel homesick, so he asked about his family. He told Henry about his wife and his seven children. He helped create an environment and a support system completely free from where guys dressed in the clubhouse and what guys said when they didn't know any better. "Growing up, I never ever heard him use a racial or ethnic slur, I think because of the way he was raised and the things he experienced as an Italian kid," David Perini said. "Dad always had that attitude—people should always feel included. Nothing historical or social should keep them from fitting in."

In turn, Perini helped Henry grow up fast. He gained confidence and began flashing his personality. When Perini praised him at a postseason banquet, Aaron asked, "Does he mean these things before I sign or after I sign?" Aaron's overall future potential was limitless, but he hadn't grown into the kind of player Willie Mays had become. Mays returned from the army as a wiser hitter, winning the 1954 NL Most Valuable Player award and leading the New York Giants to the World Series crown. The New York dynasty continued—and even after the Yankees' streak ended at five straight, the Giants took it home. The Braves were competitive but fell to third place with 89 wins, behind the Giants and the hated Dodgers. The fans didn't care. The Braves were still the hottest ticket in town and now complacency set in. "The players were treated so royally," Roland Hemond said. "They had cars loaned to them, free beer and bratwurst, and they didn't have to pay for their dry cleaning. They got free gas for their cars. It was beyond belief the way the city supported the players beyond the games. They were treated like new celebrities in town and beyond."

It added up to astounding box office receipts. The Braves drew 2.1 million fans to County Stadium and became the first team to surpass the two-million mark. They led the majors, vastly surpassing the 1.4 million fans the Yankees drew. Bushville remained big ticket.

Someone else in New York saw money in Milwaukee. Lou Perini's unparalleled financial success enticed Henry Luce, the most powerful corporate executive in American magazine publishing. Luce envisioned using the Milwaukee Braves to launch his own franchise. Luce's magazine Murderer's Row—*Time, Life,* and *Fortune*—were staples in every living room, office, bar, and barbershop in America. But Luce wanted a cleanup hitter, a guy's magazine, a glossy homage to testosterone. Perhaps someday there would be swimsuit girls in its pages, but for now, *Sports Illustrated* needed a cover boy. It needed someone Luce was certain could sell a lot of magazines to complete his self-proclaimed "American Century." He could go with Willie Mays, but Luce had to ask himself marketing questions. Would a black ballplayer on the cover of a new magazine sell in Iowa and Michigan and Wisconsin, as well as it would in New York and Chicago? He could always go with Mickey Mantle, who by 1954 had been on the front of everything except the one-dollar bill. Duke Snider was an option, but the Bums weren't drawing like they used to. If not Mickey, Willie, or the Duke, where was the biggest story in baseball for the past two years? Nobody had ever seen two millions fans come to a major league stadium until Bushville came along, so Luce copied the formula and chose Milwaukee.

The cover of the August 16, 1954, inaugural issue of *Sports Illustrated* featured Eddie Mathews taking a ferocious fully extended cut beneath the glowing lights of a capacity County Stadium. Eddie's swing was almost as pretty as the forthcoming swimsuit issues. While the magazine searched for its voice, Milwaukee and Mathews connected with the common fan. The magazine was a big seller in the Heartland, even though Braves fans were disappointed to open the magazine and discover that the cover story wasn't about Eddie. It was about Willie Mays.

Eddie and Mays. Now there was a fight Eddie would have loved to happen. Eddie couldn't stand Mays. He didn't like how he played the game and he hated Mays's obsession with drawing attention to himself. He hated how Willie fiddled with his hat to make it fly off his head when he was on the run. Eddie didn't mind Willie's talent. It was his mouth and self-importance he couldn't tolerate. Once, when the Pittsburgh Pirates were becoming the first team to regularly wear plastic shells as rudimentary batting helmets, a light-hitting backup infielder named Dick Cole was trying one out. Cole remembered Mays howling at him, "Goddamn, Cole, you don't need one of them because nobody is gonna throw at you." Mathews hated such disrespect for fellow players. He felt Mays disrespected the game when his thirst for flashy plays turned into bush league mistakes. He loved hassling Mays on the field and off it, he wasn't afraid to show his disdain.

Once, while barhopping in New York City, Eddie demanded to know why the bartender kept a framed photo of Mays prominently displayed above the beer taps. When the bartender told him Mays was his favorite player, Mathews jumped over the bar, ripped the photo off the wall, and smashed it. Two seconds later, a gang of goons was smashing the hell out of Eddie, who didn't give a shit. Fighting was fun.

Another time, Eddie went into a bar owned by a boxing trainer. He looked like an athlete, so the bartender assumed Eddie was a fighter, especially when he asked, "Where the hell is my picture?" When Eddie scanned the bar and discovered a photo of Willie at the end of the wall, well, you know what happened next. Only Eddie could be crazy enough, drunk enough, and fearlessly insane enough to piss off a bar full of boxers. Eddie landed some and took some, and in the end, thanked the guy for putting up with him. He walked out the door feeling pretty good. That was his idea of a good time.

Eddie loved Henry Aaron for all the reasons he disliked Mays. There was never a moment anyone could remember when Eddie underwent some kind of revelation about why he should care about Henry Aaron. He just did. Eddie made it known—anyone who wants a piece of Henry gets a piece of him. Eddie didn't give a shit what anybody thought about that. Henry was his man. In turn, Henry instinctively understood what made Eddie click. "Eddie was a big cat," future teammate Red Schoendienst said. "You can pet him, but don't try and corner him." Henry and Eddie's bond was strong and recognizable. "They both laughed and joked," Schoendienst said. "They'd get on each other in the right way, not in a way that was going to hurt them."

That was because, for all of Eddie's beers and brawls, he had what another future teammate, Frank Torre, called "a heart of gold." Eddie could say insensitive and boneheaded things, yes, and he could say things that alienated people of other races and religions. But this aspect of his personality did not pollute his relationship with Aaron largely because Eddie and Henry were neither allowed nor did they feel the need to socialize together off the field. They led separate lives away from the ballpark, but this was not a consideration for either of them. Henry and Eddie were not like Spahn and Burdette or even Eddie and Buhl. They were great coworkers with a tremendous level of mutual respect and had enough common ground to bond at a closer level. And the best thing Eddie ever did was to never go drinking with Henry. "Eddie was the nicest guy in the world until he was drinkin'," Torre said. "He was tough as nails and a tremendous competitor. There was no ifs, ands, or buts about him."

Henry accepted Eddie exactly for what he was, too. And that was rare at a time when black and white ballplayers, especially tremendously talented ones, were playing together. Race was never an issue between them. It was all about baseball. And both guys loved that about the other. Race, class, money, society—that was the outside world and it didn't belong in the clubhouse or on the field. Both guys had one thing in common—when they were hitting, they didn't want anyone or anything from outside world intruding.

Years later, when Eddie was scouting, he explained his admiration for Henry to fellow scout Rick Schroeder. "Eddie's feeling was, 'If you are on my team, you are with me, and we are loyal,'" Schroeder said. "He was very loyal to Hank and vice versa. A lot of it was to protect Hank. Hank felt Eddie physically protected him on and off the field. It wasn't anything ever said. It was in Eddie's actions. Hank was his teammate and he loved him."

5

THE GREAT PRETENDERS

Milwaukee changed forever on December 18, 1954. Fred Miller, his son, and two pilots were killed in a fiery plane crash at Mitchell Field. Their Lockheed Ventura developed engine troubles immediately after takeoff and crashed, killing pilots Joseph and Paul Laird and Fred Jr. Only Miller survived the initial impact. He was thrown clear of the wreckage and lay dying on the tarmac. When rescue crews reached him, they found fire had consumed Miller's skin, but he was still alive. "My God, don't bother about me," he reportedly told them. "Save my son."

For four excruciating hours, Fred Miller survived. When he died, church bells tolled across Wisconsin. Nothing would be exactly the same again, including the Braves. Miller's funeral brought the Midwest together. Notre Dame football coach Frank Leahy led the university in mourning at a memorial mass in South Bend. Lou Perini prayed the rosary at Miller's funeral and later established scholarship funds in his name. Miller's death was the kind of loss that never healed.

The 1955 season was all about the Brooklyn Dodgers, who finally beat the Yankees in the World Series and extended the New York City World Series dynasty to seven years. Fans from around the country were beginning to wonder if baseball anywhere else mattered. It did in Milwaukee, where the High Life was still flowing. Henry Aaron continued to develop into a dominant major leaguer. As a rookie Henry had worn number 5, an infielder's number, not a number that a big hitter would wear. Mathews wore number 41, so Henry wanted something closer to Eddie's number. How Henry became number 44 is the stuff of urban legend, but one version goes like this:

On a hot afternoon in 1955, while the Cubs were in town beating up on the Braves, Henry decided he had seen enough of number 5.

He walked down the tunnel and found Tommy Ferguson, the Braves visiting clubhouse assistant, who said he was filling in for home clubby Joe Taylor. "Henry took off his number 5 shirt and said, 'Hey Fergie, I want a shirt in the 40s.' I knew he didn't want that number 5 no more, he wanted a bigger number like the rest of them guys. I said, 'Lemme see what I can get.'" Ferguson rummaged through the folded-up flannels. "It was easy to find him a pair of pants, home and road, because he had the waist of a bat boy. It was hard to find him a shirt. I'm going through all them uniforms. Finally I come up with the extra shirts. These were leftovers from spring training. On the bottom of one of them shirts, it was number 44. I pulled it out. When he saw it was 44, he was happy as hell."

It made for a great story and proved that Henry's ability was enough to generate tall tales. One thing was for certain: Henry wasn't creating his own mythology. His home runs moved others to hyperbole. "Henry was so shy back then," Bobby Uecker said. "He was a shy guy. Nobody—well, who knows some guy is going to hit 900 fuckin' home runs? How do you know that? Just come out of Eau Claire, Wisconsin, and hit 900 fuckin' home runs!"

Aaron didn't quite hit 900 home runs wearing his new number 44 in 1955, but he did pretty good anyway, batting .314 with 27 home runs and 106 runs batted in. The secret was out. By the time Pittsburgh Pirates scout Howie Haak watched Aaron in spring training the following season, Henry was gaining new confidence and maturing as a man and a major leaguer. "HENRY AARON—NEGRO—Liable to lead the national league in hitting someday. Untouchable," Haak wrote.

He was a baby-faced killer. Nothing fazed him. Phillies pitching ace Robin Roberts repeated an oft-told comment, joking that Aaron "catches up on his sleep between pitches." Charlie Grimm even changed his tune. "Mays is the best out there in center field, but when it comes to hitting, don't be surprised if Henry turns out to be better."

At least you could always depend on the Milwaukee Braves and Brooklyn Dodgers hating each other. Their animosity had reached a boiling point on Sunday, July 31, 1954, at Ebbets Field, thanks partly to a borrowed bat. Joe Adcock hit a home run and then broke his bat on a single in the ninth inning on Friday night. That was like a death in the family, so on Saturday he borrowed some lumber from backup catcher Charlie White. Adcock mumbled "thank you very much" and then went out and had what at the time was the single most prolific offensive day in major league history. He hit four home runs and a double, and collected 18 total bases. Adcock was an immediate darling—he posed with a wide smile and four, long, strong wiry fingers extended off his enormous palm. Suddenly, Adcock was more popular than "Rock Around the Clock." There were so many demands for interviews that Adcock made Andy Pakfo's hotel room a hideout for the night.

But the following day, everyone knew what was coming next. In his first at-bat on Sunday, Dodgers pitcher Russ Meyer knocked him down. That was to be expected. Joe got up and hit a double that nearly went out of the park. Like many right-handed hitters, Adcock thought he'd be good for 40 bombs a year if he played in this dump. He wanted another home run when he came up in the fourth inning against Clem Labine, but enough was enough. Adcock took a huge rip at the first pitch and came up empty. On the second pitch, Labine drilled Adcock on the left side of the head, "with a distinct thud," according to the *Journal*.

Adcock was knocked cold. He laid flat on his back with his legs spread. He looked dead. All he needed was police tape and a chalk outline. Tempers flared. Both teams spilled onto the field. The Asshole Buddies were itching for a fight. Jackie Robinson was playing third base and Eddie Mathews was the base runner at second. Eddie went after Jackie, but Jackie didn't want Eddie. He was going after Lew Burdette, who came out after Labine. Jackie got to Burdette, but only because center fielder Duke Snider grabbed Eddie first.

At home plate where Adcock lay cold, Jackie and Burdette screamed and pointed at each other. Caught up in Snider's muscular arms, the best Eddie could do was yell at Jackie, whose point to Burdette was clear—we have every right to throw at your guys if you throw at ours. Jackie was very mindful of keeping this tension between the lines. This was a baseball score to settle, nothing else. Burdette mercilessly taunted Robinson, but Jackie knew that if he ever threw a punch, it could be the end of his career.

Once the Braves finally pulled Burdette back from the brink, Charlie Grimm got in Jackie's face. Jackie jawed right back, their arguing was loud and profane and the fans could hear everything. A moment later, Eddie, finally free of Snider's grasp, charged Jackie. For a moment, Eddie looked like he wanted to pulverize Jackie, but he put on the brakes, and instead the two were yelling nose-to-nose at each other. Eddie was pissed that Joe was half dead on the diamond. Gil Hodges finally succeeded in pulling Jackie off the field. They could kiss his blue number 42. Oh, how Eddie longed for just one swing at Jackie Robinson. Oh, how the feeling was mutual.

"I was watching Mathews out of the corner of my eye, figuring he might try to sneak one in," Robinson said. "He and Burdette were both berating me by that time and finally Mathews and I got pretty close. I don't know how close we were, but I was ready. I don't go around looking for fights, but when one comes up I'm not going to run away from it."

And the same was true for the Milwaukee Braves, especially the Asshole Buddies. Eddie was never as forthcoming in the papers as Jackie was. "No comment," he growled. But, further pressed for the reasons behind the fight, Eddie cracked. "Why don't you ask Jackie Robinson?" he snorted.

The fights caused gaping wounds between the Braves and the Dodgers. The 1955 Braves never seriously challenged the Dodgers, who ran away with the NL pennant, winning 98 games to finish 13 ½ games in front of second-place Milwaukee, which posted an 85-69 record, respectable, but by far the least successful season since the team moved. The Dodgers went to the World Series and beat the Yankees in a seven-game classic. But the bad taste between the Braves and the Dodgers lingered, echoed in a previously unpublished private letter written by Robinson to *Milwaukee Sentinel* sportswriter Lou Chapman on February 10, 1955.

> Dear Lou:
> I received your nice letter and am sorry for the misunderstanding. I am sure you can appreciate my position when my wife tells me over the phone there is another rhubarb in Milwaukee. It

was hard for me to picture anything I had said or done to create one. Then, to see a statement by Mathews, really made me angry. Not at Eddie, but the reports out of your city. Certainly, your story should not have created anymore of a fuss than what I said. If I in anyway cast any reflection upon you, please accept my apology, and I hope this will end the discussion. I guess regardless of what I do, it will always be the same. As one newspaperman told me, it's foolish for them to pick the good things one does because they don't make a story. Best wishes to you and I hope this does not alter our friendship.

Sincerely,

Jackie Robinson

Milwaukee's roughneck reputation concerned Lou Perini. He never told his players how to live life, but he also wanted baseball players and not a boxing team. He wanted to beat the Dodgers and he wanted a shot at the Yankees, so the first person he questioned was himself. Had he done too much for his players? Was the city coddling the players so much that they lacked the incentive to win? His baseball team was the ultimate construction job and he started to feel behind schedule. That did not sit well with him. He began to wonder if the wrong guy was in charge. "He was always thinking about where the company could go next," David Perini said. "Whatever he got himself into, he was determined to follow up on."

At a banquet before the 1956 season, a fan asked Perini and Charlie Grimm if this would finally be the year the Braves won the pennant. Perini stared at Grimm.

"Shall I stick my neck out?" Perini asked.

"Stick it out all over," Grimm fired back.

Sarcasm was not what Perini wanted.

"I will be a little disappointed if we don't win it this year," Perini said. The warning was official.

General Manager John Quinn offered a shrewd suggestion. The Braves should hire Fred Haney to coach third base and look over Grimm's shoulder during the 1956 season. Perini, as usual, listened to Quinn. Grimm was a popular figure for years in Milwaukee, but he wasn't getting it done. He was not happy that Haney was added to the staff and he laughed off suggestions that he was threatened. But Grimm and Haney both knew what was going on. The Braves started the 1956 season in first place with a 19-10 record and then staggered through a dreadful home stand, including three consecutive losses to the Dodgers, knocking the Braves to fourth place. After the last game of the home stand, Quinn entered the clubhouse unannounced. He never, ever, came to the clubhouse. He undressed the players before they could shower. Grimm actually thought Quinn's tongue-lashing was warranted, but when he asked if it was his turn to berate his team, Quinn told him that time had passed. Grimm was infuriated. He didn't know what made him more angry: the fact that the front office was taking his team away from him or the fact that Quinn accused his team of playing soft. "That is the last time anybody is ever going to come into my clubhouse and tell my players they aren't hustling," Grimm said.

It wasn't going to be his clubhouse for very much longer. Perini denied rumors that he was ready to fire Grimm, but when the Braves came to Brooklyn a week later, Perini and Quinn were sitting together next to the dugout, literally looking over Grimm's shoulder. Cholly was most definitely not Jolly. He was tight and nervous and micromanaging the pitching staff. "It got so bad, we looked over to the dugout as soon as we allowed a couple of hits," Warren Spahn said. The Dodgers made the Braves look back in two consecutive one-run losses, the sort of gut-wrenching defeats that weighed on Perini like the water pails. *Pittsburgh Courier* columnist Wendell Smith called them "Charlie Grimm's ever-threatening, never-winning Braves." Finally, on the morning of June 17, Perini made Grimm announce his own dismissal. He could do it any way he wanted, but Perini insisted Charlie light his own cigarette when he faced the firing squad. He announced his resignation in the lobby of the Hotel Commodore, quipping, "I've decided to let somebody else take a crack at the job." Milwaukee fans were glad to see him go. "Grimm treated men like boys," a housewife wrote to the *Journal*. "The Braves need somebody stricter." If ordinary fans could see the Braves were playing like drunken frat boys managed by a bartender, everyone could. "Some people are born to be tough. I wasn't and it's too late for me to change," Grimm said.

Twenty minutes after Charlie grabbed a cab out of town, Perini's solution strode into the lobby. Fred Haney announced he had been appointed manager for the rest of the 1956 season. At age fifty-eight, he had been waiting his entire career for an opportunity like this. Haney was five feet and seven inches of curses and causes, a small man in the realm of redwoods who had never won anything in the majors, but whose thirst to be a big shot drove the fierce conviction that he could push others as hard as he pushed himself.

Wrinkly, red, and gray from the years, he dressed like a studio boss, right down to the shimmering hanky poking out of his pocket. Haney was a legendary Hollywood hard-ass—he loved the attention he garnered from exacting stern discipline upon unwilling participants. He was born in Los Angeles, never met a photo op he didn't like, and relentlessly used baseball to dabble in showbiz.

He knew every writer, producer, director, starlet, and movie star in town. Hell, when he managed the Hollywood Stars, his boss was Bob Cobb, owner of the famed Brown Derby Restaurant, where a thousand careers started and a million more ended. Haney was used to being surrounded by star power and had an enormous ego himself. The High Life boys would be nothing compared to sitting around a table with Jack Warner or some other millionaire studio chief. Haney had been around big money for years, which undoubtedly appealed to Perini. Haney wasn't about to let a bunch of screwballs screw around with Perini's fortune, especially not when it amounted to ridding his own reputation as a bush league manager. "Baseball is business—big business," Haney said.

He was schooled in the finer points of the game, mentored and developed by his close friend and former teammate and manager Ty Cobb to bunt, steal bases, play correct defense, and execute the hit-and-run. Haney's sense of discipline was as sharp as Cobb's spikes. "He's just the sort Ty takes to," the *Sporting News* wrote in 1922, though some of Haney's ballplayers hated him for the same reason players disliked Cobb. Haney used their talent to compensate for his insecurity. He used the principals Cobb taught him not only to survive as a backup big league infielder in the 1920s, but as bench boss for the brutal St. Louis Browns and the last-place Pirates. "The important thing is this—you don't play baseball, you work baseball," Haney said in his introductory press conference, and it was a warning shot to the Asshole Buddies and barflies that if they ever wanted to be thought of as more than Bushers, they were going to have to shape up or be shipped out. "Baseball," Haney reiterated, "is all business."

Warren Spahn wanted to win at all costs. He had been in the big leagues long enough to sense his own vulnerability. He had a rubber arm, but even he knew he couldn't pitch forever. He sensed, as others did, that patience might one day run out on the High Life. He also began to ask himself hard questions. Had he too become complacent? Had he worked as hard as he could? "We were in Milwaukee over three years before we heard our first boo," he said. Old critic Shirley Povich of *The Washington Post* didn't hide his satisfaction in Bushville's turmoil. "The honeymoon phase of major league baseball in Milwaukee is at an end and Milwaukee fans are no longer riding their pink clouds," he wrote. "The town whose eager fans smashed all National League attendance records has become more demanding of its ball team with each passing season."

Haney's hiring caused a team-wide pause, as if none of them had ever left the tailgate party since the day the train arrived in Milwaukee in 1953. Perini replaced a bartender with a beat cop. Haney presented a challenge to their pride. The time had come for them to leave their legacy or be left behind. On his first day as manager, the Braves swept a doubleheader from the Dodgers at Ebbets Field. Joe Adcock, who always seemed to do his best work with a borrowed bat, got a loaner from Dodger outfielder Carl Furillo and hit three home runs in two games. The Fred Haney era had begun.

By July 4, 1956, the Braves were in a first-place tie with the Cincinnati Reds. Excitement rose with heat waves through the tailgate parties. Pennant fever swept the Milwaukee summer. On July 20, the Braves had a two-game lead over the Reds, and more impressively, a six-game lead over the hated Brooklyn Dodgers. In the lobby of a Milwaukee hotel, a fan cornered Perini and asked him for three tickets. Perini agreed. "Thanks a lot," the fan said. "Now we can go and root for the Dodgers. I'm sure they're going to beat the Braves!" Perini didn't know what to say and was further perplexed when the young man asked for his autograph. Three tickets down, he figured what's a signature. The kid looked at the piece of paper. He had the team owners confused. Now it all made perfect sense. "Oh, sorry," the kid said. "I thought you were Walter O'Malley."

If the Braves could put the Dodgers away, most expected the pennant would not be far behind, and at last, a shot to knock off the self-righteous New York Yankees in the World Series. World Series ticket deposits were accepted for the first time and hotel reservations filled up. Every home game was a sellout as Braves fans flooded the gates with two million fans for the third consecutive year. The ticket office, sensing a golden marketing opportunity and ignoring any traces of modesty, ordered a thirty-foot-high carved wooden Indian sitting happily atop a globe. He held a bat in one hand and his other hand rested at his knee, though one might have wondered why he wasn't holding a High Life. A big toothy smile was painted across the grinning warrior's face, suggesting he drank his beer before he climbed atop County Stadium. The well-honed hero needed only to be portrayed wearing a loincloth and moccasins, proper attire no matter the chill October would surely bring. The wooden warrior was just slightly ethnocentric, but Wisconsin didn't mind. The handsome young Brave was hoisted above the stadium's main gate to welcome the inevitable World Series to the Heartland. Nothing could possibly go wrong this time.

On August 1, the Braves remained in first place, two games in front of the Reds and three in front of the Dodgers, who were coming to County Stadium on August 27. Jackie Robinson, with his waist widening and his body giving out, came to bat and heard the unmistakable Appalachian yell of Lew Burdette, who "unleashed a stream of racial epithets," according to *Sentinel* sportswriter Lou Chapman. Robinson said nothing. When he took his position at third base between innings, Burdette howled, "Hey, watermelon!" Jackie had one final last piece of business to attend to before he retired at the end of the season. He spied Burdette hanging out in the dugout like a limp scarecrow with a dark grin painted across his face. Robinson scooped up a grounder and rifled a throw into the Braves dugout, "whizzing through the dugout and missing Burdette by inches," Chapman said. Robinson challenged Burdette to a fight after the game. Burdette declined. "Any moron can do that," he countered. Robinson prided himself on playing the game right, and though years later, Burdette said he and Robinson made amends, at the time Jackie had no love for him. "Lucky for him, I missed," Robinson said.

The Braves hoped they wouldn't miss this year, but the incident with the Dodgers should have reminded them not to count Brooklyn out. The Braves reached September in first place, two games in front of the Dodgers and 3½ in front of the Reds, but they did not play well down the stretch. Warren Spahn became a 20-game winner for the seventh time, but Burdette and Bob Buhl did not pitch well. Henry Aaron was closing in on the National League batting championship, but the rest of the team wasn't hitting and the Dodgers came charging back. Fred Haney defended his team, but also reminded them how "you can't back your way into a pennant."

But only a dramatic collapse would cost the Braves the pennant. On September 26, Reds manager Birdie Tebbetts declared, "I don't see how Milwaukee can lose." On the final weekend of the season, the Braves were 91-61 and held a half game lead over the Dodgers entering a three-game series in St. Louis on Friday, September 28. Jackie Robinson needled the Braves from afar. "(They) could get their nose bloodied in their last three games with the Cardinals," he warned. The Dodgers were rained out in Pittsburgh on Friday night, leaving the Braves a golden opportunity to take a one-game lead with two to play, if they could beat the Cardinals.

But Buhl, the former paratrooper who won 18 games, was shot down in the first inning and gave up three runs before Haney cut him down from the trees. The Braves crept back to tie the score, 3–3, after five innings, but promptly gave two runs back in the sixth inning when the usually reliable Crandall made a key error, and the Braves fell behind 5–3.

The Braves got one back in the eighth, thanks to the Alabama connection. Billy Bruton doubled and Henry Aaron singled him home stride style to cut the lead to one run, but the Braves went without a fight in the ninth, falling 5–4. The press box was filled with out-of-town writers, who had come to witness history or a funeral. Frank Finch of the *Los Angeles Times* piled on, "The Braves played like a bunch of bushers."

Saturday meant the season. It would measure all the progress the Braves had made since moving to Milwaukee. Warren Spahn knew how games like this defined decades and careers, a life's work within the game. Fred Haney asked him to pitch on three days' rest, even though he had already worked 270 innings. He was asking a marathoner to go the extra mile, but Spahn took the ball and pitched one of the best games of his life.

Billy Bruton hit a solo home run in the first inning to give Spahn a 1–0 lead, but after that, the cagey old lefty was on his own. The Braves dropped like dominos, yet Spahn soldiered on. He shut down the Cardinals on no hits until, with two out in the sixth, he allowed consecutive doubles to Don Blasingame and Alvin Dark, two slap hitters Spahn felt should have never touched him.

Spahn held the glove over his mouth and cursed loudly. The score was tied 1–1, but there was worse news: The Dodgers had defeated the Pirates 6–2 in Game 1 of their doubleheader, catching the Braves from behind there on the St. Louis grass. Spahn felt like a beggar pleading for one stinking run, but the Braves could not give it to him. In the ninth inning, Eddie Mathews hit a sharp liner to center field, where Bobby Del Greco ran the ball down. With two out and a runner on first base, Del Greco made a circus catch for the final out on a ball hit by second baseman Jack Dittmer. The game went to extra innings, where Del Greco made four more catches, helping the Braves strand runners on second base in the eleventh and twelfth innings. Bobby Del Greco became a cursed name in Milwaukee baseball lore, one that could not be said without profanity, as exhibited by Braves first baseman Frank Torre many years later: "They had their goddamned Bobby Del Greco."

Nobody could blame Spahn if he wanted to cry, but he was too tough to show his emotion. No game, no situation could touch him. He refused. He lived his life looking over his shoulder at the bridge that wasn't there. Then news came that the Dodgers had completed the sweep in Pittsburgh, beating the Pirates, 3–1 in Game 2 of the doubleheader. Now the unthinkable had happened—the Braves were a half game behind with this one tied and one to go.

There was no room for a mistake. With one out and the bases empty, the angelic swinging Stan Musial came to the plate. His red and white uniform was splotched with dirt and sweat like Spahn's cheeks and uniform. These two greats had faced each other for years and had nothing to hide. Spahn had held Musial hitless in all four at-bats, but wanted to face him as badly as an arm surgeon. They knew each other like brothers, and keeping Musial from hurting you was trying to avoid the inevitable. Spahn missed with a slow curve where Musial could reach it. He sliced the ball to right field, where it curved away from Henry Aaron's glove as though driven by a cabbie speeding away. Musial parked it at second with a double.

Third baseman Ken Boyer was next, and Spahn and Haney were in mutual agreement. They intentionally walked Boyer to pitch to left-fielder Rip Repulski, who despite his catchy name, was considered a substantially easier out. Spahn wanted a double-play ground ball to get out of the inning, so Spahn threw him a first-pitch sinker. Repulski watched it go by for ball one. Then Repulski could no longer hold back his urges. He took a round-house swing at a Spahn sinker and hit a chopping line drive to third base-man Eddie Mathews.

For all of his home runs, Eddie was still as shitty with the glove as the day Johnny Moore discovered him. For all of his beers, booze, broads, and f-bombs, Eddie still didn't know how to handle balls hit hard directly at third base. Now, with everything riding on him having even the slightest ounce of discipline to get Spahn out of his misery, Eddie, the true and natural bar-room brawler, got his ass kicked by a basic ground ball. The ball caught him on his heels and hit him in the knee, bouncing into foul territory down the left field line and into purgatory, where no Brave could reach it. Musial covered ground like he was ten years younger, cutting third and heading home, scoring without a play to give the Cardinals a 2–1 victory, taking Milwaukee's pennant right along with it.

The loss was crushing. Warren Spahn was stunned. He didn't move. He didn't twitch. Nobody said a word to him. The Braves were dead and everybody knew it. They were bush league choke artists after all. A goddamn ground ball, a couple of goddamn doubles, a couple of goddamn balls that goddamn Del Greco ran down, and that was that. Spahn was fuming. Then, Fred Haney slowly walked to the mound. They were the only men on the field. Haney whispered something to Spahnie.

And the lefty cried.

Unashamed. He didn't care if he was thirty-five years old. He had given everything and Milwaukee had nothing. He measured his career by his ability to pitch his team into and win the World Series. He was frustrated at Eddie, but he would never throw him under the bus. These were his brothers, and they had lost. Tears streamed down Spahn's cheeks and nose along with the dirt and sweat as he walked off the field. A photographer swooped in for the emotional photograph, but Spahn had one last fastball left. He raised his glove, fired it at the cameraman, and told him to get the hell out of here. Cardinals General Manager Frank Lane watched the scene with admiration and sorrow. He would have thrown the glove at the guy, too. "What the hell did they expect him to do," Lane said. "Whistle?"

He wasn't alone. Andy Pafko, an old man, cried. Taylor Phillips, an insecure young relief pitcher, cried. Spahn cried. The Braves were sobbing like high school boys who lost the big game. Lew Burdette sat forlorn, quietly smoking a cigarette down to a nub. He would pitch on Sunday, but it didn't matter. Everybody knew the Dodgers would win. Nobody knew where Eddie was, and nobody wanted to go find him, either. That was up to Bob Buhl. Henry was beside himself. "What did I finish with?" he asked. The answer was a league-leading .328 batting average, 200 hits, 34 doubles, 14 triples, and 26 home runs. "I think I can do better next season," he said. "I've had too many slumps."

Lou Perini came downstairs and put on his brave face, but it was obvious he had been crying, too. He looked for Warren and hugged him. The reporters had a soul after all. They couldn't bring themselves to write about two grown successful men crying together. Some things needed to stay in the clubhouse. "We've been together many years," Perini said a few minutes later. "And we're gonna win a lot of them."

Fred Haney portrayed the strong face. He didn't cry. He showed who he really was. The collapse gave him the clean slate and the leadership power he lacked when he first took the job. The moment that ball bounced off Eddie's knee, this became his team. Like him or not, this was his turn. "We have to face the facts about this ball club," he said, without sympathy. The Braves were 14-13 in September and terribly inconsistent. "Its principal strength was pitching depth until recently," Haney said. Lew Burdette won only once and Bob Buhl had a losing record in September. "It is solid defensively despite occasional lapses," Haney said. He knew Eddie Mathews should have turned that double play and he planned on doing something about his defense. "Its hitting has been streaky," he said. He thought Henry ran hot and cold. "Its doesn't have much overall speed," he said. He knew Bruton was getting too old to steal bases. "Also, it has lacked a take-charge guy." This time, he didn't have anybody to protect. The 1956 season was over and Haney knew he was missing the everyday player he needed to make 1957 successful. "I'm not even thinking of ballplayers I want or don't want," Haney said, but he was lying. He knew exactly what ballplayer he wanted. "I'm already concerned with the kind of team I want," he said. "We're going to play some things different from now on." That was going to be a fact.

Spahn finally composed himself. Eddie still wasn't in the room, so he allowed for a taste of truth. "I wanted Repulski to hit into a double play— and it could have been," he said. But that was as far as he would go. "We play all season for these games and then lose 'em. Let's face it. It looks like it's down the drain. I know we're a better ball club, but we just couldn't do anything right. It's a cruel truth to face, but the fact is we didn't deserve to win."

Everybody on the long, agonizing and bumpy flight home suffered. "We certainly blew it in '56," Frank Torre said. "We just were not going to win that game," Del Crandall said. "I don't understand why or anything. I don't know what the baseball gods had in mind, but we did everything in the world to win that game. We were all shakin' our heads."

When Warren Spahn saw the welcome afforded a team that had just collapsed, he felt incredible guilt. The welcome home inspired sorrow. Milwaukee loved and cried with the Braves. They were family.

"There must have been twenty thousand men, women and children, including some parents with babies in their arms," Spahn recalled. "Some of the people were crying. Many of them patted us on the back and told us not to worry." That welcome, in the cold 11 P.M. darkness on the tarmac of Mitchell Field, stayed with Spahn. Maybe the High Life had been too much.

There was no victory parade in 1956. Even football season felt subdued.

It was "sad in Milwaukee," the *Journal* reported. "The cleanup of World Series debris—mental and physical—started. Tickets had to be returned, hotel reservations canceled and deposits returned, communication facilities dismantled, and the happy celebration signs stored away for another day."

The handsome young Brave was removed for the winter and placed in a cardboard box, as though it was his coffin, and then stored in the basement of County Stadium, as though it were his tomb. Resting with him were the hopes of the Heartland, who wondered if 1957 would be any different. It would be if Fred Haney had anything to say about it. "Go home and get a rest, a very good rest," he told his players. "Get rested, because when you come to Bradenton, you're going to have a hell of a spring."

Haney spent the night in Milwaukee and then flew to New York with his wife to make an appearance at the World Series before returning home to Los Angeles for the winter. He went to Brooklyn's Ebbets Field for Games 1 and 2, because damned if he would go to Yankee Stadium unless he was going there to manage the Braves. The season was over and the little old man was already fighting mad. "I'm going because I want to show those Brooklyn guys that I'm not afraid to show up," he said. By the time Haney returned home, Don Larsen pitched a perfect game for the Yankees, Jackie Robinson played what turned out to be his last game, and the Yankees took the title back from the Dodgers in seven games.

For eight long years, the World Series trophy remained safely in the hands of the New York City baseball dynasty.

PART II

THE SEASON

6

"YOU'RE GOING TO HATE MY GUTS"

Fred Haney arrived in a thunderstorm, his little feet striding quickly through the rain and puddles. A trench coat was tied around his waist and his brown fedora was drenched. Mud specked his shiny shoes but the dapper little dictator didn't mind. The Florida winter had been unusually cold and wet, but Haney welcomed the harsh weather for what he vowed would be an unforgiving indoctrination. The old Army Air Force Bradenton barracks doubled as the Braves spring training camp and was as deserted as the day the last bomber crew departed. Haney arrived in February 1957, before the players, coaches, or the front office. He was eager to inspect the second diamond Lou Perini's construction company had built at his request. He slogged around the grounds for so long that his trench coat sagged and his fedora drooped before he tracked down the custodian to unlock his office. The groundskeeper gasped. He thought Haney was a ghost.

Alone in the dingy office, where Charlie Grimm's cigarette butts were still in the ashtray and a few bottles of the High Life were discovered stashed in a desk drawer, Haney began shaping the struggle that would define the 1957 season. When the Braves reported, would they be haunted by their 1956 humiliation? Would he have to motivate them? He recognized the vast amount of talent this team had, far beyond any team he had ever managed. At the age of fifty-eight, he finally had the horses to prove he was a better major league manager than his record of four last-place finishes in six seasons indicated. He studied college football coaches for years and loved how they tortured players, but how was he going to make this team care about winning as much as he did? He intended to find out with his dictatorial voice and his demanding schedule. He would run the boys, drill them, slide them, curfew them, and make them puke on the grass. He was not afraid to push them. He didn't care if they hated him.

It was 8 A.M. and Haney had been at the ballpark since dawn when the team arrived on March 1. Everybody but Henry Aaron and Lew Burdette reported on time. The players sipped coffee in various stages of dress, but Haney's uniform was so crisp it looked like it was painted on him. His players were foggy and drowsy, but Haney's blue eyes were burning and his voice was piercing. "You guys are going to hate my guts," he announced. "But you'll love me when you see those World Series checks."

Spring training was no longer paid vacation. Haney sent his players onto the field to get team pictures out of the way so the photographers couldn't mingle with them the way they used to. Then, the running started. The barrack ghosts were surely pleased to see new souls suffer. Haney marched like a general wading onshore. He would achieve results through humiliation and determination. He was trying to replace a sense of entitlement with a feeling of animosity. Batting practice was conducted in two big groups while pitchers worked on fielding, base runners worked on taking leads and stealing, and extra men hit against the pitching machine. A steady rain pelted the players. Haney patrolled the groups, each conducted by one of his hand-picked coaches, clutching his clipboard and stopwatch, and screaming at the top of his lungs. The veterans were motherfucking Haney between gasping for breath, but he didn't care. At the end of every thirty minutes, he blew his whistle, the groups changed stations, and Haney turned the page on his clipboard and carefully stepped over the vomit. "Running and plenty of it," the *Journal* reported, "was interspersed throughout the workout."

The next day, Haney put them through the same drills and then sprung a five-inning intersquad game on the Braves. The players were stunned. At camps around Florida, guys were golfing, drinking, and chasing college girls, and here the Braves were, treating five innings in a murky hellhole like it was Game 7 of the World Series. "I would have held out if I had known we were gonna work this hard," Warren Spahn grumbled.

On the third day of King Haney's reign of terror, he announced that he was going to train them all how to properly slide. This was like telling big leaguers how to hold a baseball bat. The players silently seethed. Haney used to run this drill as manager of the Pittsburgh Pirates, where sliding into sandpits had been one of Branch Rickey's favorite inventions. Haney thought that was too soft. You could almost hear his old buddy Ty Cobb sneering at the idea that a ballplayer should fancy his backside in favor of proper baseball. "We won't have sliding pits, either," Haney decreed. "They don't have help like that in a game and they won't have it here."

Haney made one concession to modernity and comfort. He allowed his players to wear sliding pads, which were baggy yellow diapers strapped outside of their pants legs. "Everybody will practice sliding until he can slide to his left, to his right, and head-on," Haney said. "I want everybody on this club to be able to slide all three ways when the season opens." So there were the Braves, a million dollars' worth of big league ballplayers with yellow pads affixed to their asses, lined up like a bunch of rubber ducks, sliding into the mud.

Haney brainwashed the baseball writers before the ballplayers bought in. "Every move is carefully mapped out in advance and the systematic approach results in a workout that is probably more beneficial and purposeful than any of the Braves have had since their fateful move to Milwaukee," *The Journal* said. When Haney caught second baseman Danny O'Connell screwing around, he chewed him out in front of the entire team. "I'll give you all the running you'll be wanting!" he barked. Haney never liked O'Connell, who had been his starting second baseman on the '53 Pirates. He was a good ballplayer, but when Fred hated you, Fred hated you. The feeling was mutual. O'Connell popped off and told Haney he was too tight, so Haney buried O'Connell. He wanted a new second baseman, but he was going to have to wait. Instead, he made an example out of O'Connell first chance he got. Fred Haney was no Jolly Cholly. He demonstrated to his team that he had a very deep doghouse—once you went in, you never came out—and like his friend Casey Stengel, he had trained the writers to enforce his will. "What gives with O'Connell anyway?" *Milwaukee Journal* sports editor Oliver Kuechle wrote. "That's the approach of a loser. Maybe the search for a new second baseman should be intensified."

Haney wanted his team to have a new spirit before a new second baseman, though both were high priorities. He chided newlywed Joe Adcock
into losing the weight his wife's cooking put on, and soon Adcock and the
rest of the players were wearing heavy rubber sweatshirts beneath their jer-
seys. Haney drilled and drilled, through what the *Journal* called, "the most
wretched weather the Braves have had in 10 springs here." Privately Haney
loved the rain so much that one might have wondered if he had prayed for
poor weather, so that each drop might rinse his message into his players'
pores and purge their prior habits.

Finally, he broke them down, and reluctant acceptance arrived. Johnny
Logan vowed the ballplayers wouldn't be so loose this season, promising
they would win at all costs. Warren Spahn hated Haney's hell week, but as
he rubbed his aching legs, he understood why his manager was punishing
the players. "I'm worn out after every workout," he said. "Yet I know I've
accomplished something."

When Henry Aaron made it to camp a few days late, Haney demanded
to know where he had been. Henry told Haney not to worry. Traveling by
rail through the segregated South wasn't the most efficient or timely method
of transportation, but Henry arrived ready to roll. He demanded Haney
never question his professionalism in front of the team ever again. The
players took note: Henry was growing up. Then he walked onto the field for
his first batting practice. Bob Buhl was soft tossing. That wasn't good
enough. Henry stepped in and stared down the paratrooper.

"Throw 'em," he said. "Hard as you can."

"You serious?" Buhl said.

"As serious as you," Henry said. "Let's get going."

And there in the quiet Florida sunlight there was nothing like the sound
of the gunshots that came off Henry Aaron's bat, booming predictions of
production, a home run hitter in the infant stages of discovering the magnitude of his talent. He attacked the ball and trusted his loose and explosive
wrists. Aaron's shots cracked like lightning through the humid sky. Buhl
shook his head and was so happy he didn't have to pitch to Henry for a living.

Eddie Mathews stood there watching the balls vanish into the woods
and the swamp. Henry and Eddie became a formidable tandem. "You know,

we was good for each other, as far as baseball players, you know, we complemented each other quite well," Henry said. "He happened to be a left-handed hitter and I was right. We complemented each other very well, and, you know, he hit the long ball, and I was blessed with the long ball and an average. It wasn't a matter of me doing more than him. You know, he won a lot of ball games, and I protected him. And he certainly protected me as a hitter."

Then Eddie pointed the barrel of his bat at Buhl, his drinking buddy, and announced to the team, "I'd like to hit against number 10." Haney watched Eddie hit. He had no trouble with him as a hitter, but he did have issues with Eddie's drinking. He quietly ordered veteran players to keep a closer eye on him.

Then he pulled Eddie aside, and told him he was going to make him a major league third baseman, like it or not. From there on, before every game, Fred Haney, a former infielder, was bound and determined to transform Eddie from a hack to a genius. Haney kicked Eddie's ass. He worked with him on playing different angles to balls, how to judge when he needed to charge and when he needed to stay back, when to wait for the play to come to him, and when to use his good arm to throw the runner out. Haney hit Eddie a thousand groundballs that spring, making him range to his left and right. He made him field grounders with his bare hands. He made him get on his knees, hold his hands behind his back, and block grounders with his chest. For Eddie, it was like fighting without his fists, and he hated the grouchy little asshole for putting him through this, but he respected his teammates too much not to work hard to get better. He never again wanted to let them down when they needed him most.

Haney pushed his players so they would not fall. They hated it, but realized his demands were designed to exorcise their demons. Spahn was still one of the boys, but he took winning more seriously now, giving Haney a very powerful ally. Spahn felt guilty about some of his behavior in years past, joyous stupidity undertaken with Eddie's Asshole Buddies. In quiet moments, Spahn admitted that the time in 1956 when he and Lew Burdette stole rookie outfielder Wes Covington's hat and burned it at home plate at Ebbets Field may have gone too far.

You could take the boy out of the grass but not the crass out of the boy, and maybe Haney's spring boot camp had been successful partly because Burdette was not there. He was holding out for a raise from $23,500 to $30,000, and said he was doing just fine selling real estate in Florida while the Braves were sweating and barfing in Haney's jungle. Nobody was sure how much the holdout had to do with how much more money Burdette wanted, but they were certain he was in no mood to give Fred Haney the satisfaction of running him into the ground. Burdette felt he was an old pro who would be ready. He didn't need some old Hollywood asshole telling him how to do his job after all these years. "Some players liked Haney and some players didn't," clubby Tommy Ferguson said. "You can guess who did and guess who didn't."

Haney figured out that Eddie alone wasn't so bad. Even Spahn, Buhl, and Eddie together were working hard. The wild card was Burdette, the loose cannon, who Haney couldn't win without but would have thrown off the team if he could. Haney had his own nickname for the Asshole Buddies. He called them "The Four Worst Offenders," and knew that containing their antics was the key to the High Life's success.

Even Jackie Robinson, though he was out of baseball now, believed the Braves needed to sober up. "We came into Pittsburgh just after the Braves," he said. "I was talking with people and they were telling me about two or three Milwaukee players who were visiting nightclubs and bars until the wee hours of the morning. I think there was tremendous pressure on them and maybe they weren't sleeping well. But that to me was the reason. I had honestly given up all hope of being in the World Series. But you can't mix athletics with drinking and smoking."

Haney brushed off Robinson's allegations, but they were true. Eddie's nighttime tales were legendary. "Spahnie, Mathews, Buhl, and Burdette, I was never with them, because I didn't live that kind of life," Del Crandall said. "The only time I ever went out with Mathews, he said, 'Come on, come on, come on, let's go!' So I went out and went to a place where he was and we sat there and we talked and I'm not a drinker, but I had something to drink. It got to be 2 A.M. I said, 'Hey Eddie, I got to go.' And he said, 'No, no, no, no! The girls are just starting to come in!' So I says, 'Eddie, I gotta go.' All the guys were after me to loosen up more, to go out more. The next day we had a day game and I really wasn't feeling very good at all, I took a cab out to the place, had the window down, out to the Polo Grounds. That day I went 3-for-4, hit a home run, drove in three runs. I got back to the clubhouse and Eddie said, 'See! You'd be a great player if you went out with us a little more!'"

Frank Torre also tried and failed to roll with the Asshole Buddies. "I remember so clearly, we were playing a doubleheader in Pittsburgh on Sunday (August 5th) and that was a tough town to go out at night," first baseman Frank Torre said. "And we're in this private club across the street from the hotel from where we were staying. I think I went to bed about 1 A.M. and Eddie stayed there until 4 A.M. You know, he went back, drunker than hell, but shit, he hit two home runs the next day."

Haney hated that his starting third baseman was an alcoholic. At least the other three Asshole Buddies, all pitchers, didn't play every day. Haney kept the pressure on. He believed the only way was to make the Braves work as hard as he did. "You can't beat the hours, not if you like the twenty-four-hour workday," he said. "I do." From here on, winning the pennant became a twenty-four-hour a day job for the 1957 Milwaukee Braves.

Lou Perini shook the snow off his shoulders and returned to Bradenton in March. The bulldozer relaxed on the wooden benches behind home plate and watched the Braves hustle through Haney's stations of the cross. Perini was pleased to hear the shrill voice of his new company foreman, bellowing as he looked across the field and into his boss's eye, "The only guy who sits down while practice is in progress is the manager!"

Lou Chapman, the wisecracking beat writer for the *Milwaukee Sentinel,* sat with Perini. Chapman was a quick-talking, fast-typing, hard-drinking baseball writer obsessed with his own byline. He earned every bit of his weekly $250 salary digging out stories that earned him the nickname "Gumshoe," shortened by Warren Spahn and Lew Burdette to "Gumby." Chapman was respected for his tenacity and willingness to shoot straight, though it didn't always win him friends. Once, he was walking in front of the dugout at County Stadium when a baseball whistled over his head. A hair lower would have hurt him. Chapman turned around and saw Burdette grinning at him. Another time, Spahn and Burdette greeted Gumby in the clubhouse by lifting him up and tossing him in the whirlpool to protest a story they didn't like. But Henry Aaron loved him from the start. He admired Chappie's single-mindedness in chasing the story. He could relate to a man whose focus never wavered. "He wanted to be the first one to get all the news," Aaron said.

Chapman's sentences were casual and humorous like his loose necktie and ink-stained overcoat, but he was as much of a favorite of the ballplayers as a writer could be. He lived their life—beer at the ballpark, and martinis and hard stuff on the rocks at night. He was on the road six months of the year in the era when writers traveled with the teams they covered, and when he came home, his family heard all about his job over dinner. His sense of humor fit the players he covered. Once he mailed a postcard home to his two boys, Stuart and Richard. "Dear Kids: Here I am at 30,000 feet and Bobby Thomson is sitting next to me. He'd like to say hello. Love, Dad." Chapman asked players meaningful questions about how they performed their work, and though he respected their privacy, he would still try to steal their secrets.

Once, Chapman hid in an empty locker stall in the dressing room to listen in on a closed-door meeting. All that saved Chapman from certain suffocation was his persistent banging on the door, begging players to let him out after he realized he had locked himself in. In 1956, Haney tried to have Chapman banned from the locker room, but he fought back. He protested through the Baseball Writers Association of America to Commissioner Ford Frick and had Haney's ban overturned. When the spat was over, Chapman was awarded exclusive interviews with anyone he wanted. His reputation and camaraderie made him a favorite of baseball owners, who routinely mailed Christmas cards, even though Chapman was the only Russian Jewish sportswriter in Milwaukee.

Inside Chapman's confessional, Perini professed he paid Haney to exact penance. "I'm sure a lot of these things must have gone through their minds over the winter because they look more serious this spring," Perini said. "They don't do as much talking as they used to. They're doing a lot more thinking."

By that Perini hoped a lot less drinking.

"We've got a more determined bunch this season," he said. "We've got to get serious about this thing. The boys will have to be more mean in the field."

Haney refused to let up. There were returning players from the 1956 team who figured to play more prominent roles. Frank Torre, a lanky left-handed backup first baseman from the Bronx, was so gifted defensively that it was said he could wear a tuxedo to play first base and hang it up after the game without a speck of dirt. He learned how to become a good fielder on the rough gravel infields when he served in Korea. When Torre was called out after forgetting to touch first after a single, Haney stalked him off the field, belittling, "I'm going to put neon lights up at first base after this!" Hitting coach Paul Waner nit-picked Torre's swing so he could learn to be a successful pinch hitter, scolding, "You only get one shot so it better be good."

Everything that came out of Haney's mouth had capital letters and exclamation points. He loved the left-handed home run potential of out-fielder Wes Covington, and he especially loved him because he was seven years younger than Bobby Thomson, but no jobs would be handed away for free. "Bobby is the man," Covington said. "Anybody who takes his place has to move him."

Haney liked Covington's humility, but he wanted him to be a killer, so he dispatched the feisty scout Ted McGrew, a plucky little old man who used an old sawed-off baseball bat as a cane, to teach him how to be more aggressive. At age seventy-seven, McGrew loved baseball as much as he did when he strapped it on in 1901 as a kid busher playing with Three-Finger Brown. Baseball changed, but McGrew never did. He ripped the 30-ounce bat out of Covington's hands and made him swing with a tele-phone pole, a 54-ounce bat. He leaned on his cane until the strong lad was gassed. Then he lifted the bat out of Covington's hands, flipped the 30-ounce toothpick back at him, slapped him on the ass, and told him to go make him look good. "I found out I could come around quicker on the ball," Covington said.

Few young pitchers could unleash a fastball harder than twenty-year-old rookie left-hander Juan Pizarro, signed creatively out of Puerto Rico to bypass the bonus rules, gifted with such extraordinary velocity that Roland Hemond called him "one of the great arms I have ever witnessed." Pizarro would fit perfectly if he could be consistent, and he had a roommate and companion in slick-fielding middle infielder Felix Mantilla, whose hands were so soft they could skim froth off the top of a beer.

John "Red" Murff, a thirty-five-year-old right-hander who quit his safe factory job after the war to chase the nomadic life of a bush league pitcher and center fielder, threw so soft that most teams didn't want him. The Braves bought him from the Giants at a discount price after winning his contract rights in a poker game. He was hungry, versatile, and experienced, just the sort of man Haney was looking for. He was also quirky, cocky, and very brittle. A bad back hindered him. When he collected three hits in a scrimmage and played center field, he joked, "It's a good thing Bill Bruton wasn't around. He might have been worried."

When spring training games began, the pace was already more frantic and urgent, though the Braves lost the opener, 3–2, to the Dodgers. Bob Wolf, the stoic young *Journal* beat writer, typed with a wooden prosthetic hand he received after suffering a wound in aerial combat during World War II. That made him a natural left-hander who was famous around the league for knotting his bow tie with one hand. He was Lou Chapman's best friend and biggest competitor. He wrote straight sentences with grammar as correctly placed as the part in his sandy hair and noted the Braves picked up where they left off, "a close second to the Brooklyn Dodgers."

The next day, Haney was so annoyed that he picked a fight with umpire Augie Donatelli over a close call at second base. Haney sprinted onto the field as if he was shot from a cannon. As soon as Haney beaked Donatelli with the brim of his hat, he was gone, and so was Haney's civility. He sometimes refused to use profanity while pushing his players, but this was an umpire, a moment to make a leadership example for his team, and besides, Haney was pissed. He ripped the shit out of Donatelli so loudly that parents might have wanted to hold their hands over their children's ears. Getting run from a spring training game was pretty impressive.

The Braves had yet to leave Florida and Haney was turning them into fighters. Johnny Logan hit three home runs in one exhibition and vowed he would hit twenty home runs, though he had never hit more than fifteen. "About time I started driving a Cadillac," he said. Wes Covington was hitting and working hard to become a better outfielder. Del Crandall was trying to hit the ball to all fields. Eddie Mathews had Haney's bruises, but he was getting smoother at third. The Braves lost to the Yankees, 6–5. Warren Spahn took a beating but nonetheless felt ten years younger. "I've done more running this spring than I ever have," he said.

Still, Haney was infuriated by the loss, which occurred when pitcher Gene Conley blew a pickoff play. He just could not believe that any loss to the Yankees should be taken lightly. His players thought he was insane. "Don't count, hell!" Haney shouted. "It counted in my book! Lapses like that count plenty! That's the kind of thing that beat us last year and it's the kind of thing I've been trying to eliminate this spring. I guess the job isn't done." The next morning at 8 A.M. sharp, the Braves were running five hours before their ballgame and an hour later, Haney was stepping over the puke again. Even Chapman was impressed, writing in the *Sentinel*, "The horseplay is missing," though his writing read as though he was losing an old friend.

The Braves couldn't wait to leave Bradenton for the barnstorming tour with the Dodgers that would take them through the Bible Belt before returning home to Milwaukee, where tickets were in such high demand that when a season-ticket holder died, fans crashed the funeral to get the seating assignment from the widow. The Braves would have hailed a hearse out of Florida if it meant getting away from Haney's workouts. It sure would feel good to be sneaking a drink in the back of the plane again. Barnstorming was becoming a thing of the past, made obsolete by air travel, population shifts, and technology. More people than ever were watching big league baseball on TV, and the number seemed certain to grow based on the persistent rumors that the Brooklyn Dodgers were planning to move to Los Angeles.

Henry Aaron spent the winter of 1956 barnstorming the South with Willie Mays, and though the team that marched Henry and Willie together would be invincible, not even Aaron and Mays could stave off travel ball's extinction. Everything was changing rapidly now, and the moment you caught yourself looking back instead of forward, you were behind. Henry pressed ahead and hit everything in sight. He hit so many home runs during spring training that people began using a new nickname, "the Hammer." He launched ten home runs in nine games, but didn't play like an elitist superstar. He played so hard that he banged his head against the outfield wall trying to make a catch, and a few days later jammed his ankle sliding hard into second.

Before the team left Florida, Lou Perini quietly sought out Henry. The Bulldozer whispered to the Hammer, "There's a lot of money in the World Series. A man can earn extra by trying harder. That's all it takes—a little more determination and drive." Of course, Perini didn't blame Aaron for the 1956 collapse; Henry knew the Braves could do better. He liked playing for Perini. And Perini loved watching him play.

Henry, for his part, respected Perini for his trust, but when Fred Haney announced his solution to the team's offensive woes was to begin the season with Aaron batting second, young Henry winced. Alabama stride style wasn't made for hitting second. An icy silence intensified between Haney and Henry.

Fred Haney inadvertently unlocked Aaron's strong sense of pride, individualism, and single-minded obsession shared by all great hitters. Overnight, Henry evolved from a shy kid to a defiant young man. Where Henry had been accommodating with the writers, now he was short. When he was asked if he knew his batting average, Aaron snapped, "You got a pencil there, so you do the figurin' and I'll do the hittin.'" Nothing mattered to Henry except hitting his way out of that Godforsaken two hole, and he believed the Braves would win it all if he were free to fly.

Of course, Haney thought his decision was practical. He wasn't thinking, "Hello, my name is Fred Haney, I'm going to hit the greatest home run hitter of all time second." Haney estimated that Aaron hitting second would amount to about sixty more at-bats. He believed Henry could hit .350 while giving Eddie Mathews and the meat of the order more chances to drive in runs. Henry hated that idea. He thought *he* was the meat of the order. Haney knew Henry wasn't happy but he simply didn't care if his decisions made him unpopular with his players. Haney wasn't running for mayor because he was already the dictator. "I'll probably get blasted for batting Aaron second," he said, and he was right. Columnist Red Smith wrote, "For lesser heresies than these, Galileo faced the inquisition and Joan of Arc went to the stake."

Henry didn't wear number 44 to be no table setter. Those double fours meant dollar signs for a main course hitter. "I'll never drive in 100 runs hittin' second," he said. Though he was only twenty-three, Henry began growing into his destiny. He was a home run hitter after all, and even though National League players picked Mays to lead the league in home runs, their annual player's poll revealed that the young Hammer was the clear favorite to win the Most Valuable Player award and that his Braves were favored to win the pennant, where the players predicted the Braves would face American League MVP Mickey Mantle and the New York Yankees. Henry was on his own in the two-hole until further notice. He could complain all he wanted, but Haney's will was the way. "The front office won't interfere and never will," GM John Quinn said.

So Henry put his head down and kept hitting. He hit two home runs against the Dodgers in Houston against streaky young lefty Sandy Koufax. Bob Wolf, who dressed like a math professor and sometimes wrote like one, calculated in the *Journal* that Henry would hit 81 home runs during the season at this pace. Not bad for a table setter. Maybe Henry was trying to hit enough home runs to make Haney realize that there would be nobody on base for Eddie and the boys to drive home if he got to it first.

The Braves and Dodgers could be playing hopscotch and they'd still try to kick the shit out of each other. Even their meaningless games contained the menacing fervor of a school-yard sandbox. In San Antonio, Haney made a trade for Pirates utility infielder Dick Cole, who had played for him in Pittsburgh and Hollywood. Haney loved Cole, mainly because he reminded him of himself, and the players took to calling Cole "Haney's Little Bo Bo." When Red Murff, coming on strong to make the team, pitched against veteran Sal Maglie, it was deemed the "Battle of the Ages." The Dodgers and Braves barnstormed through Fort Worth, where

Bob Buhl was eager to stick the Bums with his jump knife. Lew Burdette, who had finally signed his contract, made his first start of the spring season, and though his ankle was killing him and his arm wasn't in shape, he wouldn't admit it.

Finally, the tour ended in Tulsa, which was a homecoming for Spahn, who lived the off-season in his wife's home state, tending to the cows and the chickens on the ranch off Rural Route 2 in Hartshorne. The Dodgers, who owned Spahn, beat him again and swept the Tulsa series. Dodger right fielder Carl Furillo, who had a rifle for an arm and a cannon for a mouth, said the Dodgers still weren't scared of the Braves. With Jackie Robinson retired, the Dodgers couldn't replace his energy, but Furillo tried to replace his words. "They look exactly the same to me," Furillo said. "They ain't hungry enough." When Fred Haney heard Furillo's bullhorn, he laughed. Perhaps his drilling had done the barflies some good. "At least he said hungry and not thirsty," Haney observed.

At long last, the Braves headed to Chicago's Wrigley Field for the season opener. After almost two months of spring training and barnstorming, the regular season was finally here. The Braves yearned to prove they could win when it mattered most, to finally be better than bush league, and to prove Lou Perini right when he said, "I was never more sure of anything in my life when I said we'd win last year. I know I never should have been more right. We beat ourselves." The flight from Tulsa to Chicago was always choppy, and if the Braves could get through the cutthroat National League, the New York Yankees would almost surely be awaiting them in the World Series. New York writer Dan Daniel, writing in the *Sporting News*, predicted, "The Braves at long last demand their place in the sun. It is a rough and tumble contest, with Milwaukee finishing first by a cat's whisker and the vital fact that in June it was able to acquire a hitting infielder from another NL club. Warren Spahn, Lew Burdette, and Bob Buhl get stronger help than they received in 1956. The glass shows the New York club winning in six games."

Manager Casey Stengel wasn't willing to relinquish the New York City baseball dynasty just yet, though fans were growing tired of domination. "The Yankees win too often for the peace of mind of about 95 percent of the country," the *Hartford Courant* wrote. "People hate them as the world must have hated Alexander and Napoleon."

Stengel was the symbol. His words were as sharp as the deep creases in his sun-wrinkled eyes. He was trying to become the greatest Yankees manager of all time and he didn't care who or what stood in his way. Casey couldn't care less who the Yankees played in seven months. He was certain he knew the answer already. "The Yanks aren't going to let anybody else win," he promised.

7

WELCOME HOME, BRAVES

Warren Spahn was a few days shy of his thirty-sixth birthday when he strode into the dressing room at Wrigley Field in Chicago to change from one business suit to another. Few games meant more to him than pitching on Opening Day. "I've been pitching twenty years and I don't think I'll ever go out there calm, collected and cool," he said. "Once you stop getting nervous, you may as well quit, because, brother, you're dead."

Spahn was determined to put many candles on his cake before the hitters blew him out, though his stuff was no longer as swift as his swagger. Years and innings had shaved between five and seven miles per hour off his fastball and left him throwing 84–88 mph on the new portable "electronic scout" devices that had appeared for the first time during spring training. The *electronic scout* was a fancy term for a radar gun. The next generation of scouts turned the gun into a god and endangered pitchers like Spahn, who understood that the gun could not measure location, life, and changing speeds any more than it could gauge fearlessness, tenacity, or intellect. "My fastball," he eulogized, "is no longer my ace in the hole."

In Bradenton, Spahn very quietly re-engineered an old weapon to help him survive. He had never been taught the screwball, but he instinctively knew how to throw it. He threw it as a minor leaguer, where in 1941, he became a prospect by pitching three straight shutouts and 31 consecutive scoreless innings. In 1942, the *Hartford Courant* predicted the young busher was "knocking on the door of the Hall of Fame," thanks to the pitch that veered low and away from right-handed hitters. When Spahn came to the big leagues, he threw his fastball and curveball so hard that he didn't need the deception. "He is cocky," the *Christian Science Monitor* reported in 1947. "He thinks there isn't a hitter in the league good enough to hit him. To the amusement of some and the annoyance of others, he goes around telling you about it."

Nowadays, Spahn kept his tricks to himself. He took the mound before 23,674 fans, including his wife, Lo Rene, who wore the lucky hat she had worn every Opening Day since the Braves moved to Milwaukee. Her husband carved through the Cubs lineup, sequentially pitching backwards with reverse psychology. He threw his curveball as his changeup and saved his fastball for when the Cubs were least expecting it. Spahn loved causing confusion, creating guess hitters and awkward swings. His control got better as he went, sharpening after the Braves scored four runs in the sixth inning. Spahn could make hitters suffer with his wisdom. He alternated the pressure points on his fingertips to make the ball speed up, slow down, dive, sink or tail, the same way an artist might manipulate a brush or the way a clarinet player might finesse the reeds.

Cubs manager Bob Scheffing kept a close eye on Spahn. He had seen him pitch countless times, but Spahn was doing something different this year. When Spahn threw one version of his fastball, it wasn't straight, and it sawed off right-handed hitters. Sitting in the Braves bullpen was the veteran Red Murff, who had made the ballclub with the help of his cut fastball. He grinned proudly as Spahn took the ball by the horseshoe and occasionally threw the cutter Red showed him. But there was something else, a new pitch to right-handers, the screwball, a friend Spahn had reacquainted himself with. "Whatever he's using," Scheffing said, "he was using back in 1942."

Now he could throw a cutter inside and a screwball away. It was deviant and delicious and counterbalanced the velocity loss. If you counted up all the different pitch variations Spahn threw and multiplied them by the various speeds he threw them at, you'd discover he pitched like he had never left the war, weighed down with weapons. His legs felt strong beneath him—"I was pumping them good," he said—and Fred Haney's trials gave him better strength and stamina. Lou Perini watched in admiration from the front row, wearing a huge smile and his favorite Braves hat. "Who knows how many years he can continue?" Perini said. Spahn pitched a complete game, the Braves won, 4–1, and he bounced off the mound and sprinted into the clubhouse. "He's just like a kid after all these years," backup catcher Del Rice said. The *Journal* gushed, ready for the pennant race nine innings into the season, writing, "The World Series is still 153 games away, but for the moment at least, the Braves are headed in exactly the right direction."

Spahn wanted to win so badly that he went public in the *Saturday Evening Post* with a ghostwritten story titled, "Why Milwaukee Will Win the Pennant." He may not have thrown hard anymore, but he was still cocky as hell. "This year they can pick Milwaukee all the way and not go wrong," Spahn proclaimed without hesitation, even though he knew every ballplayer in the National League was going to read that story while they were was sitting on the john. "I'll go even further," Spahn predicted, lacking humility and exuding confidence. "The Braves will also defeat the New York Yankees in the World Series, four games to two."

Somewhere, Spahn knew Casey Stengel was shaking his head at the busher he had shipped back to the minors during spring training 1942, when he was manager of the Boston Braves. "Naturally I feel we have a better ball-club than the Brooklyn Dodgers or Cincinnati Redlegs, our chief contenders," Spahn said. Most agreed, but almost everyone agreed with their former manager, Jolly Cholly Grimm, who returned to Wrigley Field, his baseball home, to work for the Cubs. He watched the Braves in the press box that day, steering clear of Perini and his former players, but told the *Sentinel*, "I think it looks like a three-club race between Milwaukee, Cincinnati, and Brooklyn."

Milwaukee County Stadium was blanketed in early morning fog when the Braves returned two days later for their home opener on April 18 against the Cincinnati Redlegs. Of course, their name was really the Cincinnati Reds and had been for years, but in the hot years of the Cold War, when schoolchildren were trained to duck and cover in the event that the Soviet Union nuclear bombed us into oblivion, calling them the Cincinnati "Reds" was downright un-American. So sportswriters went back to base-ball roots and called them "the Redlegs," even though they could have called the Braves the Rednecks and nobody would have noticed the difference, especially when Lew Burdette went to the bump like it was a bar stool and pitched like a guy trying to clean out the pretzels at closing time.

While Burdette prepared his awkward and kooky rituals, 41,506 fans paraded though the gates, oblivious to the cold and rain, hauling beer coolers, a High Life in one hand and a hot coffee in the other, dressed in "red hunting coats" that "outnumbered the red coats of the ushers," with Braves hats and shirts hiding under raccoon coats, fur coats, fur hats, blankets, shawls, and, for one fan, the canvas of a pup tent, according to the *Sentinel*, whose front-page headline shouted, WELCOME HOME, BRAVES! The concession stands raked in the cold cash, selling hotdogs, hamburgers, bratwurst, corned beef, ham, peanuts, pretzels, French fries, taffy apples, soda, milk, chocolate candy bars, hot chocolate, beer, cigars, cigarettes (what's a nonsmoking area?), and novelties and trinkets that included papier-mâché teepees, pennants, programs, baseballs with facsimile autographs, little paper black-and-white pictures of the ballplayers, bubblegum cards and minibats. The *Journal* called it a "mine," Perini called it pure profits, and the Heartland called it home.

Some fans carried new technology—not radar guns, but portable transistor radios that could be had for $59.95 and were dialed to WEMP to hear Earl Gillespie who, thanks to the Braves, became the unofficial voice of Wisconsin. Nicknamed "Lippy," the former first sacker for the semipro Green Bay Bluejays was better with a microphone than with a mitt. He gained local fame in the 1940s for his stunning recreations of Packers-Bears football games. He later became the fulltime play-by-play man for the Packers and was hired to call the Braves in 1953. Gillespie's hometown allegiance waved as briskly as the Miller High Life flag he and his radio partner Blaine Walsh, nicknamed "the Blainer," flew out of their booth. Gillespie and Walsh hung fishing nets out of their booth to catch foul balls, and when a ball came their way, Gillespie would yell, "Get the net out, Blainer!"

Earl and the Blainer were pumped up for another opening day. A scorecard cost a nickel and gave you last names and numbers of the Opening Day roster: 1 Crandall, 2 Haney, 4 O'Connell, 5 Mantilla, 7 Rice, 8 Ryan, 9 Adcock, 10 Buhl, 14 Torre, 15 Sawatski, 16 Jolly, 17 Phillips, 18 Tanner,

19 Murff, 20 Crone, 21 Spahn, 22 Conley, 23 Logan, 25 Thomson, 30 Trowbridge, 31 Root, 32 Johnson, 33 Burdette, 34 Pizarro, 38 Bruton, 41 Mathews, 43 Covington, 44 Aaron, and 48 Pafko. "Yes, we've got a feeling this is going to be the big year for you," one advertisement proclaimed. "We've scheduled our first home game far enough ahead to give you plenty of time to cinch that '57 World Series title! This is the year!" The advertisement was signed, "Your Friends, the Green Bay Packers," who expected Milwaukee to become the original Title Town.

The pulse in the ballpark was as palpable as Burdette's jumpy energy. Everyone in Milwaukee expected this was the year. Even the crusty Fred Haney confessed his self-centered enthusiasm. "I've been in baseball since 1918, but this is one of the nicest things that could have happened to me," he said. "I'm opening with a pennant contender, and believe me, it's a great feeling."

Milwaukee society was wrapped around the Braves, its fervor at an all-time high. The Boston Store's spring campaign slogan featured a little kid talking his way out of class, claiming, "Mom, I got Braves fever." All ten writers on the *Sentinel* sports staff picked the Braves to win the pennant. Dissenters risked being shot. "Mitts of Schlitz" were promised in a cartoon of a slender wife in a hemmed dress, handing out bottles of beer to her remarkably thin husband and two additional happy characters that looked a lot like underage drinkers. A men's formal shop sold tuxedoes with star-shaped cutout photos of Spahn and others, including Henry Aaron. It was about the only time in Milwaukee you'd see a black guy in a tux. The city was informally segregated at the 16th Street viaduct and struggled with racial and social identity, even as it adopted Aaron as one of its favorite sons. His teammates played a part in that. Frank Torre and a few teammates helped Aaron get accepted into the Milwaukee Athletic Club. Lou Perini continued to take an active interest in Henry.

Birdie Tebbetts wasn't impressed with any of this. The manager of the Redlegs was a baseball lifer, a former catcher with bad knees, a big mouth, and a burning desire to get inside Lew Burdette's head. Burdette had beaten the Redlegs seven times in a row and Birdie was sick of it. He accused Burdette of throwing the spitball. The squirrel didn't care much for Birdie's tactics. "Their taunts hurt them more than it does me," Burdette said. "If I can throw hitters off stride with a little psychology, why change?"

When he took the mound in the first inning, Burdette practically skipped rope, and went through as many movements as he could to confuse and torment Tebbetts. He touched his mouth, his forehead, his cheeks, his sleeves, his pants, his brim, his glove; he'd hold his finger in the sky to gauge the wind; and he'd play up to the crowd, who ate him up. In between torturing Tebbetts, Burdette proved that he, too, had good stuff. He didn't throw hard, but everything was a sinker or a slider, and sometimes a Red Murff cutter or a Warren Spahn screwball. The sellout crowd of 43,450 cheered as though Burdette alone was responsible for the sun breaking though the clouds.

Burdette didn't throw hard enough to bruise an ego. He was another guy the radar gun would have determined could not pitch, but instead he made one of the best hitting teams in the National League look punch drunk. Many of the Braves fans were just that when Aaron hit his first home run of the new season in the sixth inning for the game's only run. Burdette made the run stand up and the Braves won, 1–0.

Tebbetts was furious. "He's a cheating spitballer," he said. "I'm sick and tired of him getting away with murder. Why should I complain? It hasn't done me any good for the last three years. I don't say he is the only man in the league who throws a spitball, but he is the only one who has utter disregard for the rules."

For the record, Lew knew Rule 8.02: "The pitchers shall not—(a) (1) apply a foreign substance of any kind to the ball; (2) expectorate either on the ball or in his glove; (3) rub the ball on his glove, person, or clothing; (4) deface the ball in any matter; (5) deliver what is called the 'shine' ball, 'spit' ball, 'mud' ball or 'emery' ball. The pitcher, of course, is allowed to rub the ball between his bare hands."

The problem was that nothing about Burdette went by the book. "In order to prove that Burdette throws a spitter you'd have to catch him with saliva on the ball and that's impossible," Tebbetts said, neglecting to mention that he had most assuredly loaded a ball for one of his pitchers when he was a catcher. "But he throws it all right. Every batter in the league knows it. I caught long enough to know the difference between a spitter and a screwball and a forkball."

Burdette gave Birdie the bird. "It's a perfect day," Lew said. "I've got Birdie chirping. It's the best pitch I've got and I don't even throw it." Tebbetts vowed he'd catch Lew in the act when the Braves came to Cincinnati. In the meantime, the Reds planned to file a formal complaint with the National League. The next day, the *Journal* ran a sequence of photos asking readers, "Does Lew Use the Spitter? Watch him and Judge for Yourself." (So much for your next-door neighbor may be a communist.) Lew rubs the ball, goes to his mouth, rubs his neck, rubs his brow, and bounces the rosin bag in his fingers. Where's the spit? Did he chew slippery elm bark like the Negro League pitchers used to do? Del Rice caught every kind of pitcher known to man and spoke for his equally innocent Braves teammates when he said, "I haven't seen him throw one yet."

Burdette lit a cigarette as easily as he roasted Birdie. He took stupendous pleasure in pissing him off. If you played with Lew, you loved him. If you played against him, you hated him. None of the Reds players accused Burdette of cheating—that would be shunning the brotherhood—and besides, if you don't check the barrel of my bat, I won't check yours.

Nobody would have accused Henry Aaron of hitting with a corked bat. If anything, Henry might have had corked wrists. He got off to a fast start in 1957, taking a .390 batting average during spring training into the start of the season. He helped the Braves sweep the Reds and hit three home runs in the first week. His third long ball came in a 8–7 comeback victory over the Cardinals and pitcher Herm Wehmeier, a taste of revenge in Milwaukee's first look at the club and pitcher that finished their 1956 pennant dreams. Eddie Mathews finally hit his first home run in that game—"I always have trouble starting," he reminded the fans—and old Cardinals rival Stan Musial promised, "Aaron will have to do better than .328 to win the batting title this time." The Braves went 6–1 on their opening home stand and played well through wet conditions before embarking on a sixteen-game road trip.

The first stop was Cincinnati's Crosley Field, where former Red Joe

Adcock could tell you that hitting a ball out at night by the 380 mark next to the big scoreboard in left field was no easy feat. Adcock was coming off a career year in 1956—38 home runs and 103 runs batted in—and he was in his prime years. Ruggedly handsome, the girls loved Eddie but the women loved Joe. He was happily married, and you could pick the blades of grass off his front lawn for a souvenir if you liked. He hit a home run to left in the second inning, out beyond the black and white scoreboard that looked like an overgrown grade-school chalkboard, flashing the power that scout Howie Haak reported made Adcock "a guess hitter," who would look bad on one pitch and crush the next. In the third inning, Adcock blasted a grand slam that vanished into the night sky beyond the 387 mark in straightaway center field.

Success almost always meant retaliation. It was a man's game then, and in the days when only one team from the eight in each league made it to the World Series and there was no playoff system that allowed a sleeper to slip through, the diamond was a battlefield. When Adcock next came to bat, a surly Southern boy from Alabama named "Buster" Freeman was waiting. They called him Buster the Duster because he was an intimidator who liked to knock guys down. The skinny righty threw his first pitch at Adcock's ankles, forcing a laborious leap. The second pitch "prompted Adcock into his personal interpretation of the highland fling," Lou Chapman wrote in the *Sentinel*. The third pitch made Adcock hit the dirt. Finally on the fourth pitch, Freeman nailed Adcock on the back leg. Adcock slowly walked to first base and sorely wanted to charge the mound and beat the ever-loving crap out of Freeman, but hesitated because league president Warren Giles, who reprimanded him for chasing Ruben Gomez off the field in 1956, was sitting in the front row. "I wouldn't have run," Buster the Duster vowed. "I might have even taken a couple of steps forward."

Lew Burdette pitched the next night with a slow-motion video camera trained on him. When he learned before the game that Red manager Birdie Tebbetts and his boss, GM Gabe Paul, were so determined to catch him in the act of throwing a spitter, he stood in the middle of the locker room wearing nothing but his jock and his socks, imitating all the illegal moves he would hide. He would have mooned the camera, but when he took the mound in the first inning, he instead tipped his cap at the camera and took a hearty bow.

The cameraman, Don Galvin, said he filmed 32,000 feet of Burdette pitching. He had nine innings to catch him in the act. "I stuck on him like glue, but I don't think he did a thing illegal out there," Galvin confessed. Giles exonerated Burdette of all crimes, Adcock and Aaron both hit home runs, and Birdie burned. "Burdette was fidgety," *The New York Times* reported. "He repeatedly wiped his brow, touched his cap, moved his fingers to his mouth and rubbed his hands." The one thing Burdette didn't throw was a loaded ball—that night at least. He was on his best behavior, maybe because his dad was in from Nitro to see the game.

The Braves completed the sweep the following day and ended April in first place with a 9-2 record and a one-game lead over the Dodgers, who awaited them on this road trip, and the last anybody checked, still played in Brooklyn. Warren Spahn won his first three starts and was thinking thirty wins. Adcock had four homers and wanted forty. "The Braves act as though they don't intend to lose," the *Journal* observed, but Fred Haney wasn't sold. He called his team "lucky and good" and dismissed any notions that the Braves would match the 22-2 start amassed by the 1955 Dodgers and run away with the pennant. There was too much talent and depth in the league for that to happen, Haney believed, and besides that, his regular leftfielder, Bobby Thomson, was hitting .083, so dismal that Thomson knew he was in trouble. "I've got practically all of my old bat speed back, but you can't stay in the majors with just a glove in your back pocket," he said.

The schedule was lucky and good to Thomson. The Braves began May at the Polo Grounds in New York to play his old team, the Giants, where the fans loved him, the archaic dimensions were forgiving, and he always hit well. Playing in the Polo Grounds was like playing ball at the pyramids of Giza, where you might get hit in the head by a chunk of falling debris. Chapman called it an "ancient bandbox," and the bird droppings in press row may have been there since John McGraw managed and Christy Mathewson pitched. The old dump was good for Thomson, who got a couple of hits in the first game to get his average over .100, but bad for the Braves, who ran into their former teammate, a punk lefty named Johnny Antonelli who missed the High Life and loved beating Lou Perini. Antonelli was a former $75,000 bonus baby who was still bitter that Perini traded him to the Giants for Thomson in 1954, even though Antonelli blossomed into a 21-game winner who helped the Giants win the '54 World Series. Left-handers were killing the Braves, an alarming trend Haney hated, and Antonelli antagonized them. "Don't let this kid tell you he don't do his best against the Braves," Giants manager Bill Rigney said.

When the Braves needed a win, Spahn wanted the ball. He got it in front of a puny crowd of 5,961, a sure sign that the home team was in danger of becoming somebody else's Giants. Thomson and backup first baseman Frank Torre, who hated his nickname "Adcock's Caddy," hit home runs in the tenth inning to give the Braves a 5–1 victory. Torre, who scout Howie Haak called "a questionable prospect," was so excited that he called his mother in Brooklyn.

Spahn pitched a complete game. He used his new screwball with great success when he faced Willie Mays four times and held him to a single. Spahn remembered that Mays's first major league hit was a home run against him on May 26, 1951, a few days into Mays's big league career. "I've got Willie hitting on the ground to the point where he can't hurt me anymore with the long one," Spahn said. The only player who knew the Polo Grounds better was Thomson, who didn't realize the Braves were showcasing him to his former team for a potential trade. When he found his swing, it was noted by the Giants, who wondered if reuniting him with Mays would be the remedy to their slumping start.

The Braves made a pit stop in Pittsburgh and took two extra-inning games against the Pirates at Forbes Field. The Pirates had a definite strategy against Henry Aaron—throw him no strikes, make him chase bad pitches, and get himself out. But Henry didn't care where the ball was pitched. He collected five hits, all singles, in six at-bats in the opener. Pirates hitting coach Frankie Frisch, the second baseman on the great Gashouse Gang Cardinals of the 1930s, hated seeing Aaron succeed with what he viewed as an inappropriate professional approach. "That sort of bad ball hitting is something that can be overcome, but apparently not by Henry Aaron," he said. The following night, when Aaron hit his fifth home run,

Pirates manager Bobby Bragan gave up. When Henry was hot, he was nearly impossible to get out. It didn't matter how you pitched to him, and he was capable of putting the Braves atop his wiry shoulders. He finished with nine hits in three days. Bragan thought the Braves were better with Henry than the Giants were with Willie. "For Aaron in trade," Bragan said, "you could get anyone but Mays."

The Pirates left the Braves with a parting gift. Crafty Vernon Law became the first right-handed starting pitcher to beat the '57 Braves when he shut them out, 1–0, on two hits. Something about Law's deception made the Braves feel ill, or perhaps it was the old habits of the High Life in the same Pittsburgh bars where Jackie Robinson heard the Braves were getting trashed last time they were here. Law walked four and struck out three with a fastball that wasn't hot enough to boil water, yet he made the Braves look like bushers, who blew a fine effort from the rookie Juan Pizarro.

Fred Haney sat with his legs crossed and arms folded, his eyes hidden behind sunglasses. The Pirates were an awful team and the Braves didn't show up to play a day before a meaningful two-game series against Brooklyn. All Haney had to do was follow the foam. "I realize there are two or three playboys on this club," he said. "I'm fully aware of our situation and will take steps to correct it." Controlling the Braves in Bradenton, where there was nowhere to go, was easy. Controlling them when they knew the directions to every bar worth a damn in the National League? That was something else. And then he understood why Jolly Cholly drank with these clowns, because if you can't beat 'em, join 'em. Haney refused to hang out with them. The only reason he cared about them was because they could play. Otherwise, these weren't his kinds of ballplayers. He would have otherwise thrown them off the train in the middle of the night.

On the journey to Brooklyn, word from home filtered through the sleeper cars that former Wisconsin senator Joe McCarthy was dead. He had spent his days on the hill pitching from the right. Before Joe, the Redlegs were still called the Reds, and nobody thought twice about it. McCarthy left a legacy of fear and paranoia in Milwaukee, where the 428th fighter-bomber wing of the Air Force reserves ran scramble drills to their Korean War–surplus F-86 interceptors, determined to shoot down the fleet of Soviet heavies headed for the Heartland. Of course, that scenario never happened, and the local residents were starting to figure out that Joe hadn't safeguarded them against anything except the voices in his head. When his body was returned to Appleton for burial, a local clergyman questioned Big Joe's final destination. "Although Senator McCarthy was a great man, we have no assurances that his soul went straight to heaven," he said.

If the Braves ever wanted to get to heaven, they had to win in Brooklyn. No pennant was ever won in early May, but confidence could be. The Braves held a one-game lead over the Dodgers. Beating their long-standing rivals was a matter of Milwaukee civic pride, as illustrated by popular *Journal* cartoonist Al Rainovic, whose game-day caricature showed pitcher Bob Buhl (*"A sparkling 8-1 record vs. Brooklyn in 1956!"*) and first baseman Joe Adcock (*"13 home runs in 17 games vs. Brooklyn in 1956!"*) pummeling Emmett, the Brooklyn bum mascot, while the poor hobo cried, *"Lay off, will yez?!"*

But when Buhl couldn't locate his slider, the former paratrooper's chute never opened. The Dodgers were an old team with a new look, figuring themselves out without their fiery leader, Jackie Robinson. But they could still hit. Buhl botched an easy ball Duke Snider hit right at him and then gave up run-scoring singles to Carl Furillo and Gil Hodges. Then Roy Campanella smoked a low line drive to left field for a three-run homer. Buhl landed with a thud, down 5–0, before Fred Haney tried reliever Ray Crone, who coughed up two more runs, and the Braves were down, 7–3, after three innings.

A lot of pitchers hated throwing at Ebbets Field, but not veteran right-hander Ernie Johnson. He hadn't pitched since early April in spring training against the Dodgers and was worried that he had somehow offended Haney so greatly that he was never going to pitch again. It was true that Haney reluctantly trusted Johnson, but this time he needed him not only to keep the Braves close, but so he could send a message by making lineup changes in the game, the most demeaning way of shaking a team to life. The Braves were 12-3 and still in first place and had played great ball, but at the first sight of turbulence, Haney tightened up. Even the players who liked him hated that. Not Johnson. His sidearm curveball was working as good as it ever had, the Brooklyn bats went silent, and he retired sixteen consecutive hitters while the Braves battled back.

The Dodgers couldn't get Aaron out. He had hit a run-scoring single in the first inning against Sal "The Barber" Maglie, who tried to bait him with garbage. But if Henry could reach it, he could hit it hard. He was spraying the ball to all fields, which made him doubly dangerous and a far more complete batter than the purely pull-hitting Willie Mays. "He has the kind of wrist power that enables him to get abundant wood on anything that shows up even close to the strike zone," the *Journal* observed. But when the stubborn Maglie again tried to sneak slop past Henry in the third inning, Aaron hit a 403-foot Alabama stride style bullet that banged against the Van Heusen sign in deep right-center, sparking a three-run inning. Henry wore out Maglie, and in the fourth, hit a three-run home run against the fringy right-hander Don Bessent to cut the lead to 7–6. The Braves scored three more times in the fifth to take a 9–7 lead in the ballpark where no lead was safe.

The Dodgers finally found someone who could get Henry Aaron out. Their third pitcher of the day was a twenty-one-year-old former bonus baby with a great arm and no earthly clue how to throw a strike. But Sandy Koufax's left arm was as loose as Henry's hands. A couple of future legends faced each other as kids—nothing fancy, me against you, bat speed against arm speed, power against power. Koufax won the first time, striking out Aaron. Aaron got him the next time with a single. Over the years, they would share many memorable confrontations, but few mattered more than the duels when Sandy pitched for Brooklyn and Henry played for Milwaukee. For the time being, even though Aaron had singled against Koufax, the young lefty threw so hard that he disrupted Henry's timing. For the rest of the month, he was going to search for it, and the Braves were going to learn that when Aaron slumped, they struggled.

While Ernie Johnson threw zeroes, Haney threw the struggling Bobby Thomson under the bus. Joe Adcock doubled to lead off the fifth inning, but as Bobby brought a .164 batting average to the plate, Haney called time. Thomson couldn't believe Haney would bench him like this, but next thing he knew, Wes Covington, the rookie, was headed up to bat in his place.

Thomson quietly took a seat at the end of the bench. There was no getting out of the doghouse now. Veteran ballplayer that he was, Thomson sucked it up. He was no longer in this team's plans and he knew it. Teammates looked away. Nobody wanted to see a grown man die.

In the bottom of the ninth, old guys ruled. Johnson, who had been perfect since entering the game in the fourth, allowed a cheap one-out single to Gino Cimoli and then walked Duke Snider. Carl Furillo came up. He was always dangerous in this park, but Johnson got him to lunge at a slow curveball and lift it softly into shallow left center field, where thirty-six-year-old Andy Pafko came charging in and slid on the seat of his pants. He cupped the ball in his palms with two hands, as if saving a baby bird falling out of a tree. Johnson waved at his fellow geezer and got Gil Hodges to ground into a force play for the third out. Final score: Milwaukee 10, Brooklyn 7.

Welcome to the 1957 National League pennant race.

The New York Times marveled at Aaron, who went 4-for-5. "Aaron was the one fellow who beat the Brooks, if one man could be selected," *The Times* believed. Furillo, as usual, made it in-your-face. He was loud, proud, Dodger Blue, and Italian—a guy who talked trash like his mouth was stuffed with pasta and you were blocking dinner. "Your club ought to kiss the ground that guy walks on," Furillo said. "That kid's kept the Braves going. Take him out and you're really hurting."

Take Henry out. Now there was an idea. Furillo had just the man for this sort of work. Tomorrow at the ol' ballpark, Henry Aaron and his .417 batting average was going to meet Don Drysdale, the boy with the messy brown hair, the killer good looks, the really nasty sidearm fastball, and a willingness to knock Jesus Christ off his sandals. The street story was that Drysdale had once been shot down when he asked out Marilyn Monroe— well, before she was Marilyn and just plain Norma Jean back at Van Nuys High School—and if a guy could strike out with one future legend, asking him to knock down another was no big deal. "If Aaron should ever get hurt," Furillo said, "forget about the pennant."

Drysdale wasn't just any headhunter, the guy practically slept with his machete. In the first inning the next day, Aaron stepped in. Drysdale didn't waste any time. He threw at Aaron's head. Henry ducked. Immediately, there were vulgar catcalls at the mound, coming from two directions. Lew Burdette was pitching that day and shouted down Drysdale. Old ballplayers never tell you exactly what they said, but a writer can: you dirty son of a bitch, you do that to him again and we'll seriously kick the shit out of you. More calls came from Eddie Mathews, who stood on deck, and seriously wanted to run out to the mound and wipe that fucking grin off Drysdale's face. Eddie's nostrils flared. Nothing pissed him off like pitchers headhunting Henry. He had three simple rules in life—don't fuck with my beer, don't fuck with my bats, and don't fuck with my boys. So what did Drysdale do? He threw at Henry again.

Now Henry was pissed. This was bullshit and he knew it, but it wasn't in Henry's nature to charge the mound. He had his own methods. "I don't know if he could do this on purpose, or did it if he got knocked down or felt provoked, but he could knock a ball back through the middle," Roland Hemond said. "I wouldn't put it past him if that was his way to get retaliation rather than to charge the mound."

On the next pitch, Drysdale attacked Henry with another fastball. Henry cracked a gunshot line drive back up the middle. Drysdale was spared the pain because Henry missed high. He nailed the ball to center field where Gino Cimoli snagged it to save his own life. Eddie was up next. He had only one home run in sixteen games. As a left-handed hitter, oh, how he wanted to see Drysdale just try to throw that hard low right-handed sidearm shit right into his wheelhouse. It was Drysdale's call. If he headhunted Eddie, he knew it would be a fight. And if he pitched to him—well, the gunshot off Eddie's bat and the trajectory of the ball told the rest of the story. Eddie rounded the bases in a hurry, his eyes fixed on Drysdale. If Drysdale barked, Eddie was coming. Instead, Drysdale turned, faced center field, and wiped the hair out of his eyes.

Eddie hit another home run off Drysdale later in the game, and even though the Dodgers kept cracking at Burdette like he was a sunflower seed, they couldn't quite break him. The game went to extra-innings, tied 3–3. Burdette got through twelve innings and faced a total of fifty batters. Fred Haney finally took pity and took him out of the game. He brought in Red Murff to pitch the thirteenth, where he, too, escaped a jam, before taking the mound in the bottom of the fourteenth with the score tied, 4–4. At exactly midnight at old Ebbets Field, Gino Cimoli led off the inning with a low line-drive home run to left field. The Dodgers had a 5–4 win, but more important, they had proven Carl Furillo's point. If you took out Aaron, you beat the Braves. Henry went 0-for-6, which happened once in a blue moon, and even though Eddie went 4-for-6 and hit two home runs, it wasn't enough. Henry was young and impressionable. "He's just a little punk," Henry reportedly said of Drysdale, though he later claimed these incendiary comments were fabricated. "The season's still early and I'll get even."

But Drysdale was absolute death to Aaron, who had trouble picking up the ball out of Drysdale's slingshot delivery. The Braves and Dodgers played twice more in May, splitting two games, each by one run. Drysdale held Aaron hitless and the Dodgers won that game, once again, completely messing up the young slugger's timing. Henry hit only one home run in the last twelve games of the month. Though he led the league, the Braves weren't good enough to win unless he was dominating all the time. Fred Haney began using his two best starters, Spahn and Burdette, out of the bullpen between starts. This was looked upon as an act of desperation. The Braves faced miserable weather and looked more inconsistent than invincible, leading some to wonder if Bushville's great pretenders of '56 were back for an encore in '57. "This could be the buildup for another September such as cost the Milwaukeeans the flag last year," *The New York Times* offered.

The fast start was a thing of the past. Eddie Mathews hurt himself in a scrum with the Redlegs and Joe Adcock's knees were so bad he could barely move. Both sluggers missed most of the rest of May, making Aaron place pressure on himself, especially after Haney dropped Aaron from second to fourth on May 25. Despite his wars with Don Drysdale, Aaron hit eight home runs in May, lifting his total to 12 at the end of the month, proving to be a murderer in the making with runners in scoring position.

In his first game as cleanup hitter, Aaron went 0-for-4 and a rookie named Dick Drott struck out 15 to lead the lowly Cubs to a doubleheader sweep. Warren Spahn couldn't buy a win and the Braves finished May with a 23-16 record, tied for third with the upstart Phillies, and chasing—as always—the Dodgers, defenders of the New York baseball dynasty. Lou Chapman of the *Sentinel*, an honorary member of the Asshole Buddies, or the Four Worst Offenders if you prefer, could be savage when he was sober and sad. "Standing there with your bat on your shoulder while the pitcher is slamming a third strike down the pipe is not conducive to improved batting averages or winning pennants," he wrote.

When Eddie saw Chapman in the clubhouse the next day, he ripped him a new one:

> Not hustling? As soon as we don't win four or five games in a row, then we're accused of not hustling? I'd like to have any of you so-called experts give me one example of any of us being guilty. We're just not hitting. Henry Aaron's been carrying the whole ball club so far. Our pitchers have been doing the job, but seems as if they have to pitch a shutout to win these days. Let's face it. We're just not hitting and it's because of the lousy stinking weather. There's nothing wrong with us that warmer weather can't cure. There's a long summer ahead. But when someone accuses us of not hustling, that's a big joke.

The Braves were thrilled to see June arrive. On the next to last day of the month, a 10-kiloton atomic bomb was detonated in the Nevada desert. The mushroom cloud was on the cover of the *Milwaukee Sentinel*. Everybody in that locker room was thinking the same thing. Please, dear God, don't let that be us.

8

"IN FOR A BATTLE"

The rain was miserable in Milwaukee during spring, flooding amateur baseball fields and saturating the County Stadium turf so thoroughly that the puddles made ballparks big and small resemble what the *Sentinel* termed "mud lots." Cold, rain, and tornado warnings accompanied the dismal weather that *The New York Times* whined, "wouldn't have drawn a corporal's guard anywhere else this side of the artic circle." Ballplayers despised the cold weather. Any batter who didn't square up the ball precisely felt his hands sting. Pitchers couldn't grip the ball right. Batting practice and side-throwing sessions were disrupted. Teams hated visiting Milwaukee and couldn't wait to leave. Neither could the home team.

By early June, the Braves were knee deep in trouble. Since starting the season 12-2, they were 12-15. More disturbing was the nine one-run losses in the first two months. Too many good pitching performances went down the drain. Nagging injuries pestered the lineup. There was no sign they were ready to pull away from the Dodgers. "There are so many things wrong," Fred Haney said. "One day we get nine runs and no pitching. The next day we get pitching and no hitting." The Braves had the worst record in May of the four pennant contenders, while the Redlegs got hot, the Phillies were a surprise, and the Dodgers were solid. The Braves looked nothing like a winner as they embarked on another marathon road trip to begin June, sixteen games in fourteen days, including a return engagement in Brooklyn. Haney said nothing less than 10 wins would make him happy.

First stop was the Polo Grounds. Whenever the Giants and Braves played, it usually meant one thing—who do you like better, Aaron or Mays?

The lowly Giants played the Braves tough, though neither team was immune from mediocrity. The Giants took the first game, 8–7, in thirteen innings, with each team leaving a city block worth of runners in scoring position, Aaron and Mays each hitting home runs and offering another opportunity to watch two great young outfielders.

Mays could throw a ball as far as he could hit one. In the fifth inning, Aaron lined a single to center field with the slow afoot pitcher, Ray Crone, on second base. Crone moved up to third and had no further intention of daring Mays. But Willie had other ideas. He charged Henry's ball in medium center and airmailed a throw that was at once awful and magnificent. Willie tried to throw the damn thing back to Birmingham. Crone watched the ball roar over his head, and if not for the saving grace of the netting between third and home, it might have carried for miles. Crone walked home and Henry dashed to third on "perhaps the most horrendous throw of Mays's career," according to *The New York Times*. In the dugout, Fred Haney turned to the eighteen-year-old rookie bonus baby Hawk Taylor, who two weeks earlier was playing high school ball in Iowa, and sneered, "Remember what you saw out there, then don't do it."

Haney was saying that a lot about his team lately, but he wasn't alone. The Braves lacked their loose cockiness and happy insanity. Veteran Giants outfielder Hank Sauer, once an MVP for the Cubs, knew something was wrong. "There's something missing about the Milwaukee club. I can't put my finger on exactly what it is," he said. The next day, the Braves tried to fix it by hitting three home runs to win 9–8, but still almost lost because they gave up six home runs to the Giants. Mays hit another one, and if it hadn't been for reliever Ernie Johnson pitching 7⅓ solid innings and hitting the first and only home run of his major league career, the Braves would have been cooked.

The Braves couldn't leave New York without looking bad one more time. Bob Buhl pitched well with nothing to show for it. He lost 2–0, and gave up a home run to Giants second baseman Red Schoendienst, who killed the Braves in the three-game set, going 7-for-14 with a home run in each game, flawlessly fielding all sixteen ground balls hit his way, running the bases like a bird, and showing his arm strength was enough to complete the double play. "The fact is Schoendienst wants to come to the Braves so badly he can taste it," the *Journal* reported. Red knew this was an audition and everyone knew that the Braves had wanted Red for years. He was an All-American ballplayer—nobody ever asked him to change his name to Redlegs Schoendienst—with a storied All-Star career behind him, spent mostly with the St. Louis Cardinals, where he helped them win the '46 World Series. When his former manager, Billy Southworth, managed the Boston Braves in 1948, he begged John Quinn to trade for him. The Braves and Giants had been close to making a trade in 1956, and after it fell through, Cardinals GM Frank Lane said the Braves would have never choked if they had made the trade. Quinn still wanted to make the deal, but the biggest concern was if Red, at thirty-four, was still the player he used to be. Pirates GM Branch Rickey scouted Red and wrote, "This player is practically through" and "not what he used to be," though he conceded, "He is dangerous at the plate." But Rickey recognized value in this player for a contending team. "If I had a club in the race, I would take him," he relented.

The front office thought Red was all that this team needed to become great, provided he could still play, and judging by a .464 batting average against the Braves this year, the answer was yes. The Braves left New York for Pittsburgh, knocked down to fourth place largely because of Red's hitting, and that was proof enough to begin trade rumors swirling anew. Fred Haney still hated his inconsistent starting second baseman, Danny O'Connell, partly because he was the kind of slap-hitting middle infielder who had just enough home run power to get in trouble. In Haney's eyes, that made O'Connell an exceptionally selfish ballplayer who bogged down the batting order. The problem was he didn't have another second baseman who was as good defensively as O'Connell. O'Connell, for his part, increasingly resented Haney for trying to edge him out of the job by auditioning every busher that came his way.

Schoendienst, a consummate pro in the Cardinal tradition of fundamentally sound baseball, performed small ball better than O'Connell. He could bunt, hit-and-run, and occasionally hit a home run. The biggest concern was his health and arm strength, but when Quinn dispatched scouts

Johnny Moore and Wid Mathews to tail Red, both reported he was ready. Now trade rumors intensified.

Lou Chapman knew the Braves were talking to the Giants, and engaged in a month's-long dodgeball game with Quinn. The Gumshoe was on the right trail—the Giants and Braves were talking—and he had the right players in mind. Chapman was a creative writer who thought like a scout. He could tell the Giants wanted three-for-one: a second baseman, a power-hitting outfielder, and a hard-throwing pitcher. "At the present time we don't have anything in the fire involving any of our players," Quinn said on May 16, but he was lying. Stonewalling again on May 28, Quinn said: "It doesn't look like we're going to make a move right now." When Quinn pulled one out of the savvy scout's handbook by staying in Milwaukee rather than watch Red play in person at the Polo Grounds, Chapman knew that a trade must be imminent. The deadline was June 15, the Braves needed help, and the deal was going to hinge on which outfielder and pitcher were going to be included. The price would not be cheap. Chapman correctly surmised that the Giants wanted one of the power arms: Ray Crone, Don McMahon, or Juan Pizarro. But the real problem was the Giants also wanted outfielder Wes Covington. It was too much youth for too much age. Besides, Ted McGrew vowed that if Quinn traded Covington away, he would beat him over the head with his fungo stick. John Quinn was a special man. He had the ability to put aside his position and ego and listen to the guys who watched ballplayers for a living.

The players wished the Braves would make a move, mainly because Haney couldn't make his mind up about a regular starting lineup. He bounced players around the batting order, from top to bottom, and was so scared that the team couldn't score runs that he would pull starting pitchers at the first sign of danger, taxing an already tired bullpen. He had a loaded ballclub but managed like they were bushers, terrified that he would be fired if the Braves didn't win the pennant. He was tight, stuffy, and had spurts where he couldn't make up his mind about anything. "Our manager is a little shaky. It's reflected in the way he keeps changing our lineup every few days. It shows his lack of confidence and results in our losing confidence," an anonymous player told the *Sentinel*. The front office further irri-

tated the team by adding two expensive bonus players to the roster early in
the month.

Bonus Babies were treated as a lower form of busher, overpaid brats
from amateur ball who hadn't earned the big bucks for doing anything
that counted and had to be carried on the big league team almost immediately or the parent club risked losing them on waivers. Bonus Babies like
Hawk Taylor and Johnny DeMerit placed strain on the roster, leaving the
Braves with twenty-three useable men instead of twenty-five, reducing
options later in games, and creating friction among players defending their
paychecks. "It's obvious that old baseball hands resent a youngster coming up fresh and drawing upwards of a $100,000 bonus," the *Sentinel* re-
ported. "The signing of two bonus players for tremendous sums hasn't
improved their mental attitude." At least DeMerit, a star from the University of Wisconsin, was a serviceable and physically mature bench player
who could fill in as a late-inning backup outfielder or pinch runner. "I don't
care who the ballplayers are as long as they can play," Haney said, but he
wasn't eager to put a bat in any Bonus Baby's hand. When Hawk Taylor
caught his first big league inning, he was so scared that he couldn't throw
the ball back to the pitcher correctly. Warren Spahn told him to get over
it, change his underwear, and write his names on his socks. Now have a
happy career.

Spahn always took it on himself to set the Braves right. He took the
ball in Pittsburgh on June 7 and scattered singles like raindrops, and when
it was over, he had the 39th shutout of his career, a 5–0 whitewashing. John
Quinn mysteriously rejoined the team. Rumors had it that he was looking
at Pirates slugger Frank Thomas as a trade target, a versatile right-hander
who could play third, first, or the outfield. Thomas was a Steel City guy all
the way, born in Pittsburgh with a workingman's genetics that could have
been a good fit, but the deal died when the Pirates asked for Juan Pizarro.
When Thomas whacked a hard line drive off Spahn's thigh in the second
inning, players on both benches winced and could hear the ball take a bite
out of his flesh. The seams cut open Spahn's thigh, leaving a welt and his
uniform pants bloodstained. Spahn absolutely loved it. He picked up the
ball, tossed Thomas out at first, and then pitched like he alone had been

ordained to turn this thing around. He walked off the mound with a huge smile beneath his crooked nose and tipped his cap to Haney, who thanked him with his new nickname. "Good work, 'Old Folks.'" When asked the last time the Braves played so well, Haney snickered and said, "I can't remember that far back."

Rain followed the Braves to Pittsburgh, washing out the Saturday game to create a Sunday doubleheader. The Braves split two, with Henry Aaron hitting his league-leading 15th home run. Lou Perini was disappointed with his team. The Braves had more potholes than he cared for. "We're playing sub par baseball for our ability," he said. "I hope we catch fire soon." It was the same June road trip to Brooklyn in which Perini had fired Charlie Grimm in 1956, but he vowed he would not can Haney, not yet at least. Perini was remarkably democratic in assigning fault this year. "You can't blame the second baseman or the left fielder," he said. "Let's face it, the entire team has been in a slump." But in his heart, he knew the four-game series in Brooklyn was huge. The Braves were 27-20, a middling fourth place team trailing the Redlegs by 2½ games with the Dodgers 1½ game in first and the Phillies one game back.

This time, handling the Dodgers would prove even more difficult. The Braves had to play the series without Warren Spahn or Lew Burdette starting. Spahn felt his new screwball would allow him to better survive at Ebbets Field, where the Dodgers' predominantly right-handed hitting lineup traditionally mauled him, but Haney didn't think he had it in him. Spahn hadn't won against the Dodgers since 1951. Burdette, whose nagging arm and ankle soreness prevented him from pitching, further irritated Haney because he thought the maladies were the result of poor conditioning associated with his spring training holdout. Another Brooklyn brawl awaited in what the *Journal* called "hand to hand encounters," this time with the direction of the season riding in the balance.

The four-game series began on June 10 at Roosevelt Stadium in Jersey City, a Triple-A park where the Dodgers played occasional home games in 1956 and 1957, owing to the age of Ebbets Field and adding to the sense of inevitability that the team was not long for Brooklyn. Don Newcombe, "Newk" for short, took the ball for the Dodgers and tried to blow up the

Braves. He was a guy who pitched like his ass was on fire and didn't like to make hitters guess. He had two speeds, fast and faster, and the compassion of an executioner. He was every bit as surly and inefficient as Bob Buhl, who pitched for the Braves. They matched zeroes for three innings until Johnny Logan hit a sharp ground ball to third baseman Charlie Neal. In years past, this would have been the province of the able Jackie Robinson, but the ball played Charlie. He couldn't make the play and Logan was safe at first.

Here came Eddie Mathews, one of the only guys in the league who could give Newk a run for his bar tab. "He was a big, tall, strong son of a bitch," Newcombe said of Mathews, and there was little doubt Eddie felt the same way about Newk. There was no room for small talk or changeups. Newk's fastball was heavy as a beer bottle, and if you hit it wrong, the stinging felt like broken glass poking your hands, but if you got him right, the ball would carry like a good tip to a cigarette girl. Newk served it up and Eddie hammered it 425 feet over the big barrier in left-center field. Newk hated falling behind, but he had to give it to Eddie. Any guy who could do that to his fastball deserved a beer.

Over the radio waves, Earl Gillespie should have announced that this 3–1 victory was made possible by the generous support of the Asshole Buddies. Eddie's ninth home run of the year was enough support for his pal Buhl, whose fastball strayed like a kid past curfew. He walked six and struck out five in nine innings. Nobody cared what his pitch count was. It was about winning. Buhl was coming on strong now, running his record to 5-2, and helping the Braves crawl into a third-place tie with the Dodgers heading back to Ebbets Field for the next three games, 1 ½ out of first.

When the Braves took batting practice the following day in Brooklyn, a little sixteen-year-old stood scared on the grass. He watched the Braves hit in the usual order: Bruton-Logan-Mathews-Aaron-Adcock-Thomson-O'Connell-Crandall. My God, he could recite them in his sleep. What the hell was he doing here? They were hitting balls out for the other kids to chase through the streets. He just happened to be the lucky bastard whose older brother played on the Braves and got his kid brother onto the field to hit with the team. After the regulars hit, Frank Torre let his little brother, Joe, swing. He wore a crisp new hat that the Braves local scout, Honey Russell, put on his head. Joe was a high school slugger of some renown in Brooklyn and hit well enough for the *Journal* to report, "Torre is batting .515 in the high school league."

The older players watched him curiously. Joe had some raw power but nobody envisioned a kid who would win a batting title. He was too fat for his own good. Dodger shortstop Pee Wee Reese told him so. When Joe changed, Warren Spahn had a look at him with his shirt off and called him "spaghetti vendor," and chided him for never missing a meal. But if Joe was looking for his big brother to be supportive, he was looking in the wrong place. His kid brother had been babied and Frank knew Joe needed to get tougher. He wanted him to learn to be a catcher, not a third baseman, because he knew he would either work hard or quit. But he also thought Joe's power and arm strength was too much to waste, so he laid it on with the older guys. "My brother really went through a period where he hated me and I couldn't get through to him," Frank said. "I knew he really wanted to play ball, but he was so damn heavy. He loved to eat. I don't know what my brother would be doing for a living today if I didn't insist that after he graduated he became a catcher."

While the Braves got ready to play the Dodgers, they got Joe Torre ready for his own career, which included the 1973 NL MVP award and four World Series titles as manager of the Yankees. His baseball roots belong squarely with the 1957 Milwaukee Braves, the team he says today, "made me who I am, though they certainly did have some fun at my expense."

Lou Perini relaxed in the front row by the Braves dugout, hosting a group of sixty-two investors who must have had more money than God, extolling them the virtue of his favorite projects. He gave them each a brand new baseball cap. Perini called them "The 62 Club" and it was clear that this was the elite, which meant everybody really better play well and make the old man look good. The 62 Club represented "control of billions of dollars of industry," the *Journal* plainly stated. Perini liked to keep his players in the dark about how much money and influence he actually wielded. He knew from his days carrying the water pails that if he told the workers how much he was really worth, they would never stop wanting. Instead, he let them be just thirsty enough.

Money and influence was not on pitcher Ray Crone's mind. He started the game with a 5.13 earned run average and was desperately trying to keep his job. Crone threw hard but was maddeningly inconsistent. He read the papers and knew he was one of the players discussed as part of the potential trade for Red Schoendienst. Crone had been with the Braves since he signed out of high school in 1949 and hated the idea of being traded away from the only organization he ever knew. So he went out and pitched his best game of the year, scattered nine hits in nine innings, and got a grand slam home run from Bobby Thomson, who always seemed to be at his best in New York City. Crone gave up Roy Campanella's 237th career home run, setting the National League record for home runs by a catcher, but not much else. The Braves beat the Dodgers again, 7–2, jumped into second place, a half game back of the Redlegs, and handed the Dodgers their fourth consecutive loss. The Braves gave *The New York Times* a heart attack, writing the slump was "a skid that would have (the Dodgers) in serious trouble but for the astounding jam in the National League flag race." For his part, Crone thought he had saved his job. The trading deadline was in three days. "I'll be able to breathe easier once it passes and I'm still with the club," he said.

The Dodgers took a deep breath the next morning when manager Walter Alston taped the lineup card to the dressing room wall. Their veteran captain, Pee Wee Reese, was back in the lineup for the first time since May 30. Injuries ravaged the thirty-eight-year-old, who was batting .205 and wondering if he would ever make it to Hoboken or Hollywood or wherever the Dodgers wound up next. When everyone saw the lineup, most rubbed their eyes. Pee Wee was batting second and playing third base, not shortstop, his natural position, because his legs were getting too slow for short. Pee Wee packed his pipe with his favorite Kentucky tobacco, folded his arms, puffed the smoke into the stale clubhouse air, and watched the years drift away.

But getting old beat sitting on the bench. Gene Conley was pitching for the Braves. The six-foot-eight giraffe hadn't made a start in almost a

JOHN KLIMA

month and walked leadoff hitter Junior Gilliam in the first inning. Then
Pee Wee, generously listed at five-foot-ten, dropped down a bunt and ran
like hell. Conley rushed and threw the ball away, a costly two-base throwing error that scored Gilliam, setting the Braves back a run before the seats
were filled, and helping the Brooks bombard the Braves for nine runs in the
first two innings. Pee Wee went 3-for-4, and his replacement at short,
Charlie Neal, knocked in four runs. They looked like the Bums of old.

Finally, the Braves got close in the ninth inning. Johnny Logan drew
a leadoff walk, bringing Eddie Mathews to the plate. He was killing the
Dodgers in the series and had three more hits tonight. Facing Eddie Roebuck, a right-hander short on stuff and long on courage, he found a fastball
to his liking, reached out, and pulverized it for the 200th home run of his
career. He was the fastest player to 200 home runs in major league history.
If anyone was ever going to catch Babe Ruth's career home run record, this
was the guy, not the kid waiting at home plate with his outstretched hand.
Then Henry came to bat and hit his league-leading 16th home run. Eddie
Roebuck thought, well, there's always scouting for me. The Braves lost, 11–9,
and five of the eight National League teams were separated by only two
games in one of the most congested playoff races anyone had ever seen.

After the game, Mathews said nobody better ask him if he was going to
catch Ruth's record. He had been hearing that shit since he was twenty, and
all he knew was that he wasn't going to be the guy to do it. Taking down a
record like that would require a special individual, and he didn't know who
the hell that was, but it sure as hell wasn't going to be him. Eddie didn't
need the headache that would accompany chasing down that record. He
admitted he'd love to get to 500 home runs, a sure ticket to the Hall of
Fame, but even that looked "pretty far away." Eddie was trying to become a
more reliable hitter in the present. Branch Rickey once wrote, "He can look
very bad against a certain pitcher and will slump for a period of several
games," so Eddie wanted consistency. "I've learned how to snap out of those
prolonged slumps," he said. Nothing got him going like a pennant race, not
even a drinking contest in a boxing bar, but tomorrow he'd get the best of
both worlds when Don Drysdale pitched for the Dodgers. Not a single guy
on the team forgot about the bastard who headhunted Henry.

It didn't take long for it to boil over. In the first inning of a beautiful day in Brooklyn, in front of only 8,778 fans who gave enough of a damn to cut work or ditch class, leadoff hitter Billy Bruton got hold of one of those Drysdale fastballs. The warm air helped Bruton's ball carry out of the ballpark. That really pissed off Drysdale, because Bruton had only hit one home run all year. Drysdale was young and hot and when he got mad, he lost his focus.

That was perfect for Johnny Logan, who feasted on pitchers in moments of weakness. He wasn't the most talented guy, but he was one of the most valuable players the Braves had. No team could win the pennant without a reliable shortstop who could play everyday, play hurt, and hurt you with the bat if you weren't careful. Besides, somebody had to hold up Eddie at third when he couldn't stand straight. "Logan was the glue," Henry Aaron said. "When the ball club got in a slump, it looked to Logan to try to ignite you. You got in a fight and everybody got kind of loose and they started playing better. You know, really, he was somebody that you loved."

Logan loved a fight. He singled off Drysdale, tricked him into a bad pickoff throw, and stole third, seemingly cackling all the way. Drysdale sneered at the pesky little Ukrainian shortstop, then struck out Mathews and Aaron to end the inning.

But in the second inning, Drysdale's sidearm fastball wasn't fooling anybody. He gave up a double to Bobby Thomson, who scored on another double by emergency catcher Carl Sawatski, a light-hitting journeyman backup catcher and recent call-up who got into the game at the last minute because Del Crandall tore a fingernail off his throwing hand. That infuriated Drysdale, who hated looking bad, especially against bushers hitting .077.

Nobody knew when Drysdale was going to explode, but he was a ticking time bomb, and when he went off, all hell was going to break loose. But Drysdale didn't go after Bruton when he came up next. He challenged him with another fastball, believing his earlier home run to be a fluke, but Billy unleashed his own Alabama stride style, sending a rocket to center field, the best ball he had hit in years. The ball carried 400 feet and tortured

Drysdale every inch along the way. It was the only time Bruton ever homered twice in a game for Milwaukee and it gave the Braves a 4–0 lead.

Then Logan stepped back into the box and aggressively waved his bat. He was the last guy Drysdale wanted to see. Fans rubbed their fists. Drysdale worked into his windup and threw a fastball.

Strike one.

Logan settled back into the box, hoping not to get a knife in his back, but Drysdale threw a dart at his elbow. "Then he hits me on the crazy bone," Logan said. "And I get an upset stomach and I get paralyzed a little bit there in that left arm. And I'm laying there and Haney comes over to me and says, 'Are you going to play?' And I said to him, 'Hey, I just got hit now. Just a minute.'"

Logan knew it was intentional. He slowly began walking to first base, growing hotter with every step, but he didn't drop his bat. "His bat was poised over his head as though he was debating whether to toss it away or use it," Lou Chapman reported.

Logan got about halfway up the line, jawing with Drysdale the whole time. "I said, 'What the hell are you hitting me for? Why didn't you hit the guy who hit the home run?' And he said, 'Hey, you got anything on your mind?'"

Plate umpire Jocko Conlan stalked Logan, warning him in his thick Irish accent to drop the bat and get on with the game. Jocko next warned Drysdale. Neither man cared what Jocko said. This was between boys and ball clubs, for pride, ego, and World Series money. Backing down would be a sign of weakness. It was a simple conversation. If you want me, come get me. All the years were boiling. "I mean we both had great teams," Frank Torre said, "But we really thought we were better than the Dodgers."

Logan stood at first base with his hands on his hips. Gil Hodges, the big Dodger first baseman, told Logan to shut up and cool off, but Johnny wasn't hearing any of that, mainly because Drysdale wouldn't stop taunting him. According to *The New York Times*, Logan barked, "I'll get you when I come into second base," to which Drysdale bellowed, "If you've got a beef come on and get it over with!"

For a second Logan hesitated. Then something snapped. The hell with this—the hell with the idea that the Braves were bushers who would never fight you for the World Series money, the hell with the idea that we were Bushville and you were the Brooklyn fuckin' Dodgers, and the hell with Drysdale! Logan charged the mound from first base, dragging that big mule Gil Hodges behind him, and he reached out and grabbed Drysdale's shirt. "I had one motive, to kick the hell out of Drysdale," Logan said. "I mean, he hits you twice, what you supposed to do, give him a big kiss?"

Logan cocked his fist. "I was going to give him a haymaker," he said, "But I was off balance and somebody pushed me right in front of (Dodgers manager) Walter Alston. And I wasn't going to hit Walter Alston." But Logan managed to spin Drysdale toward first base, creating a blind spot, where Eddie Mathews came charging in from the on-deck circle.

Eddie knew he would only get one crack so he better make it good. So what if those hands meant everything to Milwaukee's pennant hopes. This bastard was throwing at his guys! He readied his right fist, and with the same speed and hand-eye coordination that had already hit 200 big league home runs, he hit Drysdale with a gunshot right hook to the chin, leaving his feet as he threw all his weight into it, and spinning Drysdale around enough to lose his balance and fall down. Eddie had done this a million times before, though most times, not in a ballgame. He piled on top of Drysdale and unloaded on him, one punch after another, he "pummeled away at him as they rolled around the dirt of the mound," *The Times* reported. Pretty soon both teams were out in the middle of the field, kicking, yelling, screaming, punching, cursing, and spiking.

"We settled our own differences on the field," Torre said. "There was times I hit behind Mathews and Aaron and they hit home runs and I had to stand there and take it, because you knew you were going to get hit by a pitch. You settle your own differences and that's how the game should be played."

When the fight was finished, Jocko Conlan threw Logan and Drysdale out of the game, but somehow permitted Mathews to keep playing. Eddie had a sore hand, but the four runs were enough for starter Bob Trowbridge, a hard-throwing sophomore right-hander. The real hero was Sawatski, who had a career day. His three-run home run with two out in the eighth inning against Clem Labine snapped a 4–4 tie and led the Braves to an 8–5 win, taking three out of four from the Dodgers. Sawatski went 3-for-4 with four runs batted in and never did anything so dramatic, poignant, or meaningful with a baseball bat ever again.

When the game was over, cooler heads and cold beers prevailed, though Logan remained feisty and defiant. He had a lump over his eye and bruises his undershirt concealed, but he wore his wounds with unmistakable pride. Fred Haney said, "Johnny's the kind of guy who would cut your heart out to win." Somebody asked Logan why he went after Drysdale in the first place. Shouldn't he have just taken the retaliation as part of the game? "Drysdale knows he's in for a battle if he throws at somebody," Logan said. "I guess he thought I would back off."

Eddie was very clear. He fought his battles on the field, not in the newspapers. "Hit him?" Mathews asked rhetorically, hiding his hands. "I never hit him." Amazingly, Eddie said this with a straight face. Impressed, the *Journal* offered, "Never play poker with Mathews." On the Dodgers side, Drysdale was checking out the bruises on his collarbone in his shaving mirror. "I was mad about the homer, but I didn't throw at Logan," Drysdale said, his back to the writers. "It was just a close pitch and my fastball runs in on a right-handed hitter."

Now get the hell out of here.

The fight sparked Lou Chapman's poetic side. He wrote, "Logan touched off a chain reaction brawl here Thursday night that ranks high in the history of rhubarbs between his Braves and their old Dodger sparring partners."

When Chapman and the other writers hustled off to file their stories, the Braves had another argument, this time amongst themselves behind closed doors. "Mathews said to Logan, 'From here on in, you're going to have to fight your own fights,'" Torre said, though Mathews was half-kidding. Everybody got hit sometime, and if you fought anytime you got popped, you'd never get any playing done. Eddie would never say no to a fight, but still, the Braves seemed to realize that the ability to pulverize opponents with their fists paled in comparison to finishing first. The pressure was prevalent and occasionally boiled over, as it does with ballplayers and brothers sharing a bedroom. Position players bickered with pitchers. Nondrinkers called out heavy drinkers. Hitters argued with other hitters. But the frustration blew out quickly because they all had common ground—love for Milwaukee, hatred for the Dodgers, and the fierce desire to win the '57 pennant. "Sometimes we used to fight like hell among ourselves because of one reason and one reason alone," Frank Torre said. "Winning."

Blowing off steam in Brooklyn was worth it. The Braves moved back in first place, invigorated and testy, ready to sprint through the summer months. They knocked the Redlegs and Phillies into a second-place tie, a half game game back, and the Dodgers into third, one game back. The Cardinals brought up the rear, 1½ back, five teams clustered together on June 13. BRAVES IN FIRST! the *Sentinel* announced, but who knew how long it would last? It was going to be close and any team could get hot at any time. But for now, it was time for two bottles of the High Life—one to savor—and one to chill the cuts.

John Quinn learned long ago that no general manager could succeed unless he knew how to smokescreen, stall, and manipulate. For the past several months, he had talked trade with every GM he had a good relationship with. Traditional unwritten rules applied: National and American League teams seldom traded with each other because nobody wanted to give the other league an advantage in the World Series. You also never traded with your sworn enemies, which for the Braves, meant the Dodgers. And any team that was no friend of the Brooklyn Dodgers was a friend of the New York Giants, who just happened to have the player the Braves wanted most.

Quinn and his Giants counterpart, Chub Feeney, spent weeks working the puzzle. Feeney knew Quinn wanted second baseman Red Schoendienst, and Quinn knew Feeney wanted three major-league-ready players. Roland Hemond remembered the late night closed-door meetings Quinn held with Fred Haney in his upstairs office at County Stadium leading up to the trade deadline, where they fiercely argued. Quinn did not want to trade Wes Covington. Haney demanded Quinn trade Covington if he was the price. Quinn asked Haney if he wanted to lose a player who could help him. Haney had no qualms with surrendering an untested rookie for a veteran second baseman. They argued for weeks, top-secret conversations of which the best information anyone could gather was a terse Haney acknowledging, "There will be changes made, period."

The Braves left Brooklyn for Philadelphia less than forty-eight hours before the June 15 midnight-trading deadline. There was nothing but silence from Quinn. Lou Chapman tried like hell to get the scoop. He would have hid in Quinn's desk to get the real story, but the best he could get from Quinn was, "the status is quo."

There was no way Quinn was tipping the trade. He didn't want any of the other teams to get wind of what he was doing for fear they would make a corresponding move. The Braves beat the Phillies, 10–2, when Henry Aaron hit his league-leading 17th home run and Warren Spahn pitched a three-hitter to keep the Braves in front by a half game. The Braves were playing great after beating up Brooklyn and improved to 31-21, ten games over .500 for the first time since May 13. Everyone expected a trade, but after the Phillies game, no news. The next day, the Braves beat the Phillies again. Aaron was hot, and of course, so were the Braves. He hit a home run in his third consecutive game, he had 18 now, and the Braves extended the lead to 1½ games over the Redlegs. Bob Buhl walked eight and still won, but after the game, instead of news, there was nothing. The deadline was less than twelve hours away.

Quinn whittled down the minutes. He had the framework for a trade, but Chub Feeney insisted the Braves include Wes Covington. Quinn staunchly refused to include the young slugger, who was tearing up Triple-A Wichita. He desperately wanted the Giants to instead accept their prodigal son, veteran Bobby Thomson, and he compromised by offering young pitcher Ray Crone, who owned the Dodgers in his last outing. Quinn surely reminded Feeney that the Giants loved a good Dodger killer, and in Thomson and Crone, they were getting not one, but two. Besides, Thomson had just gone 4-for-5 against the Phillies—what more proof did you need that Bobby was back? For good measure, the Braves would throw in Danny O'Connell, who was younger than Schoendienst and would take over at second for the Giants, and whose home run power would almost certainly play, as long as the Giants didn't move anywhere cold, windy, or near the ocean.

The Giants pondered the deal. Three established big leaguers for a thirty-four-year-old ballplayer on a bad ball club was a pretty good offer. The Giants were going nowhere and the Braves had a chance to beat the Dodgers. If the Giants weren't going anywhere this year, neither should the Dodgers. At the last minute, Feeney relented, and Quinn pulled the trigger on both the best trades he ever and *never* made. He got Schoendienst for Thomson, Crone, and O'Connell, while hanging on to Covington, who was immediately recalled from Triple-A and inserted into left field. Getting rid of O'Connell made Haney's day. Most important, the Braves had the player they felt they were missing. BRAVES WIN, BOOST LEAD! the *Sentinel* headline read the following day. GIVE 3 PLAYERS FOR SCHOENDIENST.

"Your club outjockeyed the Reds, Dodgers and Cardinals by making that last-minute deal with the Giants," Pirates manager Bobby Bragan said. "Credit the Braves with being smart operators. If they made the trade a few hours earlier, I'm sure other deals would have been made in response. I always said the contending club that makes the big deal is gonna win the pennant. Red will give your club the spark it has always needed. He means you've become the team to beat."

The next morning, Thomson, Crone, and O'Connell arrived to pack their bags. Thomson couldn't wait to go home to New York. "I hated to be traded here the first time," he admitted, and Bushville said, buh-bye. O'Connell wanted to be loved again, and Haney still kicked his ass on the way out the door. "Too inconsistent," he growled. Crone nearly cried. All he ever knew was the Braves. "It's a blow to a fellow's ego," he said. "I didn't think the deal was necessary."

But the entire league knew it was. Red Schoendienst joined the Braves in Philly the next day. The switch-hitter walked into the room with two bats, two pairs of spikes, a lifetime .290 batting average, eight All-Star appearances, a World Series ring, and a youthful visage of "pale skin on which freckles stand out like specks of butter in buttermilk," the *Journal* wrote.

Henry Aaron loved the trade. "You know, we had myself and Mathews and some young studs over there at the time, but still, we needed someone like Red Schoendienst," he said. "Red Schoendienst came along just at the right time and gave us the spark that we really needed."

Fred Haney was waiting. "It's good to see you," he said. He called Red into his office. "He says, 'You're in the middle infield here, we could make you a captain," Schoendienst said. "And I said, 'No, no, no.' I says, 'You got guys been here a lot longer, great ballplayers like Mathews, Logan, Crandall. I'm just here to help out and that's it.'" Haney liked Red's humility, but he wasn't making a request. He was issuing an order. Johnny Logan, Red's new double-play partner, tapped him on the shoulder. "First time I met with Red in a Braves uniform, I said, 'You're the captain,'" he said.

And that settled that.

"I was pretty lucky," Red said. "I walked into a real good situation and fit right in." But secretly, Red felt more pressure than he showed. "I said to myself, 'I don't want to screw up a good thing.'" Red took number 4 and found his old chum from the Cardinals, catcher Del Rice. "He's still the best second baseman in the business," Rice said. Red was so good defensively that his .987 fielding percentage had been the National League record until Jackie Robinson broke it. When Warren Spahn saw him, he immediately talked trash. "Hey, four," he catcalled, "Your average goes up 10 points. You don't have to hit against me anymore."

Lou Chapman took a look at Red and marveled at how a thirty-four-year-old could look like a teenager. Red's bats had the knobs shaved off and were fashioned with crude athletic tape grips. He had a well-worn glove weathered at the fingertips that ground balls flocked to like pilgrims to the Promised Land. In a room with big hitters like Henry, Eddie, and Adcock, it seemed funny that this little guy could make the difference. Red was short for Alfred, D the most important letter in his name and game, a leathery wizard Chapman called "Huckleberry Finn in a baseball uniform."

Warm weather arrived with Red. It was 94 sticky degrees in Philadelphia when he made his debut in a Sunday doubleheader on June 16. He got two hits in his first game and the Braves won. "They will be tough to beat now," Cubs manager Bob Scheffing said. "Schoendienst is quite a money player and those Dutchmen in Milwaukee will really love him." Red took an "Ofer" in game two and the Braves lost, finishing the road trip with nine wins instead of the ten Haney wanted, but he came home with a new second baseman, which he wanted even more.

When Red played his first home game in Milwaukee, he went 4-for-5 with two doubles and the fans absolutely adored him. It was his first taste of the High Life. "They were all out and they wanted to see their boys win," Red said. The Braves pounded out a season-high 17 hits but gave up four runs in the top of the ninth to blow a one-run lead and lose to the lowly Pirates. It was the kind of loss that reaches down your throat and rips your heart out. Welcome to life in Bushville, Red, up one moment and down the next.

But instantly Red made everyone in the lineup better. His defense and knowledge of opposing hitters was invaluable. He was an ideal number two hitter, behind Billy Bruton and in front of Eddie Mathews. You make one mistake in the first inning and you gotta face Aaron. When the Giants were in County Stadium a few days later, that's just what happened when Milwaukee got a taste of the Aaron-Mays debate.

Aaron and Mays always brought the best out of each other. Aaron had a 12-game hitting streak and was stuck on 18 home runs. In the first inning against pitcher Ruben Gomez, Henry laced a high fly ball deep to center field. Willie took off at the crack of the bat. If you liked Willie more than Henry, it was because you thought Willie played the best center field around. He knew every inch of every outfield in the National League. Willie knew he was right in front of the 402-marker in straightway center field. His vertical jumping skills were unlike any athlete ever seen in baseball. Willie left his feet, seemingly hanging in midair, like a Christmas ornament hanging off one of the big trees planted in Perini's Forest. Henry's ball seemed destined to land in the trees growing beyond the chain link fence, but instead, landed softly and safely in Willie's glove. Henry didn't even flinch, but the entire ballpark could see Willie beaming like one of the old Birmingham Black Barons who used to play with Piper Davis when the Negro Leagues toured Milwaukee in the 1940s. "Mays got quite a hand from the crowd," *The New York Times* noted.

But Henry got quite the revenge. In the third inning, Gomez tried to smoke Henry with a fastball down-and-away, a cocky and arrogant way of Gomez backing up his manager, Bill Rigney, who vowed his pitchers had "found something out about your boy." But Henry was having none of that. If he could reach it, he could hit it. This gunshot was a high, racing line drive into the left-center gap. Mays and Bobby Thomson, the former Brave and now Giant again, gave chase, but this ball was gone for home run 19 and a 13-game hitting streak. Henry was getting hot and the Braves were warming up.

As for Bobby Thomson, he was happy to be home with the Giants, where he had been the starting center fielder before Willie showed up. The year he was traded to Milwaukee, he busted up his ankle and lost his spot to Henry. Poor old Bobby Thomson had to move again. He will always be the only ballplayer in history who can say he lost his job to both Willie Mays and Henry Aaron. Hey, Bobby, who do *you* like better—Mays or Aaron?

9

COME ON YOU, HENRY!

"Come on you, Henry!" Earl Gillespie called into his microphone. Inside Milwaukee County Stadium, hundreds of transistor radios were turned to Earl and 31,051 eyes were fixated on Henry Aaron at home plate. It was June 27, the last of a three-game series between the Braves and the Brooklyn Dodgers. The Braves trailed 1–0 with one out in the bottom of the eighth inning against nemesis Don Drysdale. Down range at second base stood Bob Buhl. Billy Bruton was on first base. The High Life flag flew in the radio booth. The fans stood and roared. The Braves were on the top step of the dugout. Hearts raced. Feet stomped. Hands clapped. The noise rumbled.

And in the batter's box, there was peace and quiet.

Henry was untouchable in moments of great concentration. The game slowed down. He saw the world in silence. Henry recognized the release point when the ball rolled off Drysdale's fingers. He could see the spin clearly and all he had to do was wait. Front foot down, hands back, weight shifting, quiet and deadly, serene and sudden, stride style. He hit the pitch on the good part of the bat and felt the wood give way as the sound of his contact punctured his cocoon.

Now Henry could hear how explosively loud the fans were as his gunshot echoed through the ballpark. The hit split the right-center field gap in the time it takes to inhale. The Dodgers outfielders, Duke Snider and Carl Furillo, ran down the ball. Henry could tell by the fans that Bob Buhl creaked home with the tying run and Billy Bruton was racing home behind him. Henry had a double for sure, but he wanted more, so he turned for third and beat the throw, safe with a slide and a two-run triple. He had no personal animosity toward Drysdale, but he loved to get him good. He had smoked the ball back up the middle, his personal touch when he wished to make a point. The Braves beat the Dodgers, 2–1, took two out of three in the Series, and finished June riding high with a six-game winning streak, 42-29, in first by a half game over the Reds, 2½ in front of the Cardinals, and 4 ahead of the Dodgers.

Henry was closing out a June tear in which he hit 11 home runs, the best month of his career, but the biggest news in the locker room was not that Henry hit, but that Henry spoke. He had responded well to Fred Haney's decision to drop him to cleanup. Henry did not seek attention, but attention found him. "I always get blurry eyes against Drysdale, but made up my mind that I had to stay with him," Henry said. "So I got hold of one." Some of the Milwaukee writers were starting to understand him better. He hit Alabama stride style and he spoke it, too. His words were brief but meaningful. "I sure ought to hit at least 40 home runs," he said, and that was a tremendous announcement on Henry's part. In 1957, Henry was growing into himself as a player and as a person. He would become a star in the summer and a father for the first time in the winter. In the fall, he wanted to win the World Series. He always knew that inside that cocoon of the batter's box, nobody could touch him. He couldn't feel anything but how loose he rolled the bat in his fingers. He was alone with his intellect and his instincts, deconstructing pitchers and their stuff, how they were trying to get him out, and how he was going to beat them.

"I think Henry made up his mind that he was going to hit more home runs," Del Crandall said. "I have no idea where he projected himself as far as how many home runs he was going to hit. But I think he decided he was going to be a home run hitter, because to me, Henry Aaron was the best hitter I ever saw. He could have been a career .350, .360 hitter, whatever he wanted to do, but I think he made up his mind that he was going to hit the ball out of the ballpark. I can't read his mind, but that's what it appeared to me."

Henry was asked why he was hitting more home runs this season, but great hitters seldom feel the need to elaborate. "I don't know," he said, though he understood his swing better than anyone. "For some reason I'm putting more lift on the ball." Henry was putting more of everything on the ball—more power, more hard contact to all fields, more clutch hits, more bravado. He realized that he alone had the ability to carry the team. His game-winning triple against the Dodgers sparked a ferocious tear. A day later in Pittsburgh, he went 3-for-4 with his 21st home run to break a tied game and lead the Braves to a win. The day after that, a doubleheader in Pittsburgh, Henry hit a home run in the first game and a home run in the second game.

The Braves fed off Henry's bat. Wes Covington, the rookie left fielder, went 3-for-3 in Game 1. Eddie Mathews hit a game-winning two-run home run in the thirteenth inning of Game 2. A rookie, Don McMahon, made his major league debut and pitched four shutout innings and became the team's closer out of the bullpen, a significant addition that shaped the Braves in the second half. And in the lineup, Henry was becoming a man. The Braves opened July in St. Louis, where the weather was hot and the memories were hell. Henry homered again, his 24th, tying him with Mickey Mantle for the major league lead. He went a day without a long ball, because nobody is perfect, then hit three more home runs in three more days. His home run at Wrigley Field on July 5 was his seventh in eight games. Lou Chapman saw the happiness in his young friend's face when he wrote, "Henry Aaron's features were creased in a big grin, like a kid who shot off a firecracker under an unsuspecting fat man and got away with it."

Babe Ruth was that unsuspecting fat man. For the first time in his life, Henry Aaron heard his name mentioned in the same breath as George Herman Ruth. He had 27 home runs in 76 games, identical to Ruth's record 60 home run season in 1927. Ruth's record was hallowed ground. Many thought Mantle or Mathews would hit 60 home runs in a season before anyone else, but now, along came Henry Aaron. Henry's teammate and father figure, Billy Bruton, believed Henry belonged in the conversation. "It's about time for somebody to start comparing Henry's homer record with Babe Ruth," he said. "With a natural hitter like Aaron, anything is possible."

While the Braves played slip-and-slide through late June and early July, absorbing beatings to the pitching staff and Lew Burdette's winless streak that stretched from May 18 to July 7, Henry remained consistent. On the last day before the All-Star break, he went 3-for-4 to extend his hitting streak to ten games. He hit safely in 24 out of 25 games. He led the league with a .347 batting average, though the Cardinals held first place, 2½ in front of the Braves. Fred Haney knew that only special hitters could single-handedly keep a team in the pennant race. These players were more than cornerstones. They were generational offensive talents. "Henry reminds me of the Babe," he said.

When Aaron went to the All-Star game in St. Louis, his hitting spree put him in heavy demand for many writers who didn't know him and came into contact with stride style for the first time. On the whole, writers did not understand the sanctuary of Henry's batter's box. *Pittsburgh Courier* columnist Wendell Smith reminded readers how "Aaron's lethargic care-free appearance is deceptive. He's not lazy, nor numb mentally. He's a quick-witted, alert young man." As more people discovered the magnitude of the young Henry Aaron, Lou Chapman became a valued friend. From the beginning of Henry's time in Milwaukee, Chapman's copy was never littered with the condescending style reporters often affixed to black players. Some writers didn't know any better. Some knew better and didn't care. Chapman was neither. Henry was a ballplayer and a ballplayer alone. "My dad was really sensitive to the race issues of the time when they were traveling and dealing with segregation," Richard Chapman said. "My dad was very positive whereas a lot of reporters were very skeptical about the black athlete's ability to play baseball."

Chapman let Henry's bat speak for him, and when they spoke, the conversations were much more substantive than the typical athlete-reporter relationship. "He was a very good friend of mine, and when I mean friend, he was a very good friend of mine," Aaron said years later. "I accepted him as a friend and he and I talked a lot about different things. And so, I looked at him, I looked upon him that way, you know, as being someone I could trust as a friend, and someone that not only looked at me as a baseball player, but looked at me as someone that was a human being."

The Braves needed Henry locked and loaded more than ever. Joe Adcock was out of the lineup indefinitely after suffering a fractured fibula six inches above his ankle on June 23 against Philadelphia. He went straight to a Milwaukee hospital, where a few hours later and popped up on painkillers, he smiled for the photographers with his leg elevated in a cast. Frank Torre went into the everyday lineup for the first time in his career. The knock on Torre was good field and no hit, but Henry Aaron disagreed. "He was a very good hitter," Aaron said. "And he played first base as well as anyone in the big leagues." Though he was possibly the slowest guy in the National League, he even legged out a few triples, nearly collapsing when he got to third. "He wasn't blessed with blazing speed," Henry noted, allowing a warm laugh. But lack of foot speed was part of the charm of the Torre clan.

Adcock's injury was the first sign that the Braves were in for a rough summer. On July 11, in the first inning of a game against the Pittsburgh Pirates, Bill Virdon looped a lazy pop into shallow left-center. Shortstop Felix Mantilla and center fielder Billy Bruton charged the ball and violently collided. Simply put, "it was bad," according to Aaron. Mantilla, a versatile and rangy utility infielder, bruised up his chest and missed most of the rest of the month. Signed out of Puerto Rico by the Braves at age seventeen in 1952, Mantilla was an old pro of twenty-two when he went down. He was Fred Haney's favorite infielder off the bench. He alone was a tough loss, but losing Bruton was worse.

Bruton's lip ripped open, pouring blood all over the front of his uniform and required eight stitches. He jammed his kneecap into his jaw and went to the hospital after the game. Bruton thought he would be back in a few days, but his knee was so damaged that it was a week before he could hobble out of the hospital. It was soon determined that he was out for the season. Bruton's loss was a devastating injury for the Braves. He was their everyday leadoff man and anchor in center field. "He was somebody we all had a lot of confidence in," Aaron said.

But so was Henry. The next day, he was in the lineup in center field. He had never played an inning of center in his big league career, but Henry took to it like a natural. The main disadvantage he had was that he was unfamiliar with the various quirks of the different outfields throughout the National League. Every outfield had its traps and angles. Henry was going to find out on his own, but he kept right on hitting. Without his bat going strong, the injuries would have further tested Fred Haney's ability to creatively manage his roster. "You're only as good as your replacement players," he said.

Billy Bruton's injury caused a chain reaction that threatened the team's makeup and the shape of the season and forced Haney to juggle the lineup. He moved Red Schoendienst up to the leadoff spot from second and Johnny Logan up from seventh to second, setting the table for the middle of the order, a left-right-left combination of Mathews, Aaron, and Covington, followed typically by some combination of Frank Torre, Del Crandall, and Andy Pafko, who at thirty-five, became the everyday right fielder in Aaron's place. Had the Braves failed to trade for Schoendienst, who hit leadoff for the '46 Cardinals, they would have lacked an experienced leadoff hitter. He was vital to the Braves if they were going to survive. "He not only knew the game," Henry Aaron explained, "But he knew *how* to play the game."

The Braves told their scouts to comb the minors for a versatile right-handed hitter who could play first base and the outfield. From Johnny Moore came a possible solution. Vernal Leroy "Nippy" Jones was a thirty-two-year-old former part-time player for the St. Louis Cardinals who hadn't appeared in the majors since 1952. When Jones left the big leagues, he returned home to Sacramento where he carved out four happy and productive seasons with the Pacific Coast League's Solons. He was five weeks shy of his major league pension and gave up hope of ever playing in the majors again. "When I couldn't get back, I figured I never would," he said. But Jones was just the kind of ballplayer Johnny Moore was looking for. He recommended the Braves purchase his contract from Sacramento. A few days later Jones walked into the dressing room at Ebbets Field. The ballplayer who swore he'd never cry fought back tears when he returned to the big leagues.

Bob Buhl loved to make the Dodgers cry, and right now, he was in a particularly nasty mood because he felt Dodgers manager Walter Alston left him off the NL All-Star team simply because he owned the Dodgers. Buhl was on his game again, especially against Gil Hodges, who couldn't figure him out. "Buhl could throw his glove out to the mound and Hodges used to strike out practically every time," Frank Torre said. "I mean, he couldn't hit his slider worth a damn." Red Schoendienst hit a leadoff home run against Sal Maglie and Buhl struck out Hodges twice to protect a 2–1 lead, entering the ninth inning. But the Dodgers had a taste of revenge in mind. Buhl walked Gino Cimoli to bring Hodges to the plate. Buhl tried to overmatch him, but Hodges lined a game-winning two-run home run into the left field stands to give the Dodgers a 3–2 victory. The 20,871 Dodger fans rejoiced as they had few times in a season marked by the anxiety and uncertainty of their future home.

The next day, a few glorious hours soothed the tortured souls of Brooklyn. The Dodgers were all powerful again, pulverizing the Braves 20–4 in the worst loss since the team moved to Milwaukee. The Dodgers ran up the score with a nine-run eighth inning against twenty-four-year-old reliever Taylor Phillips, who Fred Haney left in the game to absorb the ambush because he didn't want to tax the bullpen. The beating swelled Phillips's earned run average, destroyed his confidence, and put his career in a tailspin. Don Drysdale pitched 6⅓ strong innings and hit one of Brooklyn's five home runs, and he held Henry Aaron hitless in five at-bats to stop his hitting streak at 15 games. Lou Perini watched this humiliation from his seats by the Braves dugouts. The Braves fell into third place, 1½ behind Philadelphia. This was a loss worthy of praying Mr. Perini's rosary.

Milwaukee fans had a nervous breakdown. The *Journal* called the loss a "massacre" and a "holocaust." Rumors abounded that Perini was going to fire Haney. Some angry fans crafted a crude Fred Haney dummy and hanged him in the streets. When told of his symbolic execution, Haney responded with typical defiance. "When this club assembled for spring training, I told them, 'There is going to be a lot of work done here and you are going to do it. You may hate my guts for it, but when you get those World Series checks, you may like me.' I say the same thing to the fans who hanged me in effigy in Milwaukee."

Warren Spahn loved to pitch the day after a bad loss. He was an ace whose pride rested on righting his team's ship. The Braves had no time to wallow. They arrived the next night for a three-game series against the surprising first-place Philadelphia Phillies, a team few expected to be in contention. The Phillies were an aging team that lacked depth but had just enough starting pitching to be dangerous. Spahn pitched into the ninth inning protecting a 6–2 lead, when the Phillies loaded the bases with two outs and their pesky left-handed hitting center fielder, Richie Ashburn, at the plate. Ashburn slashed a slicing hit to right-center field. Aaron, who was swung way over to left, had no chance to close the gap. But right fielder Andy Pafko could get to the ball, if his old man legs would let him get that far, that fast. "Handy Andy" made his living eschewing what he called "rock 'n'roll" baseball. He lacked the ability to hit many home runs and he wasn't fast, but he could play both outfield corners and knew how to position himself against every hitter in the league. His crotchety defiance endeared him to Haney, who held his breath along with Spahn as they watched the old man in right field charge the ball. Pafko broke into the big leagues in 1943 and had been with the Braves since 1953, and though his knees had the mileage to show for it, he was determined not to let Ashburn's ball drop. Pafko dove and slid across the grass chest first, like a plane making an emergency landing. He rolled over, but somehow, the ball was in his glove as surely as Andy was a baseball geezer. Ballgame over. Final score: Braves 6, Phillies 2. Spahn hugged him when he came in. "It was the first time a pitcher ever hugged me," Pafko said. "That made me feel real good."

The Braves also hugged Henry, who went 3-for-3 and hit his 29th home run. The next day, July 17, Phillies fans threw cold beer at plate umpire Jocko Conlan when he ejected pitcher Robin Roberts, but Henry stayed hot. He collected three more hits to raise his league-leading batting average to .352. But in the sixth inning, Henry discovered one of the traps of a center field he was not familiar with. While chasing a two-run double by Willie Jones, Aaron tripped over a drainage board near the 447-marker in Shibe Park.

An inning later, his ankle swelled badly enough for him to leave the game. The injury terrified the Braves and the citizens of Milwaukee, who were already jittery. The *Sentinel* spent considerable inches detailing the threat of the Russians dropping a nuke, warning citizens, "For machine gun fire, man invented the trench. For the Intercontinental Ballistic Missile, the only defense is prayer." For losing Henry for a prolonged period, there was absolutely no defense. The Braves hoped Henry could come back within a week. There was nobody on earth who could replace him, so the Braves showcased teamwork.

While Henry's ankle healed, Fred Haney kept the Braves together with spit and glue. The following day, he started rookie bonus baby Johnny DeMerit, whose major league career consisted of nine at-bats, in center. Later in the game, he moved Red Schoendienst to center for a few innings, where he hadn't played in a decade, and inserted one of his former Hollywood Stars, Dick Cole at second. Andy Pafko was the unlikely cleanup hitter and Del Rice, Bob Buhl's personal catcher known for his defense but not his bat, hit a two-run home run to spark a 4–2 win, complete a three-game sweep and put the Braves back in first place on July 18. Rice, who rarely hit home runs, explained, "Before the game, Henry told me to hit one for him. So I did."

When the Braves came to the Polo Grounds on July 19 for four games, Andy Pafko was playing right field and batting cleanup, in the lineup against the left-hander Johnny Antonelli, who had beaten his former team three times this season. A big crowd came to see the Braves at the old shanty. "It's pretty good when you can get 22,000 to come out and hate you, isn't it?" Lou Perini said, but he underestimated where the hatred was directed. Giants owner Horace Stoneham announced that he planned to recommend to his board of directors that the Giants quit the Polo Grounds after the season and leave New York. The Giants fans saw the writing on the wall and came to protest. Most speculated that the Giants were leaving for Minneapolis, where the Giants had their Triple-A team, in a move that would mirror Milwaukee's 1953 relocation to the Heartland. But Stoneham's other solution seemed utterly implausible. Why would anybody move to San Francisco? Think about it, the fans argued, it just didn't sound right. *The San Francisco Giants.* Try it on for size. Willie Mays of the San Francisco Giants? Times were changing, but this didn't make sense. Then again, neither did Andy Pafko batting cleanup and playing right field for the Milwaukee Braves.

The humble Andy Pafko would tell you that pennant-winning teams do not have Andy Pafko playing right and hitting cleanup. So what did Pafko do? He made two daring and dazzling catches and hit two home runs, including a game-winning, two-run home run in the top of the ninth, to give the Braves a 3–1 win, keep them in first place by one game over the Dodgers, and give them their fourth consecutive win. "Here is a guy, Pafko, who at 36, is supposed to be ready for a rocking chair, and all he's doing is carrying a crippled ball club on his back," Bob Wolf wrote in the *Journal*.

Pafko's back was killing him the next day, July 20, so Haney sat him down against right-hander Ruben Gomez and put left-handed hitting Wes Covington in the cleanup spot and started Johnny DeMerit in center field, moved catcher Del Crandall to right field for the first time in his career, and played third-string catcher Carl Sawatski behind the plate. There wasn't much interest in the patchwork Braves—a crowd of only 7,638 attended— and they missed DeMerit's first big league RBI, Red Schoendienst's single to extend his hitting streak to 17 games, Del Crandall's error in right field that allowed the Giants to get back in the game, and Covington's second home run of the game, a two-run shot in the ninth to win it, 7–5. Talk about team effort. It was a five-game winning streak for the Braves while Henry Aaron healed, and Fred Haney decreed, "It's up to Henry," to announce his return. "I'm not going to use him and risk aggravating the injury if the ankle still bothers him."

In Game 1 of the doubleheader on July 21, there was good news: Aaron pinch-hit late in the game to test out his sore ankle. He drew a walk and was lifted for a pinch runner. That's where the good news ended. Closer Don McMahon blew his first save opportunity. But the Braves used their resilient teamwork to bounce back in Game 2. Shortstop Johnny Logan, a career table-setter, saw his name penciled in batting sixth in the lineup. The feisty New Yorker's eyes lit up. "Batting sixth? Watch Logan go!" he said. Go, Johnny, go. He aspired to be a Cadillac instead of the souped-up Chevy he really was and went 5-for-5, his first five-hit day since 1955. Red Schoendienst had three more hits, and went 5-for-9 in the doubleheader to extend his hitting streak to 19 games. The Braves scored all seven runs in the final three innings, won 7–4, and almost single-handedly ruined the Giants will to live in Harlem. "Even the group holding a 'Stay, Team, Stay,' sign in the bleachers felt let down," *The New York Times* reported. Some of the fans at the Polo Grounds must have wondered if San Francisco was far enough away for the Giants to go. The Braves had just one more stop to go on this trying road trip, back to Boston, to Lou Perini's hometown, to play the Red Sox in a charity game for the Jimmy Fund. Perini was in a bright mood as he walked down Commonwealth Avenue muttering his morning rosary. The Braves rolled back into Boston, much like the ragtag street-smart survivors they had always been, but this time, they were first-place ragtag street-smart survivors.

While the Braves rolled to Boston, they had to admit that like him or not, Fred Haney had held them together. He had an all-star team of injured players—Henry Aaron, Billy Bruton, and Felix Mantilla currently—and Eddie Mathews, Johnny Logan, and Del Crandall had also been banged up at various times. The 1957 National League was ferociously tough and balanced. Virtually every team could beat each other on any given night. Future Hall of Fame hitters were on every team, a golden age of National League talent—Roberto Clemente in Pittsburgh, Ernie Banks in Chicago, Willie Mays in New York, Richie Ashburn in Philadelphia, and Stan Musial in St. Louis. Plus, veterans Roy Campanella and Duke Snider were joined by young pitchers Don Drysdale and Sandy Koufax in Brooklyn. The Braves were in first place by one game over the Dodgers. Five of the eight teams in the National League were separated by 3 ½ games in one of the tightest NL pennant races in years, called an "astounding logjam," by *The New York Times*.

Fred Haney's career struggles had groomed him for this race. He had always been the underdog, from the time he was a short high school fullback, to the years he bounced around the bush leagues until Ty Cobb gave him his shot to play in the majors, to the losing seasons managing the Browns and the Pirates. Now he had the horses, and even if they were wounded, he wasn't going to blow his chance. "Fred Haney deserves a lot of the credit," Frank Torre said. "Somehow, someway, he'd always get the other guys into the ballgames even when everybody was healthy."

Keeping Eddie Mathews healthy was a huge priority, which meant keeping him dry. You would never get Eddie completely sober, because he didn't want to be, and he'd be out with Lew Burdette, who liked to say of Eddie, "We never ran him out of beer, but we had him workin' nights."

When Eddie returned to Boston, he was not forgotten by the small but strong contingent of Braves fans packed among the 30,572 fans. He was having a solid season, with his average high for him at .292 and his home run production, 18, a little lower than usual for him. Mathews was stuck in one of his most frustrating slumps in recent years, with no home runs in his last 14 games and four hits in last 28 at-bats. He was ready to beat the crap out of somebody, but he would have to wait.

Nobody ever doubted his power, but since Fred Haney arrived he was determined to see Mathews get more out of his skills than just home runs. His defense, while not pristine, was smoother. Playing with Red Schoendienst created a certain air of accountability defensively. Eddie was still hard-nosed, but he never cared about the finer points of his all-around game as much as he did when he played with Red. He showed his teammates commitment working long hours with coach Connie Ryan.

There was a maturation process with Eddie, who didn't necessarily always like it, but he understood what Haney wanted. He wanted him to hit for a higher average and trade a few home runs to do it. The problem was Eddie was so pull-oriented that managers shifted defensively against him. The fielders moved to the right side and the pitchers threw him slow garbage away. "I'd hit the ball hard to right field and there wouldn't be anywhere for it to drop, then I'd try to hit it to left and pop up," he said. In short, Eddie's approach was screwed up. So Haney summoned his friend, Ty Cobb, to speak to him during the season. Eddie never hit left-handers very well, so Cobb suggested Mathews stand farther back in the box to get a longer look at each pitch. "Ty talked to Eddie for quite a bit," Haney said. "When he came back to the bench, I heard him mutter to himself." That was perhaps sportswriter Lou Chapman's way of suggesting Eddie thought the old fart was full of shit. "But I had a hunch he remembered what Ty told him. Hell, he may have been following Ty's advice without even knowing it." One thing about Eddie—he wanted to win. For all the late nights and hangovers, nobody questioned his desire.

The Braves returned to Milwaukee and found another way to win through injuries and hitting slumps. Bob Buhl pitched a two-hitter for his first victory in nearly a month, a 1–0 victory over the Phillies and Curt

Simmons. Johnny Logan drove in the game's only run with an RBI triple, his seventh consecutive hit, underscoring his value to the club. "He was a big, big, part of our success," Del Crandall said. "He never got the accolades Henry and Eddie got, but we knew how important he was to us. Johnny Logan was the player who, when we needed him most, came through." Logan helped the Braves push their record to 54-38, a season-high sixteen games above .500, and maintain a one-game lead over the Dodgers.

The following day, after missing five games, Henry Aaron returned to the starting lineup. He was a sight for sore eyes, but his trigger was slightly off. He went 0-for-3, and the following night, when the Braves lost, his hitless streak stretched to 0-for-7. Phillies pitcher Jack Sanford wasn't about to take any credit for prolonging Henry's slump. He grew up in Boston where he said he played sandlot ball with Lou Perini's children and joked, "Their real estate was a little different than mine." He knew Henry's real estate as a hitter was a little different than anyone else's. "Honestly, I hate to pitch against this club," Sanford said after pitching a five-hitter and winning, 3–1. "I was just lucky. There's no way to pitch to Aaron."

Robin Roberts was as crafty as any pitcher in baseball when he faced Aaron the following day. Roberts, the venerable right-handed ace and a six-time 20-game winner, was transitioning from a power pitcher to a control pitcher. He was riding a seven-game losing streak, the longest of his career. In the first inning, Henry cracked a single to snap his slump. In the fourth inning with two out and nobody on, Roberts faced Henry again. Aaron thought Roberts had good stuff, saying he "looked like the Roberts of old," but when Roberts tried to pinpoint a fastball, Henry looked like the Aaron of old.

Milwaukee County Stadium heard that distinctive gunshot as Aaron stride styled into Roberts, rocking Robin deep to right, his 30th home run of the season. As he trotted the bases, Earl Gillespie bellowed, "Go on you, Henry! Number 30! Holy Cow!" and his partner Blaine "The Blainer" Walsh waved the High Life flag. It was Aaron's first home run since July 16. But Roberts settled down, and though he allowed a scratch single to Red Schoendienst to extend his hitting streak to 22 games, he outdueled Warren Spahn to beat the Braves 5–3 and knock the Braves lead down to a half game. The Phillies were in fifth place, 2½ behind. It was July 25 and it was still anybody's pennant race.

The Giants arrived in Milwaukee on July 26 at the same time as Jayne Mansfield, who set her pink stilettos on the Mitchell Field tarmac to plug her next movie. Wearing all pink, she announced, "There's nothing but me underneath it." The Giants, at 11½ games out, would have loved to undress the Braves and play spoiler in a five-game series, but they were all wrong to play the part. Nippy Jones, major league rejuvenation project, played the leading man. Tied 3–3 with one out in the bottom of the eleventh inning, Giants manager Bill Rigney intentionally walked Andy Pafko to pitch to Nippy, who was 1-for-12 since joining the Braves and hadn't hit a home run in the majors since May 1, 1952. So what did Nippy Jones do?

The Braves, a hero-a-day ballclub, found today's hero in Nippy Jones, who launched a three-run game-winning home run. The Braves beat the Giants 6–3 to move 15 games over .500 and hang on to first place by a spaghetti strap. A crowd of 33,743 went nuts. The Braves had recently surged past one million in attendance and were aiming for two million for the fourth consecutive season. As Nippy rounded the bases, it seemed like millions were blowing him kisses. If Mansfield could imitate Marilyn, then for one brief moment, Nippy Jones could imitate Mickey Mantle, who hit his 200th career home run that night at Yankee Stadium. Jayne Mansfield would have given him a big, sloppy wet kiss, but she'd have to peel twenty-five sweaty summery ballplayers off him first.

Wins like that kept the Braves moving though July. Bob Buhl came out the next day throwing bullets, pitching like a bully, running his scoreless streak to 21 innings before the Giants salvaged a couple of cheap runs. He won his second consecutive game. About the only good news for the Giants was that they stopped Red Schoendienst. His hitting streak wasn't very flashy—a lot of singles and 1-for-4 days—but it added up to a .340 batting average from July 2 to July 26. He raised his season average from .294 to .326, and hit .347 for the month. It was one of the best stretches of his career, hitting leadoff, playing defense, and turning countless double plays. Red played in a manner that never drew attention to himself, but the Braves knew Red was a big reason they were in the race through the rash of injuries. "Red was the missing piece in the puzzle," Henry Aaron said. "We had a good ball club, but we was a better ball club with Red Schoendienst."

Lou Chapman took great delight in playing off Red's name. Wisconsin, the state that gave the union Joe McCarthy and the Communist blacklist, had a new hero, and his name was Red. This cracked Chapman up beyond belief. His parents were Russian immigrants and he grew up speaking Russian in the house before he served in the Army Air Force in World War II and attended Marquette's journalism school. Chapman went to write a feature on Red one day and the jokes kept coming. You could feel the whimsical glee in his copy.

"Don't look now but the 'Red' influence has permeated the ranks of Milwaukee youngsters," he wrote. "Red cells have worked their way into practically every neighborhood, but in this case it's nothing to notify the FBI about. No hammer and sickle for them. They use a saw to cut their ties with tradition—and when finally comes the revolution they'll all use cut-down bats like the cult's beloved idol. Ever since the star second baseman came to town with his midget bats and choked plate stance, he has touched off a growing fad."

Turns out, Milwaukee kids were making like Red. They took the expensive bats their parents bought them at the sporting goods store, got out Dad's saw, and cut off the handles. That really pissed off a lot of dads because bats aren't cheap. Then the kids took athletic tape and made knobs like Red did. Then they tried to hit like him, but good luck. Red Schoendienst was a latter-day Ty Cobb, gifted with extraordinary hand-eye coordination and bat control, and a burning desire to not screw up Milwaukee's good thing. "I didn't want to be the guy they traded for who didn't make a difference," he said.

On July 29, anyone with a TV set outside of Milwaukee got a rare treat when the NBC game of the week originating in Milwaukee pitted the Giants against the Braves. Lou Perini refused to allow Braves games to be broadcast locally in Milwaukee for fear that he would hurt ticket sales, his club's primary source of income. The Giants weren't above selling their TV rights, however. Perini looked at the attendance on July 28—40,503—versus the attendance of the televised game—24,179—and said, *See, that's why we don't televise Braves games in Milwaukee.*

The Game of the Week was a big deal in those days and players aspired to look good in front of large TV audiences. The Braves flashed the feel of a team coming together. Eddie Mathews played third base like a poet. In the sixth inning, Ray Jablonski smashed a shot to his right. Eddie threw his glove to the backhand side, speared the ball, and finished the double play. "I may be prejudiced because he's my roomie, but hasn't he improved over there?" Bob Buhl asked. Giants manager Bill Rigney fumed. "He's making more good plays than he has a right to make." If the Braves were going to win the World Series, they would never be able to do it without trusted late-inning defense at third base.

When Eddie hit his 19th home run of the season the day before, it was his first home run in 15 games. Eddie's power numbers were killing his pride. They were good enough for any other third baseman in the league, but not for him. He took solace in his improved defense, his better batting average, and the fact that the Braves were in first place because he was sacrificing some of those home runs to be a complete ballplayer. Hell, he even stole a base on national TV. "If anybody's a team player," Buhl said, "it's Eddie." Translation: He'll trade home runs to win the pennant.

The TV audience got a look at the never-say-die spirit the Braves prided themselves on. The Braves were losing, 8–4, in the bottom of the ninth inning. But Del Crandall hit a solo home run with one out to make it 8–5. Pinch hitter Carl Sawatski singled to make it 8–6. Pinch-runner Johnny DeMerit ran for Sawatski and Nippy Jones came to the plate. He singled home two runs, including the tying run on right fielder Ozzie Virgil's error. The Braves brewed a four-run comeback to tie the score and force extra innings. The stadium was shaking. Somewhere, the New York Yankees might have been shaking, too, or at least mildly entertained.

Henry Aaron led off the bottom of the tenth inning. Once more in the broadcast booth, Earl Gillespie bellowed his familiar call, "Come on you, Henry!" Henry came on and hit a screaming line drive deep to center field. There was only one center fielder fast and reactionary enough to read that ball and make that catch, and he wore number 24 and played for the New York Giants. Willie Mays sprinted for the fence, leaped with both feet in the air, and came down with the ball in his glove. Without a question, Lou Perini was watching this ballgame on TV and dreaming of what might have been if the Braves had succeeded in signing Mays. "My dad would always talk about Mays and Aaron and how unbelievable it would have been to have had them both in Milwaukee," David Perini said.

But Henry Aaron insisted this was not a one-man team. It was a point of pride that the Braves were deep, balanced, and talented enough to pick up each other. "What makes clubs is that you know what you need to do and you know how to do it," Aaron said. Sure enough, Wes Covington drew a walk. The reliable Crandall singled. Andy Pafko walked to load the bases with two outs. With the pitcher's spot up, Fred Haney sent Felix Mantilla to pinch-hit for the first time since he was injured in the July 11 collision with Billy Bruton. Facing Giants reliever Al Worthington, Mantilla didn't do anything flashy except get the job done. He drew a bases loaded walk to score Covington and give the Braves a dramatic, comeback 9–8 victory.

It's a good bet that some of the Braves had a good time Saturday night. When you have an early game on Sunday morning, and the only guy who does anything is the church-going Mormon, Nippy Jones, the barflies were out in force. Nippy went 3-for-4, making Giants manager Bill Rigney wonder what hat Johnny Moore pulled that rabbit out of, but the rest of the ball club wore dark shades, and sucked down coffee and aspirin. Johnny Antonelli shut them out, 2–0, and Willie Mays went 4-for-4. The Braves sobered up and took the second game, though Mays hit his 18th home run and went 6-for-8 in the doubleheader.

Whenever Henry and Willie played, the debate started anew. Amid the pennant race was the never-ending public argument over who was the best player in the National League. To a man, the Milwaukee Braves would have taken Henry Aaron over Willie Mays, though practical minds wanted them the same. "If you had a chance to take one or the other, you'd take both," Red Schoendienst said. But Eddie would take Henry. In Eddie's mind, Willie answered the question with his own showboating. During the series, Henry hit a shoe-top level liner at Willie, who tried to Hollywood the ball. His flamboyance failed him and the ball skipped away, allowing Henry to glide into third with a triple. Another time during the series, Willie bounced off third base with the mouth of a trash-talking pool hustler. Eddie always tried to sneak in behind him so Del Crandall could try to pick him off, but Willie would drive Eddie crazy, screeching, "I know what'cha doin'!"

Once, while Spahn was pitching to Bobby Thomson with Mays on third and a runner at first, a trail runner broke for second. Crandall popped up to throw and Mays charged home on the delayed steal. But Crandall outbluffed Mays. He faked the throw to second and held the ball. Willie threw up his arms like he was pushing against the wind. He turned to third, and Crandall threw a strike to Eddie, who bull-charged Mays back to Crandall. The most exciting play in baseball might have been Willie Mays in a rundown between Eddie Mathews and Del Crandall. Willie twisted to avoid Eddie, his body twisting and contorting in elastic energy, until Eddie lunged to lay the tag on before he scored. Then Eddie dusted himself off, glared at Willie in the dirt like he had knocked him down in a heavy-weight bout, and stalked back to his position.

Plays like this were about winning at all costs. The Braves finished July in first place with a half game lead, but five teams were separated by four games. The convoluted pennant race sparked Lew Burdette's goofy imagi-nation. He held court in the locker room one day and announced the solu-tion to the problem: "Every team wins 77 and loses 77, creating an eight-way tie," Burdette explained. "With a best two-out-of-three playoffs for each club, the playoffs will take weeks! Then the National League victor will win the World Series because the Yankees will be out of shape after sitting around for half of October."

The Braves could dream about October now. Since the day the Brook-lyn Dodgers humiliated them at Ebbets Field, Milwaukee went 13-4 and won six of the last seven games of the month, finishing July with an over-all record of 60-41 and noting that the red-hot Cardinals went 21-10 and closed July with an eight-game winning streak, vowing to make things interesting. If you wanted a pennant race, the National League was the place to be, because the Yankees were 3½ in front of the Chicago White Sox and 11 games ahead of the third-place Boston Red Sox. The Braves had something nobody else had—the quiet and booming bat of Henry

Aaron, who batted .337 with seven home runs in the month despite missing five games and being thrown into a slump. There was a quiet confidence about Henry that could not be duplicated. He refused to take all the
credit even as it became apparent a hitter of his caliber was a force of nature, gifted with modesty. "Henry continues to be the cream of the crop,"
Frank Torre said.

10

THE MOST MEANINGFUL HOME RUN

Milwaukee County Stadium crackled with excitement as the calendar turned and the sweltering humidity fanned the feelings of a special summer. The parking lot was packed on August 2 for a three-game series against the Brooklyn Dodgers, "strictly a World Series atmosphere," according to the *Sentinel*. The pilgrims came from near and far, across Wisconsin and Illinois, where the Cubs were long out of the pennant race, and from as far away as Southeast Oklahoma, where Warren Spahn's neighbor Bill Prichard loaded the car with Choctaw beer and headed to the brew city. A curious *New York Times* reporter wandered the parking lot and reported 11,538 cars and 166 out-of-town buses, both record figures. Fans saved their ticket stubs for souvenirs of a summer they were sure they would tell their grandchildren about. The faithful flocked and the turnstiles clicked toward two million fans for the fourth consecutive year. The ballplayers were well aware of how much the pennant meant to Milwaukee and they did not want to let the city down again. Every pitch, every play, and every fan counted, and in the summer of '57, the Braves might have been bigger than the Bible, at least in the Heartland, which yearned for David to beat Goliath.

A season-high crowd of 45,840 fans filled the ballpark. There was too much excitement to think of fire hazards. "After the seats in the lower grandstand had been filled, latecomers stood two deep around the entire rim," the *Sentinel* reported. "Several score found roosting places on the ramps, where they sat with their feet dangling, or they squatted for vantage points. In the upper deck, seats were taken and small knots of fans stood together or sat on the rails. Aisles in the left-field and center-field bleachers disappeared before the game. Those late sat in a row on the gravel be-hind the wire fence and stood in a crowd of about a hundred on the pathway that separates the bleachers from the trees in center field."

More than ever, the Braves were religion, belief, and hope, but before they could bring the Yankees to County Stadium and use the World Series to show off their blossoming city, burgeoning ballpark, and community spirit, they had to prove once and for all they could beat the Dodgers, "still a magical name, still the top drawing card, still THE TEAM TO BEAT," pro-claimed the *Sentinel*.

Gene Conley, the tall lefty, was coming off a great July in which he was 4-1 with a 2.23 earned run average. He improved his slider and changeup and was getting outs yet again, locked in a tight pitching duel with Johnny Podres. The Braves scrounged together the only run in the fifth inning. Conley, the former basketball player, dribbled a single to right field, scor-ing Johnny Logan. The big crowd went crazy and Conley pitched with the fans behind him. He finished out his 1–0 complete game with a flourish to move the Braves to 61-41 and put the team in a first-place tie with the Cardinals and 2½ in front of the Dodgers.

The Dodgers would never go down easily, and the next day, they beat Lew Burdette 7–1. But the Braves once more played inspired baseball after a lopsided loss to the Dodgers. They won the final game of the series, 9–7, behind Bob Buhl, who allowed thirteen hits and six runs in 7⅓ innings. But Buhl hung in there, and the Braves got home runs from Henry Aaron, Eddie Mathews, Del Rice, and Johnny Logan, but it took Warren Spahn to save the day. Spahn wanted to win at all costs and that including com-ing out of the bullpen and into the fire with one out and the bases loaded in the ninth inning.

He hadn't pitched against the Dodgers in more than a year and hadn't beaten them in six years. He could get loose in about six pitches, and when Fred Haney determined the matchups benefited him, he gave the old man the baseball. Spahn got Don Zimmer to pop up to first baseman Frank Torre for the second out of the inning, bringing Jim Gilliam up.

Gilliam was just the kind of slap hitter who gave Spahn fits, so he at-tacked him and ran the count full. Then Spahn fooled Gilliam, placing a fastball perfectly on the outside corner. "His control was uncanny," Del Crandall said. Call strike three, ballgame over. Take that, radar gun. Location, location, location! Spahn's third save of the year showed his reliability and resilience. Modern pitchers would tremble at his stamina and durability. The 43,109 fans roared, part of the 128,317 that attended the three-game series.

Later, Haney walked out of the shower and draped his arms around Spahn, who was talking endlessly to the press about his heroic deeds. He was so happy he could have talked for years. "This guy's been asking for a year when I was going to pitch him against Brooklyn," Haney said. "Well, he got his answer today."

The day Spahn saved the day was the day prayers began to be answered in Milwaukee. For five years, they had longed for a hot streak like the August warpath they were about to witness. When were the Braves going to pull away from the National League? They were about to get their answer and see their team make the cover of the nation's sports pages in the next ten days.

Spahn's playfulness and good heart got the best of him two days after he pitched against the Dodgers. He saw two schoolboys playing catch at a stoplight and rolled down his car window. Did they want a ride to the ballpark along with him? He had a little boy of his own, Greg, and he had a touch with the little guys. Spahn was deeply amused by their star-struck acceptance. The boys eagerly piled into the backseat.

Spahn asked them their batting averages, told them that Willie Mays couldn't hit his screwball if his life depended on it, and said he'd like nothing more than to win a World Series ring for Milwaukee and let them try it on next spring. Then he dropped them off and made sure they had a couple of tickets and a dime to call their folks. He signed their gloves so the boys had playground proof of their fabulous tale.

Then Spahn, though he had pitched in relief between outings, made his regularly scheduled start and beat the Redlegs 5–4, pitching the Braves back into first place by a half game over the Cardinals. If Spahn pitched every game against the Reds, he'd have been a 500-game winner. He was 4-0 against them this year, 43-13 lifetime, and notched his eleventh win and first since July 16, a span of four starts.

Cincinnati manager Birdie Tebbetts insisted the Redlegs were still alive, but the Braves hitters were proving otherwise. On August 7, the second game of the series, Wes Covington hit two home runs and knocked in four to lead a 12 to 2 victory, the third win in a row, and help pitcher Gene Conley's fourth consecutive win. Covington now had 11 home runs, most of which came after he became the everyday left fielder in June. Covington had quickly become an important part of the Braves lineup, giving them a complementary left-handed power bat behind Eddie Mathews. Covington broke into pro ball with Henry Aaron, who always respected Covington. "Wes and I go back a long ways," Aaron said. "He could hit the ball a long ways, and I really don't know what people thought, but he was a very good left fielder. He might have missed one ball and they started saying he couldn't catch this, he couldn't catch that, but he was a very good ballplayer."

The Braves were a very good team right now. They completed the sweep against the Redlegs on August 8, when Red Schoendienst hit a clutch two-run, bases-loaded single in the eighth inning to give the Braves a 5–3 win. The Braves got help from the Cubs, who beat the Cardinals, and pushed the first-place lead to 1½ games with their fourth consecutive victory. The sweep all but pushed the Redlegs out of the race. Lou Chapman asked Henry Aaron what he thought. Henry pondered for a moment, then told Chapman, "They did look a little tight." And when Chapman asked Birdie Tebbetts, Chappie had to clean up a pissed-off manager's language. "They just kicked the shit out of us," Tebbetts said.

When the Braves arrived in St. Louis on August 9 to play the Cardinals for three games, more than the winning streak was on the line. Milwaukee had a golden opportunity to push the slumping Cardinals further behind. As the Braves took batting practice, they looked like the well-oiled machine Fred Haney envisioned. There was no horseplay, no banter, and no chatter. One man after another stepped into the batting cage and went through their swings like assassins—hitting balls the other way, then up the middle, and finish turn-and-burn—but the Cardinals weren't interested in lauding the Braves. Terry Moore, the former center fielder of the Gas House Gang Cardinals of the 1930s and now a Cardinals coach, didn't care how hot the Braves were. For as long as he could remember, Midwest baseball tradition began and ended in St. Louis. The sun never set on the Cardinal Empire as far as career Redbirds were concerned. They refused to act intimidated by the upstart team from the bush league town. Moore believed fate would be with the Cardinals. "All I have to do is remind you of last year when you came here and blew it," he said.

The Braves stomped Moore's message into the dirt. In the second inning, Bob Hazle, a newcomer recently called up from the minors to play right field, hit his first home run with the club. And then, Milwaukee's Murderer's Row took Cardinals pitching to town. Henry Aaron hit his 32nd home run in the third and Eddie Mathews and Wes Covington homered in the eighth to lead the Braves to a 13 to 2 victory, extending the winning streak to five games. Henry's two hits wrestled the NL batting lead away from Stan Musial by a few points and Eddie was warming up in August. But Hazle, the newcomer, opened eyes when he went 4-for-5. The Cardinals thought it must have been a fluke. Their general manager, Frank Lane, had passed on paying a pittance for Hazle when the Braves exposed him in the annual winter draft. Then again, so had every other club in the National League, which didn't have use for a twenty-six-year-old career minor league outfielder with a history of leg injuries. But this misfit was a perfect fit for the Braves.

There was only one question most baseball fans asked: Who is Bob Hazle? The guy didn't even have a baseball card. He was acquired from the Redlegs as a throw-in to complete a 1955 trade for first baseman George Crowe and then had two solid summers playing Triple-A ball at Wichita for manager Ben Geraghty. It took one unsung hero to know another. The Braves were so loaded that Wichita was maybe the hardest Triple-A team on earth to play your way off of. The big club was so talented that right-hander Carlton Willey, good enough to pitch on most big league staffs, won 21 games and stayed in Wichita.

The Braves wanted to bring up another outfielder for the stretch run because as much as Fred Haney loved Andy Pafko, he wasn't sure if his body would hold up. The veteran Pafko profiled as a true bench player. The Braves needed a batter who was younger and could play everyday. The first choice was to call up outfielder Ray Shearer, who was hitting around

.320, and finished the season with 24 home runs and 118 runs batted in. But despite Shearer's lofty stats, Geraghty said he was the wrong guy. Geraghty, the minor league manager who had so strongly advocated Henry Aaron's promotion in 1954, told General Manager John Quinn that Bob Hazle, a lefty outfielder hitting a modest .279, was the player he wanted.

Roland Hemond heard Geraghty's reasoning. "He said, 'Take Hazle. He's a streaky hitter and he's hot as he can be right now. You can send him back to me when he cools off.'" The decision to pass on Shearer and bring up Hazle was completely unconventional, if you went by stats alone. But Geraghty knew the nuances better than the stat sheet did. Now Hazle was in the big leagues, where he wasn't about to cool off, and as a result, neither were the Braves.

And still, the Cardinals acted unimpressed by the Braves, as though Milwaukee was chasing them and not the other way around. "You haven't got this thing won yet and you're not gonna win this thing," the Cardinals' leading trash talker Moore vowed. Inside the Braves dressing room was a sense of anticipation. "If we can sweep the next two games here," Henry Aaron said, "we can really raise a head of steam and pull away." Eddie Mathews admitted, "It's still too early to count anybody out even through we're looking better than we have this season."

Andy Pafko, who had been in the big leagues since some of his teammates were in grade school, warned them not to celebrate before it was finished. He evoked the memory of their old teammate, Bobby Thomson, whose "Shot Heard 'Round the World" home run sank the 1951 season on the last day. "I remember too vividly when I was with the '51 Dodgers and we blew a 13-game lead," he said. "It also gives me a pain when I think of what happened here last year."

The Cardinals were determined to inflict pain upon Warren Spahn when he pitched the next game. They would try it every way they could, with their bats and with their mouths. The Cardinals' old hands competed against Spahn for years and knew that bench jockeying usually did no good. The best you could hope was for him to be off his game. When Spahn walked past the Cardinals dugout to get loose, manager Fred Hutchinson was waiting. "Hutch" was a buzz-cut mad dog of a manager with tobacco-stained teeth who didn't like losing, hated black players, and would throw elephant shit at a guy if it would help his team win. "Hey, 21!" he snorted. "You'll be walking past this way by the fourth inning." Spahn tipped his cap and replied with a smirk. Then he went out in the horrid humidity, put the Cardinals in his crosshairs like he was picking off pigeons, and pitched so leisurely that neither age nor words could afflict him.

Being manhandled by Spahn was no fun, but it didn't bruise the Cardinals as much as being hurt by someone they'd never seen. Bob Hazle went 3-for-4 with another home run. Before he came to the '57 Braves, he had a lifetime big league mark of 3-for-13 and a .231 batting average, but since joining the Braves on July 29, he was 11-for-20, with a robust .550 batting average. Hazle, who thought his big league chances were through, didn't want anybody to jinx him. He made it clear—don't tell him his batting average. "Just let me dream," he said.

Spahn had the Cardinals dreaming for runs. He pitched a five-hitter in Milwaukee's 9–0 victory, extending the winning streak to six games. The victory pushed the Braves out to 4½ games in front of the Cardinals. After the game, Spahn nursed a beer and a grudge. "What gave me the biggest satisfaction was beating those guys in the other clubhouse," he said. "It's a matter of personal revenge."

The age of Spahn chasing all-time pitching records had begun. The shutout was the 40th of his career, tying the National League record. Spahn was old enough to realize an opportunity like this season would not come often, if ever again. He had spent too many summers pitching for nothing but his paycheck. He had 215 career wins and a lifetime 3.05 earned run average, numbers enough to make some wonder if he could pitch long enough to reach the Hall of Fame. People thought Indians pitcher Bob Feller would have been a 300-game winner were it not for World War II service, but as it turned out, Spahn would have been a 400-game winner were it not for his wartime career. "I've set my sights on two goals before I call it quits," he said. "Winning 300 games and retiring with an ERA below 3.00." There was another goal, it went without saying, and the way the Braves were playing, he might be living the year.

The last day in St. Louis, August 11, the Braves could smell the sweep. Pitching in oppressive heat, Gene Conley beat the Cardinals 5–1, extending the winning streak to seven and pushing the Cardinals back 5 ½ games with 45 games to go. It was the biggest lead of the season and the Braves were the biggest news in baseball. At the site of their 1956 demise, they made a tremendous statement about what kind of team they were in 1957. Conley was becoming a workhorse in his own right, pitching his fourth consecutive complete game. His infield defense made him look downright dominant. Eddie Mathews hit his 23rd home run and started one of Milwaukee's two double plays. The frenzy was building back home in Milwaukee, where schoolboys wondered if the Braves would clinch the pennant by September back-to-school time.

The Cardinals vowed to resist. "They don't have this thing clinched, not by a long shot," St. Louis GM Frank Lane said. All parties agreed that it was Red Schoendienst, the former Cardinal, who was making the difference. Still, Terry Moore promised the Braves would fold again. He thought Red would never hold up. "I got news for you," Moore said. "He's going to get tired and start petering out."

The Braves weren't scared off by threats. They were thrilled with the sweep over the Cardinals. After a hot night at the ballpark, there was only one way to cool off. "If you're in St. Louis, and we beat them, we'd have a Michelob or a Budweiser, ya understand," Johnny Logan said. "Because them cities are hot. And you're young and you can have a beer or two. And that's the key of what it is."

The Braves showed no signs of gassing out as they rolled into Redlegs town, Cincinnati, USA. Lew Burdette loved torturing the Redlegs so much that when he hit two home runs—the first two home runs he had ever hit in the big leagues—his teammates just laughed. The winning streak reached eight when the Braves won 12–4. The lead held steady at 6 ½, and back home in Milwaukee, the town wanted free hamburgers from a guy named George Webb, a local businessman who ran a chain of burger joints. Webb was a big Braves guys, and before that, a Brewers honk. Every year, he had a running bet with the public. If the Braves could run off a dozen consecutive wins, he'd spring for free burgers for the fans. The Braves had been close in 1956, but just missed it by one victory. The town hoped this would be the year, but there would be a little sorrow with those pickles and onions. Webb died just before the start of the 1957 season, some said from the heartbreak of 1956. His son took over the burger chain and continued the family tradition.

Everything was wrapped up in the Braves getting this done. They made it nine in a row against the Redlegs on August 14, as Bob Buhl won his seventh consecutive game, his 16th overall victory. You knew things were going good when Buhl struck out more guys than he walked. The Braves poured it on with an eight-run ninth inning to make it a 13–3 blowout. Wes Covington hit a grand slam in the outburst. The lead was now 7½ over the Cardinals. Some Cincinnati writers thought the hot streak was an aberration and got in Fred Haney's face. Haney loved it when the writers dared him to throw his guys under the bus. Only one guy had the right to do that, and he wasn't lugging a typewriter from town to town. "I'll be satisfied with a five-game lead with four games to go," Haney spat, and that was that.

The Braves had one last game on the road trip. Going undefeated on the road was virtually unheard of, especially in the heat of an August pennant race. Fittingly, Warren Spahn and Henry Aaron combined to make it a reality. Aaron, who had only five home runs in 22 games since he turned his ankle in Philadelphia in July, turned on a fastball from Hal Jeffcoat to spark a four-run first inning and then added his 34th of the season in the seventh. The notion that Henry was no home run hitter was fading as quickly as the thought of Spahn as a fastball pitcher. The loose lefty won his 13th game—speeding toward 20 victories yet again—scattering eight hits with just enough strikeouts, three, to keep a guy honest. As usual, he threw all nine innings to give the bullpen a rest. Red Schoendienst sat in the locker room and admired these ballplayers, who gave him all the credit in the world, of which he felt he deserved none. He admired their tenacity and determination, the regulars and the role players, and the refusal to wither. He had been through many pennant races, but this one felt different. "These fellows amaze me," he said. "They don't show the tension of the race. They play the games one at a time. We play the Cardinals next. I haven't heard anyone talking about it. These guys are used to the stress. This team would have folded a month ago if it didn't have spunk."

The Braves turned for home with an imposing 8 ½ game lead over the second-place Cardinals, who were coming to County Stadium for a four-game series beginning on August 16 that could end the pennant race, set the Braves up for another colossal fall, or bring free George Webb hamburgers to all Milwaukee. The headline above the *Sentinel* masthead told exactly where the hearts and minds of the Heartland were focused in the summer of '57: "Wow—10 in a row!"

There was another sign welcoming the team home. Workers brought the wooden mascot out of his basement tomb and spruced up his red-hued paint job. They whitened his teeth and metaphorically dabbed away the tears of 1956. He was hoisted high above the main entrance. When the ballplayers saw him, they knew the town expected them to make good this time. There were 41 games remaining in this marathon and second place wasn't good enough. The totem's return was symbolic and religious. Family processionals through the front gates saw the wooden warrior high above their heads, raised from the dead and ascended to his cloudy perch above the County Stadium cathedral. It was bad luck not to bow, or to at least wave to him.

If the ballplayers had learned anything over the years, it was to never count the World Series checks before they are cashed, but this summer was testing that patience. "We just can't flub it again," Lou Perini said, and one had the feeling he had a scorecard in one hand and his rosary in the other. "We have much too much talent, too much balance, and too much depth." The only thing the Braves didn't have was too many championships. At the first sign of vulnerability and fragility, the out-of-town writers and teams were going to pounce. The Braves may have been in first place, but there was still no love lost in the National League. It was a forgone conclusion that the winner of the National League pennant was going to play the Yankees in the World Series, and nobody outside of Milwaukee gave the Braves a chance to become the team to topple the New York baseball dynasty.

However, win ten games in a row, and the New York Yankees will begin to take notice. Word seeped out that the Yankees were thinking that this World Series would not be played between the Yankees and Dodgers or even the Yankees and the Cardinals. Instead, for the first time ever, it might be the Yankees and Braves. If you gave most Yankee fans a map and told them to find Milwaukee, they'd point to Toots Shor's in Manhattan and say "Close enough." Truth was, the ballplayers didn't give a crap about history or tradition. That was a fan and media thing. They were, however, very interested in money. The gate receipts promised by a Milwaukee World Series struck the New Yorkers as very lucrative. "The Yankees are naturally giving random thought to what team they will face in October," the *Hartford Courant* noted. "They are reported to have had a sentimental interest and professional faith in the Dodgers until recently. Now that Milwaukee has acquired that gilt-edged look in the National League, the Yankees are beginning to count possible World Series shares."

The Cardinals hated the idea that the Braves were somehow "gilt-edged." They still thought they had the best young pitching in the league and they intended to show it. They were also planning to ambush Henry Aaron, much the way the Dodgers had earlier in the season. Henry had proven himself to be the best young power hitter in baseball. Praise and fear followed him. The only way to stop him was to hope he tripped on a drainage pipe in the outfield or to hunt him down with high-and-tight fastballs. The Cardinals decided they would attempt to intimidate him. They were so flippant and cocky that they posted a bogus batting order—a coach's kid batting leadoff, the clubby hitting cleanup, old fart coaches and snot-nosed bonus babies in the middle, and Stan Musial ninth. The Gas House Gang Cardinals were riding again, in spirit at least. They didn't give a shit about Milwaukee's winning streak. And they didn't act like they had a nine-game losing streak.

Lindy McDaniel, a twenty-one-year-old Oklahoma bonus baby, was just the kind of cowboy country boy the Cardinals loved. He had a baby face, big arm, and bad attitude, and his jaw looked like a cement mixer when he swirled his chewing tobacco around his mouth. He signed for fifty grand out of high school in 1955 when he had the body of a fully grown man and a fastball that didn't take shit from anybody. He was on his game and shut out the Braves for six innings before he turned the lead over to the Cardinals bullpen comprised of a knuckleballer (Hoyt Wilhelm), a guy with one of the best nicknames in baseball history (Vinegar Bend Mizell), and a gas-throwing rookie bully (Billy Muffett), who completed the 6–2 Cardinals victory when he achieved the nearly impossible feat of throwing a fastball past Henry Aaron. Muffett howled with delight. Henry, frustrated though he was, kept quiet and made a very serious mental note for retribution.

The winning streak was over at ten games and the Braves had fallen flat in front of 45,437 fans. The Cardinals still trailed by 7 ½ but had made a significant point. They ruined Milwaukee's parade and that was a good start. That was Gas House Gang baseball. But it would be less than twenty-four hours before Billy Muffett received his retaliation.

The next day's weather was murky and miserable, and yet, most of the 39,694 fans withstood a lengthy rain delay; their faith would be rewarded as surely as they would be riled up. Facing Cardinals starter Larry Jackson, a right-hander with a sneaky fastball and a devilish smirk, Henry hit the dirt when Jackson came high-and-tight. Then Jackson had the nerve to stand there with his arms folded as if Henry was holding the game up. Jackson's body language infuriated Henry as much as the pitch itself. Jackson tugged the brim of that road black Cardinals hat like he was a part of some death squad sent to Milwaukee to put these bushers in their place. Henry stood up, dusted himself off, and then struck out. He did nothing for the rest of the afternoon except invite speculation that his batting average, which had slipped from .352 to .330 in the last month, somehow meant he had topped out.

The Braves trailed the Cardinals, 4–3, in the bottom of the eleventh inning. With runners on the corners and one out, Henry again faced Billy Muffett. The Cardinals had a base open and could have walked him to set up a double play or a force play at home. But Hutch and Muffett were having none of that. To beat the Braves out of the pennant, they had to beat Henry. The surest way to demoralize Milwaukee was to make that little kid with the fast hands look bad, but to do that, your fastball really had to have something.

Muffett didn't mess around. He threw hard, tailing fastballs on the outer half. If he walked Henry, so be it, he would take his chances with Wes Covington. But Muffett was playing with fire. If you were going to get Henry out on the outer half, the pitch needed to be a foot outside and an inch off the ground. Anything else was fair play, and even if you threw him that pitch, Henry might still surprise you. Muffett wound up and spun a two-seam heater on the outside corner. He swore the damn pitch was in Hal Smith's catcher's mitt, but instead of a pop in the pillow, Muffett heard the gunshot at the last millisecond. He couldn't say "shit" that fast. He couldn't believe his eyes and Smith couldn't believe his hands. Henry had literally hit it out of the catcher's mitt and driven it hard down the right-field line. Hawk Taylor and Eddie Mathews came flying home, Henry had his revenge, and the Braves had a 5–4 win. Muffett was beside himself. Nobody had ever done that to his fastball. He stopped short of shaking his fist at Henry, but he knew there would be another time and another place.

Henry was still hot when the game was over. He was certain Larry Jackson knocked him down intentionally. "It's getting so now you can't even hit a long fly ball without getting one thrown at your head," he said. "I get a base hit and the next time I'm flat on my back."

The writers hustled over to the Cardinals side and read the quotes to Hutch. "Aaron doesn't know what it is to be knocked down," Hutch huffed. "He wants to take that long stride toward the plate and complains if you pitch him inside. Hasn't he been around long enough to know the difference between a beanball and a brushback?" Translation: Stupid boy got shit for brains.

When asked if he purposely threw at him, Jackson said that if he had really been meaning to hit Henry, he wouldn't have missed. Translation: Can I take my hunting rifle to the mound? Terry Moore called Henry's complaints "strictly bush league."

"Bush league, huh?" Aaron said. "Real big league pitchers don't throw at you, only gutless ones."

Hutch shook his head. He lied like he smoked, one after another, until there was so much haze in the room that you couldn't see his eyes. "Our pitchers read about him and maybe some of them wanted to see how good he really is," Hutch said. "I don't know what they are doing out there, but they don't have orders from me to knock him down."

Henry was furious. In his mind, between the lines, you should take race out of the equation. If the Cardinals wanted to knock him down because he got a big hit, that was one thing. If they wanted to knock him down just because he was a big hitter, it was something else. Every knockdown pitch should have a meaning, but that meaning should have nothing to do with the color of a guy's skin, white or black, big or small, who cares? Play the damn game! And the St. Louis Cardinals, well, they played by the rules of the Gas House Gang, the 1930s boys bred from Texas and Arkansas and Alabama and Louisiana. Henry was a new ballplayer for a new time. The Cardinals needed to get with the times.

A doubleheader was scheduled against the Cardinals on August 18 with rain falling throughout the morning. Bob Buhl warmed up twice, once before the two-hour rain delay and once after, and by the time he got into the ballgame, he was spent. He left the game in the first inning with his shoulder killing him, snapping his winning streak at seven consecutive starts. The Braves could not afford to loose any of their four starting pitchers and needed home runs from Eddie Mathews and Bob Hazle, now nicknamed "Hurricane," to get the game to extra innings tied, 6–6.

In the tenth, it was Stan Musial's turn. At age thirty-six, he was closing in on 3,000 hits, and was every bit as dangerous as he had been a decade ago. Juan Pizarro, the hard-throwing rookie who spent the season shuffling between Milwaukee and Wichita, challenged him with one of those good fastballs. Musial uncoiled his graceful left-handed swing and knocked the ball out of the park for a game-winning two-run home run. The Cardinals won 8–6, and had a chance to inflict more damage, if the rain would ever let up.

The rain stopped but Musial didn't. He went 2-for-5 again and finished the doubleheader 4-for-10, regaining the NL hitting lead, and, more significantly, surpassing 5,000 total bases for his career. The achievement alone guaranteed almost certain election to the Hall of Fame. As for the game, Vinegar Bend Mizell pitched a four-hitter. The rain never bothered him. He was one of those guys who did better the worse the weather was. After eight hours and forty-eight minutes, two rain delays, Johnny Logan's infected shinbone, which he suffered when he was spiked at second, and Aaron's tepid swings, the Braves were swept. This, in baseball, is what they call a shitty day. The lead was back down to 6½. It should have provided enough comfort, but it did not. The Cardinals left town convinced that it was just a matter of time before the Milwaukee Braves became the great pretenders all over again.

Fred Haney hated losing, but he liked keeping his players humble. Training them not to get ahead of themselves was one issue, but conditioning baseball-mad Milwaukee was something else. He ordered his players to try to avoid discussing the pennant with the press and told the fans to stop sending World Series ticket orders. The front office returned ten thousand such requests and it wasn't even September yet. "Anyone who is predicting a pennant for the Braves or any other team in baseball is a damn fool," Haney snapped. "I don't want my players thinking this thing is all wrapped up, because it isn't."

The Braves had 36 games to play, in which they would play the soft teams in the league in the ultimate salary drive, an opportunity to pad personal numbers for next year's contract and to secure a share of World Series money. But there was also a rare emotional investment in this team. "I don't think I could go through another series of disappointments like we had last year," Warren Spahn said.

Winning the pennant would be the culmination of all the dreams since the team moved to town. "We all have to keep our fingers crossed," Milwaukee mayor Frank Zeidler said. "It would bring a terrific lift to all the people of Wisconsin who have supported this team."

While Haney was putting on his best Hollywood stage persona to convince the Braves nothing was finished, the New York Yankees weren't buying it. They quietly assigned two advance scouts, Bill Skiff and Johnny Neun, to begin tailing the Braves when they arrived in Brooklyn on August 22. Change was in the air. A few days earlier, the New York Giants had officially announced they were leaving for San Francisco. The first thought that went through most players minds was, well, that makes for a hell of a road trip. The next thought was that the Giants were going to need a rival. It didn't make much sense for the Giants and Dodgers to fly across the country to play each other now, did it? Players thought the Brooklyn Dodgers were history. The public kept praying, but the ballplayers sensed the money moving.

The Braves took two out of three in Brooklyn to keep the lead at 6½ over the Cardinals and 7½ over the Dodgers. The once-simmering rivalry between the clubs was empty now, gone from this pennant race. Lew Burdette beat the Dodgers for the first time at Ebbets Field since 1954, and it was sure to be his last. Henry Aaron hit his 35th home run and Hurricane Hazle had three more hits, prompting a 6–1 victory and Dodgers farm director Fresco Thompson to wonder how a busher like Bob was carrying the Braves as the everyday right fielder. Hazle was hitting a nice, round .500 in 16 games. "Our scouts reported he was weak with the bat," Thompson said. "This is a funny game."

The Dodgers were out of it and started planning for the future. The *Los Angeles* Dodgers? It sounded strange, much like the idea of a baseball owner gouging for parking, divorcing his wife, filing for bankruptcy, and suing the commissioner's office. Manager Walter Alston gave the ball to Sandy Koufax for his first career start against the Braves. Koufax was starting to find himself, a frightening sign of things to come. He struck out eight in seven innings, and the two runs he allowed could be traced to the only hitter who could get the barrel around Koufax's arm.

The Aaron-Koufax meetings were legendary, even before the players were. Sandy wasn't about to get beaten with anything less than his best pitch. His curveball may have made him famous, but he didn't lead the league in strikeouts per nine innings for nothing. He loved to save the hard curveball for the left-handed Eddie Mathews, who hated facing lefties, especially ones who threw hammers that traveled as fast as heaters. As for Aaron, Koufax dispensed with pleasantries. He threw too hard and his ball got to the plate too quickly for movement or deception. He wasn't trying to trick Henry. He was trying to overmatch him. It was his pure heat against Henry's hand-eye coordination. You could scout for a million years and never find two kids who could do this, unless you were in the right place at the right time.

In the second inning, Henry was just feeling out his timing. He grounded out to second base. In the fourth inning of a scoreless game, Henry had Sandy solved. He took a fastball on the outer half and rifled it hard to right field. It was like two atoms colliding. The solo home run was Henry's 36th, and more significantly, his 100th run batted in, the second time in four major league seasons he had reached the century mark.

In the seventh inning, Eddie managed to lay off the high heat and the low curves. He drew a walk and took second on a wild pitch to Aaron. That put Sandy in a hole. The last guy you wanted to be was the pitcher who had to throw Henry Aaron a fastball in a fastball count. Henry waited patiently, as if he were waiting for ducks to cross the road. Then Sandy came back with another fastball, a foot off the plate and an inch off the ground, and Henry lined it to right field for a triple. There were only three guys in the league who could hit that pitch in that location. One was Willie Mays. One was Roberto Clemente. And one was Henry Aaron.

The Braves blew the lead and lost 3–2 in the bottom of the ninth, but bounced back to take the final game, 13–7. Aaron hit his 37th and Duke Snider, closing in on his last of five consecutive 40-home run seasons, hit his 34th. It was the last game the Milwaukee Braves would ever play at Ebbets Field. Jackie Robinson watched the Braves and believed this was their year. Maybe he would have given anything for one last crack at Lew Burdette. The Brooklyn Dodgers hadn't been the same team without him. They were older and slower, and nobody could replace Robinson's fire. Manager Walter Alston was in denial about the decline of his star players. *Atlanta Daily World* columnist Marion E. Jackson wasn't. He had been a strong voice for baseball integration and a staunch supporter of black ballplayers for more than a decade. He identified the end of an era as surely as he previously helped usher in a new one. "Defunct, demised, or any other word you care to use to describe a club that has had it. We repeat, the Dodgers have grown fat and rich and must rebuild from scratch!"

The hell with the Dodgers—they weren't the problem anymore. The Braves left town, with the two Yankees scouts stalking them. They had already started compiling notes. They liked how Sandy Koufax attacked Eddie Mathews and would urge their left-handers to off-speed him to death. They still couldn't figure out how to get Henry Aaron out, but neither could the National League.

There was a great misunderstanding about Henry Aaron, a notion that he simplified hitting, and that he didn't understand how he did what he did simply because he didn't like to talk about himself. But saying Aaron was talented by dumb luck was a huge misnomer. He was, in fact, consumed with each and every at-bat. Frank Torre was wise enough to know that he was not the hitter Henry was (who was?), but he was smart enough to talk to him about hitting. Ballplayers, after all, are big believers in performance by osmosis.

"Here Henry was having this sensational year and he used to tell me all the time, 'You know how important that last at-bat is? You know, if you're 0-for-3, there's a big difference between 0-for-4 and 1-for-4. Or if you're 3-for-3, there's a big difference between 4-for-4 and 3-for-4," Torre said. "Too many hitters, including myself and so many others, we give away at-bats. They go up, they get a good pitch, they take a half-assed swing."

Henry never gave away at-bats. To him, they were savored and milked for all they were worth. Wasting an at-bat was like leaving money on the sidewalk. Years later, when asked about his passion for talking hitting with hitters, Henry Aaron modestly smiled. "Well, that may be true," he said. "And I think that's what makes ballplayers."

The Braves took a pair in Philadelphia, with Warren Spahn winning his sixth consecutive start and earning his 16th victory. Then the Braves returned to the Polo Grounds one last time. They split two games there, winning the first, 4–3, on August 27, to move 30 games over the .500 mark and maintain a 7½ game advantage over the Cardinals with 30 to go. Lew Burdette won again, and he, too, was rounding into form as September approached. He had not lost since August 3 and notched his 14th victory. The Braves got help from Willie Mays, who was playing out the string, distracted by the emptiness of the Polo Grounds and the loneliness he felt over leaving New York City. In the sixth inning, he beat out an infield single to Burdette. Lew lacked the arm strength to throw out the flying Mays, and in his haste, deposited the ball down the line, sending Mays to third.

Eddie Mathews was waiting for him. Eddie always loved seeing Willie in his corner of the diamond. The next hitter, Ray Jablonski, hit a hard smash to third. Willie was gone with the contact, and that really pissed off Eddie, because Willie was telling him two things: you can't make that play and you can't throw me out. But Eddie's hands were softer now and he stayed with it, fielding a difficult ball with ease, much to the delight of Fred Haney. Eddie set his feet and threw a strike to catcher Del Crandall. And there he was, the great Willie Mays, trapped once more in the hot box. Eddie ran him down and made the tag, prompting the *Journal* to offer, "Willie Mays is the heart and soul of the Giants, but hardly the brains."

The Yankees scouts, Bill Skiff and Johnny Neun, made their notes. For fun, they marveled at how talented Willie Mays was, but damn, why did he still make so many rookie mistakes? Casey Stengel would have killed him, but he would love some of these Braves. Eddie Mathews was a better defensive third baseman than the American League gave him credit for. Lew Burdette could still spin it, whatever "it" was. Skiff and Neun recognized that this Braves team was different for its depth, determination, and sense of destiny. "This is a far better team than the one of a year ago," Skiff reported. "These boys have more spirit and seem to be improved in every respect. Schoendienst makes a big difference. And I don't see how they're staying up there after losing so many regulars to injury."

The Yankees scouts also saw the technical proficiency of the Braves infield and noted that this team was a machine wired to make opponents pay for mistakes. That, more than anything, made Fred Haney proud. "We practiced that rundown play for twenty hours in spring training," he said. "It was one of those examples of improved execution of fundamentals that is paying off for us." Giants manager Bill Rigney simplified it. "If the Braves don't win this year, they'll never win."

The Braves were sad to see August go, but September arrived with a bang. The Braves played a Labor Day doubleheader against the Cubs at Wrigley Field, and outslugged them 23–10 in Game 1, and blanked them 4–0 in Game 2. In Game 1, (with the wind blowing out, taking earned run averages and pitchers' self-esteem with it), the old Eau Claire duo, Henry Aaron and Wes Covington, had a day, knocking in six runs each. Eddie

Mathews hit his 29th home run, his fifth in six games. Bob Trowbridge pitched the only shutout of his major league career in Game 2 and Henry made two tough catches in center field. Another ball popped out of his glove, but he bare handed it, very Willie Mays–like, for the out. Henry always loved the daytime baseball at Wrigley Field and enjoyed the Midwest rivalry between the Braves and the Cubs, even when the Cubs were hopelessly out of the race. "I thought the Cubs, since they were only ninety miles away from us, I thought that's where the sticky point come in," Henry said. "We had to do better than the Cubs, but for some reason, the Cubs never did pan out to be the kind of club they should have been."

But the Braves were doing everything right. They finished August 19-7, their best month of the season, thanks to their 10-game winning streak. They were hitting, pitching and playing defense. Even Joe Adcock's broken leg healed in time for him to return. Cubs manager Bob Scheffing called the Braves the hottest team he had ever seen, but warned the Braves not to get cocky, reminding them that the Cardinals were ten games behind Brooklyn on Labor Day in 1942, and charged back to win the pennant. Nonetheless, players inquired reporters about the magic number needed to clinch the pennant, but were very careful not to let Fred Haney hear them ask.

Rogers Hornsby, the ancient Cubs bench coach, didn't mind running his mouth. He said the Braves were ready for the Yankees. Hornsby, of course, was a National League man all the way. He said the National League was tougher, harder, and more balanced than the American League. Hornsby saw the Yankees as stagnant. He thought their pitching wasn't as good as it used to be. He felt the Braves had more power and that Red Schoendienst made the difference. "The Yankees aren't the Yanks of old," he said. "They are ready to be taken and you have the team to do it."

Nothing terrified Fred Haney more than the thought of the Braves losing focus, but his team was performing. The Braves finished the three-game sweep of the Cubs when Spahn won again, his seventh consecutive victory and 18th overall. Henry Aaron hit his 39th home run, knocked in his 118th run. The Braves had an 8½ game lead with 23 to go. Now, two more big games in St. Louis on September 4 and 5 awaited them.

The Cardinals hadn't waved the white flag and were getting hot. In football terms, they were a fourth-quarter team. They staunchly refused to concede and won both games. Herm Wehmeier, the pitcher who beat them out of the '56 pennant, pitched a complete game, not withstanding Eddie Mathews' 30th home run. The Braves lost 5–4 in 12 innings when Bob Hazle clanked a ball in right field.

Then the Cardinals pummeled Lew Burdette, 10–1, and sliced the lead to 6½ with 21 to go. St. Louis was second in the league and first in trash-talking. "A couple of more losses and you might find momentum carrying you in the other direction," Cards coach Stan Hack said.

Any time the Braves lost in September, the choke birds came out. A guy like Hack was trying to get in Milwaukee's head; a guy like Fred Haney was trying to keep him out. Fred Haney's worst fear was that the Braves would turn cold at the wrong time of year. Their two losses in St. Louis started a slide. The Braves lost the next day to the dismal Cubs, 5–4, the first time they lost three consecutive games since early July. Any sign of weakness was enough to start a nervous breakdown in Milwaukee, and when Warren Spahn's winning streak was snapped at eight a few days later, the air raid sirens went off. Henry Aaron managed to hit his 40th home run on September 10 against the Pirates, but Spahn was stuck on 19 wins and the Braves were stuck in neutral. Even Aaron's bat was questioned. He had hit only .255 in August, but he did have eight home runs, and now with 40, he fulfilled the promise he made at the end of June. It was the first of Aaron's eight 40-home run seasons in his career.

When the Dodgers came to Milwaukee on September 12, the Braves lost two out of three and dropped eight of their last eleven, whittling their lead over the Cardinals to 2½ games. "Milwaukee must be worried now," Cardinals star Stan Musial said. "They've got to be, right?"

Dodgers right fielder Carl Furillo's opinion was as prickly as fresh-cut grass. He spent much of the season goading the Braves into doubting themselves and ripping them for daring believe they would dethrone the Dodgers. Now he faulted the Braves for failing to believe in themselves when they needed to most. It was a classic Furillo rant. "The Braves have to kick each other in the ass and hustle," he said. "They can't tell me they're not under pressure. I've been through too many of these for them to fool me. And another thing, we're out of it, but we're not going to give it to them. They're going to have to win it for themselves. Nobody's going to give it to them as a gift."

Furillo was right. The Braves were playing tight and tired. Don Drysdale beat them for the third time on September 13 and snapped Eddie Mathews's 11-game hitting streak. Warren Spahn was denied his bid to win 20 for the second consecutive start when he lost 3–2 in ten innings to the Phillies on September 15. Bob Buhl's shoulder continued bothering him, making his stuff a far cry from the pitcher who won eight in a row in the summer months. Worst of all, Henry Aaron had moments where he was ordinary. You'll have to forgive him. He was mired in his worst slump of the season, a 1-for-14 stretch that was part of an 8-for-37 drought over 10 games. Not coincidentally, the Braves were 3-7 in their last 10. Aaron's batting average fell to a season-low .316 and scared everyone but him. "Nah, I'm not worried," he said. "The bat is always heavier this time of the year anyhow."

The pressure weighed on the Braves. Struggles in May are called growing pains, but September slumps are called chokes. Big-city reporters began tailing them, expecting a great story one way or another. The Braves would either bring Milwaukee the city's first World Series or stunningly blow it again. Fred Haney was at his best when writers doubted his team. When reporters gathered around him during the slump, he was defiant. "Well, well, well," he greeted the ensemble. "Here come the pallbearers."

Haney had his game down. While his players dressed and left the ballpark, he stalled the press for so long that his players could escape, and on top of that, he never let the writers get a word in. The New York writers were used to Casey Stengel's babbling bullshit, and they kissed his ass for it, but the very moment Fred's club proved human after playing nonstop baseball since February, they were chokers? That was bullshit in Fred Haney's book. He flashed his teeth and stopped short of whipping a riding crop across a map of Europe. "We're not going to blow this one, we're going to win it," he said. Out of the corner of his eyes, he could see his players, showered and dressed, walking out. He knew he was on a roll now. "Hey, look, how do I know why we aren't getting any hits? If I knew the answer to that one I'd put a stop to the slump in a hurry."

The accounts in the papers removed the profanity from Haney's tirade and served diet Fred to the public. "We lost last year because the boys were trying too hard." You could almost hear Haney screeching, "I have a question for you assholes" when he said, "Why is the term *choke* used on us so much? I didn't hear anybody say the Cardinals choked when they lost nine in a row in August!" Haney's tirade got better. Oh, for the days before TV, radio, and Internet in the clubhouse, when a manager could curse blue until he was red in the face and the writers had his back. "Remember that bad throw by Red? Remember that game where Spahn walked five guys? That's a bunch of nonsense," though the smart money had Fred really saying, "That's a bunch of bullshit."

The prejudices that followed the Braves from Boston to Milwaukee in 1953 resurfaced strongly as the Braves tried to win the pennant in September '57. For all their achievements, it was clear to *Sentinel* columnist Lloyd Larson that Milwaukee still was a second-class citizen. He hated that the big city writers thought Milwaukee was strictly bush league. The Braves had the best record in the National League and a team loaded with talent, yet he shared an out-of-town writer's confidential rip job: "The average Milwaukee fan goes to the ballpark to drink beer, to try to catch a foul ball, to drink more beer, to boo the Dodgers, to spend time with his family, and to drink more beer. Most of these fans don't pay attention to the game and just want to be able to say in the office the next day that they were part of the big crowd."

Larson was never one to hide it when his sensibilities were offended. His views reflected the Milwaukee populace who, on the whole, said don't offend us *or else*. He wrote that Wisconsin fans were savvy baseball connoisseurs. Larson knew it by the reader mail he got and by the conversations he had with fans. They knew all the players. They knew which umpires squeezed the strike zone. Sure, they loved to drink . . . are you kidding, who didn't? Did they think Yankee fans didn't get shit-faced at ballgames? You went to the ballgame for the beer, the brawls, and the batters. Maybe the babes, but don't let your wife catch you looking. Larson also knew that the fans didn't need anybody to tell them that the series with the Cardinals at County Stadium starting on September 23 would be historically significant, for better or worse.

The Braves couldn't escape the pressure. They could wake up in the morning, have a cup of coffee, put the slippers on, and pick up the newspaper on the porch to read the September 16 *Milwaukee Journal* header screaming: ONCE ROSY PENNANT OUTLOOK GROWS DIM. Damn reporters. The Phillies were in town long enough for their GM, Mayo Smith, to remind Wisconsin not to blow it, though he sure sounded like he was pulling for the Cardinals. "Don't expect the Cardinals to fold now," he said. "They've had their slump and the Braves are just having theirs. It's amazing how the Cards have come along and they'll make a battle of it all the way. It's up to the Braves."

The ballplayers didn't need anybody to tell them that, but Fred Haney did anyway. Before the start of their September 16 game against the Phillies, Haney closed the doors to the locker room and let it rip. Nobody knows exactly what he said, but he was going to flog this horse down the stretch. The pitchers would go on short rest. The hitters would play through slumps. If you were hurt, too bad! This was money time, make history or be forgotten, Bradenton all over again. Just like he said to the ballplayers in spring training and to the fans after they dragged his dummy corpse through the streets, "You're going to hate my guts, but you'll love me when you see those World Series checks." He did such a number on his ballplayers that nobody dared recount it six hours or almost sixty years later.

But whatever he said, it was enough. After a few innings of the game against the Phillies, Eddie Mathews had enough. His asshole buddy, Bob Buhl, was pitching and hadn't won a game in a month. That alone really pissed off Buhl, who saw his shot for becoming a 20-game winner fly out the door. The Cardinals were idle and the Braves could gain half a game. Nobody was hitting and everybody was dragging. So Eddie stood on the top step of the dugout and picked up his teammates. "Come on, let's do something, even if it's wrong!" he shouted, and who were they to tell him no? For all his beers, brawls, and home runs, all his profanity and all his punches, Eddie was still fighting for his guys. Warren Spahn looked on in admiration. "He asked no quarter and he gave none," Spahn said. "He wouldn't take anything from anyone. I'm glad he was on my side."

Eddie's wrath woke the Braves, who collected 14 hits. Buhl won again, Aaron got two hits, and the Braves stretched the lead to three games with

11 games to go. Fred Haney didn't always care for Eddie's style, but he loved him more than ever for the leadership he showed. "Priceless," Haney said.

You can't put a price tag on confidence. The Braves did it the next day, too, with Aaron hitting his 41st home run and Joe Adcock, back from the broken leg, getting his first home run since June 11. The Cardinals pounded the Dodgers, 12–2, but the Braves beat the Giants, 3–1, to keep the lead.

Then it was Lew Burdette's turn to get his act together. In front of a crowd of 31,566 that lifted the Braves season attendance mark past two million for the record fourth-consecutive season, Burdette gave up Willie Mays's 35th home run, but that was about it. He always had a flair for pitching well against the New York teams, especially the Giants, who hadn't beaten him since September 16, 1954. The Braves even beat Johnny Antonelli, the left-hander who caused them great angst over the season.

To top it off, Brooklyn did the Braves a favor—finally—by beating the Cardinals to extend the Braves' lead to four games and making the magic number six. Lou Perini, on business in New York, watched the Dodgers and Cardinals on TV and listened to the Giants and the Braves on the radio at the same time. He was planning to be in Milwaukee for the big series against the Cardinals. He, too, couldn't stand the prospect of heartbreak. He wanted history. "I feel better now," he said. "The World Series doesn't seem so far away."

The Braves had never been closer, and now they were hot, winners of three in a row and the Cardinals were getting worried. This pennant race would be one big mood swing until the bitter end. The Cardinals desperately wanted to get into Milwaukee on September 23 with a shot to still win it. Cardinals manager Fred Hutchinson wasn't above playing mind games through the media. "I still think the pennant will be decided in Milwaukee," he said.

The Braves beat the Cubs the next day, their fourth consecutive victory, and at long last Warren Spahn had his 20th win of the season. He pitched through the rain and mud and could not care less. He would have pitched in a tornado or an earthquake. The Braves gave him five runs in the seventh to snap a 2–2 tie, including Wes Covington's 20th home run, and the Braves won, 9–3. Spahn was the highest-paid pitcher in baseball, but he would trade it all to pitch in the World Series one more time. When told he had joined Lefty Grove as the only left-handed starter in baseball history to win 20 games in a season eight times, his honesty overmatched his hubris. "Sometimes I wonder if I'm really that good," he said. "Or do hitters give me more credit than I deserve? Is my control an asset? Is the catcher so good? A pitcher just has to believe. You don't ask if you're going to get the hitter out. You tell yourself you're going to do it. Either you do or you don't."

Bob Buhl came back on short rest the next day to beat the Cubs, 6–2, making it five in a row. Buhl matched his career high with his 18th victory, but his strikeouts were down because his arm was killing him. Still, he sucked it up, and Henry Aaron helped him out when he knocked in his 125th run. The lead was extended to five games. Most significantly, the Braves reached 90 victories, the second team in baseball to reach that magical number. Only the New York Yankees had more victories than the Milwaukee Braves.

The Braves persevered through one last downpour at Wrigley Field and poured on the power with home runs from Henry Aaron (42), Eddie Mathews (32), Wes Covington (21), and Bob Hazle (7). The Braves rallied from a four-run deficit and did what good teams do for an angry little field general—they cut the guts out of bad teams. The sweep was complete, and at long last, the Braves were coming home to face the Cardinals and once and for all resolve this marathon National League pennant race. The lead was five with six to go. The magic number was one. Win and the years of anxiety lift away. Lose and nobody will ever forgive you.

The September 23 teaser in the *Sentinel* said it all: "Tonight's the night for which we've been waiting! Braves Can Clinch Pennant by Defeating Cardinals." The Braves were ready to explode. Warren Spahn had a message for Milwaukee. "I want to see the people in Milwaukee tear down the stands tomorrow night! And they can do it," Spahn laughed. He figured Lou Perini, who was at the ballpark early that day to greet his players, would be happy to foot the bill. Fred Haney wanted to get it over with. Lew Burdette would get the starting nod, but Haney put all his pitchers on call. "We're going all out," he said. "I'll use Spahn and Buhl if I have to. All we have to do is win one of those games."

Henry Aaron was already dreaming. He had proven so much this season. He was no longer the shy black kid from Mobile who could hit line drives and keep his mouth shut. He was, in fact, a dominant middle-of-the-order major league home run hitter and prolific run producer. He had earned the right to stand up for himself. For all those Alabama ballplayers who came before him but never got the chance, Henry spoke with his bat, and when the mood struck him, his words struck hard. He loved to tell the story of the time he played hooky as a child to hear the radio broadcast of Bobby Thomson hitting the "Shot Heard 'Round the World" home run. Henry dreamed of his own significant shot, a most meaningful home run that he would cherish forever, a home run that would mean more than any record, any number, anything else, because it meant as much to Milwaukee as it meant to him. He was young, but wise enough to sense that this opportunity might never come again, and the veteran players he had grown up with had seasoned his instincts well. "There should be a little excitement tonight, don't you think?" Henry told Lou Chapman. The smile across his face was wide and joyous. Lou captured young Henry's mood. "Boy, that's what I've been looking for all year," Henry said.

The Cardinals played the Braves inch-for-inch in a closely fought game typical of this marathon pennant race. Lew Burdette pitched ten innings, spinning success against everyone but Stan Musial, who went 3-for-4. The crowd was loud but apprehensive as the game reached the bottom of the eleventh inning, tied, 2–2. Johnny Logan was at first base with two out when Henry sauntered to the plate. He was facing Billy Muffett, the baby-faced right-hander whose dimples turned dour when he had the ball in his hand. Muffett could throw so hard that he might rip the zipper off the front of his flannels. Muffett made his big league debut on August 3 and had yet to allow a home run in 44 innings, but he was just the right kind of young fastball pitcher Henry loved to face. Velocity did not scare him.

When Henry stepped in, the stadium fell silent. In the radio booth, broadcaster Earl Gillespie paced the mood. *So here comes Henry Aaron. And Henry has two hits in three official trips. He has walked twice, singled to left,* *singled to center, and he has grounded out to the shortstop. Bob Trowbridge, a right-hander, and Taylor Phillips, a left-hander, warming up for Milwaukee. The pitch to Henry Aaron—*Muffett was too much of a gamer to headhunt Henry. He reared back and paid Aaron the ultimate sign of respect, a first-pitch curveball, a violently hard 12-to-6 downer, a hammer for the Hammer with furiously tight rotation, the red seams scorching the air, blistering the night. The pitch usually decimated big league hitters and made them feeble and cry for their Mamas, but Henry never winced, he waited, like his line was in the water and he knew he'd get a bite. Aaron let the ball travel deep into the strike zone, enough for the ball to finish its break, and then snapped his wrists like he was flicking a fishing pole. *A swing, a drive—*The ball was within Muffett's reach for only a split second as it raced over his head, but nobody could touch a ball coming off a bat at more than 100 miles per hour—*back into center field, going back towards the wall—*the ball gained altitude and acceleration faster than naked eyes could calibrate, 40,926 fans rising as it climbed, Gillespie's voice peaking, Wally Moon in center field backtracking—*it's back at that fence—*Moon's athleticism against Aaron's ambitions—*and is it caught or not?—*the ball cleared the fence before the crack of the bat finished echoing in the ears, planting itself safely in the pine trees in Perini's Forest. *It's a home run! The Braves are champions of the National League! Henry Aaron just hit his 43rd home run of the year! Holy cow!*

The ballpark organist played "Happy Days Are Here Again!" Henry ran the bases with his head down, until he heard the roar and lifted his head to see confetti falling from the upper deck and the defeated Cardinals walking off the field. He slowed his trot by a heartbeat to savor his own Shot Heard 'Round the World, his enormous smile illuminating Wisconsin, crossing second base as the organist played, and the fans joyously joined arms and sang the lyrics, "All together, shout it now, there's no one here can doubt it now, let us tell the world about it now, Happy Days Are Here Again!"

Henry turned second and headed to third and fans streamed onto the field toward him, but he was not scared. He welcomed the love, admiration, and the safe feeling of home and happiness Milwaukee had given him. Before he reached third, the Yankees scouts, Bill Skiff and Johnny Neun, turned tail amid the music and cheering, "slightly stooped under the weight of their bulging notebooks," the *Journal* reported, in awe of Aaron and singing his praises but warning Milwaukee to enjoy the moment. "We don't expect anything else from the Braves," Skiff said.

Henry's long lean legs reached third. He toed the bag with the tip of his black cleats and turned home. Here was a twenty-three-year-old black kid from Mobile, the hero of Milwaukee, and in front of him waited his joyous teammates. Eddie and Spahnie out in front, beaming like they were kids, the 4–2 victory stuffed in their cheeks like a big, fresh, fat wad of pink bubblegum. In September '57, while the black kids were being shoved out of Central High School in Little Rock, the Heartland's hero was the skinny little boy who hit Alabama stride style and vanished into the waiting love of his teammates. *They are carrying Aaron away from the plate! He just hit a home run over the center field fence! We did it! National League champions! Henry Aaron mobbed at the plate! A two-run home run and it's all over! It's all over in the National League!*

Lou Perini cried. He found Henry Aaron in the clubhouse and gave him a tremendous bear hug. The slender Henry vanished in Perini's burly body and when he emerged, a photographer snapped a picture of them smiling and laughing together. Both men, unbeknownst to each other, for years after, hung that very photo in their homes in places of importance— Henry in his undershirt and a wide, relaxed smile, Perini in his business suit with his round features and warmth. Lou Perini had seven children, but in some ways, he thought of Henry as his eighth. "Well, he showed an interest, no question," Henry said years later. "I accepted it as being young, innocent myself, and naïve, and just had somebody older that was caring about me. That's all."

Henry fulfilled Perini's vision, what David Perini called his father's "tremendous faith in the underdog." Now Milwaukee saw what it always dreamed about, and so did Henry, a most meaningful home run, one that time could never touch and would carry deep and wonderful meaning for the rest of his life. Home runs would come and go, but this one stayed with him forever.

"Yes," Henry said in 2011, his voice growing husky and emotional. "Yes, yes, yes, very much so. It was the happiest moment of my baseball career. Yes, sure did, yes. Mmmmhmmm that's true."

During the County Stadium celebration, Earl Gillespie asked Lou Perini for a live interview. "If I have got any voice left, I will," Perini said. Over the noise of the locker room celebration, Perini tried to comprehend his feelings. Gillespie helped him along.

GILLESPIE: It's wonderful to think, Mr. Perini, that next Wednesday, we'll be playing the New York Yankees at Yankee Stadium.

PERINI: Oh, that's wonderful, that's a dream, Earl, that I've been waiting for, for an awful long time. All I can say is I'm so thankful for Fred and his boys and the great job he's done managing, Earl, and for the ballplayers, and the spirit. I'm sure that the people of Milwaukee are just as proud of them as they can possibly be. I think we've got a great ball club, and another thing, Earl, we beat a great ballclub.

EARL: Well, thank you very much, Mr. Lou Perini, and I want to congratulate you again, sir, we are very proud of you because you gave us major league baseball back in 1953.

PERINI: Well, we're very grateful and we'll never forget the wonderful support that they've given us, Earl. That's all of you people listening to me. I think you've done a tremendous job in building up the spirit of this ballclub. I'm sure we're going to have a great ball club for many years to come.

EARL: I think so, too, Mr. Lou Perini, owner of the Milwaukee Braves. Here's the guy who won it tonight, Henry Aaron. Congratulations.

HENRY: Thank you, Earl.

EARL: That was a great thrill, I know.

HENRY: That was one of the best home runs I hit all year!

EARL: Those boys carried you right off that field, didn't they?

HENRY: Right off that field. That's right.

EARL: You feel real good, buddy?
HENRY: Oh, I feel wonderful!
EARL: Well, it's on to the New York Yankees now.
HENRY: I'm ready for 'em!

A Humble Visionary: Lou Perini created the Jimmy Fund, moved the Braves to Milwaukee, and ushered baseball into the twentieth century and beyond. *(Perini Family Collection)*

A Thirst for Baseball: Fred Miller, president of Miller Brewing, was the driving force behind baseball in Milwaukee. Here he studies blueprints for Milwaukee County Stadium, the first postwar major league ballpark. *(Chapman Family Collection)*

To Milwaukee, Young Man: Still wearing his Boston Braves hat, Andy Pafko is concerned about heading west as writer Lou Chapman circles the wagons. *(Chapman Family Collection)*

Eddie Mathews: If you thought Mickey Mantle was the best big-league ballplayer in 1953, Eddie might fight you on the spot.
(National Baseball Hall of Fame Library, Cooperstown, NY)

Warren "Spahnie" Spahn: A gangly, goofy, cocky, combative pitching savant, he could do everything with a baseball except throw hard, and then tell you how good he was at it.
(National Baseball Hall of Fame Library, Cooperstown, NY)

"God Done Sent the Braves a Miracle": Henry Louis Aaron arrived in Milwaukee in 1954, confident that no pitcher could beat him. *(National Baseball Hall of Fame Library, Cooperstown, NY)*

The Busher Beats It Hence: Casey Stengel buried Lew Burdette in the Yankee minor league system in 1950. Seven years later, Burdette buried him. *(Chapman Family Collection)*

The High Life: Milwaukee fans took Schlitz from nobody and savored the flavor of the town, team, and time.

Roll Out the Barrel: Lou Chapman and cronies chronicle the Braves, who became the first team to draw two million fans, then did it four years running. *(Chapman Family Collection)*

Old Rivals: Yankees manager Casey Stengel and Braves manager Fred Haney had a long friendship and rivalry.

Careful with His Hands! Lou Perini (left) loved young Henry Aaron (center) and fired manager Charlie Grimm (right) in 1956. *(Chapman Family Collection)*

Old Red: When Red Schoendienst joined the Braves in June '57, the All-Star second baseman provided the missing link to make the team great. *(National Baseball Hall of Fame Library, Cooperstown, NY)*

The Most Meaningful Home Run: Lou Perini and Henry Aaron share a moment they would never forget, moments after Aaron's dramatic home run to win the '57 pennant.
(Perini Family Collection)

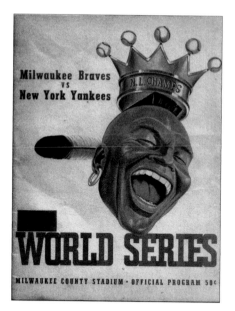

Got Fifty Cents? The Braves in the Promised Land, and the World Series program cover sold at County Stadium.

You're Asking What Now? Mickey Mantle's head, shoulder, and ankle were killing him during the '57 Series, but Lou "Gumshoe" Chapman wanted to know: Can You Play? *(Chapman Family Collection)*

Nippy Gets First: Plate umpire Augie Donatelli is satisfied that the pitch has hit Nippy Jones (25), as evidenced by the shoe polish left on the ball. Yankee catcher Yogi Berra (8) can't argue with the evidence. *(National Baseball Hall of Fame Library, Cooperstown, NY)*

Yankee Killer: Lew Burdette beat the Yankees three times in '57, pitched consecutive shutouts, and won Game 7 at Yankee Stadium on two-days rest. Henry Aaron believes he should be in the Hall of Fame.
(National Baseball Hall of Fame Library, Cooperstown, NY)

Finally: The long-suffering Braves win Game 7 at Yankee Stadium. Eddie Mathews, Del Crandall, and Lew Burdette hug as Frank Torre (14) and Del Rice (catcher's glove) lead the charge. Umpire Jocko Conlan rushes off the field.
(National Baseball Hall of Fame Library, Cooperstown, NY)

We Did It!: The Old Red Head (Schoendienst) and Spahnie (Warren Spahn) savor the moment Milwaukee won it all.
(National Baseball Hall of Fame Library, Cooperstown, NY)

Four for the Room: Long-time roommates, best friends, drinking buddies, and pitching aces Warren Spahn and Lew Burdette win hardware after the '57 Series.
(Chapman Family Collection)

Hooks, Rooms, Hurricane, and Hammer: Warren Spahn, Lew Burdette, Bob Hazle, and Henry Aaron earn honors after the '57 season.
(Chapman Family Collection)

There Is Joy in Bushville! The Mighty Yankees have… STRUCK OUT!
(Milwaukee Journal-Sentinel)

PART III

THE SERIES

11

THE SMELL OF MONEY

The World Series was this town's big moment, Milwaukee's opportunity to prove it was a citizen of the world. Ballplayers are often uneasy ambassadors of great causes, but the Braves understood the motivation behind this tremendous civic pride, identified with the great longing for acceptance, and masked fierce pride with love for beer, brats, and brotherhood. "Those people were so good to us," Henry Aaron said. "We felt like we were going to win, but we really wanted to win for those folks."

So, the city of Milwaukee shut down to send the Braves off to New York, "bolstered by a hero's send-off seldom accorded to any David of old," the *Sentinel* exclaimed. Fans crammed the Wisconsin Avenue parade route, excitement from clinching the pennant was still fresh, and the crowds were so large that the cops lost count at around 80,000 people. They were screaming and shouting, climbing light poles, hanging out of windows, chasing girls, drinking in the streets, cutting class, and playing hooky from work. Vendors set up shop in the streets, peddling colorful feather headdresses and joke-shop arrows to wear through the head, mugs, lighters, and ashtrays. One guy made up phony labels over cans of Schlitz and hawked Braves beer. Scalpers and counterfeiters did brisk business. Nobody had seen so much bootleg merchandise in the Midwest since Capone ruled Chicago.

The ovation was tremendous and never let up. Some hid cotton in their ears to soften "one of the most enthusiastic spectacles in years," according to the *Sentinel*. The parade reached the War Memorial Center for another rally, where ten thousand more fans crammed the joint. Many of the ballplayers were overwhelmed all over again. "The fans, you just can't say enough about the fans," Del Crandall said. "They were with us 100 percent. I don't think that whole scene could ever be duplicated again."

Fred Haney was made for these moments. Comfortable in front of big crowds and bright lights, he spoke for his ballplayers with élan, and revved up the fans with the same fire and passion he brought to the field. "We are touched," he told the crowd. "But we've only paid half the debt. We've got the other half to go." He was presented with a gold trophy inscribed, TO FRED HANEY, IN APPRECIATION FOR MILWAUKEE'S FIRST NATIONAL LEAGUE PENNANT. Then he put his hands over his head like a champ and bellowed, "This is one of the greatest things that has ever happened to me!" The fans ate it up. Haney walked off the stage, but as he passed a reporter, he confided that his team couldn't return empty-handed. How could they break Milwaukee's heart? "We can't let them down," he said.

The Braves hopped back into their convertibles and inched toward Mitchell Field, where maybe another 10,000 fans lined the route and crammed the airport. Milwaukee would give anything—*anything*—for a glimpse of their Braves. A woman ran up to the car carrying Warren Spahn and Lew Burdette and held her baby up for the pitchers to kiss for good luck. A fan shouted at Spahn to win one, and he shot back with two fingers, shouting and smiling, "Not one, two!" All the economic firepower of the Braves was on display—they had drawn an average of 29,725 per game in 344 home dates since moving from Boston, crossed the 40,000 mark in a game forty-six times and surpassed the 30,000 mark 181 times. They were the most powerful fan force in baseball, but as the big turbo props on the United Airlines Radar Line spun to life, nobody in New York City knew exactly what to make about the secondhand stories of this crazy town's wild parties or about the baseball team that must have won the pennant by beating the Toledo Mud Hens.

The Braves were flying into the future. The 1957 World Series was the first Fall Classic to be played by a western team since the St. Louis Cardinals beat the Boston Red Sox in 1946, but this World Series was about more than geography. It was also about technology. It would be the first time a Braves home game would be televised into Milwaukee and the first time in the television age that the World Series would have national interest because it was not an all–New York City affair or, with the exception of the 1950 NL champion Philadelphia Phillies and the 1954 AL Champion Cleveland Indians, strictly a Yankee-Dodgers affair. The Braves represented fresh blood with plenty of room on the anti-Yankee bandwagon. They were coming to town to take on the New York baseball dynasty the nation was hungry to see end. There was a real marketplace for beating the Yankees, according to *New York Herald-Tribune* columnist Red Smith, who believed it was "high time for the Eastern monopoly on success to be broken. Those repetitious charades involving the Yankees and the Dodgers are getting downright monotonous."

For the first time, NBC would employ new cameras with powerful zoom lenses that would allow viewers to see a ballplayer's eyes and expressions. You could see Mickey Mantle's eye black and Yogi Berra's catching glove, or examine the wrinkled map that made up Casey Stengel's face. Fans would see the calm expression on Henry Aaron's face, the wild-eyed insanity of Lew Burdette, and Warren Spahn's glare. The Gillette Safety Razor company sponsored the broadcasts and offered flipbooks that illustrated how to read a catcher's finger signals to a pitcher—promising an opportunity to decode "The Secret Language of Baseball"—something else fans had never before seen on TV. Players questioned the logic in that, wondering how easy it would be to steal signs.

Baseball and TV were entering a new frontier, and like he had many times before, Lou Perini was thinking ahead. Seeing the Braves in the Series at Yankee Stadium was a dream come true, but he was terrified that it would create demand for televised regular-season home games in the near future, putting a dent in his lucrative sacred cow. Why would fans want parades if they saw their heroes on TV every single day? Giving away games for free went against his baseball roots and business sense. He resisted making lavish deals to sell broadcasting rights to his home games, as the Brooklyn Dodgers had for $750,000 and the New York Giants had for $600,000. Perini was quick to point out that both teams had dwindling attendance and waning interest despite the idea that broadcasting the games was supposed to entice fans to come to the ballpark, not keep them at home.

But Perini knew his opinion couldn't keep up with technological demand, so he had a plan. Since he predicted the rise of free television would be a risk to his business, as far back as 1952, before the Braves even left Boston, he had approached production companies with the idea of creating a closed circuit Braves cable television network.

Perini envisioned subscriber-based baseball channels decades before they came into existence. He borrowed the idea from boxing, noting that in October 1952, the pay-per-view fight between Rocky Marciano and Joe Walcott attracted 125,000 viewers, paying a total of $400,000. Perini envisioned that figure multiplied over a 154-game season, writing to one producer, "Our network offers profitable possibilities," but nobody else saw his vision.

Maybe one day, he dreamed, the rest of the country would watch the Braves on their own network and root for them as Milwaukee had. Perhaps rooting for the Braves would spark communal interest beyond Milwaukee and ignite the international baseball market Perini had dreamed of. Why stop at a team in Toronto, for instance? What if the best players from Japan, Cuba, Mexico, and other outposts in Latin America all had exposure to major league baseball and all nations sent forth their players and fans to the majors? What if they wanted to play for the Braves instead of the Yankees? In another respect, Perini's '57 Milwaukee Braves were frontiersmen enabled by technology.

For the first time, World Series games would be seen in Japan via kinescope through a Tokyo TV station. Kinescope was a process by which a movie camera recorded a TV show. Films of the game broadcasts would be made at NBC in Los Angeles and rushed to Tokyo by plane. There, Nippon TV, Japan's national network, would air the games during evening hours the following day so the majority of the country could watch the World Series. That was good news for the baseball-crazy Japanese, whose prime minister, Nobusuke Kishi, threw out the first pitch at Yankee Stadium before a June doubleheader with the Chicago White Sox. He wore a Yankees hat, sat with Casey Stengel's wife Edna and commissioner Ford Frick, and inscribed a ball, "To baseball fans of America, my best wishes." The two countries had come a long way in a short time, and even though the newspapers were still referring to Kishi as the "Jap Premier," baseball and the world went hand in hand. When White Sox manager Al Lopez saw Kishi wearing the Yankees hat, he gave him a Sox hat and said, "This is the hat you should be wearing." But Kishi didn't budge. When other nations thought of American baseball, they thought of the Yankees, not of the Midwest. But this October, Tokyo was going to learn about a little city called Milwaukee.

Kinescopes would also be flown to Hawaii, Anchorage, Fairbanks, and Guam. Canada would see the World Series live for the first time, thanks to the new "over-the-horizon" relay system. The World Series would also be transmitted in Spanish to Mexico for the first time and telecast live in Cuba via over-the-horizon, where hometown revolutionary and former pitcher Fidel Castro would listen to play-by-play man Buck Canal while hanging out in the hills with Che Guevara. Things were changing—and the 1957 Milwaukee Braves were at the forefront of it all.

Inside the airplane, the Braves thought of none of this. All they knew was they wanted to beat the Yanks. Even if nobody outside of Milwaukee believed they could, they did, and their opinion of themselves was all that mattered. The Braves had earned their ticket to the big dance, Games 1 and 2 to be played in the neolithic Yankee Stadium, its broad white stone façade in the Bronx having served as a tombstone for dozens of dreamers before them. The Yanks were in their twenty-third World Series in thirty-six years. These Braves represented Milwaukee's first pennant winner and only the third time the franchise had been in the World Series since 1900. This was a historically lopsided World Series pairing. The Yankees had seventeen World Series championships to the Braves' one, including an unprecedented five consecutive crowns from 1949–1953 before recapturing their perceived birthright in 1956. These Yankees were veteran and cocky. They had power and speed. Their pitchers were crafty, cunning, and threw hard. Braves scouts Wid Matthews and Ted McGrew had spent weeks tailing the Yanks. Matthews shuddered, "This team has the smell of money . . . It likes those World Series checks."

There was enough time on the flight for dozing, dreaming, reflection, and anticipation. Before the Braves left Milwaukee, Fred Haney had settled on his World Series pitching rotation. It would be his big three in succession, Warren Spahn, Lew Burdette, and Bob Buhl, with Spahn aligned to pitch Game 7 in Yankee Stadium if necessary. Spahn had never pitched in Yankee Stadium, but that didn't bother him. He pitched well in the 1948 Series against the Indians, losing his only start and winning in long relief. His son, Greg, was born a few days before the 1948 series started. Now Greg, almost nine, could be found on his dad's leg in the dressing room. This World Series was important to Spahn because the 1948 Series had been more worrisome than rewarding. "The series wasn't as important to me personally as it should have been," Spahn recalled. Since 1948, he had achieved much and wanted more, and in his opinion no great career could be complete without winning a World Series ring. "They can't take it away,'" he said.

Haney warned his players to behave in New York City, cautioning them that "they're living in glass houses and that one beer after the game becomes twenty," but he was less worried about his team's behavior than any time since he became manager. He didn't need to remind them again that they would love him when they saw those World Series checks. They didn't need to be reminded that they had something to prove to the rest of the country, and thanks to the wonders of modern technology, to the rest of the world. Haney's fan mail had multiplied, and he tried to read as many of the messages as he could. But these letters sounded different than typical ballpark mail. They weren't autograph requests or critiques of his managerial style and they weren't from around the corner. They weren't even baseball cards.

They were prayer cards.

They came by the armful, from every faith in the Midwest, Catholic and Protestant, and from white and black fans in the South, the Baptists. The Irish, Germans, Poles, and Italians were all behind the Braves. There were prayers in Hebrew and Latin, images of saints and synagogues, which came from not only Wisconsin but from around the world. "Look at this," Haney said to Lou Chapman. "I've heard from people in every state, many places in Canada, and other countries clear around the world. It's absolutely amazing the way people of all faiths are doing all in their power to help us succeed. I'm deeply grateful for what I consider the most sincere type of backing. I've never seen or heard anything like it."

Everybody was praying for the Braves . . . everyone except Yankees manager Casey Stengel. Among the stack of letters was a message from

Casey and his wife, Edna. The Haney and Stengel families, each with deep Los Angeles roots, were close friends. "All the Yankees are pulling for the Braves," the note read, "until the World Series starts." Haney got a chuckle. He knew Stengel well and their career paths had been very similar until Casey got the break of a lifetime, transforming himself from a twice-fired National League manager into the most influential manager of the decade. They shared many adventures together over the years, and Stengel had been genuinely happy for Haney when the Braves won the pennant. But the time for pleasantries was over now and Haney knew it. When he finally met Stengel at Yankee Stadium on the workout day before Game 1, he would shake his hand, smile warmly, and maybe even hug the old son of a gun. Then he would try to cut Casey's crooked legs off before Casey could do the same to him.

The Braves left Milwaukee to shouts and arrived in New York to silence. When their DC-6 rolled to a stop at Idlewild Airport at about 4:45 in the afternoon, the only noise was the wind. Whatever the Braves were expecting, this wasn't it. Nobody cared that they were here. There were no crowds, not even the curious. There was a group of about twenty reporters and photographers waiting on the ground. Big deal. The old hands who had played in Boston had flashbacks. It had been a long time since nobody cared about them, and frankly, they liked being loved. They didn't expect the red carpet, but, after all, they were the National League champs, and nobody treated the Dodgers with this sort of disrespect in this town.

The Braves marched down the stairwell surrounded by silence. The only noise was their own murmuring and the memories of the thunderous applause in Milwaukee. Fred Haney, adorned in his trench coat and fedora, a pint-sized Bogart, marched at the front of the team. The first reporter got in his face and asked, "Are you guys going to choke?"

Haney turned red hot and his bright-blue eyes widened. The nerve! He was ready to kill the guy. "What the hell's matter with you?" he barked. "You gotta lotta guts, make a crack like that. You ever try to get into our clubhouse, I'll throw your ass out."

Welcome to New York City, Milwaukee Braves.

Haney refused to answer any other questions. This was war. The players knew Haney was doing it to motivate them. He wanted them mad and not scared. Let New York think we can't play—we'll show them. As the players filed onto the bus, Lou Chapman tapped Haney on the shoulder. "I thought you were going to slug him," Chapman said. Fred was downright giddy. He wanted this fight! "I thought my answer slugged him pretty good," Haney said.

When the Braves arrived at their midtown hotel later that evening, Haney held court. The odds favored the Yanks, 8–5, so New York sportswriters, some of whom had gambling habits and were always fishing for inside dope along with quotes for their stories, wanted to know what Haney thought. "I hope they are favored," he said. "When we win, we get more credit." Reporters wanted to know Haney's pitching plans. "It'll be day by day after Spahn," Haney replied. Then he flashed a winning smile and held up two fingers, "V" for victory, like he was Winston Churchill, and strode off for more pressing matters.

The little showman was acting again, so the Milwaukee writers kept the sly grins to themselves. They were in on the joke. If they were going to gamble, it was going to be on the Braves and on how long they could keep a straight face around the New York writers. The workout day tomorrow was scheduled for the Yanks to take the field at 11 A.M. and the Braves at 1 P.M. In between, there would be plenty of time for drinking and bullshitting and betting at the media headquarters at the Waldorf Astoria.

To the Milwaukee writers, New York's condescending air was palpable and immediate. They longed to wire their stories home and to report to the heartland how the big-city slickers thought Milwaukee was a bunch of brat-eating, beer-drinking, shitkickers. The morning edition of the *New York Daily News* said it all. "A bunch of strangers seemed to have sneaked into the World Series. It's not like it used to be with the Yankees playing the Dodgers and everybody knowing everybody else. Now the Yankees are playing the Braves and some of you AL fans probably never saw a lot of them, or even heard of them."

The *Sentinel* fired back. Red Thisted, the veteran columnist, picked the Braves in five. His words reflected the storylines Haney sold the Milwaukee writers. "These generally awesome Yankees are just another baseball team which put on their trousers one leg at a time," he wrote. "Here is a solid vote for the Braves, a club completely unperturbed by their tremendous assignment, Yankee Stadium, the crowds, or the efforts of the local press to belittle them."

And while the New York and Milwaukee writers were bickering and the Braves were holed up in the hotel, playing cards and staying out of trouble, few noticed that there was an unusual visitor at the Braves hotel. Milwaukee writer Ray Grody, who had covered Casey Stengel when he managed the Milwaukee Brewers, spotted the Yanks manager milling through the lobby. Grody smelled a scoop. He hoped to corner Casey for a comment.

Grody was one of the few National League writers with experience in speaking with Casey, and understanding the peculiar dialect he spoke. The New York writers coined a famous term for it—*Stengelese*—described by one writer as "part English, German, Indo-Iranian, Gaelic, and parakeet." The New York writers spoke fluent Stengelese, and in return Casey embraced them with familiarity that the New York scribes felt was exclusive to them. Casey represented the institution of baseball itself. He called the Yank beat guys "My Writers," and fashioned the friendship as the king and his chroniclers. Grody, hell, he could speak Stengelese in his sleep. How many guys in this lobby had downed beers with him in the American Association? The curiosity was killing him. What was Casey doing down here?

But Casey blew off Grody when he asked him for an interview. Get me at the ballpark, Casey told him. Grody thought Casey looked "more harried than we have ever seen him in the thirty some years we have known him. He doesn't walk like this is going to be a cakewalk." Maybe that was true, or maybe he was visiting Fred Haney. All of Casey's friends—and there were a lot of them, many whose names he didn't remember—called him Case.

Case was a perplexing fella. He called his own ballplayers "fellas," and anyone who wasn't on his team a "feller." Trained ears could tell the difference. Case loved to kick your ass first and buy you a beer later. He had known that feller in the Milwaukee Braves managerial suite since 1940, when Haney's St. Louis Browns and Stengel's Boston Braves held spring training together at San Antonio. They had a lot in common. Both guys were undersized scrappers from the dead-ball era who usually couldn't hit a home run if you put a dollar in their pocket and a cork in their bat. They had bad teams as young big league managers, so most people thought they had road apples for brains.

That was another piece of Stengelese—road apple. It really meant a lousy ballplayer or any baseball person with poor skills. The truth was his writers cleaned it up. Case wasn't saying, for example, "People thought Haney and I were road apple managers." No, he was saying, people thought Haney and I were horseshit managers.

But they sure had some good times together, and maybe Case and Fred were going to relive the old times before they tried to knock the shit out of each other. Their San Antonio stories were their favorites. The governor of Nuevo Leon visited San Antonio to entice Haney and Stengel to bring their teams barnstorming to Monterrey. Behind closed doors, you could almost hear the ghosts flying. "I brushed off the Mexican by demanding an exorbitant $10,000 for Casey and $10,000 more for me," Haney said. "Then I forgot about it. A few days later the Mexican returned and had Stengel and me join him at the bank. He had 10 grand each. At $20,000 this was a gala trip."

The boys packed the buses and hit the road. When Stengel saw the great crowds lining the streets in Mexico, his brow crunched into the used baseball glove glare that made him famous. "Aw shit, Fred, look at all these people," Case said. "We're doing this too cheap."

When the teams arrived at the ballpark, Stengel wanted more money, based on the big crowds the Braves and the Browns brought out. "Señor, believe me, the people know nothing of baseball," said the Mexican host. "They are cheering for the bus because this is the first time they have seen these grand American buses."

The Browns and the Braves drew huge crowds on Friday and Saturday and then played in front of nobody on Sunday. "The folks had gone to the bullfights," Haney said. "It was the first and only time Casey felt happy without a crowd. He knew he hadn't been taken." In one humorous sweep Haney had identified Case's lusts for attention and money through his great love, baseball. Haney wasn't any different. In the last game in Monterrey, a Browns runner injured his ankle sliding safely into third base. Haney wanted to bring in a pinch runner, but Stengel said Haney couldn't do that. Mexican League rules, he said. Of course, Fred knew Case was fulla shit, so he fibbed right back, and said, well, the Mexican League rulebook says the manager can pinch run for an injured player. Case had to hand it to Fred—that was no road-apple managing.

Wasting no time, Haney marched to third base. The batter hit a short fly ball. Haney tagged up, put his head down and came charging home to score the winning run. The story made the two of them laugh until they had tears in their eyes and beer in their blood, two old farts laughing because they missed being young, always with Case grumbling about Fuckin' Fred, and how he'd never play by Mexican League rules again. When the night was over, both men could wish each other luck, say see you at the ballpark in the morning, and Case could remind Fred—since he ain't never been to a World's fuckin' Series—that they don't play these fuckin' things by Mexican League rules, ya know.

The next morning, Case was in fine form. His ballplayers were out on the field getting loose in full uniform—none of this modern-day, half-assed, sun-glass wearing, backward hat, music playing in the background bullshit—they looked like Russian tanks rolling through Red Square. His writers surrounded him, a social order in its own right, a caste society determined by circulation, reputation, and how well you could hold your liquor on deadline. There were at least seven New York newspapers that covered the team on a daily basis, compared to two papers in Milwaukee.

There was Dick Young of the *New York Daily News*, the bitterest, foulest, most snarling scribe of them all, who demanded his young writers treat everyone like dirt and taught them that writers knew baseball better than the players. He taught his protégés to never change with the times, and to never let technology rob the power of the typewritten word. There were the wise guys like Jimmy Cannon and Milton Gross of the *New York Post*: Cannon ran his mouth like a Ring Lardner imitator and Gross liked to arrogantly needle anyone in his path. There were the old hands, guys like Dan Parker and Ken Smith of the *Daily Mirror*, old beat guys who usually bought and sold the Yanks company line, sometimes with a knife. The *New York Times* guys, John Drebinger and Arthur Daley, had more power than a lot of hitters and usually used it to root for the Yanks. Dan Daniel of the *World-Telegram* had an enormous ego and clout and wrote for the *Sporting News.* Then there was the poet, Red Smith of the *Herald-Tribune,* whose intellect and perception would make him an outcast instead of a star in sports media today, and whose prose would be better spent in books than in banter. Smith was a fan, but he also had the ability to see beyond jocularity. He sensed some of Casey's bluster hid his magnanimous fear of failure. "The job of running the Yankees seems like heaven on earth—except for the man who has it," he wrote. Taken together, these were Case's writers, a bunch of fellers he liked, and sometimes, he might even remember their names if it would make them feel good about themselves. And in that dugout, the Stengelese was flying.

The Yanks were "coked up," which meant they were fired up to face Warren Spahn in Game 1, who Case said could really 'dime ya,' which was to pitch with exceptional control. Of course his own pitchers—guys like Whitey Ford, Bobby Shantz, Don Larsen, Bob Turley, and Bob Grim could really dime ya, too, so long as there weren't no "blind toms," Stengelese for road apple umpires, stealin' strikes from any of his fellas. He was worried about Mickey Mantle's bum ankle and Moose Skowron's bad back. He checked on both fellas in the trainer's room. "Can't say I liked what I saw," Case said. He had Elston Howard bring out his catching glove, first baseman's glove, and outfielder's glove just in case. He had Harry Simpson to play at first base, Enos Slaughter to fill in defensively in the outfield, and versatile Milwaukee native Tony Kubek. The writers marveled at Case's ability to pull a rabbit out of the hat. As the *Post* put it, Case can "tap anybody who happens to be sitting next to him with reassurance of a cold, professional job."

The writers wanted to know his lineup, but Case wouldn't even tell his fellas that. One of his former fellas who was just a feller now, Kansas City infielder Billy Hunter, said sometimes Case would write out a lineup card with only Mick and Yogi penciled in. He'd leave the rest of the lineup blank for the other players to see, then post it again a few minutes before first pitch. Case did that because he didn't like to "take the pipe," which meant to lose the ballgame. He didn't want no "Ned in the third reader," Stengelese for dumb ballplayers, cluttering up his plans.

Case would screw with any ballplayer's head if he thought it would help him avoid takin' the pipe. His baseball daddy was John McGraw, his managerial idol who he played for in 1921–1923 with the New York Giants. Case treated many of his fellas the way McGraw did—like road apples. Case became just like McGraw, a sometimes cruel and always demanding and sarcastic boss who loved the limelight and never bothered to learn any names except those of the boys he really loved. Case was like a baseball itself—he had a hard center, but to view it, one had to unwind the complex threads of his own ego, insecurities, dreams, desires, fears, and passions. Above the twine was the shiny coat, which most of the outside world saw, sometimes glossy and sometimes scuffed. More than anything, Case despised soft players, men who couldn't follow his orders, play the game, or shriveled up at the first sign of a challenge. He hated ballplayers who didn't play hard for him, and he hated players who made him look bad. He called these fellers "Cherry Pies." That was another phrase the writers cleaned up for Case. He might say a player was a Cherry Pie for the out-of-town press, but his writers knew it was code for what he might privately call a ballplayer who really turned him off for a lack of fire. Case was vulgar at heart. He called those guys pussies. So the writers had his back, and a soft ballplayer became a Cherry Pie.

Case's writers couldn't see any cracks in the Yanks armor. They felt the Braves, in Stengelese, were "green peas," young and inexperienced players, and "culls," inferior players, bushers. Case had his "Grand opera son of a gun," Whitey Ford pitching Game 1 and the player Case called "my assistant," Yogi Berra, catching him. Milton Gross of the *Post* thought the Milwaukee Braves were Cherry Pies. "The Braves are so shy of Series experience that they won't know how the spit will dry in their mouths until they're out there looking at the packed, flag-bedecked stadium tomorrow knowing the Yankees historically and habitually beat you down."

Fred Haney didn't care what any New York writer thought about his team. A guy like Milton Gross wasn't the only New York hack sullying his

Braves. "Having beaten all seven other National League teams, it behooves them now to wrap up the Braves of Milwaukee," Dan Parker wrote in the *Daily Mirror.* "The Braves have acquired the reputation of tightening up under pressure. I suppose it would be worth a Milwaukeean's life to admit in public that he has doubts about the Braves." Parker had a point. Back home in Milwaukee, for all the parades, the hometown fans were nervous. After all, they were facing the Yankees. Parker wrote an entire column dealing with all the great National League clubs the Yanks had destroyed in Octobers past. Such dominance wasn't lost on the Milwaukee populace. "A lot of people thought the Yankees would run through the Braves like crap through a tin horn," offered Robert Kumferman, then a thirty-five-year-old mechanical engineer at Milwaukee-based American Motors. "I said, 'You're crazy.'" He picked the Braves in seven, perhaps inspired by Red Smith, who did the same. But even the more baseball-savvy fans were worried. Bobby Uecker, then twenty-two, had just finished his second minor league season in the Braves organization, spent mostly at Eau Claire. He returned home that winter to work for his uncle's carpeting business. He was a Milwaukee Brave by blood, but he looked at Case's club, and wondered how the Braves were going to pull this one off. "Casey had a great team," Uecker said. "I mean, how can you lose with those guys?"

Similar thoughts might have crossed Haney's mind as he watched the Yankees take batting practice. There was no meaningless chatter, only the solid sound of hard contact resonating over the city's daily rush. Every hitter was a threat and every gunshot off the bat reminded the Braves what they were up against. *Bang!* Mickey Mantle hit .365 with 34 home runs, pretty good for a guy practically playing on one leg, and was so feared pitchers walked him a league-leading 146 times. *Bang!* Yogi Berra still had it at age 32, with 24 home runs and a fearsome reputation in the clutch. *Bang!* Gil McDougald hit .289 with 13 home runs, good numbers for a shortstop who was so gifted defensively that he also played second and third. *Bang!* Hank Bauer was a rugged outfielder with 18 home runs. *Bang!* Elston Howard was good enough to play every day for any other team, but here, the first Yankee black player was probably the best hitter in the big leagues without a regular starting job.

Haney sat with his legs folded and watched Case's guys. They were talented, methodical, professional, loose, and cold—everything Haney knew they would be long before the scouting reports came his way. The Yankees had a detailed book about the Milwaukee hitters, too, but Case wasn't much for scouting reports. He preferred to follow his instincts and to listen to this season's hired gun—former Dodgers and Giants pitcher and longtime National League rival Sal Maglie, a cagey right-hander purchased from the Dodgers for $50,000 in September for the sole purpose of educating Yank pitchers on how to attack the Braves batting order. Whitey Ford, the Yanks ace, had taken a liking to the pitcher nicknamed "The Barber," for his numerous high-and-tight heaters, taking long conditioning runs across the outfield track while the Barber served up scouting dope.

Case closed the workout by putting his players through a crisp infield-outfield practice. He was sixty-seven years old, but he could still swing a mean fungo bat and looked like an old wizard waving a wand. This was psychological warfare as much as it was preparation. Haney's players filtered onto the bench and had their first look around the stadium just as the Yanks were finishing up. They were so graceful and elegant that you could get swing music in your head just watching them. Haney paid close attention to how Mantle was capable of moving in center field and how well the veteran Slaughter could still get a jump on the ball and cover ground. Haney watched for arm strength because he wanted to run on the Yanks.

After the outfielders made their final throws to home plate—strong online throws with carry from every position—Case jogged back behind home plate with his "assistant," Yogi, and began smashing ground balls to the infielders. Case was chippy and chatty with his fellas, "attaboys" and "eat you up!" flying out of his mouth like the grounders rocketing off his wand. His middle infielders took ground balls like surgeons and together shortstop McDougald and second baseman Jerry Coleman had such quick feet, soft hands, rapid releases, and strong throws that they looked like ballerinas with bullfighter faces.

Taken together, the Yanks had depth, firepower, experience, home field advantage, confidence, swagger, and Case calling the shots. Case could pick 'em, play 'em, and win with 'em. Even Haney's hero and mentor, Ty Cobb, thought Casey already belonged in the Hall of Fame. Dan Daniel wrote in the *Sporting News* that "Casey knows more baseball than any other manager now in the majors. He will follow a hunch. He will take a big chance. He moves in response to reasons which in his mind are already clearly defined." Nobody in New York had ever second-guessed Casey. He didn't remember what it was like to be doubted.

And right there, Fred Haney sensed Milwaukee's advantage. All anyone had ever done since the Braves got off the plane was doubt his boys. All the New York writers knew about Fred Haney was that he was the smallest manager in the majors, a fitting leader for a team that didn't belong here in the first place. Let them have it, Haney decided. Let them kiss Case's ass. Let Case think he can do no wrong. Let him think the Milwaukee Braves can do no right. So what if the Braves hit 124 of their major league-leading 199 home runs on the road, or that they had been in first place for 110 days of the season, compared to 108 for the Yankees, in a fierce five-team race, not some forgone conclusion two-team race, or that they went 95-59 in the regular season, their .617 winning percentage second only to the .636 mark of the Yanks, who went 98-56. Both won their respective league by eight games, but somehow, New York's eight games meant more than Milwaukee's eight games. So what if Ted Williams said the Braves didn't have a chance. So what if Case constructed his team as a hybrid American League-National League squad, both fast and strong, quick and cumbersome, aggressive and static, and arrogant and nonchalant. Their pitching staff was so deep that six pitchers won in double digits and they had a better bullpen than the Braves, with the best closer in baseball, Bob Grim, who led the AL with 19 saves. This was Milwaukee's kind of fight.

By the time the Yanks were showered and off to play golf for the day, the Braves were in the batting cage. Case wasn't waiting around to see all of the hitters. He only wanted to see one. *Bang!* Henry Aaron. *Bang!* What a hell of a year he had, leading the National League in home runs (44), runs batted in (132), runs (118), and total bases (369). After all the worry about his batting average, Aaron still hit .322, and finished fourth behind Stan Musial, who fulfilled his promise to take the batting title back from Aaron. Henry thought he could do some damage in this yard, though he noted the vast dimensions, especially to center field, weren't exactly hitter friendly. Henry, as usual, wasn't bothered. He hit two balls to the opposite field, planting two into the upper deck in right field. "Man, this ballpark wasn't built for any hitter, was it?" he observed, and somewhere, Babe Ruth was asking what the hell he meant by that. "But we'll do OK. It looks like I'm going to get a lot of doubles and triples."

Henry could have played for Casey any time, and that was a huge gesture of respect on Case's behalf. Maglie had told all the Yank pitchers the same thing—if you don't want him to hurt you, hope his car gets a flat tire on the way to the game. No pitch was safe. He'd swing at anything. The best strategy, according to Maglie and seconded in a scouting report authored by Pirates GM Branch Rickey, was to do the unthinkable— throw him a fastball right down the dick. Then close your eyes and pray. Aaron "will take three strikes down the middle and in fact frequently acts frozen on pitches," Rickey wrote.

Eddie Mathews wasn't going to act frozen and neither were the rest of the boys. He couldn't wait to take a shot at the right-field porch and didn't care what anybody thought of him or his team. He wasn't scared. He didn't know what scared meant. He didn't even give a shit if Stengel thought he couldn't hit or run. Hell, Stengel thought Eddie was still a road-apple defensive third baseman. When the workout was over, Eddie left the ballpark with the Asshole Buddies to tour the town. Lew Burdette hung his arm around Eddie's shoulders. "I have always felt sorry for you, running around with three pitchers," Burdette once said. "We had more time before starts than you did."

But that never bothered Eddie. He was itching for a good time, which for him meant a fight. Johnny Logan remembered a time when he and Eddie were walking and Eddie said he wanted to knock some guy on his ass. No reason. Eddie picked the fight. Johnny gave the guy a Heimlich maneuver while Eddie knocked the crap out of him. No reason. The moment Eddie said, "Get the hell out of here," he was ready to start some shit. But the buddies kept the loveable asshole out of trouble. They walked through midtown, where *West Side Story* was the hot new Broadway show commanding $25 a ticket, scalpers wanted $150 for four grandstand seats to the Series and the bell captain at the Hotel Commodore sold a couple of NYPD detectives four sets of tickets with a face value of $117.50 for $400. They told Eddie, no fighting in the World Series. He would have to find another way to channel his energy. He ought to hit instead. Play some defense.

Spahn was already mentally dialing in to pitch Game 1, so the boys dragged him along, too. It was great—they could walk through the streets of midtown and nobody knew who the hell they were, much less where they played. The players found that highly amusing and comforting. The locals were talking an awful lot of trash. Casey seemed to respect Spahn, but thought the Yanks could beat him. Burdette and Bob Buhl didn't get the same courtesy. Burdette and Spahn were road roommates for years, so Spahn called Burdette "Rooms," and Burdette called Spahn, "Hooks," a nod to his crooked beak and breaking balls. Burdette and Spahn couldn't stop bantering about it. The truth was they both wanted a piece of Casey. They both felt he had jeopardized their careers as young pitchers. They wanted revenge, but they couldn't resist the opportunity to screw around in the Big Apple first.

Lew had the perfect plan. It would make the buddies laugh so hard that Eddie would forget about fighting for a few minutes. Lew possessed a high-pitch whistle. It was shrill, ear-shattering loud. Once, he claimed he stood in the middle of traffic in Chicago and almost started a pileup. Here in Manhattan, Lew started whistling like mad. The pedestrians thought the cops were flagging somebody. Wouldn't it have been something if the pitching staff of the Milwaukee Braves caused a traffic jam? Take that, home field advantage. Besides, nobody knew who they hell they were anyhow. Probably just some redneck fans in from Wilmaukee, or wherever it was the Braves came from.

Then Eddie told Lew to shut the hell up for a second. He spotted a novelty shop, where something caught his eye. Here were the Milwaukee Braves, the little underdogs in the big-city World Series, supposed to be overwhelmed and intimidated, boys from the sticks scared lifeless by the Yanks. Nope. Eddie was eyeing the fake vomit and rubber dog shit. Then he saw a rubber snake and bought it. He thought it was a wonderful use of his meal money. He had a great idea for a good time.

12

Games 1 and 2   **THE BUTTON MEN**

The fans back home in Milwaukee were ready and waiting. Game 1 would be broadcast in black and white, and for the lucky four thousand or so fans with the newer TVs, in color for the first time. Around Milwaukee, everyone made plans to be in front of a TV, and if you didn't have a TV, you'd find a radio, and if you didn't have either of those, you would improvise.

For the first time, fans could call numerous special telephone lines to get score updates. The *Journal* and the *Sentinel* begged readers not call the newsroom to badger their beleaguered clerks and reporters for score updates. The full radio broadcasts would be heard on WEMP and WTMJ in Milwaukee and WTMJ-TV, the *Journal* station, would televise the NBC broadcasts, with Milwaukee's Earl Gillespie on the call along with Bob Neal.

Around town, it was good business to open up free TV viewing for customers. Wisconsin National Bank put TVs in the lobby of every branch. Gimbels put big-screen TV sets—twelve inches!—on several floors of the flagship store on Wisconsin Avenue. Insurance companies, police stations, and even hospitals provided TV sets for customers, clients, and patients. It was a pretty good bet that nobody was going to die or get mugged during the World Series. Breweries allowed workers to listen to their own transistor radios during work hours, causing a rush of buyers to Woolworth's drugstores, where the price for one was knocked down to a $21.95 World Series special.

Schoolteachers across Wisconsin knew they might as well give up trying to teach the kids anything when the Braves were playing. And for the few who worked outside and couldn't get to TV or radio, such as a downtown Milwaukee construction crew or any of Lou Perini's men digging on various projects, a crude chalk scoreboard on a brick wall or the side of a building would do just fine. Some technology still couldn't beat chalk.

One of the first TV images the Milwaukee fans saw was Warren Spahn heating up. Spahnie was locked in. "The fans could see the concentration on his face as though he were only a couple of feet away," the *Journal* reported. All of Milwaukee could see Spahn, holding his glove in front of his face, covering his mouth and the tip of his nose, but not his eyes. His hat and his face were both weathered with mileage, but fresh in vibrant color. Then there were the eyes. They showed Spahn's razor-sharp focus. But there was so much more in those eyes, such focus only hinting at Spahn's devotion to his craft, to his city, and to his causes.

Then the cameras panned to the Yankees side. There was Casey, bantering and bullshitting with his players, dressed in his pinstripes and high socks, wearing his horn-rimmed glasses, and if you wrapped ivory-handled pistols around his hips, he'd be damn like Patton and smack anyone he thought was a Cherry Pie.

"The fans had a close look into the Yankee dugout on the first base side and saw the Yankees, veterans of more World Series games than any other team, looking as excited as a group of rookies," the *Journal* reported. "It was a sunny and mild day in New York and hundreds of fans in the stands were in their short sleeves and many others carrying topcoats they hadn't needed. Yankee Stadium was decked in red, white, and blue bunting and appeared to be jammed to the rafters."

The camera flashed back to Spahn's deep eyes. He resented New York's overall disrespect for Milwaukee and the Braves. He disliked the strong air of superiority and the sharp and nasty condescending tones the city generated toward Milwaukee and the Midwest. Old biases that accompanied the move from Boston to Milwaukee surfaced again. "A guy will buy a ticket to Minneapolis instead of Milwaukee," *New York Post* columnist Jimmy Cannon wrote, "and not discover his mistake until he lands there."

The Braves wanted to win for the Milwaukee people because they needed to finish what they had started in 1953, and because beating the

Yanks meant more than just ending the New York baseball dynasty. It meant a victory for the little guy coming into his own, a celebration of hard work and individualism, of unity and passion. Spahn had learned something about the people of Milwaukee and Wisconsin—never believe that the working class wouldn't stand up and fight when it felt oppressed by big money, big bullies, and big power. A day before Game 1, the Schlitz hit the fan when a button man, whose job it was to start and stop the conveyor belt at one of the city's many breweries, was unexpectedly and without reason laid off. The workers had a response for that. The next day, 2,200 walked off the job and said "Go Schlitz Yourself." A day later, the button man was back at work, thanks to 2,200 of his best friends.

Spahn saw himself as a button man. He never forgave the way Casey Stengel pushed him off the assembly line as a rookie in 1942 and called him a gutless Cherry Pie. Spahn remembered the time in spring training that season when he was hit in the nose by a line drive. Case wouldn't let Spahn go to the hospital. To Case, that made Spahn soft. Spahn couldn't believe that. How could you call a guy who took a liner off the nose and bled all over the field a Cherry Pie? It was clear the damn thing was broken and he was bleeding. Asking to have the nose set, that made him weak? That infuriated and traumatized Spahn, who voiced his complaints, but Casey never forgave young players who told him what to think.

Nonetheless, Spahn made the 1942 Braves. It was a big jump, coming up from Evansville in the Three-I League, and Spahn wasn't ready. Maybe Casey knew that. On April 20, at Ebbets Field, in only his second big league game, Case caught the Dodgers stealing his signs—and they didn't even have a zoom camera to help them. Case was furious. He couldn't fathom anyone smarter than he was, which Spahn always thought was part of Stengel's problem. So Case told Spahn to knock down the next hitter, shortstop Pee Wee Reese.

"I stuck my first pitch under his chin and Pee Wee twitched his head," Spahn said, but it wasn't enough to make Case happy. "I wound up again, cut loose, and grazed Reese's chin. Pee Wee shrugged it off." But Stengel had wanted to see Pee Wee go down. He was furious at Spahn. This busher feller was a road apple Cherry Pie! Stengel marched out to the mound, every bit as mean and gruff as John McGraw, took the baseball from Spahn, and in Spahn's eyes, tried to take his career away from him, too. Two pitches! Stengel didn't just take Spahn out of the game, he sent him back to the minor leagues. "Casey was mad," Spahn remembered. "He stormed to the mound, took me by the shoulders, and said, 'Son, you'll never make a big league pitcher.'"

Spahn went to Hartford and won 17 games, came back at the end of the season and got shelled, and then missed three years to military service. He didn't establish himself until he won 21 games in 1947 at age twenty-six for manager Billy Southworth, but nobody considered him young anymore.

As the camera pulled away from Spahn, they saw a determined man, pitching for the people, and very quietly, pitching to get even with Casey Stengel, who stole some of his youth. Edward Spahn, Warren's father, was thin as barbed wire and just as prickly. When he spotted Casey walking through the lobby of the Hotel Commodore before Game 1, he made it clear that the Spahn family had a score to settle. "My grandfather saw Stengel, ran over to him, dragged him by the shirt, threw him against the wall and said, 'Now what do you think of my son?'" Greg Spahn said. "He hated that Casey told my Dad he didn't have the guts to be a major league pitcher. He held that resentment in for all those years. If my dad had a score to settle, he didn't show it, but things that were important to him ate on him. He'd do something about it. My father was not afraid of a fight. I can promise you that."

Casey considered his crowd a lot more high-class. His wealthy admirers made a last-minute entry into Yankee Stadium, indifferently shunning the Milwaukee population, the very people Spahn loved and represented. The wealthy New York crowds came fashionably late, hobnobbing in from midtown in black limousines escorted by chauffeurs polished as brass. Gents crisp as mint hundreds paraded with mink darlings on high heels and red nails to expensive box seats. The men wore Christian Dior and left topcoats in the car to sit in warmth and love baseball. They did everything but wear spats and tails and tap dance in front of mirrors. *New York Daily News* sportswriter Jimmy Powers was out of his tax bracket, admiring the money and the beauty. "I doubt any city in the world could produce an assemblage to compare with the one that sat in the sun-steeped stadium. The sleek custom built limousines bore the plates of ambassadors and United Nations personnel. Coming through the turnstiles one heard phrases in French, German, and Spanish." Powers admired the long, leggy blonds, "convoys of Veronica Lake types," he wrote. Dressed up like a million bucks, the well-to-do expected the Yanks to make like million-dollar men and dance all over the Milwaukee Braves . . . wait a minute, the who from what? You could almost hear their million-dollar brains grinding to a five-cent halt. Where are the Dodgers this year?

Casey liked to walk the line to say hello to them—he didn't dare call them "fellers" or "fellas"—that was shtick for the lowly sportswriters. Some of them were the friends of "his owners," his Stengelese term for his bosses, owners Dan Topping and Del Webb. Casey was a banker at home in California and he was always looking for new investors. You should bring your money to Glendale, he would say, where he and Edna could make your money grow as comfortable as your stay at Yankee Stadium.

Case was always using baseball to angle for a buck and create his own legend. The cameras caught him working the Park Avenue set. Then, they flashed back to Spahn, who finished his warmups with catcher Del Crandall. He slung his jacket over his left shoulder, and slowly walked onto the outfield grass to the dugout. He, too, had done well for himself financially, but he was a button man at heart.

The Yankee Stadium crowd was eclectic, diverse, and excited. "There were so many people on the field, you couldn't loosen up," Frank Torre said. A few hours before the game, before the TV cameras were rolling, comedian Danny Thomas, Fred Haney's Hollywood crony, was on the field. He waited for Haney to walk away before he told the press he was picking the Yanks to win it all. The photographers wanted shots of Spahn and Ford together. One guy asked Spahn to hold Ford's arm up. Spahn asked, "Can I twist it?" They also wanted photographs of Henry Aaron and Mickey Mantle together.

The image of Aaron and Mantle, black and white sluggers standing together in peace, carried special significance. At Central High School in

Little Rock, where nine black students were attempting to integrate in the face of hostile local protest, President Dwight Eisenhower dispatched armed Federal National Guardsmen to escort the "Little Rock Nine" to class. Newspapers around the nation found front-page space for the black student hung in effigy alongside Game 1 previews. The protestors screamed slurs and obscenities, foreshadowing the Civil Rights Movement and helping to awaken citizens around the country. "Christianity has failed in Little Rock," a reader wrote to the *New York Post*. "The rioters have not understood that all men are created equal. It appears that the moral issue involved in this Civil War is yet to be settled. It is also evident that some Southerners have adopted the superior race philosophy reminiscent of Nazi Germany. Nowhere as in Little Rock has such a malicious crime against children ever been perpetuated by any state because of a difference in skin color."

Yet, the Milwaukee Braves were a shining example of cooperation in a troubled time. On September 23, the day after the Braves won the pennant, the *Journal's* front page featured a black reporter being shoved down the steps of Central High. On the *Sentinel's* front page, you could see Eddie Mathews, Henry Aaron, Bob Hazle, Don McMahon, and Wes Covington locked arm in arm, smiling and laughing for a shared goal. Baseball could show us the best in ourselves.

Jackie Robinson was among the celebrities and dignitaries on the field before Game 1. It was his first World Series out of baseball, but he put aside his phantom pain as a retired ballplayer to support the Little Rock Nine. He wanted the students to know they were not alone in the fight. "The least I could do to help those kids was to offer what little encouragement I could," Robinson said. "I talked to each of the nine and told them we're extremely proud of the way they have conducted themselves in the face of tremendous odds."

Jackie searched out his old pals who were hanging around on the field, former Dodgers teammate Roy Campanella and Giants outfielder Monte Irvin, who had also retired after the 1956 season. "Wouldn't it be wonderful if one of the three boys among the nine turned out to be a first-class athlete?" Irvin asked. The news from Little Rock unified Robinson and his friends, but they also had business to attend to. Very quietly, all three of them summoned Henry Aaron and Wes Covington. They had never played in Yankee Stadium before, a perilous place for a young outfielder, where fly balls were lost in the sun. "Jackie said if I go looking for the shadows, I'll find them," Covington said. "I made up my mind not to go looking for them." Now, the three former Negro League ballplayers who became big league stars made sure that a member of the next generation was prepared for the challenges awaiting him.

Brooklyn Dodgers owner Walter O'Malley was safely entrenched in his field-level box, similarly envisioning the challenges of a new generation. He was finalizing the deal for the Dodgers to move west, where he had plans to develop an impoverished Los Angeles neighborhood called Chavez Ravine. History would remember the Dodgers as pioneers, when in fact it was Lou Perini's Milwaukee Braves who made O'Malley's vision possible. When the Dodgers played their last game at Ebbets Field, it had the feel of a sparsely attended funeral. Ballpark organist Gladys Gooding played "After You're Gone," "Thanks for the Memories," and "Auld Lang Syne." O'Malley was the most hated man in New York at the moment, "looking as unctuous as a funeral director and dreaming of oil wells," wrote the *Daily Mirror*. O'Malley made it a point to say hello to his star catcher, who would accompany the team west, but it was the last time Roy Campanella ever stood on a baseball field.

It was the last fall of the New York Giants. Their season-ticket holders received letters that read, "Our ticket office very presently will be established in San Francisco and at that time we will contact you." Owner Horace Stoneham said, "I hope the people of San Francisco will like us. I know we are going to like the people of San Francisco." That statement was a dagger in the heart of New York Giants fans. Somebody asked Willie Mays to turn out the lights in the Polo Grounds. The groundskeeper shoveled out a ceremonial clump of turf from the outfield grass to be shipped west. The transfer to San Francisco was well underway, and when paired with the Dodgers inevitable departure, this World Series had a more depressing feeling to New Yorkers. The fans were losing their two National League teams, leaving them with unwanted feelings, like the child of a divorce. They didn't root for the Yanks, nor could they bear the thought of the Yanks losing. "It's the Yankees against the world," the *Daily Mirror* proclaimed. The *New York Post* chimed: "We are all Yankee fans or we are nothing."

But losing two teams did not equate to unity behind the Yankees, nor would it supplant the passionate and rampant gambling on the 1957 World Series, estimated to be the largest single gambling event in baseball history, according to the *New York World Telegram & Sun*. Nationally, wagers were expected to exceed $300 million, fueled by a new era of color TV World Series baseball and the national interest of baseball's traditional power against an unknown. Thanks to technology, wagering on baseball eclipsed the five boroughs and spread coast-to-coast with some estimates expecting total wagers to soar past $60 million per day if the Series exceeded four games.

The World Series was unparalleled as a spectacle, the high holy week of American sporting life, and now it was growing bigger thanks to color TV and the Milwaukee Braves. Before the Super Bowl, the World Series was the most important event in any fan's life. Such interest gave newspaper baseball writers phenomenal power to share information and shape the narrative arc of the game's history. Locker-room scrums between TV crews and longtime print journalists broke out for the first time. Fans wanted to know as much as they could, but most of them thought they knew baseball well enough without the help of advisers such as British astrologer Fay Naylor, who said the cosmos picked the Yanks in six. There was no cottage industry of baseball analysts or "insiders." Gambling fans prided themselves on winning their bets based on their institutional knowledge of baseball trends and histories. They trusted their instincts and believed in the value of wisdom passed down through generations. Their betting slips were slivers of their souls.

New York cops said it was the biggest early World Series crowd they had ever seen. Nearly four thousand fans were waiting when the first come-first served bleacher seating box office opened at 8 A.M. Many of the fans drove in from Milwaukee and other Wisconsin towns. Their Braves hats and feather headdresses gave them away. Two hours later, when the remainder of the gates opened, almost all of the 14,000 cheap seats were sold. The brave Milwaukee fans sat among the apathetic New Yorkers, but as game time neared, Yankee Stadium snapped with energy. "The cameras carried the fans to deep center field where the ceremony of raising the American flag signaled the moment was close at hand," the *Journal* reported. Only a small crowd of Milwaukee fans had the money to fly in to New York for the first two games. During the national anthem, they announced their presence and loyalty by singing loudly, especially the part about "the land of the free and the home of the Braaaaaaves!"

Arthur Daley, the *New York Times* columnist, was looking for fear in the players. He couldn't find any. "The Braves showed no signs of jitters or stage fright," he wrote. Whitey Ford was ready to go. It was the first Game 1 matchup of left-handed starters since the 1938 World Series when Carl Hubbell of the Giants faced Lefty Gomez of the Yanks. Both were in the stands watching this one. Next, Earl Gillespie spoke the words the nation and an expected worldwide television audience of 75 million were waiting for. "We'll be right back with the first pitch of the 1957 World Series."

In Milwaukee, they prayed. In New York, they thought they didn't have to.

Whitey Ford stood on the mound and stared down the pipe to Yogi Berra. Red Schoendienst heard his name announced and walked to the plate. As he did, he could see the white rafters in the upper deck decorated with patriotic bunting and a banner announcing the Yanks were World Series champs seventeen times over. The place was packed but rather polite, 69,476 strong. Half the field was in sunlight and half the field was in shade. The grass was bright green, as manicured as the fingertips of the Veronica Lake set. The ballpark scents were a mixture of beer and grilling in the concession stands, cigarette and cigar smoke, the low murmur of individual conversations, and the scratchy sound of transistor radios. Along the third-base side was a small contingent of Braves fans consisting of Lou Perini, John Quinn, and their families. Surrounding them were Yankees fans in short-sleeve white shirts, well-established professionals, the GI Bill generation. They were conservative fans, pay-your-share types, not the rowdy type, fortunate but not as wealthy as the super-rich Casey courted. For most of them, this was the first time they had seen the Milwaukee Braves, and the same could be said for the majority of the world.

Red dug in his feet and scratched away the back line of the box. He nodded a hello to Yogi and to plate umpire Joe Paparella, an American League ump. Courtesy never hurt, especially in an arena like this. Red choked up on the bat, and back home in Milwaukee, thousands of schoolboys choked up along with him. The big manual scoreboard in left field, with its black-and-white letters and numbers, looked just like an oversized elementary school blackboard announcing AT BAT 4, POS 4, meaning number four, Red, the second baseman. Red hit from a slight crouch, knees never shaking. Yogi squatted his big rump on an invisible stool, the chest protector strapped just below the black number 8 on his back. TV viewers could forget trying to read his signs, because Whitey called his own game. Paparella was hunched behind his pillow chest protector like it was a bulletproof vest. The outfield signs were washed off—the bright red and white Coca-Cola billboard shimmering against the harsh left field sun, next to the Burma shave bomb, the FLY NATIONAL to Florida and Cuba, and BUY AMERICAN FLYING GASOLINE signage. Red was ready and so was Whitey, but they had to wait and realize that TV time-outs in big games were about to become a lot more commonplace. Finally, Paparella pointed at Whitey.

He rocked into his windup. Red was thinking fastball, but instead, Whitey pulled a string. He threw a big, slow, over-the-top tumbling curveball, it looked like a boulder rolling down the mountain, and Red watched the ball into Yogi's glove, heard the leather pop, and heard Paparella bellow *Strike!* A World Series like no other began.

Red sized Whitey up in an instant. So this was going to be a lefty's game. Everybody knew Whitey could throw hard, but he was one of those cagey guys who liked to save it for when he wanted to surprise you. Whitey was 11-5 in 1957 in an injury-shortened season in which he made only seventeen starts and pitched 129 innings. He was twenty-eight, but he had been in the big leagues since he burst onto the scene with a 9-1 record in 1950, cracking the best rotation in baseball and earning immediate respect as a key player on a historically significant team. Casey loved him from the moment he saw him. He made other Yankee pitching prospects look inferior and expendable. Whitey was cocky as hell and nobody blamed him. He was burly and sturdy, and though he stood only 5-10, he generated tremendous power from a low center of gravity. His release point was so high hitters could lose his left arm in the blur of the right-field porch. His curveball was devastating for a guy set so low.

Whitey and the curveball were made for each other. He could slow-dance with her or he could tango. He could have his way with her, speed her up or slow her down, rock around her clock, alternate the angle of the break, change the shape and depth, screw with the batter's eye levels and depth perception. Whitey was planning to waltz the Braves to sleep. The game plan was Sal Maglie's inventive and devious deception. A few slow curves later, Red grounded to third, and the Braves went quietly thereafter in the first inning.

Now, Milwaukee took the field. Many of the Braves emulated Red's composure. "It's fun no matter where you play a World Series," he said. "I'd been in that ballpark and when you go in there you try to do your best and you're playing a World Series, you're playing against the best, so that's it." Behind the plate, Del Crandall wasn't feeling so calm. "When we took the field, I'm surprised people didn't hear my knees knocking, because I was, I was nervous," he said. "I can't speak for anyone else, but I was nervous. And when Spahn threw his last warmup pitch, he usually threw a screwball, and he threw it in the dirt, and I picked it up and threw to second base, my nervousness was all gone."

Now it was Spahn's turn to take the tomahawk to the mound. He worked up-tempo and aggressive. Casey had juggled his lineup, choosing, as he occasionally did, Hank Bauer to hit lead off. That was always a different look—Bauer ran as fast as a city garbage truck—but Spahn knew what Casey was trying to do. This was all about threatening him with right-handed firepower. So Spahn put one under Bauer's hands and got him to hit a lazy fly ball to Andy Pafko in right field for the first out. But then Spahn rolled into trouble. He gave up a hard single to right to Gil McDougald, bringing Mickey Mantle to the plate.

Spahn had faced Mantle in All-Star games and in spring training, but this was different. Mick's knees were killing him. He walked like he was on hot coals, but there was no disputing his raw power. He wore that big black number 7 on his back, and when he swung the bat, he swung as hard as he could. His hands, wrists, and forearms were genetically strong. Watching Mick hit was a unique experience in itself, a strong boy whose body felt older than his twenty-five years and whose bat speed made a noise like a jet fighter screaming across the sky. He waved at Warren's next pitch and hit it hard deep into the hole at short. Johnny Logan's fast first step allowed him to range to his right and backhand the ball, but as he set his feet to throw, he could not get the ball out of his glove fast enough. Mantle, even with a knee thoroughly taped, could still get down the line. He was safe with an infield single and McDougald ran the bases for blood, cutting second, dashing past Logan, and taking third.

Spahn was no different than any other pitcher in the thinking that any time you could keep Mantle in the ballpark was a good at-bat. Spahn was in admiration. How could somebody in so much pain still be such a good hitter? "He can't be hurt too much, not by the way he swung. He took some pretty good cuts," Spahn concluded later, but it didn't change the fact that he was in trouble with runners on the corners and one out.

Everybody thought the Braves secretly must have stage fright. "I don't think any club can beat the Yanks by playing tight," said Leo Durocher, the former Giants and Dodgers manager on hand to watch the series as a commentator. "Tight is a nice word for scared." Moose Skowron was next, another right-handed *BANG!* guy, 17 home runs, and in the lineup despite a sore back. McDougald, who ran well, jumped off third base, eager to score.

The Yankee lineup was so right-handed heavy that Fred Haney might have never let Spahn pitch against them if they were in the National League. But he didn't have that choice now, and neither did Spahn. He took a deep breath and fooled Skowron. He got him lunging and Skowron hit a ground ball to second, where the ball went home to Red's hands. Red fielded effortlessly and cleanly. Skowron ran even worse than Bauer, giving Red ample opportunity to lock his glare on McDougald at third and command him to stay before he flipped to second to force Mantle.

That brought up Yogi. This was still a dangerous matchup, but a more advantageous lefty vs. lefty matchup for Spahn. Writers made Yogi out to be a dunce, but his baseball instincts were off the charts. Yogi was the exception to Casey's assembly line—the one guy with the dumpy body who didn't look like he had been assembled at General Motors. Yogi never cared if he was facing a lefty or a righty, a submariner or a side-armer, black or white, underhand or overhand. Spahn knew that throwing Yogi a fastball with a runner at third base in a scoreless World Series game was about as smart as handing a pickpocket your wallet. So that's exactly what he did.

But Spahn missed his spot. He knew it was a mistake the way it rolled off his fingertips. Yogi's eyes opened up like he was watching showgirls. Spahn was terrified. Yogi took that magnificent, sweeping left-handed cut and lifted the ball high into the blue Bronx sky. Spahn's eyes closed for a moment, he thought he had just given up a home run, but then, he heard sweet safety in the sound of Schoendienst calling for the ball in shallow right field. The ball floated into Red's hands for the final out of the inning.

As Spahn walked off the mound, he crossed paths with Berra and vowed he'd "never in your life see me give you another fat one like that." Spahn called it the worst pitch he ever threw in a World Series. When Spahn came up to bat later in the game, Yogi had a message for him. He grumbled through his steel birdcage. "I get one pitch like that a year," Yogi moaned. "And I do nothin' with it." Spahnie apologized with a smile and a lack of sincerity. Millions of TV viewers wondered why Spahn and Berra were laughing. Spahn had lived to tell the tale.

Whitey went back to work, carving through the Braves. Henry Aaron, batting cleanup and playing center field, flipped his bat at a breaking ball and rolled it to second base to start the second inning. Joe Adcock was next and he was similarly confused. He flew out to right field, and Whitey was on his way. He retired the first seven Braves before Del Crandall singled in the third. Milwaukee's first World Series hit brought cheers throughout Wisconsin, where streets were empty as fans holed up in front of TV sets. The happiness was promptly erased when Spahn hit into a force play to erase Crandall at second. The Braves couldn't get a feel for Whitey.

Henry was the one guy who showed signs that he might figure him out. In the fourth inning, Whitey tried a curveball outside and down in the dirt, but as many National League pitchers had already learned, if you couldn't get the ball lower than a groundhog, Henry could hit it. He rifled a single to center field, sending Eddie Mathews, who had walked, racing to third base. The moment revealed something about Eddie that the Yankee scouting reports compiled by Bill Skiff and Johnny Neun failed to identify—Eddie could really run. He went from first to third like a gazelle, and this should have been a wakeup call for Casey Stengel and the Yankees, but it wasn't. It was a golden opportunity for the Braves, runners at the corners with one out in a scoreless game.

Now Adcock was up, but Whitey really made him uncomfortable. "Ford would show you the fastball once in a while but he wouldn't let you hit it," Adcock said. Before he went to the plate, Red told Adcock he had already identified exactly what this Grand Opera Son of a Gun was doing to the Braves. He was just like facing Preacher Roe of the Dodgers, a little lefty with a lot of different curveball looks and a ton of guts and tenacity. Adcock hated facing Roe. Sometimes Whitey got a big smirk on his face when he was sure he could get a guy out. It didn't matter who it was or what kind of home run power they had. It wasn't a sign of disrespect. It was a sign of Whitey's enormous confidence. As Case would say, Whitey ain't no Cherry Pie.

All Adcock wanted was a fly ball deep enough for Eddie to tag up and score. The one thing he did not want to do was put the ball on the ground, especially to the left side of the infield, where Case's vacuum cleaners would be no match for Joe's aching wheels. Whitey danced and nibbled until Joe could resist no more; his hands started the bat too soon, he was way out in front of a slow curve and tapped it to McDougald at short. Fred Haney was so frustrated he could have turned corn into dust the way he was grinding his molars. Joe was such a slow runner that you could hear him coming—*thud, thud, thud* down the line—as McDougald and Jerry Coleman turned the inning-ending double play. The Yanks were jogging off the field before Adcock was halfway up the line.

Spahn went to the mound with the game scoreless in the bottom of the fifth. Coleman, the slap-hitting right-handed second baseman who had flared a cheap opposite field double and been stranded in the second inning, got Spahn again, nicking a single to left, "another of those pitches I'd like to take back," Spahn said. It was always the pesky guys that got him.

He could look like a Hall of Famer against other Hall of Famers, but put him up against a little slap artist with bat control and brains and Spahn got played like a cheap date. Coleman moved to second on Tony Kubek's sacrifice bunt. Whitey Ford grounded out for the second out, bringing Hank Bauer back to the plate.

The last time Spahn faced Bauer, he made a bad pitch, but Bauer grounded to shortstop Johnny Logan to lead off the third inning. That didn't bother Case, who leaned forward on the top step of the Yank dugout. This was just what he wanted—Spahn with no choice but to execute against a fearsome right-hander. Spahn knew it, too. These were the moments that separated the culls and the road apples from the Grand Opera Son of a Guns. Spahn got the pitch just where he wanted it—low and away—but Bauer rolled the pole right over the outer half and smoked the ball on a high arching drive to center.

Henry Aaron got a good read, but the ball was hit too hard. Bauer scorched a clean, clutch, run-scoring two-out double, giving the Yanks a 1–0 lead. The fans in steerage, up in the bleachers and rafters, cheered. The Park Avenue set politely applauded, as if they couldn't understand why it had taken the Yanks so long to score against this National Leaguer clearly spending his last two bits of energy trying to beat the Yanks. Spahn had to tip his cap to Bauer. He had been around the block long enough to know baseball could do this to a guy. "Best hit in the game and he got it off a pitch I made just as I wanted it," Spahn said.

Down 1–0, the Braves felt they had to respond immediately in the top of the sixth inning. Whitey walked Johnny Logan and Eddie Mathews to begin the inning, bringing Henry back to the plate. It was the same as it had been all season. When Henry hit, the Braves were hot. The stadium went silent. The wealthy fans grew as worried as the everyday fans. As Leo Durocher said, "If Henry is on the beam, he will do something for the rest of the club." Casey didn't want to walk Aaron, that would load the bases, and besides, if he could get past Aaron, he liked Whitey's chances against Adcock and Pafko. Henry watched his first butterfly-breaking ball flutter into Berra's glove and Joe Paparella belted a high-note strike call you could hear in Harlem.

This game was the first look at this young hitter for most of the country. His stoic mannerisms were not what white folks thought they might be. Henry didn't bounce around the box like Mays and he didn't anxiously pick at the dirt with his feet like Jackie. All Henry did was swing one leg out of the box, bend over to sweep his hand through the dirt, and stand up to get a better grip on the bat. This demeanor was no surprise to Milwaukee, who had seen Henry's supreme focus and intensity be characterized as calm and lackadaisical. But as every hometown fan crowded into third, fifth, and eighth floor of Gimbels or planted at every tavern, lodge, and bar in town could tell you, Henry was dangerously easy to misunderstand. Henry swung the other leg back into the box and was ready for Whitey.

Henry was standing in shadow. It was the hardest time of the day to pick the ball up. Roy Campanella had warned the Braves, "There's no other park where the shadows around home plate bother a hitter like they do at the stadium." Whitey rocked into that tightly closed windup, wrapped up like a fist and then exploding toward the plate, throwing curveballs that were as difficult to see as dice in the dark. Whitey could spin it and Henry struggled to read the pitches, until with two strikes, he picked up the low-and-away curveball too late. The ball was outside just enough to fool Henry. He started to swing and then stopped. His check was no good here. Paparella rung him up for the first out.

Henry hated the call. "It wasn't over the plate," Aaron later said. "He said I swung, but I didn't." If Henry thought his manager was going to come out and argue for him, he was wrong. "You can't argue something like that," Fred Haney said. The *Journal* was rough on Aaron, who was "supposed to do something on such occasions." Whitey hadn't missed—he put that pitch where he wanted and framed Henry to perfection. "Beautiful control and changing speeds," Red Schoendienst said.

Whitey wanted to finish the inning with a flourish. He got Adcock to ground out, allowing Mathews to take third and Logan to advance to second. Pafko was next. Casey came to the mound and said he didn't care if Whitey walked the right-handed hitting Pafko, because he'd rather have Whitey face Covington. But Whitey shook his manager off. He wanted nothing to do with Covington, so he bore down on Pafko, who was playing in his third World Series. Whitey fell behind in the count, 2-1, but rallied to escape the inning when he struck out Pafko. He skipped off the mound and jogged off the field with Yogi. Casey would have killed any other pitcher who defied him like that. Though Whitey needed twenty-four pitches to get through the sixth, the Braves couldn't break him and Casey couldn't complain.

In the bottom of the sixth, the Yankees broke Spahn's heart. It started well enough with Mantle flying to center field for the first out, but then Elston Howard, who had entered the game as a defensive replacement in the third inning for the sore-backed slugger Moose Skowron, singled up the middle. Spahn walked Berra to make matters worse, putting runners at first and second for the right-handed hitting third baseman Andy Carey, a rail-thin infielder and part-time player. He was just the kind of fringe hitter that always burned Spahn. Carey singled sharply over second on a pitch that was out of the strike zone. Howard thundered home to make it 2–0 and Berra scooted to third.

Fred Haney had been grinding his teeth for hours. He threw the chaw out of his mouth and went to the mound to get Spahn. He had Ernie Johnson ready in the bullpen. All of Milwaukee let out a groan of sorrow as Warren walked off the mound. The small crowd of Braves fans in the upper deck at Yankee Stadium cheered for him. Spahn flicked his right index finger at the peak of his cap to acknowledge them. That was the best he could do. He didn't think his performance warranted a tip of the cap. He would have to wait for Game 4 to get even with Casey Stengel. Then Spahn vanished into the dugout and the rest of Milwaukee wondered if the rest of the Series was going to be a vanishing act. Nobody wanted to say it, but everyone worried that it was the beginning of the end. The feeling didn't improve when Jerry Coleman laid down a perfectly placed suicide squeeze bunt between the mound and first base. Johnson shifted directions and barehanded the ball. He only had the play at first. Berra scored standing and the Yanks led, 3–0.

The Braves needed something. If they weren't going to come back, they at least needed a shot in the arm, something to build off, a big moment or a spark. In the top of the seventh, Wes Covington gave it to them. The twenty-five-year-old leftfielder, built like the granite façade of Yankee Stadium, doubled sharply to left. The Braves hopped off their bench and onto their feet to cheer for the hardest ball any of their boys hit thus far. Covington had become a vital part of the machine, his 21 home runs proving that Ted McGrew had been right in his insistence that John Quinn not include the young outfielder in any trade for Red Schoendienst.

After Del Crandall and pinch hitter Nippy Jones grounded out, moving Covington to third, that left it up to Red himself. He was 0-for-3 with a pair of ground balls and a fly out. He had seen everything Whitey had to offer. Whitey could dime or gas Red, nibble or challenge, it didn't matter to him. Red was determined to get the run home. The first time Whitey left a pitch where Red could reach it, he slapped it back up the middle for a run-scoring single. It made the score 3–1, but one run represented a huge moral victory. The Braves could score in Yankee Stadium.

But Whitey bent no more. He struck out Logan to end the seventh inning and retired seven consecutive hitters to end the game, leading the Yanks 3–1 over the Braves in Game 1. Within a few hours, the evening editions of New York tabloids carried cartoons to illustrate the results. Many papers depicted the Milwaukee Braves as a fat, dumpy, bald, half-naked Indian with a large nose and huge teeth; readers could imagine his stinky breath crushed out of him by gargantuan images of Yankee muscle. The Braves had beaten nine left-handers in a row to end the regular season, but Whitey was something else. He needed 128 pitches, 78 strikes, to complete the game. Casey never thought about taking him after the sixth. Pitch counts were for Cherry Pies. Whitey scattered five hits, walked four and struck out five. It ran his lifetime record in the World Series to 5-2. As Casey once said, "If you had one game to win and your life depended on it, you'd want him to pitch it." Whitey might have never been better. "Slow ones, fast ones, curves that break a little, curves that break a lot," Fred Haney said. "His slow curves have slower curves. He must have thrown 85 percent curves." Told this, Wes Covington scoffed. "Try 90 percent," he said. Henry Aaron tipped his cap. "Oh, he was good," Henry said. "He was very good."

The writers poured into Whitey's locker stall. He said he had a harder time with Mathews and Covington than he did with Aaron and Adcock. Then, with a grin and a nod at Sal Maglie, Whitey informed them, "I had a helluva book on them. Maglie's stuff didn't vary much from the reports we got from the scouts."

Casey Stengel was impressed with the Braves, perhaps more than he let on he would be. A careful observer might have called him worried. "That pitcher Warren Spahn is a tough boy," Casey said. That was the nicest thing he had ever said about his former busher.

Spahn took the loss and wished for a better fate than 5⅓ innings, seven hits, three runs, and no strikeouts. No cold beer could sooth his sorrow. He wished he hadn't walked Yogi Berra in the sixth inning, but said, "I wouldn't have pitched a different ballgame if I had to do it all over again." He might not have cried in public, but some of the Milwaukee fans in New York did. A street vendor outside Yankee Stadium tried to sell them "crying towels," but the Milwaukee fans weren't amused. They grabbed his merchandise and threw it into the street, according to the *Sporting News*.

All of this tense energy was just too much for some fans, but what, Lew Burdette worry? Game 2 was a must-win for the Braves. The writers circled Lew, who sat calmly with a cold beer in one hand and a warm cigarette in the other. The writers amused him and he knew what they were going to ask. Do you throw a spitball? Are you nervous about pitching in Yankee Stadium? Are you out for revenge against the Yanks?

"Hey Hooks," Lew said to Spahnie, "All these guys should be talkin' to you."

"Hey Rooms," Spahnie said to Lew. "I'm dull."

Spahn and Burdette, the longtime roommates, had a motto for the room: anything you can do I can do better. The writers loved it. Burdette and Spahn were Dean Martin and Jerry Lewis, but from Milwaukee. As Spahn recalled years later, Lew "kept me young," and the New York writers had never encountered a character quite like him. He was every bit the button man Spahn was. Burdette put down his beer and told them he drank chocolate milk on days he didn't pitch and white milk on days he did. He said he didn't finish school because he stepped out to shave one day and they wouldn't let him back in class. He told them that his ability to squirrel whistle actually had the capability of stopping midtown traffic. He advised them of his affinity for throwing confetti into electric fans to celebrate a big occasion, such as Milwaukee winning the pennant. He was also the master of the hot foot, so all the sportswriters had better watch their shoe laces so he didn't set them on fire.

Lew had every intention of lighting up the Yanks in Game 2. The writers asked him if he had read the scouting report on the Yanks. Lew said, oh, yes, he had studied it up and down, though he later confided, "The reports made Spahn and I laugh." But Lew also had a sharp baseball mind. He explained years later that he always knew he lacked natural talent. He didn't have tremendous raw arm strength or naturally explosive stuff. But he did have the gifts of movement, location, and deception. His will to win dwarfed other men with superior gifts. His fearlessness set him apart. The radar gun could not measure what made him a success. Few pitchers in the history of baseball have been more gifted at playing with the minds and emotions of hitters. Burdette's ability to breakdown a lineup was beautiful to hear. He elaborated on what he saw in the Yankees, concluding, "All these things are warnings for me to be alive."

Yes, but do you throw the spitball?

"I am not a cheat," he declared. "I do not throw a spitball."

Then, of course, came the doubts he sowed into hitter's minds through the writers. He possessed the ability to use baseball writers to his advantage, to cultivate his mystique and mound persona, especially against the Yankees, who had never faced him before. "If they want to think I throw a spitball, let them. It gives me an extra pitch, even if I don't happen to have one." That was Burdette's act. How could he throw a loaded ball if he didn't know what he was doing? "It's my psychological pitch," he said. "The batters are so busy worrying about it that they usually get something they aren't looking for."

There was a kernel of truth in that statement. Burdette wanted the Yankees to think he was cheating, because when they did, he would sense it, and he would vary his arm angle to get different movement, and he would spook them. "I think the talk about him throwing the spitter got inside their heads before the Yankees even took the field," Del Crandall said. "They had read all this stuff and heard all the stuff and that got him in there right away, before the game started."

When pressed further, Burdette might deviate again, and manipulate the matter by questioning his own intellect. He suggested that maybe he wasn't smart enough to throw the spitter. "They talk as if all you had to do to throw a spitball was to crank up and throw one. Don't they know it's the hardest pitch there is to control? It takes lots of practice and you just don't throw one when you figure it might get the hitter out."

That was as close as Lew might have ever gotten to an admission, but it wasn't close enough, and the New York writers kept right on coming with more questions. Lew didn't give a shit. He used them and they didn't even know it. He could play pepper with these guys all day long and they weren't going to outsmart him. He was screwing with Casey Stengel's mind, too, and he loved it. The Milwaukee writers knew this. "He is tongue-in-cheek, but not an insincere talker," the *Journal*'s Cleon Walfort wrote for the *Sporting News*. "He fixes you with his cold blue eyes and says what he thinks. Then it is up to you to decide what he means."

As far as Lew was concerned, they were helping him play mind games with the Yanks. "I'd love to use the pitch, if I knew how," Lew said. He was having a hard time hiding the smirk now. The New York writers pressed more. Didn't Burleigh Grimes, the last pitcher to legally throw a spitball in 1934 after it was outlawed in 1920 and grandfathered into extinction, teach Burdette how to throw it back in 1950, a year before Lew came to the Braves as the throw-in for Johnny Sain? "Grimes told me years ago not to monkey with it, but to let them think I monkey with it," Burdette said.

The baseball writers didn't go down that path to find the truth, but they should have. Grimes, who won 270 games with the wet one in his Hall of Fame career, pitched for player-manager Charlie Grimm on the 1932 and 1933 Chicago Cubs. When Grimm became manager of the Braves—and Burdette's first manager in the big leagues who actually liked him—his pitching coach was Charlie Root, another former Cub who pitched on the same staff as Burleigh Grimes. Besides, Grimes lived near Grimm in the off-season. The greatest spitballer of them all, Grimes, lived and died in Wisconsin. He never confessed to teaching Burdette the pitch. So in other words, Burdette (maybe!) threw a grim reaper pitch taught by a guy named Grimes for a manager named Grimm. No wonder he was grinning all the time. Maybe the spitball was a fairy tale.

Some wondered if Burdette actually learned the spitter from Jim Turner, the Yankees pitching coach, who had pitched for the 1930–1932 Hollywood Stars with Frank Shellenback, the last great minor league spitballer. Turner didn't throw hard, just like Burdette. He won 21 games for the 1930 Stars and had to wait until he was thirty-three to get to the big leagues with the 1937 Boston Braves, where he won 20 games with a great deal of durability and virtually no strikeouts, a stunningly odd combination for somebody whose career gained traction after three summers spent with the greatest spitballer in the history of the Pacific Coast League. No matter what he said, the facts were stacked. The spitball was in Burdette's baseball blood.

Then there was the matter of revenge. Lew danced around that one, too. He gave the writers truth, but only pieces of it. Lew never admitted he wanted retribution any more than he admitted he loaded up the ball. "There just wasn't any place for me there," he said. "It was a good break when I got traded." That part of it was also true. The Yankees were loaded with pitching depth in the early fifties. Burdette spent most of the 1950 season in the same pitching rotation with Whitey Ford at Triple-A Kansas City. Whitey was the chosen one; Lew the forgotten one. The Yanks pitchers all looked alike: thin and square jawed, no smiles, no senses of humor, they were white-bread strong boys who threw hard, pitched inside, obeyed orders, said "yes, sir" and "no, sir," and acted like they revered Casey and his pitching coach, Turner. Lew wasn't one of those guys. He couldn't afford to be. He didn't throw hard enough to act like the other guys did, so he created his own image as a crafty and cunning warrior. Conformity wasn't in his blood, and even when he pitched well for the Yanks as he did in spring 1951, when he gave up one run in nineteen innings, Casey thought he was just another feller, a road-apple busher. Casey wasn't going to give Burdette a sniff at the big leagues, and Lew knew it. That grated at him for the last seven years. "Casey didn't even know I was around," Lew said. "Whenever he wanted me, he'd yell, 'Hey you, get in there and warm up.' It was always 'Hey you.' He never knew my name."

Lou Chapman knew it helped make Burdette tick. "He won't admit it, but the loquacious right-hander from the hills of Nitro, West Virginia, has nursed a private grudge against the Yankees in typical mountaineer style from the day they let him go," he wrote. Finally, in Game 2, Burdette would get his chance against the little lefty with the big curveball, Bobby Shantz. Burdette never got nervous. He wasn't capable of it. He asked the writers if they were done, then finished his beer while it was still cold.

Johnny Logan, however, was a bundle of nerves. He hated to lose more than anything. After Game 1 ended, he was still tight. Eddie Mathews, on the other hand, had already forgotten about the game. He hated to see Johnny so upset. He slowly reached his hand into his locker. Burdette, Spahn and Buhl knew what was coming next, but showed poker faces. "Hey, Johnny," Eddie shouted, "you scared of snakes?"

"Scared to death!" Logan shouted back.

"Then meet my new friend," Eddie said.

"He then thrust a realistic-looking rubber reptile in the shortstop's face," according to the *Sporting News*. Johnny practically jumped out of his pants. The obvious jokes were plenty. Talk about a wet one. Or, the ball ain't the only thing loaded now. Johnny screamed and dodged away to the delight of the ballclub, the *Sporting News* thankfully recorded his reactions. He wanted to kick the hell out of the Asshole Buddies, but then thought twice. It was a big league gag. Red Schoendienst observed much of this brand of horseplay. "What a bunch of funny guys," he recalled. "They sure did have fun around each other."

The Yankee Stadium crowd of 65,202 was already fidgety by the time Burdette began his ballet of the absurd. He really put it on for the New York crowd. Standing on the mound at Yankee Stadium was supposed to give a pitcher the feel of being alone in the bottom of the Grand Canyon, or worse, on the floor of the Roman Colosseum. But if Burdette wasn't putting anything on the ball, he was putting everything into his show— talking to the ball, the sky, the batters, grunting, shrieking, taunting, gesturing. Casey Stengel hated it when somebody else was the center of attention. Lew relished pushing Case's buttons, but what he really wanted was three or four runs in Game 2.

The Yanks didn't like Burdette's routine and let him have it. They thought his act was bush league and let him know, "bench jockeying in good voice, needling and insulting," the *Post* wrote. Burdette wasn't bothered. "Doin' their best to do a little agi'tat'in,'" he said. When the Braves came to bat, the Yanks rode them mercilessly, too, "like they were going to run us out of the ballpark," Del Crandall said. "In the second inning, the Yankee bench was riding us hard. I could hear it all. I came back to our bench and told our boys about it. We had been kinda quiet till then."

Enough was enough. The Braves could bark, too. "I think, because of the way some of the players of the Yankees conducted themselves, that we really did not like them," Del Crandall said. "And that gave us a little extra motivation." Soon they were on the top step, jawing right back. Eddie Mathews wanted a piece of them right now. He thought the Yankees were a bunch of fuckin' assholes! Threats and profanity flew across the field. "The boys got mad and began yelling back," Crandall said. "I guess we began fighting back, too." The mood was clear. This was going to be an emotional game and players were going to be knocked down. The Dodgers might be leaving New York, but the Braves couldn't come to town without a fight. Henry Aaron was ready to hit next. Rivals learned the hard way. Anyone who wanted a piece of Henry got a piece of the Braves.

Aaron walked to the batter's box to lead off the second inning against Bobby Shantz, the lefty generously listed at five-foot-six. "Bobby has three curves and each is distinctive," Pirates GM Branch Rickey wrote. Bobby threw a get-it-over curve, a slow curve, and then a fast curve, which was his strikeout pitch. He could also vary the spins and speeds and was the 1952 American League MVP. Henry, who was 1-for-4 in Game 1, sorted Shantz's curves and found one to his liking. He drove the pitch on a sharp line to center fielder Mickey Mantle. The ball was a gunshot. Mantle had only a millisecond to measure his reaction, but the ball was hit too hard for his aching knees to forgive a slight hesitation. "I'd say I hit it straight over his head," Henry said.

The ball sped over Mantle's head, rolling all the way to the center-field wall, the deepest part of Yankee Stadium. A groan went up. Jaded Giants fans thought Mays would have made the play. But Aaron could run, too. By the time the Yanks got the ball back in, Henry was safe at third with a triple. Mantle was beside himself. "It carried better than I thought," he said.

The Braves were proving that they could carry their weight better than the Yanks gave them credit for. Joe Adcock was next. Whitey Ford's curveballs had prepared him well for Shantz. Adcock had a game plan and fulfilled it when he singled to center field, scoring Aaron to give the Braves a 1–0 lead. Mantle raced to cut the ball off, but he looked labored and in pain. He couldn't pick up the ball cleanly, committing an error that allowed Adcock to take second with nobody out. Half the Yankee fans missed the play, instead eyeballing a "monstrously pictorial blonde in tight white," milling in the stands, according to the *Herald-Tribune*'s Red Smith. Shantz, however, kept his focus on the game, turning Milwaukee's golden scoring opportunity into squat. They could solve him no further in the second. It was a small victory for the Yanks but also a disturbing warning. Their best player could barely run.

In the bottom of the second, Burdette nearly let the game get out of hand before Wes Covington saved him. He walked Enos Slaughter on a full count, then whiffed Harry Simpson with a dashing slider. But Tony Kubek singled and the ever-pesky Jerry Coleman singled home Slaughter to make the score 1–1, leaving two runners aboard with two out for Bobby Shantz.

Shantz wasn't supposed to have a chance. He hit .179 in 1957 and hadn't hit a home run since 1950, but he drove one high and deep to left field, where Covington had been playing shallow. The ball came out of the shadows and into the sun. Covington backtracked as he shielded his eyes. He heeded Jackie Robinson's warning not to let fear influence his play. He didn't have time to be scared. If the ball fell behind him, Kubek and Coleman, a couple of rabbits, would easily score. "I said to myself, 'You better get on your horse, you can't afford to let that one get behind you,'" Covington said. Fred Haney recalled his thoughts: "If he can't get that ball, we're in trouble."

With his red number 43 to the crowd, Covington, at full stride, outstretched his left hand, turned his glove to the backhand side and lunged like he was trying to pull down a light switch. Milwaukee held its breath,

Covington held onto the ball, the lights were out on the Yankee threat, and Milwaukee cracked a cold one. The score remained 1–1 after two innings.

Johnny Logan waited on deck in the top of the third as Red Schoendienst battled Shantz. As he loosened up, Logan silently muttered the prayer to St. Jude, mouthing the words as Red lofted a lazy fly to Mantle for the first out. *Make use, I implore thee, of that particular privilege accorded to thee.* The Braves needed a run. *Come to my assistance in this great need.* Logan worked the count to 2-1 and then got the pitch he prayed for. He hit a high fly ball that hugged the left field line. Enos Slaughter raced over, hoping he had a play, but St. Jude stayed fair. The ball cleared the left field stands by about six feet. The Braves led 2–1 and had the first home run of the series. Logan circled the bases like an express train. "You should have seen the guys in the dugout when he got back," Henry Aaron said. "To me, it looked like the biggest morale pickup since we clinched the pennant."

If the Braves had prayers, the Yanks had power. In the bottom of the third, Hank Bauer, who was moonlighting as a spokesman for Arthur Murray Dance Studios and insisting ballroom dancing wasn't for sissies, crushed a manly leadoff home run twenty-five rows deep into the left field stands off Burdette to tie the score, 2–2. Burdette had given up three hits and two runs in three innings. He looked like he was anything but invincible. Were it not for Covington's catch he might have been out of the game. In the Yankee dugout, Casey Stengel might have felt justified in letting this feller go to the Braves six years earlier.

But the Braves flashed their resiliency in the top of the fourth, picking away at Shantz. Joe Adcock singled again, this time to left, and Andy Pafko dropped a single into shallow left field. Adcock put down his anchor at second and Covington came to the plate. Casey Stengel liked this matchup but Fred Haney didn't. Haney ordered Covington to bunt. He squared up, but popped the first pitch foul for strike one. Haney could have taken off the bunt sign but unpredictable managing wasn't his strength. He issued the bunt order again and grinded his teeth when Covington popped foul for strike two.

Now Stengel thought he had the advantage, but Shantz was on a short leash. Right-hander Art Ditmar was heating up in the bullpen for the next four Braves hitters, all right-handers. Logic forced Haney's hand and he gave Covington the green light to attack. His big swing belonged in a New York nightclub, but the cue shot off the end of his bat belonged in a pool hall. The ball flared off the end of his bat to shallow left field. Shortstop Gil McDougald and third baseman Tony Kubek chased the ball, but it dropped behind them and in front of Enos Slaughter. Adcock was slow, but it was enough for him to score from second, giving the Braves a 3–2 lead, and sending Pafko to third. Stengel's annoyance multiplied when Kubek, the Milwaukee-born Yankee rookie, let Slaughter's return throw get past him. Pafko alertly scored and Covington charged all the way to third on Kubek's error to make it 4–2. Well, whadayaknow. The Yankees had proven they could make a mistake just like the next guy. The relief in the Braves dugout was palpable. Stengel huffed out to the mound, his cleats dragging the dirt as he went, to remove Shantz and call for Ditmar. Before Stengel left the mound, he issued an order.

Del Crandall was waiting, followed by Lew Burdette. Crandall had been very solid and could hurt the Yankees with one swing—he hit 15 home runs during the '57 regular season—and the Yankees had a base open. Ditmar threw high, knocking Crandall down. That was a clear warning from Casey Stengel, who thought Crandall was loading the ball for Burdette. There were jeers from the Braves bench and no emotion from Ditmar. Crandall said he didn't think Ditmar threw at him, but that was just the kind of pro Crandall was—what went on between the lines, stayed between the lines. "If he did, what's the difference?" Crandall said.

After Ditmar finished the top of the inning with no further damage, Burdette strutted back to the mound like a new man. He had a 4–2 lead and he intended to make it stand up, especially if that meant making a Yankee lay down. He struck out Enos Slaughter to begin the inning, bringing Harry Simpson to the plate. Burdette returned the favor for knocking his catcher down and threw high. Simpson hit the dirt. "I guess it looked like a knockdown party was starting," Burdette said.

The Yanks bench was all over him, but Lew loved it. He dared them to come out and carry him off the mound. He taunted them with cries of "Here comes a spitter!" when the ball was clearly dry, at least so far. He sneered and swore and smirked and smiled, and every move was intended to drive a stake through Casey's heart. Jocko Conlan, the venerable and vaudevillian National League umpire working the plate, maintained order by ignoring protesting players. He had once been a ballplayer, too, and he knew players whined. Jocko didn't play that game. He ruled ballgames like a Pharaoh. He never permitted players to climb all over him. Everybody knew Jocko didn't give a shit about the concerns of mere mortals. He let the boys be boys and made it known they were not larger than the game. Burdette bowed to Pharaoh, rolled him the ball, and then pitched out of the bottom of the fourth unscathed.

When Logan led off the top of the fifth, Ditmar did everything short of licking a stamp onto the baseball and airmailing the first pitch into his crazy bone. The pitch hurt like a bitch and might have been retaliation for St. Jude's home run, but the feisty Logan wasn't going to charge the mound, insisting, "I wasn't mad, I was happy to get on base." Besides, it was not wise to upset the Pharaoh. Mathews promptly hit into a double play, prolonging his miserable slump to start the Series. He hadn't done a damn thing and it was bothering him.

It brought Aaron to the plate with two out and the bases empty. Even a road apple baseball fan could guess that Henry would pay the price for Burdette's bull. Sure enough, Aaron hit the dirt when Ditmar came high-and-tight. Henry stood up and let it be known he would never be intimidated. "It didn't bother me," Henry said. He then meekly popped to first baseman Simpson, to end the inning, "Intentional or not."

Nobody could question Burdette's devotion to protecting his teammates when his first pitch dusted Jerry Coleman to start the fifth inning. The message was sent. Burdette was the big bopper in this knockdown party. Coleman didn't even glare at Burdette. Both teams sensed runs were too valuable to pick a fight. Coleman dusted himself off and settled down to draw a leadoff walk. But Casey Stengel wasn't happy. When Hank Bauer stepped in the box moments later, Stengel barked from his bench. He wanted Bauer to have Conlan check the ball. Jocko was completely annoyed. Casey was holding up the game; Bauer offered his apologies; Lew looked in the dugout with a satisfied smirk. Checking him only made him stronger. As far as he was concerned, when you tried to undress him, he had you down to the jockstrap.

The score remained 4–2 in the bottom of the sixth when the big bopper ran into a jam. He lost Mickey Mantle on a full-count leadoff walk. Burdette jawed at Jocko, who ripped off his mask to reveal his square Irish features and whiskey smooth voice. The cleft in his chin was deep enough to open a bottle of beer. His jaw was as durable as his fists. The Pharaoh told Lew to shut up and pitch. Fred Haney didn't like what he saw, but he didn't argue. Instead, he pointed to the Braves bullpen, and Juan Pizarro and Gene Conley quickly heated up. The thought of coming out of the game infuriated Burdette. One time, when Haney came to the mound to take him out of a game, Burdette said, "You got anybody better out there in the pen?" Haney looked at him and said, "No, but maybe I got someone luckier." Lew was convinced he was lucky and good. He wasn't going to give into the Yanks and he sure as hell wasn't going to give the ball back to Haney.

The trouble was Yogi Berra was at the plate. Like Eddie Mathews, Yogi was overdue in the first two games. He had only a single in five at-bats. Burdette wanted a ground ball and that's what he got, but it was hit fast enough to have tail fins. Yet, first baseman Joe Adcock handled the ball with ease. He aimed at his roommate Johnny Logan's glove and hit the target to force Mantle at second. Mick got up slowly and everyone in the ballpark could see he was hurting. He jammed his shoulder on the play. Yogi wished he had gotten a hit out of the deal but at least he was on first base. The force play proved pivotal moments later when Enos Slaughter hit a ball down the left-field line, past the diving Mathews, sending Yogi rumbling to third. Burdette had himself quite a mess—runners at second and third with only one out and two good hitters, Harry Simpson and Tony Kubek, coming up.

There was no letup in the Yankee lineup. Everybody could hurt you. At age thirty-one, Simpson was the veteran of more games than he could count, but he still had enough power to be dangerous. He took a long swing but missed most of the ball, nudging a slow roller toward third. Mathews had no chance to get to the ball. He was playing deep and guarding the line. Burdette knew he had the only chance. He sprinted off the mound and barehanded the ball, looked the runners back, and fired as hard as he could to first base, nipping Simpson by a step. But he wasn't out of the shadows until Kubek hit a grasshopper to second base. Red Schoendienst charged and made the play look easier than anyone had a right to, nipping Kubek for the final out of the inning. As Burdette walked off the mound, the players thought they heard something strange. There were cheers from the Braves fans in the far reaches of the stadium, but there was also a scattering of nearby applause. The players were perplexed. Could some Yankee fans actually be rooting for the Braves?

Burdette wasn't ready to tip his cap quite yet. He might not have had invincible stuff, but his resolve was untouchable. His sinkers and sliders gained more movement, flustering the Yanks. In the seventh inning, Burdette threw a fastball past Hank Bauer for a strike. Bauer couldn't believe he missed the pitch. He was a fastball hitter, but this fastball had extra late life. Bauer asked Jocko Conlan to inspect the ball. Jocko was annoyed, but he wondered if his own eyes were fooling him, too. Low strikes were the hardest pitches to call. When Conlan inspected the ball, there were no cuts, no scuffmarks, no traces of spit or jelly or pine tar. The ball was dry and the surface clean. All Jocko could do was toss the ball back to the magician.

Lew gingerly went back to his routine—take the sign, tug the bill of his hat, run his fingers past his lips, stall, pick up the resin bag, and let it dance between his finger and thumb, ample time to dry off any moisture. Bauer ended up popping up to short. Red Smith called Burdette's true talent, "an actor's gift for stirring up enemy suspicion."

But perhaps the Yankees had complained too much. In the eighth inning, there was more applause as Burdette prepared to face the heart of the order. This time, it was clearly field level, where the Yankee fans sat. Maybe it wasn't for the Braves—maybe it was for another blonde, this one, "in a form-fitting white dress," who "wiggled her way through the aisles along the first base side to the accompaniment of wolf whistles," the *Pittsburgh Post-Gazette* noted. Maybe it was another Marilyn looking for her Joe, but Red Smith wasn't sold. Was it the blonde or was it the Braves? He sensed the Yankee fans growing tired . . . of the Yankees. In all his years, he had never seen that. He had the feeling that "the majority of the people in the stands wanted someone else to win."

If the Yankee fans felt that way, their ballplayers didn't. They wanted their money. They didn't care if you were sick of them beating up on the world or not. And if this goofball junk dealer beat them with his antics, then so be it. The Yankees would take the train to Milwaukee and kick the crap out of the Braves for all of the Midwest to see. All of the world would watch that beating, from Tokyo, perhaps, all the way to Moscow.

But the Yankees wouldn't give away Game 2 until the bitter end, and in the ninth inning, they kicked again. Clinging to a two-run lead with his pitch count well past hundred, Burdette gave up a one-out single to Tony Kubek. Stengel sent up left-handed pinch hitter Joe Collins to bat for Coleman. Burdette loved to face a guy who had been sitting on the bench, and he popped him up to short for the second out. The Braves were one out away from tying the Series, but Elston Howard complicated matters. He hit a hard line ground ball up the middle, seemingly destined for center field, enough to get Kubek to third.

But Johnny Logan ranged to his left and dove for the ball. St. Jude must have stayed with him. Logan knocked the ball down and kept it in the infield. It didn't prevent Howard's single, but it kept runners off the corners. It was a typical Logan play—a hugely valuable yet inglorious moment. "Johnny's a clutch man," Aaron said. "That play is overlooked. If Howard's ball gets past him, things look a lot darker for us."

Casey Stengel wanted speed on the bases so he put Bobby Richardson in as a pinch runner. That left Hank Bauer, the ballroom dancing pitchman, coming to the plate. He was 1-for-4 with a little bit of everything—a strikeout, a home run, a ground ball, and a pop-up.

Burdette was a card dealer on the mound—would he throw overhand, three-quarters or side arm? Would it be a sinker or a slider? Would it be a fastball? A spitball? Bauer didn't know, but he was certain that Burdette wouldn't throw him a curveball. He hadn't seen one from him and all the Yankee scouts indicated that Lew never threw one. Bauer settled in ready for whatever was waiting for him, but he was pretty sure it wasn't going to be a curve. Burdette had thrown 120 pitches. No curveballs. So what did Burdette throw him? A goddamn curveball! Bauer was so unsettled that all he could do was hit a bouncer to short. There was Johnny Logan, who fielded, flipped to Red for the force, and the Braves had a 4–2 victory.

Burdette ran to Crandall to get a great big bear hug. The Braves were in business. They had a victory in New York and they were coming home with the series tied. The Braves were right—there were New York fans cheering for them. Perhaps Midwest baseball fever had spread to the Bronx. Or perhaps the young fan that swiped the hat off Burdette's head wanted to take away his good luck charm. Burdette didn't take that lightly. He grabbed the kid and ripped his hat right back. Then he headed to the locker room to let the High Life flow.

The writers found Lew a few minutes later freshly showered and rubbing aftershave onto his chin. He masterfully downplayed the significance of the victory. "I'd just as soon beat Cleveland," he said. He was asked if he was intentionally knocking down the Yanks. "That's a regular part of baseball," he informed the reporter, before cautioning, "if something like that happens, I guess they should know we can be as good at it as they are."

That was the significance of the victory for the Braves. It meant the Yanks were not gods. They played shoddy defense and were baffled by a guy they gave away. "Those errors show they're like everyone else," Burdette said. "What are they supposed to be—superhuman? Well, they're not."

The Braves were heroes in Milwaukee, where the fans were already partying and planning another parade even as Fred Haney gave the New York writers a hard time and kept his eye out for that jerk who asked him if his team was going to choke. The Braves had turned downright feisty. "They found out we can beat them," Logan said. "We're going to win, that's all there is to it, because we've got a better team than they have," Schoendienst said. The New York writers couldn't believe the Yankees could beat themselves. "They aren't supposed to do that, not ever," the *Post* wrote. The writers implied there was no way Burdette could win on the level.

But Casey Stengel never said Burdette threw a spitball. He hated to lose, but he knew when he had been beaten. He said Burdette reminded him of Bob Lemon, a seven-time twenty-game winner for the Cleveland

Indians. "He's got the same sharp sinker," Stengel said. "We figured we'd get him before the finish, but we couldn't. He had us beating the ball in the dirt. You gotta give him credit. He knows how to pitch."

Burdette was very satisfied, but he didn't dare let on how happy he was to win. "I have no malice against them," he said, but he was determined to prove that Stengel and the Yankees screwed up when they buried him six years ago. One win was nice. He wanted another. "Don't make it like I hate them," he said. "They treated me right when they sent me here. The Braves were building and I got a chance to pitch. Anyway, I'd rather play in Milwaukee than in New York."

The Braves couldn't agree more and couldn't wait to get out of town, partly because New York City was teeming with the flu virus. There were 5,729 cases reported a day in October and more than 16,000 stricken in a week. The 1957 Milwaukee Braves were the first team to travel to and from the World Series by airplane. They would be home in Milwaukee in a few hours and sleep in their own beds tonight, and they hoped the flu bug wasn't coming home with them. The Yanks were still in the Stone Age—they would roll into Wisconsin on rail on the first scheduled travel day in a World Series since 1948. It was a murderous all-nighter, and by the time the Yanks rolled into the Heartland, there was no guarantee Casey Stengel would be in a good mood.

13

Games 3 and 4   **WELCOME TO BUSHVILLE**

The world was changing during the 1957 World Series. As the Braves flew from New York following Game 2 to bring the Series home to Milwaukee for the first time, the Soviet Union made final plans to launch the first pitch of its own. One had to wonder if the Kremlin was following the Braves and Yankees, or perhaps if the Soviet ambassador to the United Nations reported that there was a rare travel day scheduled during the World Series. What a magnificent opportunity for a headline grab. Their propaganda device looked archaic and nonthreatening by future standards—a silver globe the size of a basketball with antennas attached that emitted an innocent-sounding signal, as crude and rudimentary as the first known baseball from 1854. That sphere, rough shaped and without seams, was marked NY KNICKERBOCKERS BASEBALL CLUB, abbreviated to B.B.C. This ball was marked U.S.S.R.

The first man-made low-orbit satellite had a strange-sounding name to most Americans, but when Sputnik went up a few hours after the Braves touched the tarmac to 10,000 fans at Mitchell Field and another 200,000 fans crowding the streets awaiting another parade, a new era had begun. Warren Spahn shoved Lew Burdette out of the plane first. He stuck his head out the door and was greeted by thunderous applause, flashbulbs, and newsreel crews. Burdette shrugged his shoulders, figured the hell with it, and blew kisses to the crowd. The High Life was flowing cold as the Cold War warmed up, the space race was on the horizon and millions of Americans cranked their necks to the heavens. But all Milwaukee wanted was a glimpse of the Braves.

The Yankees lagged behind, traveling by train, as though it was 1937 and not 1957. The long trip gave Casey Stengel time to ponder his future and past. Milton Gross of the *Post* believed Stengel, at age sixty-seven, desperately wanted to beat the Braves because it would tie him with Joe McCarthy—not the recently deceased former Wisconsin senator and anti-communist crusader, but rather the former New York Yankees manager—with seven World Series crowns. Stengel was returning to Milwaukee for the first time in thirteen years and he thought he would never have to come back here again. His vision of Milwaukee was set in the summer of 1944, when he took over the American Association Brewers in May for popular manager Charlie Grimm, who briefly took the Cubs job for the second time. The Brewers still played at old Borchert Field, a wooden time traveler from the Victorian age, a ballpark with the feel of a high school diamond, where local homes protruded behind the one-level grandstand.

Back then, Stengel was considered by many to be a washed-out former big league manager with good jokes and bad judgment. But he led the Brewers to 102 wins, their best record in years, and the town warmed up to him. Casey had forgotten how Milwaukee could love a guy and how much the town had done for his own baseball career. The '44 Brewers drew 235,840 fans, a good achievement in the war years, and his success in the field and box office helped revive his career. Stengel's season with the Brewers helped him land the Oakland Oaks job in 1946. After three successful seasons and a Pacific Coast League championship in 1948, he was hired as Yankees manager in 1949, succeeding McCarthy, inheriting his talent-laden team, and launching the New York baseball dynasty.

But as Stengel steamed to Milwaukee, he had forgotten where he came from. Borchert Field had long ago gone to ballpark heaven, where Ebbets Field and the Polo Grounds would soon be joining it. Otto Borchert, the former Brewers owner who had once promised a pennant and then dropped dead of a heart attack, was a distant memory when the New York Yankees and the former manager of the Milwaukee Brewers came to town for the World Series.

The sixteen-hour, 1,100-mile train ride was a haul, but the Yankee ballplayers didn't seem terribly worried. It was a huge traveling party of 160, comprised of players, staff and reporters. All of Casey's fellas were playing cards, having a few beers, and having a good time. Yogi, Mick, Whitey, and the boys were shooting the shit as the day turned into night. They thought Burdette was loading the ball, but they couldn't prove it. "I'll swear the ball almost exploded in Crandall's glove once," Hank Bauer said. Somebody asked Yogi if he ever faced a spitball pitcher. Yogi beamed and shrugged his shoulders. "They tell me I did today," he said. But he wasn't worried very much. "The loss to the Braves was a temporary red light in their date with destiny," the *Pittsburgh Post-Gazette* reported. Gil McDougald liked the Braves, calling them a team with "well-distributed power and excellent pitching," but Bauer was more blunt. "We're still going to win," he promised.

The Yankees stopped in Chicago for breakfast a few hours before rolling into the train station at Sturtevant, about twenty miles South of Milwaukee. The New York writers found the Sturtevant name to be amusing for the close similarity between the name of the town and Yankee lefty Tom Sturdivant, who was scheduled to be the starting pitcher in Game 4. Sturtevant was the train stop closest to the resort in Brown's Lake, where the team was staying. The natives found it odd that the Yanks were not staying downtown like every other team. It made them wonder if the Yanks thought they were too good to stay in Milwaukee. The story was that the Yankees traveling secretary got lost downtown the year before and ended up in Brown's Lake, about thirty miles southwest. He saw a golfing and drinking paradise where the sirloin was medium rare, perfect for the pinstripes.

The curiosity ended when the Yankees peered out their windows and were stunned to see a crowd of about two thousand excited Wisconsin fans. A large WELCOME YANKS banner hung in the train station and many other fans held homemade signs. The big city ballplayers were amused but disinterested. The St. Catherine High School band of Racine played a choppy "The Sidewalks of New York," followed by a vigorous "On Wisconsin." A little league team, bravely called the Yankees, awaited a glimpse. Abe Kirkorian, the village president, took time off from his job at a Racine machine shop to lead the greeting party. The volunteer fire fighters shined their silver badges. There was a seventy-one-year-old farmer, Adolf Kutsner, wearing overalls and a straw hat. He brought his cow, Rosie, to the train station and invited the Yanks to milk her for all she was worth. After all, you can't come to the dairy land and not learn to milk a cow. He was standing with a photographer and held a sign reading, C'MON OUT! WE GOT A COW FOR YOU TO MILK!

Inside the train, Yogi deadpanned, "Hey Mick, they got a guy from Commerce here to see you!" a reference to Mantle's hometown and his country-bumpkin roots. Mick was amused, but after an all-nighter, he was in no mood. "Tell the guy to bring the cow in here," he drawled. Whitey Ford slipped out of the car for a moment to greet the kids in Yankee uniforms, but that was the extent of the outreach program.

The Yankees weren't in New York anymore. They had been hoping to get off the train to stretch their legs, but the local hicks were more than they wanted to deal with and something they had never experienced. "The New York Yankees—the big boys from Broadway—are not accustomed to such treatment," the *New York Morning Telegraph* reported. "In New York, they are accepted as one segment of the city's idle replete with great theatres, museums, educational institutions, and manufacture. New Yorkers regard them within the context of a great town." After all, the Yankees had twenty-three pennants and Milwaukee had . . . a milk cow?

There was no use in trying to make the village's day, so the city slickers dumped the women and children, told them to take cabs to the resort, and decided to continue onto the Milwaukee train station, where they would board buses to go to County Stadium for a workout. "A groan of disappointment swept the crowd, along with some choicer epithets," the *Sentinel* reported. A local business owner shouted for the Yanks to at least let a player step off the train to say few words to the crowd, but a club official shouted back, "Not a chance." The welcoming warmth quickly turned a sour brew. "I hope you lose—and you're going to!" the fan bellowed back. Casey Stengel forgot that snubbing Wisconsin courtesy was a Cardinal sin. The Yanks big leagued the businessman, the band, the little leaguers, and the farmer, although Edna Stengel did try to make nice and milk Rosie once the Yanks rolled away. Nobody had ever seen a woman wearing a mink coat try to milk a cow. She gave Rosie a good squeeze but the cow wouldn't put out. The crowd gave her a hand anyway. You can't blame the cow for stage fright. They were not as forgiving to her husband.

When the train stopped in Milwaukee, a polite crowd of about three hundred waited, including the formal welcoming committee of Albert Davis, Mayor Frank Ziedler's deputy, District Attorney William J. McCauley, and Circuit Judge Robert Cannon, who swore he knew Casey from his days managing the Brewers. But Casey was annoyed. He didn't have time for this small-town stuff. Three buses were waiting to take the Yanks to County Stadium. He wanted everybody moving fast. The crowd called his name, but Casey was crabby, and there was no compromise. The ballplayers followed orders, hurrying from the train to the buses, shunning the fans, walking like stoic soldiers.

They plopped in the bus and laughed at the glossy "Milwaukee, USA" chamber of commerce magazines placed on each seat. The wise-ass sarcastic ballplayer remarks flew. "Milwaukee USA?" the *Daily Mirror* quoted one ballplayer. "I thought this place was supposed to be out of this world." Another ballplayer joked that the Yanks shouldn't complain. This was high class! "See, here we get a pretty magazine on every seat. In New York, you're lucky if you can find one lousy old newspaper."

Meanwhile, the locals were stunned at Casey's callousness. The face of the Yankees was big leaguing them. It reminded folks of the time Eddie Stanky blew off the Braves when the team moved from Boston in 1953, but worse. The locals were shocked that the Yankees were too Broadway to so much as say hello to Wisconsin.

But Davis and Cannon didn't give up easily. They began boarding each of the three buses until they picked the winner with the ballplayers aboard. When they found the team bus, they announced they were looking for Stengel, who was hiding in the middle aisle and slouching in his seat instead of sitting upright in the front row as managers customarily do. Gil McDougald, Casey's snarky street-smart shortstop, shouted, "He ain't here! He's too old to make trips with the club!"

Cannon, in particular, wouldn't give up. After all, him and Casey were old buddies, right? The least Case could do was come out and pose for a photograph. Finally, Cannon found Stengel, who looked mad. "We gotta get to the park," Casey groused. If he stopped to say hello to everyone he knew from his days managing the Brewers, the Yanks would never make it to County Stadium. When a Yankee official boarded the bus and found Cannon begging Stengel to come outside, enough was enough. The bus aisle was jammed with reporters and photographers. Yankee officials wanted everyone off the bus and they began pushing and shoving. Before they kicked him off the bus, Davis shouted, "Gentleman, whether you know it or not, you've been welcomed to Milwaukee!"

Then came the words that fired up Milwaukee and became the battle cry that rattled the heartland. Some attributed the words to Stengel himself, but it didn't matter if he said it or not. His actions said it all. Some attributed to the words to coach Charlie Keller. Some thought it was trainer Gus Mauch. Another leading candidate for the deed would have been Bill McCorry, the traveling secretary, a crony of Stengel and GM George Weiss, and a former player and scout whose claim to fame as an ivory hunter was the 1947 signing of a right-handed pitcher from the University of Virginia named Lew Burdette. "This is bush league!" the Yank official said.

Bush league. It was the greatest snub of all to a city, a state, and a region—an insult to underdogs everywhere, a bully's punch. It was made worse in that it came from the bus carrying the high-and-mighty New York Yankees, who would not even deign to grace downtown Milwaukee with their presence. The story moved on the AP wire nationwide within a few hours. The press was all over Stengel, who fumed that the team bus needed a police escort just to escape the train station. "Don't start anything," he insisted, but the beer had already spilled. The next day, while the rest of the country was worried about going to sleep under the light of a Soviet moon, Milwaukee refused to sleep under the light of a Stengel moon. They would not be insulted or intimidated. YANKS IGNORE 'BUSH LEAGUERS' was the *Journal's* headline on October 5, the morning of Game 3. It was one of the biggest days in Milwaukee history and Casey Stengel had given the entire city a huge vendetta. The next three games would be the longest days of his career. Milwaukee made it their mission to ruin him, to torment him, and they wanted their Braves to sweep the Yankees in Milwaukee and take the World Series title in front of the most loyal fans in America. Casey was public enemy number one. Have you see this man? Bow-legged, craggy, cranky curmudgeon with six World Series rings and an air of superiority, scrooge in spikes.

Stengel refused to recognize or acknowledge that he had hurt Milwaukee's feelings. In doing so, he intensified the insult. He was more upset that the Yanks were inconvenienced. "Do you have a parade before practice?" he asked. You did if you played for the Braves, but Casey was no diplomat, and that was your problem, not his. "That's silly," he said. "There's nothing wrong with what we did."

But in the eyes of Milwaukee, there was. Casey spat in Wisconsin's eye and they were coming to get him with pitchforks, torches, baseball bats, and beer bottles. Packers and Badgers and Braves, oh my! Young Bobby Uecker was back home for the winter after his minor league season. "I mean, it was already unbelievable," Uecker recalled. "That made it even better. For whatever reason, he said that. I mean it really enraged the people when the Yankees came here to play. Casey Stengel called Milwaukee Bushville or whatever he called it. It made it funny. The fans were aggravated about it, because he said it and then he tried to back off. But Casey didn't give a shit. He didn't give a shit about anything. Fuck, he was taking meals on wheels, what did he care? He didn't give a shit what he said. He was asleep half the time."

The Milwaukee writers came after Stengel, too. The Milwaukee fans were downright hospitable, but calling them bush was unforgivable. "The people had a right to resent everything implied by that bush crack," Lloyd Larson wrote in the *Sentinel*. "Bush can mean many things, like hicks, dopes, nitwits, clowns, and inferiors."

Milwaukee took Bushville as its dual identity—if they were Bushville, then the rest of baseball ought to strive to be like Bushville, too. Bushville drew ten million fans over five seasons, an unprecedented attendance record. If Milwaukee was Bushville—brawling, beer swigging, screwball, spitballing, bar-stool buddies, and no, they *don't* play "Roll Out the Barrel" at Yankee Stadium—then maybe baseball needed more Bushvilles—more passion, more fun, more tailgating, more fans staying longer, more beer flowing togetherness, more dancing in the aisles. Welcome to Bushville, Mr. Stengel, enjoy your stay in Milwaukee, USA.

The town hated Stengel for all he represented—that New York could step all over Milwaukee, the big guy could bully the little man—and Casey didn't give a shit. He bitched to his writers, the same ones the Yanks toted out in first class on the team train. Dick Young did Case's dirty work for him, his own superiority complex on display, writing in the *New York Daily News*, that Milwaukee fans "are provincial people out here. They are proud of their Braves, who have given them the illusory feeling of being 'Big League,' and they resent all others." But Dan Parker in the *Daily Mirror* realized that no matter what Stengel said, the power of the Wisconsin people could not be underestimated. He was critical of Stengel's behavior, but he still worshipped him. He thought baseball would be better if more towns treated their teams the way Milwaukee or Madison or Green Bay did. "Maybe Milwaukee is bush by big league standards," he admitted, "But if there were more cities like it, big league baseball wouldn't be as bush as it has become in recent years." He also admitted, "It is almost impossible to believe how deeply hurt all here felt by the unthinking slur."

On the bus ride from the train station to County Stadium, the Yankees witnessed firsthand the way Milwaukee felt about this team. The city was wall-to-wall Braves. Storefronts pushed out their regular merchandise to create shrines. Big cardboard Indians decorated the flagpoles on Wisconsin Avenue, and bunting and pennants were decorated everywhere. Lou Perini paid the bill for the city's decorations because he believed the taxpayers had done enough to help his boys. The team erected two big thirty-foot tall tee-pees above the main entrances to the ballpark. A line of tens of thousands snaked around the stadium hoping to get one of only a few thousand standing-room-only tickets. Many fans had been camping in line for days. Retailers took out full-page newspaper ads to wish the Braves luck. All the people wore Braves gear and all they talked about was Milwaukee Braves baseball.

During the workout day, the Braves privately hoped the city hadn't shaken the Yankee hive, though you'd never know it by watching Mickey

Mantle. He walked around the field with a phony Braves arrow through his head. His shoulder, knees, and ankles were getting worse and Milwaukee's cold weather wasn't helping. Moose Skowron's bad back was so stiff he could barely swing. Casey expounded Stengelese: he said he had enough depth and flexibility to survive the injuries. A New York writer who had never met Bob Buhl asked him how he would fare as the Game 3 starting pitcher. Buhl wanted to kick the crap out of the guy. "There's no better fastball-hitting team than the Dodgers," he seethed. "And I beat them twelve times in two years." The Milwaukee fans even came out for the workout day, which was open to the public, and allowed many of them without tickets a chance to see the boys in person. Such devotion and warmth continued to break down jaded New York hacks, like Ken Smith of the *Daily Mirror,* who wrote, "The Yankees have beaten everybody and have seen about everything, but not quite. They have yet to come in contact with the Milwaukee fan and there aren't any others like him." Smith seemed culture-shocked. He sought Warren Spahn, who explained to him how, "the most solid guy couldn't help but be affected by the intensity of the Wisconsin people."

Some Braves ballplayers reacted differently than others to the Bushville remark. For example, it was all business in the hours before Game 3 for Red Schoendienst and Henry Aaron. "As far as Bushville or whatever they were calling us, that's mostly the press, you know," Schoendienst said. "You just throw that aside and try to do your job."

Henry was completely locked in. He wanted to perform and he wanted to win, and he had the ability to brush aside name calling. "I think it was a nonfactor for me, really, more than anything," Henry said. "I mean, we were playin' the New York Yankees and somebody happened to say 'Bushville,' or said something, and it just caught on, it wasn't really givin' Milwaukee enough respect. You know I don't think there was that much to it."

In Henry's batter's box, there wasn't much to it. But outside of it, there was. What was said in the outside world about any subject, anywhere, any time, simply didn't factor into the equation of Henry versus the pitcher. Hitters like Henry had the right of way. They could view the world the way they wanted to, because nobody could hit the way they could. But for the ballplayers who fed off the fans' emotions, Bushville was a lightning rod. "When that came out, I think it angered all of us," Del Crandall said. "It just kept us at a peak, emotionally, where we just weren't going to get beat."

There were, however, a great many distractions to throw aside. The morning edition of the *Sentinel* said it all: Today We Make History! The gates opened at 10:30 A.M. for a 1 P.M. start and the seats filled quickly. Tickets were nearly impossible to come by. When somebody called from Minneapolis begging Braves PR man Donald Davidson for a ticket, he replied, "Listen, buddy, I could get you into the starting lineup easier than I could get you into the ballpark." The only guy who could get into the ballpark at the last minute, President Eisenhower, declined an invitation, indirectly citing the Sputnik and Little Rock crises. License plates from Wisconsin, Minnesota, Michigan, Iowa, Illinois, Indiana, and Ohio were spotted among the nearly 12,000 cars in the County Stadium parking lot. Makeshift bleachers upon the knoll in right field, nicknamed "Mockingbird Hill," were packed. Two large television towers were erected by NBC for the broadcast. The team installed one hundred additional telegraph lines and created makeshift darkrooms in the basement. The media overflow had never been seen before. Only the Milwaukee guys got their regular seats. Fans snapped up World Series programs for fifty cents a copy and saved them as family heirlooms. Inside the program were congratulatory notes from the Schlitz, Pabst, and Blatz brewing companies, but the back-cover ad in full color was reserved for Miller High Life, the "national champion of quality," brewed *"ONLY* IN MILWAUKEE, WISCONSIN," just like Milwaukee's passion for the Braves and the bitter beer face reserved for Stengel and the Yanks.

The Braves were robustly cheered and the Yankees were lustily booed. The Yankees didn't have to do a damn thing to be booed—when they walked on the field, they took the heat. The Braves players were shocked. They had never heard such vitriol from Milwaukee fans. "I mean, it was ridiculous," Frank Torre said. "Those were the greatest fans in the world and they never booed *anybody*. They were so kind to everybody. Of course, the home players were gods, but when those comments came out about

Bushville, USA, and all this kind of stuff and how inferior, and what are we doin' here type of thing, that really inflamed the people. He really made the comment, whether he was kidding or not, I don't know, but it was a big help. It was electricity at the ballpark. It was one of the few times I ever heard booing toward Casey Stengel."

The animosity grated Stengel. The fans were yelling at him constantly with Bushville inspired catcalls. It was a new feeling for him to be treated as a villain instead of a warm funnyman. Milwaukee's hatred revealed a darker side of his personality New Yorkers rarely saw. Bob Cooke, a reporter for the *Herald-Tribune,* overheard Stengel yelling at his players to, "belt their brains out." Casey was a cutup, but he had a mean streak. He wanted to rip the shit out of the Braves and he wanted to shut the fans up. His best revenge would be for the Yanks to sweep the three games in Milwaukee and shove New York's Eighteenth World Championship down their throats, so he could look forward to another parade down Canyon of Heroes in New York City, the only good place for a parade in his book, and read his writers celebrate the accomplishment of tying Joe McCarthy as the greatest Yankee manager of all time. He longed to turn Bushville into a phrase Milwaukee regretted putting in his mouth. As Dan Parker warned before Game 3, "A Stengel scorned is a Casey to beware." It didn't take long for the Yankees to execute Stengel's demands.

Bob Buhl got his brains beaten out and gave up three runs before Fred Haney shoved the meat hook in his back and pulled him out of the game in the first inning, already trailing 3–0. Buhl had his fastball, but he had no clue where the hell it was going. Tony Kubek, the twenty-year-old Milwaukee boy, pulled a home run to right field, where the wind was blowing out. So what if he was from Milwaukee. Not even his own family was rooting for the Yankees. He trotted the bases in dead silence. Buhl also walked Mantle and Berra, then gave up a sacrifice fly and a run-scoring single, and Haney had it. Buhl was incredibly pissed. A fan told his wife that childbirth was easier than watching him pitch. Eddie Mathews, as usual, was the only guy who could console Buhl. Nobody knows how many beers it took to bring the former paratrooper back to earth.

The Yanks kept on coming and beat up on the bullpen. They flexed their power. They took the capacity crowd of 45,804 out of the game. The Milwaukee fans didn't move a muscle. There were boos and grumbles, but mostly uncomfortable silence. The Yanks got two more in the third and two more in the fourth when Mantle launched a home run to right field to make the score 7–1. Casey wasn't too patient with his starting pitcher, Bob Turley, and yanked him after he walked four in less than two innings.

His replacement, Don Larsen, was having a pretty good year. He threw a perfect game in the World Series in '56 and was planning to marry a stewardess after the '57 Series. He was lights out the rest of the way, though Henry Aaron hit a two-run home run against him in the fifth inning. It seemed fitting that Aaron hit the first World Series home run in County Stadium, but it was nothing more than a footnote. Henry trimmed the lead to 7–3, but the Yanks blew the game open with five runs in the seventh. Three walks, followed by Hank Bauer's two-run single and Kubek's second home run of the game, a three-run shot, turned out the lights inside the teepee. The local burghers were so angry at the hometown kid that people drove their cars past his boyhood home, threw trash out the window and made harassing phone calls to the residence. Kubek even claimed a cross was burned on the front lawn. It didn't help that the *Sentinel* ran the kid's family address in the morning paper. Final score: Yanks 12, Braves 3. The Yanks led the Series, 2–1. On Saturday night, the Yankees partied. On Sunday morning, the Braves prayed.

Faith and this team were quiet partners. From the prayer cards Fred Haney received in the mail, to Johnny Logan muttering a prayer at Yankee Stadium, to the Negro League manager who once called Henry Aaron a miracle, to the Franciscan missionary priest from Wisconsin who was a guest of Lou Perini and his family during the World Series, divine intervention was seen as the body and blood of Braves baseball. On Sunday morning, while the Yankees slept off the celebration and bused to County Stadium past fans taunting them with cries of Bushville, the Braves ballplayers, regardless of denomination, attended a service and joined together for meditation. There were Catholics, Lutherans, Protestants, Baptists, and even a Mormon (Nippy Jones). They were all in this together. Baseball wise, they needed to win Game 4 to stay in the Series. And if they were to lose, perhaps not even a miracle would save them.

The Braves weren't worshipping alone. Across Wisconsin that Sunday morning, worshippers of all congregations prayed for them. "Braves fans aren't ashamed to admit they pray for their team," the *Sentinel* wrote. Lou Perini, never baptized but deeply spiritual, prayed on his knees at night. Even the New Yorkers were struck by Wisconsin's devotion. "They are spectacular in their faith," *Post* columnist Jimmy Cannon observed. He noticed the articles of faith published in the Milwaukee papers. There were plentiful references to Milwaukee's "Burning Bush." The hardened metro columnist got the feeling that New York should respect this passion, even if dramatically different from its own.

Warren Spahn closed his eyes in front of one altar and a few hours later opened them standing atop another. It was Sunday, October 6. He had pitched more Sunday games at County Stadium than he could possibly remember, but this was the biggest of them all. He swung his arms into his windup, his big leg kick poking a hole in the clouds, with the shiny tip of his polished black cleat scraping the sky, and from the first pitch, he had his stuff. Pinpoint fastballs, late sinkers, low screwballs, down and in, down and away, never down the middle, never up and away, never up and in. He changed looks on different looks, but before the afternoon was over, Milwaukee's faith would be tested as never before.

Spahn gave up a run in the first inning on a two-out single to Gil McDougald, but settled into a calm and aggressive streak, retiring eleven Yanks in a row. Then the Braves answered prayers when they scored four runs for Spahn in the fourth inning against one of Casey's favorite fellas, lefty Tom Sturdivant, a guy he called "my dipsy-doodler." But Sturdivant didn't dipsy and he didn't doodle. He walked Johnny Logan, to lead off the fourth. That brought up Eddie Mathews. He was having an awful Series, 0-for-8, and he wasn't hitting anything hard. A superstitious Pittsburgh sportswriter, Les Biederman, stuck three pennies in Eddie's back pocket before the game. Usually, Eddie would think to beat the shit out of a sportswriter looking at him funny before a game, but Biederman was a National League guy, so that helped his cause, and he explained to Eddie how he tried the three-penny trick with Pirates sluggers Ralph Kiner and Frank Thomas to great success. Eddie might have asked Les if he was touching those guys' asses, too, but Eddie was feeling so shitty about his at-bats that he was generally willing to try anything. Hell, he even let the clubhouse kids, Charlie Blossfield and Paul Wick, apply a generous amount of black shoe polish to his cleats, just like they did for everyone else. When the Braves lined up for the national anthem before the game, they looked like tap dancers. It was for good luck and plus it made you look snazzy. Eddie was all for that.

Eddie was on his best behavior during the series, but perhaps the karma from his rubber-snake gag with Logan after Game 1 was taking a bite out of his production. His mother was in the stands, as was his high school coach, who proudly boasted that he had been smart enough not to touch his swing. But nobody was harder on Eddie than Eddie. He bitched himself out before the game. He couldn't live with himself if he couldn't help his team win. Hell, he would even pray. If God could cure a slump, by all means, Eddie needed all the help he could get. The calluses on his hands had opened up and his blisters were killing him. He decided to use Joe Adcock's bat, which he had occasionally done during the season. It was 35 inches, 32 ounces, the same as his, but Eddie liked the feel of Joe's 35-32. He felt like the weight of the bat was more evenly distributed. Maybe all he needed to answer his prayers was a soft-throwing lefty. Sturdivant served one up and Eddie roped it down the line for a double, sending Logan to third, at last, his first base hit of the Series. Eddie was thrilled and the crowd came alive—runners at second and third with nobody out for Henry Aaron.

The Hammer was leading the Braves offensively, hitting .357 in the Series, 5-for-14 following an infield single in the second inning. Sturdivant wasn't fooling him. He tried to sneak a 1-1 changeup past Aaron, which was a tremendously poor decision. Henry waited that split second, then put his good swing on the ball, Alabama stride style, and it carried through the cold air into the packed left-field bleachers, a three-run home run above the 355-foot marker to give the Braves a 3–1 lead. The stadium was loud and rocking. Casey Stengel sat quietly with his arms folded.

One hitter later, it was Frank Torre's turn. He had proven he could swing the bat enough during the regular season to earn Fred Haney's respect and a start at first base against the left-hander. Torre had never hit a home run at County Stadium, but he turned on a fastball and lined it into the right-field stands to give the Braves and Spahn a 4–1 lead. Sturdivant was out of the game after the fourth inning.

Spahn went back to work, bolstered by a Braves defense that had never been better. With one out and a runner on first in the fifth, the inning ended when pinch hitter Harry Simpson grounded to Red Schoendienst. The trustworthy second baseman skimmed the ball on one hop, tapped second, and threw to Torre to complete the 4-3 double play. In the seventh inning with one out and a man on first, Johnny Logan fielded Elston Howard's shot and flipped it to Schoendienst, who completed a 6-4-3 double play. And in the eighth inning, when Spahn was really in trouble, the defense answered his prayers once more. He gave up a leadoff double to Andy Carey followed by a one-out single to pinch hitter Jerry Lumpe, putting runners on the corners with Tony Kubek coming to the plate. Spahn, who hadn't walked a batter since the first inning, put the bait exactly where he wanted. Kubek hit the ball hard on the ground to short.

There was Johnny Logan. His tools were as glossy as a hammer and nails, but he prided himself on building up his pitchers with his defense. Logan fielded cleanly and hurried the ball to Schoendienst, who finished the relay to Torre. It was the third inning-ending double play in four innings and one of Logan's World Series record ten fielding assists in the game. The Braves ran off the field to a thunderous ovation. Hotels in New York City began receiving reservations for Games 6 and 7. Maybe the Braves could answer Milwaukee's prayers. They weren't dead yet.

Spahn went to the mound in the top of the ninth inning, cradling the 4–1 lead. It would not be easy. He would have to pitch through the heart of the Yanks order: Hank Bauer, Mickey Mantle, and Yogi Berra. Spahn bowed his head behind the mound for a moment before the inning began. He cleared his mind and took a deep breath. The crowd was louder than he had ever heard it. The TV cameras zoomed in on the concentration stitched across his face. First up was Bauer, 0-for-3 with three ground balls. Spahn worked carefully and menacingly. The fans weren't leaving their seats. He kicked and delivered. Bauer lifted a lazy fly ball to center field. Henry Aaron drifted under and made the catch for the first out of the ninth.

Next was Mantle. He, too, had been feeble against Spahn. Mick shook his head. Spahnie's stuff wasn't overpowering, but his control and movement was. Mick was running on a bad leg and he hadn't gotten a ball out of the infield against Spahn—a couple of comebackers and a strikeout. Spahn wound his grandfather clock delivery, let loose something with sink and Mick dribbled one to Logan at short, who easily threw him out for the second out of the inning.

The fans were shaking the rafters as Yogi Berra came to the plate. The prayers of Milwaukee, it seemed, had almost been answered. But Yogi wasn't a clutch hitter for nothing and the Yankee fans were praying, too. Yogi was one of those rare guys born with the gene that seemingly always prevented him from being the final out of a big game. Spahn tried smoke and mirrors, but Yogi smoked a single to right. Then Gil McDougald mirrored Yogi's hit and singled to right, too, putting Yanks on first and second with two out. Elston Howard was coming to the plate.

The crowd, while loud, hesitated and became edgy. Fred Haney called time and slowly walked to the mound. In almost any other situation, Haney might have yanked Spahn rather than let him face a twenty-eight-year-old right-handed hitter with home run power. Haney had his rookie closer, Don McMahon, a hard-thrower averaging a strikeout per inning, warm in the bullpen. But Spahn deserved different consideration. This was "Old Folks," and this was his ballgame. In Fred's mind, this was no spot for a rookie.

If Howard—who was 0-for-3 with three grounders—could somehow get Spahn's pitch in the air for a three-run homer, the score would still be tied and the Braves would still hit in the bottom of the ninth. It wouldn't be much fun, but Haney and Spahn both hated the idea of walking Howard to set up a potential grand slam that would give the Yanks the lead. So the decision was made. They would attack Howard with sliders low and outside. They would get him lunging and only come inside if they had to, but if they did, they would try to catch him hanging over the outer half and cut his hands off. "I wanted him to hit it," Spahn said. "Low and out-side all afternoon and he had been my man." What he wanted was a grounder. Not much to ask for.

Spahn wound up and threw a first-pitch slider. Howard didn't bite. He watched it all the way into catcher Del Crandall's glove for ball one. Spahn nodded and said, OK, this guy is going to make this tough. He rocked and fired again. It was another slider. Casey Stengel had the take sign on all the way. Make the old man throw a strike. Howard took the pitch just outside, ball two. Spahn cursed. The ballpark noise was too loud to hear him.

He was in a 2-0 hole. The crowd grew increasingly uneasy. Fred Haney paced in the dugout. He was a ball of pain—his ulcers were burning and he was grinding his teeth so badly his jaw hurt. Howard took a strike and then a ball to run the count to 3-1. Then Spahn went backwards. He tried his screwball, which cut across the inside corner to a right-hander. Howard blinked. Spahn was trying to jam him though the backdoor, but How-ard took the pitch. Plate umpire Augie Donatelli hit the high G note with his strike call. Full count.

Now the runners would be off. The Braves fans stood up and roared to will Spahn to the final out. Spahn lived for this. He once said he wouldn't throw his eight-year-old kid a good pitch to hit in a big situation. Some fans couldn't bear to watch. Haney stood on the top step, calm, though his guts were raging inside him. Stengel kept his eyes glued on the field. Spahn, whose control had been so perfect, knew Howard needed to pro-tect the plate and swing at anything close. He knew that gave him the advantage. His pitch count was up past 110, but he felt strong and cocky. The old heater was gone but his youthful arrogance and defiance was power-ful. His infielders, Johnny Logan and Red Schoendienst, slapped their hands in the gloves and yelled for him. Crandall pounded his mitt, urging Spahnie for one more strike, hit the glove, let's get this guy. Eddie was guarding the line and playing deep. Henry was playing a few steps to pull. Spahnie had the ball behind his back. He frantically wiggled it in his palm. Milwaukee was up on its feet, in the ballpark, and in bars, in front of TVs and radios, a city banded together praying once more. Oh God, Spahn loved it! He was going to go back low and outside. He reached back and the adrenaline put something extra on the ball.

But Spahn overthrew and missed badly. He didn't get the pitch low and away, he got it middle in. Son of a bitch! That pitch was right in Howard's wheelhouse. Spahn knew it when he threw it. He didn't want to watch the ball. "I knew by the way it was hit," he said. All the Brave fielders knew it to. Haney knew it. So did Stengel. Howard crushed the ball, a gunshot that killed Braves fans, resonating as his ball rose and their hearts fell. He pulled it high and deep to left field. Wes Covington went back, but there would be no miracle catch today. The ball was gone, a three-run home run, the Yanks tied the score, 4-4, and Milwaukee collapsed.

The only noise in the ballpark was the sound of the Yanks hooting and hollering. Spahn stood silently on the mound. His hands were on his hips. He looked in the dugout for a split second—that was his way of asking Haney if he wanted to come get him. But Fred said no with his eyes. Spahn stayed in the game and got Andy Carey to fly out for the third out. He walked off the field dejected. God, how he loved the game, but God, how he hated it right now! He felt worse than he did at the end of the 1956 season and he never imaged he could feel worse than that. "The greatest disappointment of my life," he said. He called the pitch "a sinker that turned out to be a stinker."

The home run should have beaten the Braves. With one swing of the bat, Elston Howard swept away five years of momentum and a million Milwaukee prayers. The score was tied but it was a crushing moment of defeat. Some fans tore up their ticket stubs, threw them in the air, and stormed out of the ballpark. Others compared the feeling to getting a flat tire at full speed. Champions didn't blow the game with two out in the ninth. Chokers did that. Bushers did that.

The Braves went quietly in the bottom of the ninth and Spahn went back to the mound for the tenth inning. There would be more heartache awaiting him. After a ground ball and a strikeout to the first two batters, leadoff hitter Tony Kubek came to the plate. He hit a slow and cheap twenty-seven-hopper back up the middle. Red Schoendienst charged to his glove side and got off a decent throw, but Kubek beat out the infield single. Around Milwaukee came the thought: Here we go again.

There were more grumbles from the crowd. Some fans wanted Haney to take Spahn out of the game. But Haney refused. He would win or lose on this horse. Hank Bauer came back to the plate. He was 0-for-4, but Spahn's impeccable control was fading. Without it, he was nobody. Bauer got one good and crushed it deep to center field. Henry Aaron gave it a good chase, but the ball carried over his head. Kubek walked home. Bauer lumbered into third with a two-out RBI triple. The Yanks had come all the way back—this is why they were the Yanks and you were not. They led 5–4 now, the comeback from 4–1 with two out in the ninth inning complete. Milwaukee was quiet as a mausoleum. New York was New Year's Eve noisy.

Faith was falling. Instead of a baptism this was a wake. In the press box, the New York writers chortled. The Milwaukee writers were silent. "A neat hole, two feet wide, six feet long and six feet deep had been dug at home plate," the *Journal* wrote. "A plain but permanent looking pine box sat beside it. The American League press extended somewhat insincere condolences." The Braves had been through a lot, but their resiliency was about to be tested. All year, they had heard what a bunch of choking, small-town losers they were—the Bushville Braves of Bushville, USA—and now they were facing the prospect of going down 3 games to 1. Spahn finished the inning. He had worked ten full innings and thrown 126 pitches. His spot in the order was leading off the bottom of the tenth inning, but he obviously wasn't going to bat. The lefty Tommy Byrne, one of Casey's favorite crafty old fellas, was the fourth Yankee pitcher of the game and would try to close it out. If he got into trouble, Casey had his closer, Bob Grim, heating up in the bullpen. Fred Haney needed a pinch hitter. He called on Nippy Jones.

County Stadium was quiet as Nippy took his practice cuts. He had been a good find, coming off the bench to hit .266 with two home runs in 79 at-bats. He eyeballed Byrne, the oldest pitcher on the Yankees staff, who had been pitching in the big leagues since some Braves were in grade school. At age thirty-seven, Byrne was an old-school fella Casey loved so much that he brought him back for a second tour with the club. He called him "my train man," because he held railroad stock (quite possibly suggested to him by his investment-savvy manager), loved riding the rails and detested flying because he, like Casey, felt it robbed the ballplayers of some of their greatest memories. Tommy could still dime ya, and right-handers only hit .240 against him. Nippy sized him up, clanked the barrel of his bat against his shoe that was polished as black as his dark hair, and walked to the plate.

Nippy knew he needed to get on base. He didn't care how he did it. The Braves were down by one and had Schoendienst, Logan, and Mathews coming up next. If the Braves could prolong the inning, cleanup man Henry Aaron would hit. Stengel computed possible sequences and concluded he did not want to face Aaron. He would rather let the Braves tie the score than give Aaron a chance to win the game.

That made Jones the man to get. He had limited power and he couldn't run. He would have to crush the ball to hurt the Yanks. Anything else in play would be an automatic out. Jones reported himself to plate umpire Augie Donatelli as a pinch hitter for Spahn and dug his shiny polished cleats into the dirt. Byrne had pitched well, entering the game in the eighth inning with two on and two out to strike out Wes Covington. He didn't throw hard and he wasn't going to give Jones anything good to hit. He wound up, throwing sidearm and across his body. The screwball came sweeping down-and-in. Nippy didn't move a muscle. Byrne knew he nicked Nippy, but it was close, and he wasn't going to say anything. The ball skipped past Berra. Donatelli called ball one.

But Jones immediately thought Donatelli was wrong. He felt the ball graze his right shoe, his back foot in the batter's box. He swore the ball hit him and pleaded with Donatelli to award him first base. "When I saw the pitch, I did not know that it hit him, either," Del Crandall said. "The ball didn't redirect. It didn't do anything. It just kind of skipped on by to the backstop. There wasn't anything to tell us or the umpire that the ball hit him."

But thanks to the heavy coat of shoe polish, there was. The batboys, Charlie Blossfield and Paul Wick, alertly retrieved the ball and ran it to home plate, where Nippy showed the ball to Donatelli, who saw it was smudged with a nice blur of black shoe polish. Donatelli was satisfied and pointed Nippy Jones to first base. Casey Stengel didn't raise a fuss. The proof was in the polish.

The ballplayer who said a prayer of thanks when he returned to the big leagues might have often wondered why the Lord had chosen him to join these beer-swigging screwballs. He stood at first base for a brief moment and soaked it all in—the crowd, the feel, the passion, and the ballplayers—as Haney dispatched speedy infielder Felix Mantilla to pinch-run for him. Nippy smiled. He slapped Mantilla's hand and said so long. Then Nippy walked off a big league field for the last time in his life. He's 0-for-0 in his final box score, but his footprints live on.

The Braves were still breathing. Casey had seen enough of his "train man," so he went onto the field. The Milwaukee fans gave him hell. When he brought in Byrne in the eighth, thousands of fans mocked him by counting his crooked steps to the mound. A fan in left field belted through a bullhorn, "Hey, bush leaguers! Hey, You bush league Yankees!" When Casey walked off the field, they counted louder. Casey had enough. He decided to respond to the fans. "I think Casey, as only Casey could do, lit the fire," Frank Torre said. When Casey reached the dugout, he blew the fans a kiss. That was part showmanship and part flipping Milwaukee the bird. The Bushville fans jeered him, wearing their headdresses with "scalp the Yankees" slogans printed on the headbands. As Casey paced to the mound to take Byrne out of the game and summon Bob Grim to face Red Schoendienst in the tenth inning, they taunted him louder and harder. Casey dropped the ball in Grim's hand with immense confidence. The orders were simple: get us the hell out of here with a win. Casey walked back to the dugout and the Braves fans rode him harder. Casey returned the favor, gesturing to Milwaukee with his arms wide open.

The switch-hitting Schoendienst was made for a precision moment like this. The situation called for a sacrifice bunt. He turned around to bat left-handed against Grim, who threw a sneaky fast heavy ball, and was tough against lefties. But Red squared the bat and pecked the ball softly and sweetly. Very few batters possessed hand-eye coordination like Red. He nudged the first pitch to the right side of the infield, moving Mantilla up to second. It was a textbook perfect sacrifice bunt—Fred Haney's will and Red Schoendienst's way. The energy in County Stadium rose again. Two pitches and the Braves had the tying run on second base with one out. Prayers were still in play. The beer lines were empty. Nobody wanted to miss anything.

Johnny Logan was up next. Casey vigorously clapped his hands. He loved this matchup because he didn't think Logan had the bat speed to get around the good gas. But Casey wasn't finished meddling. With a one-run lead, he wanted a lockdown defense, and he couldn't have it with Mickey Mantle hobbling in center field. So he walked out to home plate to talk to Donatelli. He had his lineup card and a pen in his hand, the artist with his ink. The Milwaukee fans flogged Stengel, but he was concentrating too hard to pay attention.

One reason Stengel loved Tony Kubek was his defensive versatility. He could play the infield or outfield and played left field today. Stengel quipped that he would play Kubek at the position where his family could see him best, but that was a classic example of Casey cracking a joke to hide his true motives. Mantle couldn't run and cover ground like he was capable of— Aaron's triple over his head in Game 2 was still fresh in Casey's mind. So he removed Mantle from the game, taking his bat out of the lineup, which alone was an acknowledgement that he didn't believe the Braves had a comeback in them. Then he moved Kubek over from left to center and called on the veteran Enos Slaughter to finish in left field. The Braves fans remembered Slaughter very well from the Cardinals. He was a part of Milwaukee lore; the center fielder who in 1953 couldn't quite catch Billy Bruton's home run on the city's first major league opening day. Slaughter, who had been in the American League since 1954, was forty-one now. Though he couldn't run like he used to, he was still supposedly a smart defender. Still, many observers wondered what Casey was thinking. Wouldn't a banged-up Mantle be better than a full-speed Slaughter? Casey didn't give a shit what anybody thought. Then he did one last thing that really pissed off Johnny Logan: he told Slaughter to play shallow.

Logan saw the entire scenario as a slight to him personally. Fucking Casey. Guys had been picking on Logan his whole life. This was no different. Logan had a home run and two singles in the Series, though he was 0-for-3 with a walk in Game 4. Johnny had spent his entire career with the Braves, but he was still a feisty New Yorker at heart, a hard-nosed grinder who played when he was hurt and lived to make the other guy suffer. "All I could think of when I went up there was, 'base hit, base hit, I gotta get a base hit,'" he said. He reminded himself to keep his swing short and not aim for the fences. He needed discipline. He always felt like he had something to prove to the hometown fans following him on TV and radio back home. And besides, the Braves fans were loud again. He couldn't bear the thought of letting them down. "They don't know our Johnny," the *Sentinel* wrote, "A tough little guy in his own right."

Grim fired two pitches out of the strike zone. Johnny laid off and thought, good, now this goddamn guy gotta throw me a strike. Grim did and Logan was ready. He smoked a shot to left field . . . but Slaughter was shallow! The ball got behind him! It was like Johnny Logan reached over and punched Casey Stengel in the eye! Slaughter turned and struggled to run the ball down in the corner. Felix Mantilla could fly; he touched third and turned home. The score was tied, 5–5, but Logan wanted to rip Casey's heart out. He spiked second for a double and then took a wide turn around the bag. God, how he wanted third, because all Eddie would need is a sacrifice fly, but he couldn't risk getting thrown out at third for the second out. So Logan slammed on the brakes and hurried back to second with a run-scoring double, his biggest hit of the season, more important even than St. Jude's home run. He pounded his hands together, the ballpark pumped fists along with him.

Now it was Eddie's turn. County Stadium was thunderously loud beyond belief. The Braves were back in business, all tied up. Eddie strode to the plate. This was a barroom brawl on a baseball field and he was ready. Grim was going to take the gloves off and Eddie knew it. He would get nothing but heat and he knew where it would be—in on his hands. Eddie would take that trade—give him velocity instead of crafty, nibbling shit. He wanted pitchers who came for a fight. With only one out and a runner on second, Grim was going to have to pitch to Aaron anyhow, so he might as well attack Eddie. Stengel didn't think walking Eddie to set up a double play against Aaron was a good idea. Besides, nothing in the bottom of the tenth inning had unfolded as Casey planned it. He felt suddenly human, worse yet, he felt like a horseshit manager. So he said the hell with it. He shouted at Grim through the frenzy of the ballpark roar, as loud as a Redstone Rocket, to get the gas under Eddie's hands, to make it impossible for him to turn and burn into the brisk wind blowing out to right field, to wipe him out and humiliate him, to bury him!

Eddie waited for Grim. He cranked up and began firing fastballs. "When anyone talked about Series flops, [Mathews] had been the first name mentioned," the *Journal* reported. Grim missed with a pair and Eddie saw two strikes. "To expect Mathews to come through was more than they could reasonably have asked," the *Journal* insisted. Grim peered down the pipe. Yogi wanted the 2-2 pitch low and inside. Eddie loosely held Joe Adcock's bat at the ready, not too tight, careful not to hurt his blisters. The noise was deafening in the ballpark. The prayers were pumping through Wisconsin. "A million watt beam of wish power throbbing from the stands," the *Sentinel* reported.

Grim humped up and fired a hard fastball, but he missed the mark. Instead of getting the ball inside, he elevated the fastball over the heart of the plate. Eddie decked the pitch. He put the best swing of his life on that ball, the most memorable swing of his career. It was a high, fast, rocket into right field. Eddie dropped the bat and began running for his life. He wasn't sure if it was gone. He was scared when he saw right fielder Hank Bauer beating on his glove as though he had a play. But Eddie had misread Bauer's body language. Bauer wasn't hitting his glove because he had a play. He was hitting his glove because he didn't.

The ball was gone! A three-run home run! The Braves had pulled it out, 7–5, in a game that would be remembered in Milwaukee lore as the "Shoe Polish Game," and it tied the Series at two games each and assured that the Series would return to New York. Eddie practically danced around the bases in his shiny shoes. "I felt ten feet tall," he said. Three lucky pennies jingled in his back pocket. The faith of millions could touch the soul of the hardest brawler, the drunk with a heart of gold. "I never believed in charms before," he said. "But this makes a believer out of me."

This was Eddie's moment, just like Henry Aaron's special moment had been the home run to clinch the pennant. "Reports of Braves Deaths Were Exaggerated," the *Journal* reported, while the *Sentinel* wrote, "Fans Entitled to Whoopee After Win." The rafters rocked the bunting loose, hats and scorecards and programs flew into the air, confetti fluttered from the stands as Eddie's teammates poured out from the dugout and gathered around home plate. Sputnik's sensors could hear the joy. Prayers had been answers around Wisconsin. In downtown Milwaukee, fans streamed out of bars, taverns, and stores, and crushed into the streets screaming and hugging, horns blowing, boys kissing girls, sailors climbing the light poles, cops too busy crying for joy to care about the crowds. In Green Bay, where the Packers were losing to the Lions, a shockwave swept through the City Stadium rafters as fans carrying transistor radios heard the home run and spread the news. Beer flew through the air in Green Bay and splashed in Milwaukee, where Eddie rounded third and headed home.

After all his agony, Warren Spahn finally had a World Series victory in a game he had started and finished. It wasn't exactly what he had in mind and he hoped he'd get another shot to win a game the way he wanted to. But he would trade his pain for his city's pride and admitted that maybe there was more to this team than conventional baseball could explain. He was too excited to notice that he was starting to feel under the weather. "There's no lift like coming from behind," Spahn said. "Maybe this was a blessing in disguise." And as Eddie touched the plate, the Asshole Buddies—Spahn, Lew Burdette, and Bob Buhl—mobbed him. Burdette was pitching Game 5 on Monday. Spahnie and Burdette rubbed Eddie's head. But the biggest hug came from his best friend, Buhl, who some actually swore, smiled for the first time in his life.

It was starkly cold and quiet in the Yankee clubhouse, where players answered questions with distant gazes. "For the first time in the series, Yankee poise seemed shaken," the *Journal* reported. That wasn't just the first time in this World Series writers could remember seeing the supremely confident and cocky New York Yankees rocked at their fragility. That was the first time anyone had seen this in the 1950s. They always looked infallible under Casey Stengel. Even when the Dodgers finally beat them in 1955, well, you figure the Dodgers were due. But to loose like this in a town like this against a team like this . . . the Yankees were never supposed to be, as the *Post*'s Jimmy Cannon put it, "human beings same's you and me."

Casey Stengel wasn't telling jokes. He looked tired and worn. He explained his decision-making process without passion or performance. The

Braves had achieved a first in baseball history—they made Casey a boring interview. "They won it themselves," he said. "Both those guys (Logan and Mathews) hit the ball real good and we lose."

Stengel told the team to leave the park without him. He sat in the visiting manager's office for about an hour. When he thought the crowd was gone, he slowly showered and changed, putting on his black fedora and overcoat, and slowly trudging out of the clubhouse. He walked mournfully slow; he resembled an undertaker at his own funeral. But when he neared the exit gate, there was a crowd of about a hundred fans, mostly teenagers, just waiting for him. The kids tore him up. *Busher! Busher! Busher!* Casey tried to make nice. He signed an autograph for one kid, who took the piece of paper, and said to Casey, "Thanks, Busher!" Casey gave up and hurried back into the Stadium. He asked for the cops to walk him out. They did, though the kids still burned him. *Busher! Busher! Busher!* A shy little girl hid behind the mob. She was scared but curious. She wanted a look at this Grand Opera Villain. Then Casey walked past the curtain, a stooped old-timer with a sad look on his exhausted face. The little girl's surprise resembled Dorothy when she met the wizard. "Why, you're just an old man," she said.

The little girl was scared no more.

14

Game 5 **ONE PARTY RULE**

Maine governor Edmund Muskie watched Game 4 and like a lot of baseball fans, decided that he had seen enough of the Yankees. "I used to be a Yankee fan, but you know I'm against one-party government," he said. More and more fans were starting to agree with him especially after the Shoe Polish game captivated the nation and reduced the mighty Yankees to choirboys. A *Sentinel* reporter overheard a New York writer say, "You can call this 'Bush' if you like, but if we had a little of it in New York, the Giants wouldn't be on the way to San Francisco."

The sports editor of the *San Francisco Call-Bulletin* understood what made this town tick and hoped San Francisco would take to the Giants the way Milwaukee adopted the Braves. "Milwaukeeans like four things— parades, fireworks, baseball, and beer. They aren't naïve people—they merely think the world will come to an end if the Braves don't win the World Series." The sports editor of the *Toronto Globe & Mail*, where some people dreamed that one day they might get baseball too, wrote, "Milwaukee has to be seen to be believed. For undiluted enthusiasm, it tops Louisville on Kentucky Derby Saturday and Indianapolis 500 Sunday."

Many out-of-town reporters thought it was funny and strange that on the day Sputnik launched, the *Sentinel*'s "We Make History" headline referred not to the satellite but to the Braves. They found it funny that Milwaukee was not preoccupied with the Little Rock Nine crisis or the recent election of labor leader Jimmy Hoffa. After watching two World Series games in Milwaukee, they understood why this World Series had such meaning and significance to their people. They also understood why Wisconsin fans made it their mission to torment Casey Stengel, though columnist Arthur Daley of *The New York Times* remained appalled at the treatment of his beloved Bronx Bombers. He wrote Milwaukee fans "have a deep distaste for the Yankees," and that "Ol' Case takes the fiercest booing."

Yes, booing the symbols of status quo. The 1960s were definitely on the way. Cities that didn't have major league teams looked at the Milwaukee Braves and saw a shining example of what they wanted to become. They, too, believed that there was power in their communities and that symbolic obstacles like those the Yankees represented could be overcome if everyone worked together. The 1957 World Series was becoming about more than baseball. It was about everything Americans wanted to be.

The Birmingham News realized the passion of Milwaukee Braves fans resonated with their readers. Their correspondent, Eddie Glennon, the general manager of the Birmingham Barons, dreamed of the day major league baseball would come to the South—just as long as it didn't get to Atlanta first. Glennon wisecracked his way through the Series, but the paper's editorial board saw this World Series as more than Milwaukee against New York. It saw it as a symbol of much greater struggles ahead. The Braves had given "a memorable exhibition in coming back against adversity. It was the kind of demonstration that should be heartening to all of us in this time of many troubles. The Braves did not let thoughts of Yankee invincibility get them down. They kept on fighting and out of the woods came one of the most thrilling Series victories. It's good to have that sort of example in days like this."

All this insanity and introspection did not bother Lew Burdette one bit. Nope, a lot of people thought Lew must have had a screw loose, but he didn't think so. A lot of pitchers got up in front of a big crowd and got away from what got them there in the first place. Not Lew. When he walked to the mound to start Game 5, he stood there like he was supposed to be here, and all this attention just came with the deal. The louder the crowd, the calmer he got. You could look at his picture and almost hear the West Virginia accent speaking through a tobacco wad. He was a hero for winning Game 2, finishing strong with six shutout innings. This time he was matched against Yankee ace Whitey Ford, Casey's Grand Opera Son of a Gun, the toughest left-hander the Braves had faced all year.

The crowd of 45,811, Milwaukee's largest crowd of the series, screamed. It was Milwaukee's last home game of 1957. All of this pressure might have bothered another man. But if it bothered Burdette, you'd be damned if you could get that out of him. The most anyone ever got out of Burdette was in a 1991 interview, when he confessed, "The tough game was the fifth game, pitching against Whitey."

Burdette was in trouble from the beginning. His fastball was up and the Yankees were hitting him. They knew if they didn't get him early, they might never get to him at all. "We thought we would get one pop at him," Casey Stengel said. Burdette's first pitch of the game was a sinker to Hank Bauer, who wasn't fooled. He singled to extend his World Series hitting streak to twelve games. Bauer moved to second on Tony Kubek's sacrifice bunt, bringing Gil McDougald to the plate before all the Milwaukee fans had arrived in their seats.

McDougald was hitting third in place of Mickey Mantle, who was held out of the starting lineup because of his sore legs and shoulder he hurt sliding into second base in Game 2. He was no slouch, and he had a plan. McDougald knew trying to pull Burdette would be a bad idea, so he waited for one of those little sliders on the outside corner and flicked the ball into shallow right field. Andy Pafko was playing deep. He charged and picked the ball off at shoe-top level for the second out. He came up throwing to keep Bauer at third. Pafko's catch was all the help Burdette needed to get out of the first unscathed. The tone was set: Game 5 would be a series of very big small moments, a succession of bang-bang plays that would determine the path of the Series.

Leading off the second inning, Enos Slaughter dribbled a ground ball up the middle. Red Schoendienst ranged left behind the bag and lunged for the ball. He got his glove on it, but he came up lame. Slaughter had an infield single and Red stood up slowly. County Stadium fell quiet. He was clearly in pain. Red aggravated the same groin injury that he had suffered playing for the Cardinals in 1953. The injury had been creeping up on him in September and into the Series. He waved off concern and tried to stay in the game, but when Del Crandall caught Slaughter stealing after Burdette struck out Harry Simpson to complete a double play, it was clear that Red's groin was murdering him. He came out of the game at the end of the inning and Felix Mantilla took over at second. Mantilla went into the game in the third inning and promptly fielded the first two balls of the inning for clean outs, but Red was a tough loss for the Braves to absorb. "I don't know that our ball club could have succeeded if we didn't have Red Schoendienst," Henry Aaron said. But the Braves didn't have time to cry. Nothing had ever been easy for this team. Why should it be easy now?

The Braves needed all the help they could get—Red was the only Brave who drove in a run against Whitey Ford in Game 1. Whitey was dealing again, his curveball was working, and the Braves still couldn't figure him out. "Hell, he could pitch any time," Schoendienst said. "Big games or no big games. He always had good stuff."

But Burdette needed help, too. In the fourth inning of the scoreless game, McDougald solved Burdette yet again. He got him good this time, drilling a sinker high and deep to left field. Wes Covington had to hurry. He back pedaled at full speed, fighting the sun, until he was up against the left-field fence. In one sweeping motion, the outfielder who had once turned down offers to play college football and had a look from the New York Football Giants, left his feet at full speed and made the catch falling backward. It was a Sunday catch on a Monday afternoon, the touchdown Covington never scored. His back banged against the waist-high steel fence and he bounced off the hard railing like a linebacker had speared him. Covington fell forward, somersaulting, wincing in pain, landing hard. On all fours, he slowly got to his knees and showed the ball to the left-field umpire, Nestor Chylak. McDougald was the first out of the inning. The crowd roared. Burdette pumped his fist. Just as Covington had saved him with a fine catch in Game 2, he had saved him here in Game 5. "Wes is my good left fielder," Burdette said affectionately.

The play loomed larger moments later when Berra hit a routine grounder to first baseman Joe Adcock. Big Joe was almost always reliable, but not this time. He bobbled the ball for an error, allowing Yogi aboard first. Then Slaughter, whose ability to put the ball in play got him a lifetime .300 average and a plaque in the Hall of Fame, flipped a single over short to put runners at first and second with one out for Harry Simpson.

This was a bad setup for Burdette. The Yanks were putting the ball in play, but more alarmingly, they were lifting the ball and redirecting it. Burdette had just about had enough of this. His feelings of resentment and revenge toward Stengel had not expired. He wanted to get the Braves out of town with a one-game Series lead, but he needed to make his sinker start sinking, not in the next inning, not against the next batter, but now. He knew that Simpson was an average runner, so anything on the ground and the infielders would have to hurry. That's what Burdette wanted. He threw what the *Journal* termed a "weird spinner" and watched Simpson take a roundhouse swing. Simpson hit a high chopper to third base, a brat with a lot of mustard on it, but Burdette wasn't sure if it was made to order.

Eddie Mathews had almost no time to make a decision. The ball was a bounder on an in-between hop. The mustard slowed the ball down just enough, so Eddie made a jump for it. Casey Stengel, a former infielder, watched Mathews and didn't think Eddie was good enough to finish that play. He urged Simpson down the line like he was a guy playing the ponies and clutching his betting slips. But Eddie would never let Burdette down. He speared the ball in the air and landed, set his feet, and fired a strike to Mantilla at second, whose strong throw to first nipped Casey's horse by a hair. The inning-ending 5-4-3 double play brought the crowd to its feet and kept the game scoreless. Casey threw his ticket in the air and wondered how Eddie picked it. That feller wasn't supposed to be so good an infielder. When Eddie charged into the dugout, Fred Haney was waiting for him with a smile and a handshake, instead of a fungo bat and a bruise, proud of him for the hard work he put into fixing his defense.

The Braves weren't doing much at the plate against Ford, but their defense kept Burdette alive. In the top of the fifth, with the game still scoreless, Burdette found his good sinker and began playing pepper with Yankee batters. He felt confident with Felix Mantilla at second base. Mantilla darted to his left to backhand Jerry Coleman's sharp grounder behind the bag. Mantilla turned in one motion and fired a strike to nail Coleman.

Burdette slapped his glove with that silly smirk of his, and figured the more grounders he could roll to this kid, the better. Mantilla's soft, sure hands and nimble athletic actions up the middle were tremendous assets. Burdette set down the top of the Yanks order in the sixth on three grounders, the last two to Mantilla. He was Milwaukee's most versatile infielder, having come off the bench to hit .236 and play second, short, and third during his rookie season. When Juan Pizarro, who had pitched an inning in Game 3, and Mantilla debuted against the Yankees, they were among the first Puerto Ricans to play in the World Series. Pizarro and Mantilla signified the coming age of Latin power arms and agile middle infielders, players with skills that changed the way baseball is played. It was in sharp contrast to the Yankees, who had no Latin players, and a manager who couldn't pronounce their names.

The Braves couldn't hit Ford's curveball in any language as the game moved to the bottom of the sixth inning. Aside from two singles from Andy Pafko and a single from Henry Aaron, the Braves had only moved one base runner into scoring position in the first five innings. With two out and the bases empty, Eddie Mathews came to the plate. He was 0-for-1 with a walk and a strikeout. Whitey was murder on Mathews. In the fourth inning, Whitey sawed off Eddie so badly that the barrel of the shattered bat flew beyond first base. Whitey was supremely confident but pitched with caution. He threw a breaking ball and Eddie hit a high bounder to second base. He got a good first step out of the box, and even though he figured he was out, the Series was too close not to run a hard 90.

The ball was right at second baseman Jerry Coleman. It was a room-service hop, but for some reason, Coleman stepped back on the ball. Eddie couldn't believe his luck. He lowered his head and ran like hell. "When I saw that Coleman wasn't going to charge the ball, I knew I was going to make it," Eddie said. He accelerated down the line and even the *Journal* noticed his "great burst of speed." Burdette knew it when he saw it, too. "Coleman backed up!" he blurted. Speed was the most overlooked part of Eddie's game. The Yankees swore the scouting reports grossly underestimated Eddie's speed. Had they put the stopwatch to him? Eddie was flying. He was an A runner on the era's grading scale. The Yankees who had never seen him run thought he was as fast as Mantle. Coleman realized this was no ordinary play anymore. He had wasted time. He hurried his throw, but with one final lunge, Eddie's front foot touched the bag a shade under four seconds. Jocko Conlan, the first-base umpire, emphatically called Mathews safe. The photographic evidence proved Jocko right. "I guess they didn't figure on me getting down there so fast," Eddie said.

Stengel didn't even come out of the dugout to argue. He loved Jerry Coleman, but as a former infielder, he knew his fella had screwed up. Coleman, who had been a steady and solid veteran Yankee infielder for a decade and who was playing in what turned out to be his last season, did not hide from his mistake. "I should have charged it," he said.

Coleman gave the Braves the break they needed. Henry Aaron was next. He had hit Ford hard both times with a line out and a single. This time, whatever Ford threw fooled Henry. All he could manage was a cue shot off the end of the bat, a pop fly into shallow right field. But the blooper had eyes and luck. Coleman backtracked into shallow right. Tony Kubek sped in from center, and Hank Bauer barreled in from right. Henry's hit fell for a cheap single, the crowd shook the rafters, and Eddie Mathews raced from first to third.

Whitey was in a mess with runners at the corners with two out for the right-handed hitting Joe Adcock, who hadn't done much in the Series. He was 2-for-14, hitting a skeletal .142, and he had grounded out twice against Ford in the game. The park was swaying. Even in the press box, the writers were rooting for the Braves. "Come on, Joe, for your sake as well as for all of us, you have the guts," *Sentinel* columnist Lloyd Larson wrote with pom-poms laced to his wrists. Adcock was 0-for-6 against Ford, all ground-ball outs. Adcock's ankles hurt and Mathews had just broken one of his bats. Whitey had made him look bad enough times. Joe had constantly been trying to pull him, so he committed to making an adjustment. He would try to shoot the ball to right field. Whitey wasted no time attacking, throwing a sharp curveball on the inside half. Joe pulled his hands inside and shortened his stroke. He intended to inside-out the ball to right field. The man was a fearsomely strong right-handed hitter who finished his career a decade later with 336 home runs, but on this fine day in October 1957, nobody had ever seen a better singles hitter than Joseph Wilbur Adcock, who flicked a single to right field, and scored Eddie Mathews to give the Braves a 1–0 lead.

With a one-run lead, Burdette turned nasty. "I mean, he pitched his whole career that way," Del Crandall said. "He was just really sharp against the Yankees, the pitches he threw were crisp, and he was not afraid to pitch inside." The *Journal* called him a "mean-looking gentleman." He wasn't knocking anyone down, yet he owned the inner half of the plate, and the Yankees hadn't dared knock any Braves down with Burdette on the mound. Burdette knew he had found his stuff. A long line of zeroes collected on the scoreboard behind him. Each zero was a feather in his headdress, and as he pitched deeper into the game, his face turned as red as the number 33 on his back. Burdette was no slouch, but he looked taller than six-foot-two, an imposing "rangy tower of muscle with sandy hair and cold blue eyes," Red Smith wrote.

His defense never let him down. Burdette allowed a leadoff single to Yogi Berra in the seventh, then rolled a ground ball against Enos Slaughter and watched Johnny Logan field, step on the bag for one, and fire to first for two. Then Burdette got a ground ball to close the inning to make it a lucky 13 straight shutout innings against the Yankees. The cameras caught Mickey Mantle sitting quietly on the bench with Casey Stengel. Mick didn't know what hurt worse: the fact that he couldn't run or that he couldn't take a crack against this crazy bastard.

Mantle finally got his wish and got into the game in the eighth inning, with Burdette and the Braves zealously protecting the 1–0 lead. He allowed a one-out single to Jerry Coleman. Casey called Coleman off the field. He sent Mick out to pinch-run. Then, with the pitcher's spot due, Casey pulled Whitey Ford. He sent Elston Howard to pinch-hit.

Everyone remembered what Howard had done to Warren Spahn in the ninth of Game 4, but Burdette came after him. He threw two quick strikes to jump ahead of the count. Burdette was firing and working fast. Howard had barely settled back into the box when Burdette cranked into his windup, but this time he had a surprise—he dropped down to throw a sidearm fastball that tailed across the outside corner and froze Howard for strike three. It was the first time Burdette had given the Yankees that look, reflecting his advanced feel for thinking ahead of the hitters.

There was still the question of Mantle on first. Burdette knew Casey hadn't put him in the game to fetch him a beer. Even banged up, Mantle could still run, especially in short spurts. He thought it was only a matter of time before Stengel sent him. Burdette had to hand it to Case—it was no road apple move. Burdette would split his attention between Mantle at first and Hank Bauer, who came to the plate with two out. He could give the Yanks a lead with one swing of the bat and had hit Burdette well in this ballgame already, going 2-for-3 with a pair of singles.

The idea of putting a hurting runner in motion with a hot hitter at the plate and down by a run late in the game would have been frowned upon by most managers and armchair tacticians. But Casey didn't give a shit what anybody thought. He had a hunch he should send Mantle. Casey knew Burdette would nibble against Bauer and would never give him anything to hit. That would translate into a good pitch for Mantle run on. Casey knew Burdette only had one magic trick in him this inning—that was the side-arm look against Howard—and Casey knew Burdette would never dare try it again.

Early in the count, Stengel saw his chance. He put the steal sign on. Mantle got a decent jump. He winced and willed his bad knees to second. Burdette grunted as he threw a fastball in the dirt. Bauer took a hearty swing and came up empty on an awful pitch for catcher Del Crandall to handle. Mantle should have had the base stolen.

But Crandall two-handed the ball as it skimmed the dirt and popped into proper throwing position. The great quickness scout Johnny Moore had seen on the Southern California sandlots a decade ago came into play. Crandall's transfer from his glove to his throwing hand was rifle rapid. He threw a bullet to second base. The ball snapped into Felix Mantilla's glove just as he slapped the tag down when Mantle's foot dislodged the dirt as he came flying in. The second-base umpire, Bill McKinley, called Mantle out with operatic grandeur. You could read Casey's lips. "The throw had to be perfect," Casey said. "Otherwise we've got the tying run on second and who knows what happens." Henry Aaron, charging in to back up the play, admired Crandall's quiet reliability. "He didn't have the strongest arm in the world, but he got rid of the ball quickly," Aaron said. "His pitchers believed in him. Very intelligent behind the plate and called a very beautiful game."

Burdette roared into the ninth inning protecting the 1–0 lead. He finished every pitch with a flourish, leaping forward like a bullfighter, holding the red cape in front of the Yankees, daring them to touch him. Come hit him, check him, check the ball, look for spit, look for grease, or look for a nick. Try to get inside of his head because he was already inside of yours, "keeping his stuff low and evil, like the minds of those who question his principals," Red Smith wrote. Burdette was wincing, grunting, howling, screaming, fidgeting, and absolutely wired and pitching with his fingers on fire. The Yankees countered by never asking for the ball to be inspected, which, while it made Burdette lonely, did not dissuade him. "I kind of missed that squawking," he said. "Not a darn word about spit. Too bad."

He struck out Bauer to begin the inning and then fanned Kubek with the best screwball he had thrown all day. Then, of course, came one final obstacle. Gil McDougald singled, bringing Yogi Berra to the plate.

Burdette had fared decently against Berra, who was 1-for-3 with a single. He had thrown him nothing but low sliders despite the fact that Berra was a notorious low-ball hitter. Most pitchers tried to climb the ladder on the lefty Yogi, but Burdette would have nothing of that. He refused to change his game for anybody. He always heeded the advice of Bucky Walters, a former big leaguer who won 198 games and was Burdette's first pitching coach with the Boston Braves. Burdette could always recite Bucky's stern warning to "keep the ball down, work in and out, and don't come in against lefties. Don't throw up and away unless you throw ninety-five. You are a sinker-slider pitcher. If you miss, miss down. Don't miss up. And if you come up, come up and in."

Yogi walked to the plate, and before Burdette could throw a pitch, Yogi, a master at controlling the minds of pitchers, asked plate umpire Joe Paparella to check the baseball. It was as dry as the smile on Burdette's face. Yogi, however, wasn't laughing. He was desperate to keep the Yanks alive. Del Crandall asked Yogi why he wasn't smiling. "I ain't smiled since the tenth inning yesterday," Yogi said. And right there, the Braves knew why they were winning.

Yogi quickly realized that Burdette was going to stay with low sliders. "Berra's bat kept getting longer and longer and we'd stay away from him, we'd throw screwballs and we'd throw sinkers, and then I gave Burdette a slider," Crandall said. "I wanted to crowd Berra, because he was going out after the baseball and he's a notorious bad-ball hitter and clutch hitter. And when I gave Burdette the slider, he looked, and he actually changed his facial expression in surprise. His eyes got big and his head went up. He went and threw a perfect pitch that jammed Berra and he hit that little bitty pop-up to Mathews and that was the game."

The Braves had done it. Burdette had defeated Whitey Ford and the Yanks 1–0, to give the Miracle Milwaukee Braves a 3-2 Series lead going back to New York. Burdette needed only 86 pitches to complete a seven-hitter with no walks and five strikeouts. He had now pitched 15 consecutive scoreless innings. "When I pitch, I throw away the book," he said. "I can't pitch to a hitter's weaknesses with my own weaknesses." Then, when the writers wanted to know how he knew to throw a slider to Berra, Burdette winked at Crandall, the quiet guy sitting next to him. "No, no, he calls all my pitches," Burdette said. "I never shake him off."

This was a tough loss for the Yankees to shake off. "This is new and startling," the *Journal* wrote, echoing the nation. "Never before in this series had the Yankees found it necessary to refer to future games or their possible outcomes." The Milwaukee fans were too giddy to worry about losing the Series. The outpouring of love and cheers continued and the Braves tipped their caps to their home crowd for the final time in the 1957 season.

The Yanks were stunned. Never before in the franchise's illustrious World Series history had they lost back-to-back one-run games on the road. Only once had they rallied from a 3-2 deficit to win the Series, when in 1952, they broke Brooklyn's heart by winning Games 6 and 7 at Ebbets Field. In 1955, they had trailed 3-2, won Game 6 in New York, but lost Game 7 at Yankee Stadium to the Dodgers. In 1956, they led 3-2 after Don Larsen pitched a perfect Game 5, lost Game 6 in Brooklyn, and then buried the Dodgers in Brooklyn to win Game 7.

It was always a bad idea to count the Yankees out, especially in New York, but that did not dissuade enormous joy in Wisconsin. "The Braves have just about convinced the New York Yankees that 'bush league' Milwaukee has quite a ball club," the *Journal* wrote. "The Braves are making the big plays in the tight ball games and always hustling. The Yanks aren't always." The *Sentinel* was a little more humorous and blunt in its cheerleading for the Braves, which had the Series lead for the first time. There was no semblance of objectivity, though the Braves had a huge task at hand. No team outside of New York had ever taken the World Series away from the Yankees in Yankee Stadium. "Come on, Bushers!" the *Sentinel* urged. The Yankees checked out of Brown's Lake with a $30,000 bill and, for the first time in the World Series, flew home instead of taking the train. The ballplayers couldn't wait to leave. The sportswriters were right there with them. "The sports journalism here has an innocence I thought was obsolete," *Post* columnist Jimmy Cannon observed. "It may belong in a high school paper, but it suits the mood of the town."

Casey Stengel hated everything about the last three games. He hated the way the fans and press treated him and the Yankees. "Disregard all that stuff you read about New York being sugar bush," he said. "Some Milwaukee fans and writers are very much closer to being sugar bush. We've been a success for many years and now they're just gaining it. If we lose, we'll go out like champions." But even just acknowledging the possibility of losing the World Series was news. Casey respected Fred Haney and his team for playing and winning two excellent close ballgames. That much he did not resent.

But Stengel feared losing grip of himself. He hated that Burdette, a pitcher who he alone had been responsible for the Yankees losing, had beaten him twice. He hated it when his managerial maneuvers backfired. He hated it when fans jeered him. He had a lot of John McGraw in him— ego, pride, arrogance, and insecurity. Success had spoiled Stengel. He knew people would eventually start wondering if he was getting too old. He dreaded the day when age became the reason to take away his uniform. All the money in the world couldn't replace Casey's need for a jersey on his back, with a manager's low number, of course, and here he sat, wondering if the Milwaukee Braves had just opened the door to the decline of his career. "Up to now," Stengel lamented, "it ain't anybody who lost this pennant but me."

Ain't nobody gave Milwaukee a better shot to win the World Series than Burdette, who improved to 2-0 and mixed in 12 groundball outs. Burdette became only the second Brave to win two World Series games in the same Series, following Dick Rudolph in 1914. He was also the third Brave to throw a shutout in the World Series, following Johnny Sain in 1948 and Bill James in 1914. The writers learned after the game that Burdette had never been the pitcher the Yanks intended to pass off on the Braves, who were ready to accept a busher named Wally Hood before Johnny Moore insisted the Braves get Burdette instead. Wally Hood was a losing pitcher with a 5.42 ERA in the minors in 1950 and his major league career consisted of two innings. Moore, the scout responsible for Burdette, Eddie Mathews, and Del Crandall, had his fingerprints all over the field. "Johnny Moore was very important to our team," Crandall said. Nobody knew Moore's name, but they were learning Burdette's. "Stengel Must Know Lew's Name Now," the *Sentinel* headline read. "How could he ever forget it?" Lou Chapman asked.

Warren Spahn was waiting for his roomie. "Nice going, Rooms," Spahn said. He didn't mention that he was running a fever.

"That's three for the room, hey Hooks?" Burdette jawed back.

Burdette should have been done for the Series, but Spahn looked pale. Perhaps he had brought the flu virus back from New York City. Potentially losing Spahn was cause for great concern. "Conceivably, if the Braves were to lose the sixth game, Burdette might come back in the seventh," the *Journal* reported, and that wasn't a bad guess if Spahn couldn't go. Burdette would be a likely alternative, though it would be asking him to pitch Game 7 in Yankee Stadium on two days' rest.

Burdette walked out of the trainer's room to face the reporters. He had just called his wife, who two weeks before had a baby. There was a horde of reporters from around the country: print reporters, radio guys, newsreel crews, TV guys—it was a new age of baseball media—so much for a nice relationship with one guy and his pencil and notepad. Most of them were strangers Lew had never seen before. They spoke in the same nasally manner: "We're standing here with Mr. Lew Burdette, hero of the Milwaukee Braves and of Nitro, West Virginia, twice the winning pitcher over the New York Yankees in the 1957 World Series, including today's stunning 1–0 triumph over Whitey Ford and the Bronx Bombers."

Then, of course, they asked a most penetrating question: "How does it feel?"

"I'd a lot rather just crack a beer," Burdette said.

15

Games 6 and 7 **FOUR FOR THE ROOM**

Lou Chapman and a buddy caught a cab from the Commodore Hotel in New York City to Yankee Stadium the first day the Braves were back in town. It was a miserable, murky October day and the city was in a lousy mood. The Yanks were trailing the Series and now the news that had been anticipated for months was finally official—the Brooklyn Dodgers were outta here, off to Los Angeles. The cabbie, though a staunch Yankee fan, was beside himself. He couldn't imagine New York City as a one-team town. Who would the Yankees beat up on?

Tough break, Chapman said, but everyone knew it was coming. That was no solace. Maybe they ought to get cracking on that new ballpark in Flushing. New York without a National League team was as unthinkable as a team in Minneapolis or Atlanta or Toronto. Chapman consoled the guy the best he could. His buddy kept his mouth shut and let the cabbie do the crying.

On the day the Milwaukee Braves should have been the most hated guys in New York City, they were beloved compared to the city's loathing of Dodgers owner Walter O'Malley, called by Dick Young of the *Daily News*, "the most momentous manipulator baseball has ever known." The city was on the same page. One of the New York tabloids ran a cartoon depicting the New York cityscape with a large hand marked LOS ANGELES ripping a heart-shaped parcel of land out of Brooklyn. *The New York Times* treated the news like a funeral, complete with a full-fledged memorial. "Preliminary diagnosis indicates that the cause of death was acute greed, followed by severe political complications," Young wrote. "Surviving are millions of fans and their memories."

No use crying over spilled beer. The cabbie noticed Chapman's press badge and asked him who was pitching Game 6 for the Braves.

"Bob Buhl," Chapman said.

"Buhl?" The cabbie chortled. "The Yanks will beat his brains out. He's a fastball pitcher. Casey's boys eat those guys up."

Chapman's companion, a big dark-haired guy with bushy eyebrows, didn't react, so Chapman spoke for him. "You know he kills the Dodgers, right?" Chapman said. "Best fastball hitting team in baseball and he's beaten them twelve times in the last two years." But the cabbie was unimpressed. Finally, after miles of banter, Chapman could hold the joke no longer.

"I'd like you to meet Bob Buhl," he said.

Buhl was not smiling, though he was laughing on the inside. He saved his beer sneer for the cabbie. He didn't speak. He growled. Chapman remembered the cabbie turning red and almost losing control of the cab—or at least the story sounded better when he told it this way. Why shouldn't he? The guy was driving Frankenstein, but the monster had a heart. The cabbie got a good tip, Chapman reported.

The ballplayers had all day to laugh about it. Tarp covered the field and a steady rain wiped out the workout before Game 6. Fred Haney confidently predicted the Braves would win in six while Yogi Berra assured New York this thing was going seven. The big question for Casey Stengel was if Mickey Mantle could play. "I dunno," he said. "We sure need the kid but if he ain't fit to play, that's that. Nothing we can do."

The weather was no good for Warren Spahn, who was scheduled to pitch Game 7. The flu bug in New York and around the country bit Spahn, whose temperature had risen to 103 degrees. He developed an upper respiratory infection. He was supposed to throw a routine side session, but he felt as lousy as the weather, so Haney sent him to the hospital while the Braves went back to the hotel and played cards. Haney later held a team meeting. The ballplayers showed up with smiles on their faces. Haney loved that about his players. How many teams could lose two players like Red Schoendienst and Warren Spahn and still be so loose? The Braves didn't like losing their boys, but if the kid ain't fit to play, he ain't fit to play. They believed in each other and they'd only worry if they had to.

The Braves slept well, waiting for another crack against Yankee right-handed Bob Turley, who they had knocked out early in Game 3. They knew what they were getting with him—big right-hander, throws hard, good curveball, surly disposition. The Braves had just the man to combat that sort of pitcher, but they hoped Buhl would forget his lousy performance in Game 3, not put too much pressure on himself, and pitch Game 6 like he was born for the mound at Yankee Stadium.

One thing was for certain: the Yankees weren't so worried that it got in the way of a good time. Lou Chapman caught another cab back to the hotel later that night. While at a stoplight, he glanced at the cab next to him. There was Mickey Mantle and Whitey Ford shit-faced in the backseat and having a blast. It became one of Chapman's favorite war stories. "They exchanged greetings," Chapman's son Richard said. "But then again, those guys probably told him to fuck off." But they probably had a smile on their faces while telling Chapman off.

Mantle liked Chapman enough that he allowed him to visit his hotel room for an interview. Chapman wanted to know if Mantle could play. Mantle, laid up in bed, several sheets to the wind, was blurry, bloodshot, and hung over, but he was a helluva guy. Mantle respected how Chapman went the extra mile to get the story. They didn't call Chappie "Gumshoe" for nothing. Mantle mumbled a vow that he would be ready to play. Then his eyes glazed closed and he blacked out. Chappie, sport that he was, made sure that the photograph taken of him interviewing Mantle while he was completely hammered was never published. He saved the photo for the rest of his life. That was the way of the world then—good writers and good ballplayers trusted each other—and they had each other's backs.

The following day, Milwaukee camped out in front of TVs and radios to follow Game 6. They were itching for a party and enjoyed their new-found nickname. "Downtown TV fans expect the value of hayseed to skyrocket on the nation's baseball market Thursday when our 'Bushville, USA' team goes to harvest," the *Sentinel* wrote. The first toast of the day came when Bushville learned Stengel had decided to keep Mantle out of the lineup. The second toast went up to Buhl as he took the mound. He treated himself to a John Wayne movie, *Jet Pilot,* the day before to get himself riled up. Buhl could tell he had good stuff. His fastball was as heavy as a stout and his glare as a dark as a porter. His complexion blended in with the shadows and the gray sky, and he started well enough, with a couple of strikeouts in the bottom of the first inning.

But the problem with Buhl was that when he lost his control, he lost it fast. He walked Enos Slaughter, gave up a single to Yogi Berra, threw a wild pitch to advance the runners, and then struck out Gil McDougald to end the inning. It was a great way to strike out the side if you liked ulcers.

Buhl struggled again in the second inning, allowing a leadoff single, and only surviving on a strike-'em-out-throw-'em-out double play, courtesy of his personal catcher, Del Rice. But in the third inning, with the game scoreless, Buhl's inability to throw strikes caught up to him. He got himself in trouble with two out, walking Slaughter again to bring Berra to the plate. Yogi was hitting .315 against the Braves. Buhl kept the pitch lower than the subway system, but Berra reached down, hit it out of the gutter, and got it in the air down the right field line. The ball would have never carried out of County Stadium, but if it stayed fair it had a chance. This was New York, where things tended to go the Yankees way. The ball landed in the lower deck, a 296-foot home run that gave the Yankees a 2–0 lead.

The home run unscrewed Buhl. He reached back and threw hard out of aggression and frustration, but after allowing another single and a walk, Fred Haney had to come to the mound to get him. He walked like a man tasked with shooting a horse. Buhl, an 18-game winner who should have won more than twenty, put up a 10.80 earned run average in his only World Series. His stats looked like a six-pack: six hits and six walks. "He did a hell of a job for us during the season," Haney said. He called on veteran reliever Ernie Johnson to quell the storm. He recorded a strikeout to end the inning, but after he surrendered a leadoff double in the fourth, he settled into the most magnificent groove of his career.

Turley was dealing, too. The ball was coming out of his hand well. He had four strikeouts in four innings and pitched his way around Eddie Mathews's double in the fourth. Nothing distracted him, not even the fan who dumped pro–Fidel Castro leaflets on the field, showering third-base coach Connie Ryan. But in the fifth, he was finally tagged when Bronx native Frank Torre drove a 350-foot home run into the right-center gap to cut the lead to 2–1. Turley carried the lead into the top of the seventh inning, with Henry Aaron coming to the plate.

Nobody had ever had such a great Series so quietly. Aaron had hit safely in all five games with two home runs. He had two hits each in Games 3, 4, and 5, but Turley handled him in his first two at-bats of Game 6. He struck him out on a curveball in the second inning and got him on a ground ball in the fourth. That had lowered Henry's average to .380 in the Series, an 8-for-21 spell in which he was swinging the bat so well that keeping him off base twice was a moral victory. "I was seeing the ball well," Henry said, and he didn't need to say any more than that.

All season long, Aaron listened to critics call him an undisciplined free swinger. The way the chorus made it sound, you'd think Henry would try to drink a High Life with the bottle cap still on. But Turley knew Henry had a very good knowledge of the strike zone when he tried to bait him. Henry laid off and Turley fell behind in the count, 3-1. Aaron was the lead-off guy and Turley still led by one run. This was a fastball count. There would be no secrets, no surprises. Turley was nasty—broad shoulders, thick trunk and thighs, and a loose arm—he was just the kind of fire-throwing short arm the Yanks built their firing squads around. No need to dime Henry—Turley reared back and challenged him with a letter-high fastball . . . and Henry cracked a gunshot that sounded like Mickey Mantle at his best. The ball was out of the ballpark faster than Eddie Mathews could pound a beer. It was the hardest ball Henry had hit in the Series, a home run to left-center field over the 402 mark. Some estimated the ball traveled 425 feet. Braves Pitcher Taylor Phillips caught it while standing in the bullpen. Aaron thought he hit the ball about as hard as he had hit a ball back in St. Louis in 1955. New York partisans said the only right-handed hitters who hit a ball that far in that direction were Joe DiMaggio and Hank Greenberg. No matter how many feet it traveled, all that mattered was the one run that tied the score, 2-2.

Henry took Buhl off the hook and now the decision belonged to Ernie Johnson. He had retired ten consecutive Yankees following Jerry Coleman's leadoff double in the fourth. He had also succeeded in stopping New York's

Hank Bauer, who was 0-for-3 with a pair of strikeouts, one against Buhl, and the other against Johnson. Bauer thought he would never see a fastball and he was right. The count was 2-2 when Johnson spun a curveball and Bauer connected. He hit a high fly ball down the left field line. The ball was hit too high and deep for Wes Covington to make another clutch catch. It would either be fair or foul. Home plate umpire Jocko Conlan followed the flight of the ball, but the ball made the call for him. It hit the screen attached to the left-field foul pole and bounced back onto the field. Bauer slowed up at second, unsure if the ball was in play. Only when he saw Conlan circle his index finger did he realize that he had homered to give the Yanks a 3–2 lead.

This is what they mean when they call baseball a game of inches: the screen on the foul poles had only been installed at Yankee Stadium at the start of the 1957 season. They were installed to help umpires make the correct call on balls like the one Bauer hit. Without the screen, Bauer's shot could have been called foul and the Braves might still be tied. But instead, it could be chalked up to another World Series first: the first World Series home run to hit a foul pole screen—the ancestor of Carlton Fisk's home run down the left-field line eighteen years later.

With a one-run lead, Turley wasn't about to give it back. He was coked up, throwing hard, throwing strikes, working ahead of the count, getting bad swings, putting the Braves on the defensive, making all of Milwaukee sad. He struck out two more in the eighth, and in the ninth, he walked Eddie Mathews with the tying run to bring Henry Aaron back to the plate.

The *Casey at the Bat* moment of the Series had arrived. Once again, there were no surprises, a fastball pitcher against a fastball hitter, the game and the Series in the balance. Turley was covered in sweat, his heavy white flannels hanging off him like the branches of a tree. Henry cradled his lumber and expected a first-pitch fastball. He got it and took a violent rip, fouling it straight back for strike one. The crowd reaction at Yankee Stadium told the story of the emotion. The fans back home pounded their beers on the tavern bar in frustration and anticipation. Prayers and crossed fingers flew from both sides of the field. You could have called in the fielders and let them take a knee. This was going to be decided man against man.

Turley reared back and threw another fastball. There was a little something extra on it, so quick that it made the previous pitch look like a changeup. Henry flinched. He never flinched. That's how strong Turley's arm was. Jocko Conlan's call sounded like a Supreme Court judge banging his gavel. Strike two!

Aaron never stepped out of the box. He just wanted the next pitch. He was always a guess hitter and admitted so. He had seen all of Turley's stuff and he knew there was no way Turley was going to throw him a fastball for the third consecutive time. But as Henry Aaron's Alabama stride style forefather Piper Davis once bellowed, "Element of surprise, my dear brother!" Turley stunned Henry when he did just that. The bat never moved an inch. Conlan called strike three. Nobody—*nobody*—had managed to take the bat out of Henry's hand the way Turley had. "He threw me a beautiful pitch—a fastball about at my knees," Henry said. "I was expecting something inside. I was sore at myself, not Turley."

If the Braves couldn't win with Henry, they didn't deserve to win the game. Turley finished the game off by himself. Wes Covington hit a hard smash back up the box, but Turley picked it cleanly. He fired to Gil McDougald to start the 1-6-3 double play to end the game. The Yanks had proven Yogi Berra right. There would be a Game 7. Final score: New York 3, Milwaukee 2.

Warren Spahn watched in his hotel room. He had always dreamed of pitching Game 7 of the World Series. Now it was here, but the decision wasn't his. He was still sick, but he thought he could pitch through it. He had no idea what Fred Haney was thinking. Back at the ballpark, when the Braves trudged into the clubhouse with worried faces, Haney walked into the middle of the room and answered the question before anyone asked. "Burdette tomorrow," he announced.

The writers scurried to Burdette's locker. He had the calm demeanor of a man who knew he was pitching Game 7 of the World Series at Yankee Stadium. It was the single greatest plum in all of pitching, but there was a catch. Burdette would have to come out on two days' rest, which even in days of the four-man pitching rotation was uncommon. The short rest didn't bother Burdette one bit, or at least that's the way he made it sound. He played catch before the game and everything felt good. He had only thrown 86 pitches in Game 5, in contrast to the 121 pitches in Game 2. Pitching on two days' rest hadn't bothered him before. He recalled pitching on two days' rest against Brooklyn in August 1955, but omitted mentioning that the Braves lost both games. Fear was simply not a part of Lew Burdette. He would take his 15 consecutive scoreless innings and his two World Series complete game victories and put them on the line in the name of carrying the Braves on his back. "I'm not going out there to lose, so you figure it out," he said. "Besides, my roomie may be sick today, but I hear he'll be in the bullpen backing me up." Then somebody wanted to know if Burdette was a better pitcher now than he had ever been. Lew's big eyes lit up and a big sarcastic smirk came over his face. He looked a little unstable, but that was part of the act. At least people though it was part of the act.

"Yeah," he said. "I'm bigger, stronger, and dumber."

On the bus ride to the ballpark the following morning, the Braves were unusually quiet. This team was known for its voice, individuality, and passion. But as the players boarded at the Commodore Hotel and left for Yankee Stadium, there was uneasy silence. Everything they had worked for came down to one game and one guy pitching on two days' rest. Nobody needed to remind the ballplayers what was at stake, least of all, Fred Haney. He was chewing a steady diet of antacids to treat his ulcers. After Game 6, he excused himself to find a dentist to perform emergency oral surgery. In his angst during the Series, Haney had so violently grinded his teeth together that the molar collapsed.

Burdette sat quietly by himself. He was alone with his thoughts and a pack of Camels. He chain-smoked, but that wasn't out of the ordinary. He anticipated Casey Stengel would stack the Yankee lineup with left-handed bats and that Mickey Mantle would be back. There was never much room to be ordinary against the Yankees. There would be less today. Don Larsen would be his mound opponent, exactly one year and two days removed from pitching a World Series perfect game against the Brooklyn Dodgers. These were the games that made the Yankee who they were. It was the moment the Braves needed to steal away to bring the World Series home to Bushville.

Back home in Milwaukee, the streets were quiet and tense. People went about their daily lives, but life would stop when the first pitch was thrown at 1 P.M. at Yankee Stadium. They had never been champions and they wanted to be winners now and to complete their long journey from bush league to major league city. Milwaukee never wanted to lose its small-town identity, but times were moving forward. It was time for a new era and a new World Series winner. Perhaps even the Yankee fans sensed this. As 61,207 fans trooped into the ballpark, they were serenaded by the 42nd Infantry Division marching band, which played, of all things, *On Wisconsin*.

Casey Stengel might have thought the song selection was bush, but he liked his chances in Game 7. "I've got a good one," Casey said, talking about starting pitcher Don Larsen, one of his favorite fellas. He really liked the idea of a hard thrower going against the Braves in a winner-take-all game, as opposed to his old pal Haney, who was asking his sinker-slider-screwball-spitter guy to become the first pitcher to win three starts in one World Series since 1920. Though Burdette had proven himself to be more than the busher Casey once considered him, Stengel still believed he had the better man pitching. The odds of Burdette beating the Yanks three times in the Series were very steep.

Casey could smell history in the air. Thirty-four years to the day, Stengel hit the very first home run in World Series history at Yankee Stadium. How could he forget? It was Game 1 of the 1923 Series. Stengel came to bat with two out and the bases empty in the top of the ninth inning. He was an old fella already, at thirty-two years old, the veteran of eleven big league seasons in a playing career that was soon to be overshadowed by his managerial record. His legs didn't work so good anymore, but he got hold of one, and hit it where they ain't. In his scrapbook, you would likely find Damon Runyon's narration:

His mouth wide open, his warped legs bending beneath him at every stride, his arms flying back and forth like those of a man swimming . . . Casey was muttering to himself . . . to greater speed, as a jockey mutters to his horse . . . People—sixty thousand of 'em, men and women, were standing and roaring sympathetically, "Come on Casey!" The warped old legs, twisted and bent . . . barely

held out until Casey reached the plate . . . then they collapsed . . .
he suggested a huge crab down there, his arms and legs wiggling
in all directions.

Casey could still remember the cheering as he filled out his lineup
card the way he liked it, with Mantle hitting third and Berra cleanup. It
was time once and for all to beat Milwaukee back to Bushville, to reassert
the Yankees after a Series that suggested that Casey was slipping. But had
Casey told the story of his home run to completion, he would have had to
include the name of the pitcher who surrendered the most famous, glorious, and magnificent moment he ever accomplished with a baseball bat.
The pitcher, a fella for the Yankees, was Bullet Joe *Bush*.

Lew Burdette was playing a few blocks away from the birthplace of
the popular term *Bush*. The earliest known published reference to a
"busher" occurred in 1905 in a poem written by *New York American* sportswriter W. E. Kirk and subsequently published in the *Sporting Life* as a
tribute to the famous New York Giants pitcher Christy Mathewson, who
pitched three shutouts in the 1905 World Series. The feat had never been
duplicated. No pitcher had even thrown two World Series shutouts in the
same series since the fabled Matty. History was the furthest thing from
Burdette's mind as he tuned up his sinker, slider, screwball, and maybe his
spitball. But even in 1905, in the age of the dead-ball era and the invincible starting pitcher, when two day's rest was routine and guys loaded the
ball with everything imaginable, writers like Kirk realized that most of
them would be dead and gone by the time anybody saw any pitcher do
something so spectacular again in the World Series.

Perhaps in years to come a strapping lad
May twirl like Matty, showing no fatigue
And crowds in this same ballpark may go mad
O'er some green busher from a minor league.

The poet had the city correct, though he would have to wait for his
children to see Yankee Stadium. Burdette was the busher, the team was the
Braves, and the city was Milwaukee, its heart open to the term *Bushville*.

They had won over the nation and were sentimental favorites. The New York dynasty had nine innings to prove Bushville was a fluke.

The first question most fans had was if Larsen had another perfect game in his right arm. Facing him took some getting used to because he had no windup. He was tough to get used to for hitters who had rarely faced him, like Bob Hazle, the Braves leadoff guy in the first inning who took a first-pitch strike. The game was on and the bets were down. The Braves were getting even money now. The country slowed to a stop. Nobody was watching anything else. Game 7 at Yankee Stadium still evoked the Mount Olympus of American sporting life, a moon shot before anybody coined the term. The Russians could have launched another Sputnik and nobody would have noticed. They watched Hurricane Hazle foul away the next fastball, then saw Larsen blow him away. Johnny Logan grounded out on the first pitch and then Larsen threw three fastball strikes past Eddie Mathews. As Casey might say, that was a good way to take the pipe to the Braves.

Burdette ambled to the mound. He was the ultimate "squibber" in Stengelese—a soft thrower with deception. Lew was unusually wiggly. Back home in Nitro, the town of three thousand gathered around his mama's front porch to hear the radio broadcast. Hank Bauer hit leadoff for the Yanks. The very first pitch Burdette threw him was hit hard down the left field for a double. Bauer had now hit safely in all seven games and extended his career World Series hitting streak to 14 games. Burdette was already in a mess.

Enos Slaughter came to the plate. He was tough because he always put the bat on the ball. Burdette checked Bauer at second. Then he threw a sinker that Slaughter slapped back to the box. Burdette speared it with quickness and agility. Bauer was halfway between second and third. Burdette's instincts took over. Red Schoendienst always thought Burdette was a better athlete and a better baseball mind than he ever got credit for. Burdette saw the fear and uncertainty in Bauer's eyes. Burdette held the ball in his bare hand and ran directly at him. Bauer fled for third.

The Braves executed a flawless rundown. A novice baseball fan would have seen perfection in motion—Burdette charged Bauer and flipped to Eddie Mathews at third. Bauer turned tail and ran for second, where shortstop Johnny Logan was waiting. Eddie flipped the ball back to Logan, so Bauer turned for third again. Guess who he saw waiting for him? There was Lew Burdette. A refugee running out of breath, Bauer turned around. He slid back into second base just in front of Logan's tag.

But Slaughter, a smart country ballplayer, ran the bases country dumb. He thought Bauer would be out so he kept coming around first. And there it was, ladies and gentlemen, two Yankees standing at second base at the same time in Game 7 of the World Series. It was stupidity in action. The scorecard read 1-5-6-1-6. Across Milwaukee, cheers and laughter rose. *Excuse us,* the city asked, *we're the bushers?*

Bauer owned the bag, because it was his in the first place. Burdette went back to work to pitch to Mantle. The best the mighty slugger could muster was another nub back to Burdette, who stabbed the ball and gave Bauer a nice long look at second base. It was practically an invitation to try for third. But Bauer stayed put, Burdette tossed Mantle out, and Yogi Berra came to the plate. This was a no-brainer. The Braves intentionally walked Berra to bring up Gil McDougald. Burdette fell behind in the count 3-1, but he fought back to get McDougald to pop up to Mathews to end the inning. If Fred Haney had any hair left, he might have pulled it out along with his tooth.

Henry Aaron led off the top of the second inning. The rest of the country had officially discovered him now and knew he belonged with Willie Mays. Henry's Alabama stride style had served him well. He was 9-for-23 and had hit safely in all six games, bringing a World Series average of .380 to the plate. Larsen wasn't nibbling, only challenging Henry with hard low strikes. Aaron smoked a single and the Yanks would take that any time. Most of the pitchers still felt Mathews was the more dangerous home run threat at Yankee Stadium. The Braves moved Aaron to second and stranded him there, but in the third inning, they found the combination they wanted.

Larsen allowed a one-out single to Bob Hazle. When Johnny Logan hit a sharp grounder right to third baseman Tony Kubek, no Milwaukee fan expected anything good to happen. But in his haste, Kubek threw wild to second, blowing the force play, leaving Hazle safe, and putting runners at first and second with nobody out for Mathews. The play was close enough to infuriate Stengel, who charged onto the field as fast as his shaky legs could carry him, to go jaw to jaw with umpire Joe Paparella.

Casey was very cautious. He held his hands behind his back as though they were tied and made certain that the brim of his cap did not beak Paparella, which would mean certain ejection. Then Casey let "Papa" have it. That was a horseshit call in the biggest fuckin' game of the year. Stengel was livid. All his frustration came seething out, all the old rivalries of years past, the hostile feelings between the leagues, Milwaukee's rejection and treatment of him, his ballplayers acting like stupid players making stupid plays and making him look stupid, or as Casey would say of a dumb player running a dumb play, making him look like "Ned standin' up in class." Casey never stood up in class.

Paparella warned Casey that if he didn't shut up right now and get off the field, he would be standing in the shower instead. So Stengel retreated to the dugout. The Braves had him by his jockstrap and he knew it. If he pitched around Mathews, he'd have to face Aaron. Stengel lowered his head and counted his crooked steps as he walked back to the dugout. At least nobody counted his steps aloud in Yankee Stadium, but they were banging beer bottles, one for each step, back home in Milwaukee.

Eddie's .222 Series batting average wasn't much to look at, but unless Larsen could get an inning-ending double play, this was probably going to be his last batter. Casey had his pitchers on a choke chain and he had lefty Bobby Shantz warming up to pitch to the right-handed Aaron. The noise in Yankee Stadium intensified, but with a different feel. The crowd lacked the hostility Yankee fans often spewed toward their mortal enemies. The cheering wasn't confined to the wealthy Braves fans from places like White-fish Bay who could afford the last-minute airfare and hotel accommodations in New York City or the blue-collar fans who dug deep into their pockets for gas money and motels in New Jersey. The energy came from all over the ballpark, from the rich seats to the cheap seats, from the bankers and the bakers, from the book editors to the bookmakers, from the social-ites and the secretaries. New York loved an underdog, and for maybe the first time, they felt like one, too.

"Homeless Dodger and Giant fans seem to have adopted the Braves, at least for this World Series, and even some of the true-blue Yankee fans of New York are beginning to grow tired of their monopoly," the *Journal* wrote. If they had to root against Casey to fill that void, they would, and no memories of a home run against Joe Bush could change that. "I suppose, deep down in my heart, I really want the Braves to win," a Yankee fan told the *Journal*. Then someone asked him why he considered himself a Yankee fan. "It's sort of like religion," he explained. "I was born into a Yankee family." Casey couldn't buy a cheer or a prayer. So he turned self-centered in his motives. If he had to be the bad guy to win, he'd do it. Casey didn't give a shit about what the fans wanted. He demanded a fastball low and inside against Mathews. The fastball had to be located in the right spot to beat him.

Don Larsen was perfect in 1956, but not in 1957. He missed, but Eddie didn't. He banged a high fastball for a hard line drive over first base, where a jumping Joe Collins came up empty. The ball rattled into the right-field corner. Hurricane Hazle came rolling across the plate with Johnny Logan at his heels. Eddie stood at second base and clapped his hands. He had a two-run double, the Braves had a 2–0 lead, and Casey had enough of Don Larsen.

Stengel summoned Bobby Shantz. "His willingness to work should not be abused," Branch Rickey once wrote. Casey took Rickey up on that offer. All Casey asked Shantz to do was to keep the game close, but he had to face Henry Aaron. So obviously, there was no pressure. The little lefty who learned to spin his curveball at Pottstown High School in Pennsylvania tried the quick curve, but Henry hit a scorching line drive single back up the middle to score Mathews and give the Braves a 3–0 lead.

Milwaukee was going crazy and the inning wasn't over yet. Wes Covington dumped a Texas League single into shallow center, sending Aaron racing from first to third. Frank Torre was next. He looked over his shoulder because he was certain Fred Haney would pinch-hit for him against the left-hander, but Haney let him hit and put on the suicide squeeze bunt. There was one problem—Torre realized he missed the sign after the pitch was on the way and he saw Aaron charging down the line. If he didn't make contact, Aaron was a goner.

So Torre slashed a ground ball to second base and ran like hell. Now, the Torre family is not exactly known for leg hits. Frank was so slow that he swiped four bases in seven years. He hit a tailor-made double play ball that forced Covington at second, but miracle of miracles, Torre ran like a new man. "I think the fact that I missed the sign gave me some extra speed to beat the throw," Torre said. "I was determined to get that run home. And I did beat it out."

Aaron scored to give the Braves a 4–0 lead and Torre caught his breath at first, safe on a fielder's choice, the greatest ground ball of his life. Frank's kid brother Joe jumped out of his chair and wildly cheered. Casey Stengel wondered what else could go right for the Braves and wrong for the Yankees. He couldn't have imagined that the slow first baseman's kid brother would one day have his job, winning titles for this team in this ballpark.

When the inning was over, Lew Burdette was loaded with confidence. Everything he had ever wanted to be as a big league pitcher was six innings away from being his, thanks to the defensive help from Eddie Mathews and Frank Torre. Eddie made a backhand pick on a smash by Kubek in the second. A batter later, he almost threw away a routine grounder, but Torre scooped the ball out of the dirt. When the Braves gave Burdette a lead, he turned nasty. His flawless bottom of the third greeted the Yankees, extending his scoreless innings streak to eighteen.

Burdette had to wade through the heart of the order in the bottom of the fourth. Every strike was significant and every out important. Mickey Mantle led off the inning. He was playing on painkillers and pride. He took two magnificent swings at Burdette and missed both times. On the 0-2, Mick lifted a fly ball high enough to have window washers, but Bob Hazle made the catch in shallow right field. Yogi Berra lined one to right field right into the Hurricane, where Hazle caught the second out. Then, Gil McDougald put another good swing on a Burdette mystery pitch and hit it hard to right-center field. It was Hazle's ball all the way. He got a good jump, picked it out of the air on the run, and got a slap on the back from his center fielder, Henry Aaron, for handling all three chances. Now, Burdette had 19 consecutive scoreless innings.

Aaron had beaten the Yanks with the long ball. When he led off the top of the fifth, he tried to beat them with little ball. With third baseman Tony Kubek playing him deep, Henry dropped down a bunt. Yogi Berra pounced on the ball, but he could not field it cleanly. His throw was too late. It was the third error of the game for the Yankees. Stengel was hurting inside. Even his beloved catcher, the kid he called his "assistant," was making mistakes. The Yankees got out of the inning without any further damage, except to their reputations.

Burdette got the first out of the bottom of the fifth to retire his 11th consecutive hitter. Then, after Jerry Coleman fouled a sinker off his front foot, he singled to center to snap the streak. But Burdette wasn't licked, and as far as the Yanks could tell, he wasn't licking the ball, either. Joe Collins, the veteran lefty hitting first baseman, wasn't sure. He made a big fuss and asked plate umpire Bill McKinley to check the ball. McKinley had a look and said the baseball hadn't been drinking. Collins wasn't convinced. He grounded to short, forcing Coleman, and found himself safe at first. He spent all his energy eyeballing Burdette, but he couldn't figure him out.

With two out and Collins at first, Casey went to his bench. He wanted Moose Skowron to hit no matter how bad his back hurt. If Casey was going to lose, Burdette and the Braves were going to have to beat him with all his guns in the lineup, no matter how sickly, sore, or slumping. If Fred Haney wanted to pry the World Series away from his old buddy Case, his tiring pitcher would have to do it against a lineup with Bauer, Mantle, Berra, McDougald, and Skowron. Burdette had to fight through the lineup not once more, but twice. They had all seen his stuff. There were no more secrets.

Burdette was getting tired, but he concealed his fatigue in his body language. Nobody could imitate him, not his stuff and not his shtick. He always pitched like a guy who drank too much coffee, but this time he poured it on. He needed deception and deflections. He needed mirages and miracles. He needed the Yankees to not catch onto the fact that he didn't have enough left in his arm to reach back and throw harder when he needed it. Burdette was completely alone in the most hostile environment baseball can possibly create. Game 7 on the road, at Yankee Stadium, all the Bombers in the lineup, a city on his shoulders, two days' rest, the hopes and dreams of Bushvilles everywhere. The situation required a guy who couldn't feel human emotion on the mound, but his veins ran as cold as his fastball, and when Skowron grounded into a force play to finish the fifth, he walked off the mound with 20 consecutive scoreless innings.

The gauntlet resumed in the sixth with Burdette facing the top of the order, still leading 4–0. Burdette got two quick outs, but he was laboring, going into deep counts against almost every batter. Behind the plate, catcher Del Crandall tried to nurse him home. They switched up pitch sequences and worked to stay one step ahead of the hitters. Getting Hank Bauer and Enos Slaughter out to start the inning was crucial, because it allowed Burdette to face Mickey Mantle with the bases empty.

Mantle had not been himself in this Series, batting .235 to this point, 4-for-17 with one home run. With nobody on, Burdette pitched to contact. If he gave up a home run, so be it, but instead, Mantle singled to right to bring up Berra.

Casey's "assistant" had been a constant. He would finish the Series with a .320 batting average. Burdette got what he wanted, a grounder to third, but it took a tough hop off the cut of the grass. The ball handcuffed Mathews, who in the day's parlance "scrambled" it. His error put runners at first and second for McDougald, who was 0-for-2, but had hit the ball hard to right in his last at-bat. But he didn't hit this one hard. He rolled a ground ball inside the bag at third, a tailor-made ball for Mathews, who stepped on third base for the third out. The streak was at 21 consecutive scoreless innings. "Everyone is relieved again," the front-running *Sentinel* reported. "And how have you been around the homeland?"

As Burdette and the Braves jogged off the field, they earned a healthy ovation from the Yankee Stadium crowd, a "tremendous roar," according to the *Sentinel*. This time it was clear that it was too loud to only be Wisconsin natives. No, these were the bandwagon fans who were pulling for the Braves even if they wore Yankee hats, and especially if they wore Dodgers and Giants hats. The National League fans would always root for the National League, and many of the Yankee fans liked good baseball, period . . . and what they were seeing from Milwaukee was better baseball than what they were seeing from New York. In between innings, Burdette sat alone in the dugout with his right shoulder draped in his jacket. He sneaked a smoke in the tunnel to keep his energy up. The Braves kept trying to get him one more run, grand-slam protection, but couldn't do it in the top of the seventh.

Burdette would have bypassed his seven warmup pitches in the bottom of the seventh if he could have, so instead, he tossed the ball so lightly that Del Crandall could have caught the ball barehanded. Tony Kubek led off the inning and got Burdette in trouble again, spoiling a 1-2 pitch with a leadoff single. Jerry Coleman, who had been a pest all Series, was ending his playing career with a bang, finishing with a .364 average, the best mark of his six World Series appearances with Casey Stengel. He put yet another ball in play, hitting a high bounder to the right side, but Burdette jumped off the mound and came down with the ball. He threw out Coleman and Kubek took second.

With the pitcher's spot due up, Casey Stengel tried to disrupt Burdette's rhythm. He would obviously use a pinch hitter. He needed runs fast, so the best choice would be Elston Howard. But Casey stalled. He fiddled with his lineup card. He tied his shoelaces. He walked down his bench pretending to interview different men for the job. This charade continued for a minute before Fred Haney yelled across the field. They were friends, but not right now. Haney knew Casey was stalling and he demanded Case pick a hitter and get the game rolling. When Casey further loitered, Haney had enough. He marched out onto the field and demanded that home plate umpire Bill McKinley speed up the game.

McKinley was an American League career man. He shrugged his shoulders at Haney and indicated there was nothing he could do to hurry Casey along. Haney pointed at Stengel and yelled at him to get a hitter out here. Quit playing Mexican League rules and get the game going again. Burdette didn't mind. He knew Casey was only trying to disrupt his rhythm and he knew Casey was going to send up Elston Howard to pinch-hit. He struck him out in Game 5. Once Howard was finally announced, Burdette struck him out again. After Moose Skowron grounded out to end the seventh, it was 22 consecutive scoreless innings, the 4–0 lead intact, and Burdette had his second wind.

Then, in the top of the eighth inning, against Tommy Byrne, the fifth pitcher of the game for Stengel, Del Crandall got the extra run. Del hadn't done much offensively in the World Series, his .211 average not his favorite, but he saved his best hit for last when he blasted a solo home run. "Oh, my goodness, yes," Crandall said. "I guess I touched all the bases."

When Burdette, who was up next, came up to the plate, something special happened. All 61,207 fans at Yankee Stadium gave him a standing ovation the *Sentinel* believed "he won't ever forget." There was no such thing as the designated hitter in 1957. Burdette had batted three times in Game 7, and after seven shutout innings on two days' rest, he drew a walk. Pinch hitter Andy Pafko popped up to end the inning and that was probably intentional. He didn't want to make Lew run the bases so late in the game.

By the eighth inning, with the Braves in command 5–0, the Yankee Stadium crowd lost it. Burdette got a standing ovation, not for walking off the mound, but for walking onto it. The crowd was unabashedly pulling for a Bushville win. In their minds, Milwaukee had already won. They had pitched better, played better, hit better, were better in the clutch, played hard in all seven games, and made their city, state, and indeed, the entire Midwest proud. That was as all-American as a story could get, and even if Burdette somehow gave up a run in the last two innings to lose his scoreless innings streak, even if he couldn't complete one of the most remarkable pitching feats in modern World Series history, they would still applaud him. At heart, the New York fans were baseball fans, just like the Wisconsin fans, proud of the game and of their people.

Burdette could fulfill the poet's prophecy and become the busher who won three World Series games in New York City. Bauer, who the *Journal* called "the best .250 hitter in World Series history," popped up to Logan for the first out of the eighth. Burdette was thrilled to be rid of him. He needed five more outs when Enos Slaughter came to the plate. The Yankee batters were dead men walking against Burdette's stuff, which was getting better as he got closer to ending the game. Slaughter popped out foul to Crandall. Two down and four outs to go—the Burdette beer-drinking game was on.

Mantle hobbled to the plate one last time, again, with nobody on base. It was a simple strategy—nothing but sinkers and screwballs to Mick, hitting left-handed. Lew was locked in. He didn't care if Mantle hit a home run. He wanted outs. And if he left one where Mick could get it, and he did, then he'd tip his cap to a fellow pro. Mickey got a ball he could handle and put that gorgeous swing on it. When he did it right, it didn't matter if he was in pain, he was perfect—his hands started quickly and effortlessly, the bat sped up so easily, his arms extended like he was giving Burdette a hug, and he finished with a flourish, a sweeping uppercut that resembled a fancy curlicue at the end of his autograph. He lifted the ball high and deep to left field, one of those majestic opposite field shots that made adults feel like children. But Mantle's ball did not have enough behind it and came to rest in Wes Covington's glove for the final out of the eighth inning. The scoreless streak was up to 23, but all that mattered was one—one inning, the bottom of the ninth.

In the Braves bullpen, Warren Spahn had been throwing all afternoon in case Rooms got in trouble, but he never had. Now, Spahn knew that was it. He sat on the bench and got ready to watch the ninth. Much raced through his mind—all the years and innings, all the ups and downs, the close calls, the time he was almost killed. He looked onto the field and saw these guys who he had played so many games with, in Boston and Milwaukee, throw the ball around like kids one more time: Eddie, and Johnny, and Del, and Andy, and Henry . . . and especially Burdette. Spahn would have loved to be the man on the mound, but if it couldn't be him, he would have wanted his best friend, the guy his son considered a second dad. Burdette was more than his roommate. Burdette was his brother.

Yogi Berra led off the bottom of the ninth. Old-time Yankee fans swore they had never felt an atmosphere like this. Yankee Stadium, one might suggest, was as loud as Milwaukee County Stadium. Yogi hacked at the first pitch, lifting it foul and into the sun, where first baseman Frank Torre made the catch. One out.

Yankee Stadium roared, but in the streets of Milwaukee was complete silence. Traffic signals changed colors without cars on the road. Cops and crooks sat elbow-to-elbow at bars and taverns watching the ninth inning.

There were prayers and tension and beer on ice. Everyone stopped working. "I was watchin' Game 7 on TV, just like everyone else," Bobby Uecker recalled. "I was working. My uncle and I were at a job somewhere. We didn't even have to ask people to turn the TV on during the World Series. We were just sittin' on the carpet spellbound during the ninth."

At Yankee Stadium, owner Lou Perini muttered a silent rosary. The old man knew when to pray. The Midwest huddled together, hoping the Braves would win one for the road, before this country changed, and left everything in the past. Gil McDougald was next. He worked the count to 2-2, then lined a sharp single to left field. It was a veteran at-bat. Not so much for the next hitter, rookie Tony Kubek. He swung at the first pitch and skied a routine fly ball to center fielder Henry Aaron. Two outs.

Jerry Coleman was a good guy for the Yanks to have up. Burdette's soft stuff simply hadn't fooled him. He had a single and nearly had base hits on his other two grounders. "Oh, my thumping heart," *Sentinel* columnist Lloyd Larson wrote. In the vast reaches of the outfield, a gang of bleacher fans climbed over the fence and began to swarm the field. Time was called as the cops shoved them back. A minute later, Burdette had the ball in his hand again. Coleman, in what would be his last major league at-bat, carried a defiant gleam in his eye. He was too proud to accept the idea that he would go out like Jackie Robinson did in 1956—the last out of Game 7 in his last major league at-bat. Coleman got what he wanted out of baseball one last time. He singled to right field, putting runners at first and second.

Burdette wasn't out of it yet. Spahn nervously began playing catch again. Haney inched to the top step of the dugout. The Yankee pitcher, Tommy Byrne, was the next batter. He had pitched the eighth and the ninth inning. Many pitchers were easy outs even in the days before the Designated Hitter, but not Byrne. He was a lifetime .238 hitter with 14 home runs. Casey Stengel never thought once about hitting for him. Moose Skowron was on deck, which meant if Byrne could get on and load the bases, Skowron could get the Yanks back into the game with one swing of the bat.

Byrne would not give this at-bat away. It was the last moment of his major league career, too. He had come to the big leagues with the 1943

Yankees and become a favorite of both Stengel and his predecessor Joe McCarthy. Byrne had walked off the mound for the last time in the top of the ninth, and like Coleman, he was determined not to be the final out in the bottom of the ninth. With the count 1-1 on the left-handed hitting Byrne, Burdette threw him a backdoor slider. Byrne gave up on the pitch and then watched it cut across the outside corner for strike two. Burdette tried it again on the 1-2 pitch, but Byrne showed his years and wisdom. He hit a hard smash to second base, off the glove of Felix Mantilla, and was safe at first with a single to load the bases with two out in the ninth.

It was 1:34 P.M. in Milwaukee and there was a tense silence, and in Yankee Stadium, fierce roaring, all of New York pulling for the feel-good Milwaukee kids. Moose Skowron was an aggressive slugger who never smiled, a quintessential Yankee villain with a face as charming as a rusty nail. "The home run I hit didn't seem to be important until they loaded the bases," Del Crandall said. "I knew at that point that at least he couldn't hit a five-run home run."

Burdette bore down. He stared into Crandall for his sign. All he could see was his catcher and all he could hear was his breath. All he wanted to know was what pitch to throw. Crandall gave his sign while in the crouch. Burdette coiled up and threw Skowron a first-pitch fastball. Skowron took a vicious cut and fouled it straight back. Crandall ripped his mask off and saw it go foul. He had no play. Crandall and Burdette's hearts both missed a beat. Plate umpire Bill McKinley put a new baseball in Crandall's hand. Crandall asked McKinley an innocent question. Where was that pitch? As he did, he rubbed the ball in his hands. McKinley gave a bland answer, so as Crandall continued rubbing the ball with the sweat accumulated on his glove hand, he asked McKinley another question. Would that pitch have been a strike in the American League? McKinley gave a bland answer and hurried the game along. Such boring conversation was never heard of in the bottom of the ninth of Game 7.

Burdette observed halfway between the mound and the plate. Crandall turned around, and still standing, threw back to Burdette, who caught the ball, looked at it, and shook his head in agreement. "He would give me that little peek and then go about his business," Crandall said.

Burdette looked utterly unbothered on the mound. He was so laid-back, yet so determined to win, that even the guys who had played with him for years, marveled at how the pressure that would kill other men couldn't touch him. "Burdette was such a loosey-goosey guy, the crazy joker always pulling stuff, and with men on base, he was impossible," Frank Torre said. "He would always figure out a way to finagle his way out of the damn thing."

Once more, Burdette went through his dance. His arm was damn near ready to fall off, but he wasn't letting on. He stared into Crandall for his sign for a long time, but he already had it. This pondering was purely for show. Burdette was ready for his beer and champagne shower. He was ready to get wet. He reached back for one last fastball and threw it as hard as he could. The pitch was a heavy and fast sinker with a tail on it—late, late, late down-and-away movement. Most hitters either missed it or topped it into the ground. Skowron took a menacing rip and hit a hard chopper to third baseman Eddie Mathews, very similar to the in-between hop that devoured him in St. Louis at the end of 1956, but all of Eddie's hard work paid off. "It was hit good and Eddie got it on the short hop," Crandall said. For one shining moment, Edwin Lee Mathews from Santa Barbara, California, was the greatest defensive third baseman anyone had ever seen. He made a smooth pickup and now it was a footrace to the bag. This was a fight Eddie wasn't going to lose. "He went right to the bag," Crandall said, forcing Jerry Coleman at third base for the final out of the 1957 World Series, and then turning toward Burdette and Crandall. The Braves poured out of the dugout, and Henry Aaron jumped for joy in center field.

BUSHVILLE WINS!

EPILOGUE

It was 1:35 P.M. on Wisconsin Avenue on October 10, 1957, when the Milwaukee Braves defeated the New York Yankees, 5–0, in Game 7 to win the World Series. Windows rattled and people poured into the street, heat and energy and passion waving through the city like an A-bomb, rippling and rumbling from the epicenter, north to Green Bay, south to Chicago, west to Los Angeles and San Francisco and beyond, and yes, east, back to New York, where on the Yankee Stadium grass, Eddie Mathews vanished into a group hug with Lew Burdette and Del Crandall.

Roland Hemond, who turned a job sweeping the bleachers at a minor league baseball park in Hartford, Connecticut, into a career as a Hall of Fame baseball executive, always loved the lasting image of Mathews, Crandall, and Burdette. "Johnny Moore's boys," he called them, a shining example of why teams must carefully cultivate their scouting staffs and then listen to courageous and creative thinkers who possess the ability to predict the future. Hemond never forgot Ben Geraghty, the minor league manager who should have managed in the big leagues, who proved the value of correctly profiling roles for young prospects to become productive major leaguers.

Bob Wolf, the iron-man *Journal* beat writer who never missed a game, pounded his typewriter with tears in his eyes. "The Yankees Are Dead! Long Live the Milwaukee Braves!" he wrote. He turned around in the press box and gave his best friend and biggest competitor, Lou Chapman of the *Sentinel*, a tremendous hug. As they typed, the conga lines and bunny-hop dances were in full swing on Wisconsin Avenue long before the reporters filed their final copy of the season and penned one last—30—for the season.

Henry Aaron never forgot Chapman. When Chapman retired from full-time sports writing in 1979, Aaron wrote to him, "You were a great human being and I am so happy that I had a chance to be a friend of yours for all these many years." When deadline beckoned for Lou Chapman at the age of ninety in 2004, he was laid to rest on a hill overlooking Miller Park in Milwaukee, not far from his old press-box perch at Milwaukee County Stadium, which itself went to ballpark heaven after the 2000 season.

Lew Burdette got a big hug from Fred Haney and mumbled that he felt, "just sort of wonderfully tired." He affectionately pinched his kewpie manager's cheek. Fred Haney was right—his players loved him when they saw those World Series checks. The World Series full share was worth the princely sum of $8,900 to each Braves player, a plum when the average major league annual salary ranged between $8,000 and $15,000. Burdette won a Corvette as World Series Most Valuable Player and made an additional $20,000 in endorsements. Nobody could say he didn't earn his reward. He was the only man to ever pitch a Game 7 shutout against the New York Yankees at Yankee Stadium on two days' rest. Burdette won three games in the series, pitched two consecutive shutouts and 24 consecutive scoreless innings. It was the best World Series performance by a starting pitcher since Christy Mathewson's legendary three-shutout performance in the 1905 World Series. He remains the last pitcher to throw consecutive complete-game shutouts in the World Series.

Burdette's accomplishment is standing up well in history. As of this writing, it has been fifty-five years since he made like Matty. There had been only fifty-two years between Mathewson and Burdette. He won 203 career games and twenty in a season twice, but his World Series brilliance has yet to be equaled. He is not in the Hall of Fame, and this bothers his most famous former teammate. "Burdette is a pitcher I think should be in the Hall of Fame," Henry Aaron said in 2011. "That's my opinion. I think he pitched well enough that he should be in there."

Lou Perini was moved to tears. He was one of the last great owners in baseball history, a visionary who believed in the fans and who, like Burdette, belongs in the Hall of Fame. If you are reading this book in a major league city outside of New York, Boston, Chicago, St. Louis, Pittsburgh, Philadelphia, Cleveland, Detroit, or Cincinnati, then you owe your baseball team to Lou Perini's bold decision to move the Boston Braves to Milwaukee in 1953, which sparked the evolution of the game you know.

Baseball became a truly national game because of the 1953–1957 Milwaukee Braves. They ignited evolution. Before Lou Perini and the Braves, the thought of major league baseball teams in Texas or Florida or Arizona was far-fetched. The Braves victory in 1957 brought balance back to the game. New dynasties emerged in new markets. Baseball eventually came to Canada and the Pacific Northwest and the Rocky Mountains. The Pacific Coast League towns became big league cities. Get your map and find your teams. There were five franchise relocations in the years immediately following the Braves, and that was just the start. New ballparks sprouted across the land and have since spawned replacement parks in the same cities. Teams demand new ballparks before they reach the crumbling status of Boston Braves Field or New York's Polo Grounds or Brooklyn's Ebbets Field. Hey, they even got rid of the original Yankee Stadium. One day, Fenway and Wrigley will bite the dust, too. You can cry and so will I. But you can thank the team that is now the Atlanta Braves for proving that population shifts and emerging markets are not to be ignored. Someday, when the Major Leagues expand to Japan and put the Japanese Leagues out of business the way they did the Negro Leagues, you'll be able to point to Perini's Braves. Someday, when Major League Baseball has a Caribbean Division that plays in-season, you'll be able to thank Perini's Braves. Once baseball got global, corporate and economic expansion in its blood, it never lost the lust. I'll stop short of predicting a team on the moon, but look me up when the travel technology catches up. I hope they play in a domed stadium. Otherwise, the sun glare will be brutal.

Then, now, and in the future, Lou Perini's contributions remain vast and strong. International play, interleague play, expanded playoffs, roster diversity, the age of new ballparks, competitive balance, teams outside of New York and Boston getting a chance to win—all are Lou Perini's baseball legacies. Bud Selig, who grew up with Lou Perini's Milwaukee Braves, later became the owner who brought the Brewers back to Milwaukee and restored Milwaukee as a National League city. As commissioner, he initiated the revolutionary ideas that had their origins not with Major League Baseball, but with Lou Perini. The humble Perini always kept his personal touch. When Perini died in 1972, Henry Aaron gave tribute at his memorial service:

> I'm awful proud that I was invited here to pay tribute to one of the greatest men that I ever had the chance to know in baseball. I'd like to say that at the time I knew Mr. Perini when I was playing in Milwaukee, of course, and in Atlanta, he'd done an awful lot for me. I can remember the time—in 1957, of course, when we won the pennant—that we shared some of the greatest moments—I still have the picture hanging in my basement. I was also happy to have the chance to talk with Mr. Perini and sit down with him, because he was particularly concerned about me, because when I came up I was a very young kid and he would often speak to some of the baseball writers about me and, of course, he always said a kind word about me. I remember when my daughter was born with a little infantile paralysis and he was particularly concerned about her. He would often speak about her. He would often speak about Children's Hospital here. He would also speak about the Jimmy Fund. He would want the ballplayers to come here and play in this Jimmy Fund game and, of course, every ballplayer that I can remember willingly came here with his heart open to play in this Jimmy Fund game. I would just like to say to Mrs. Perini that I'm happy to have known such a great family and happy that I was associated with such a great man. Thank you very much.

The Milwaukee Braves were the dynasty that could have been. They blew it by one game in 1956, won it all in 1957, blew a 3-1 World Series lead against the Yankees in 1958, and lost a one-game playoff to the Los Angeles Dodgers in 1959. "We would be getting a lot more credit than we got, because we should have been in four straight World Series," Frank Torre lamented. But when foam comes off the beer, it stays flat. Milwaukee never drew two million fans again after the 1957 season, and you can thank a lot of factors, starting with the genius idea of banning carry-in beer to the ballpark, the practice that put the Braves on the map. In the years follow-ing 1957, everything the Braves had done right, they were doing wrong. By 1960, Fred Haney was gone, and Charlie Dressen was manager. He loved to talk about how great the Dodgers were, and Spahn and Burdette hated the guy so much that they said they'd lose games if it helped get him fired. John Quinn, the general manager, was forced out and went to Philadel-phia. Lou Perini sold the floundering team to an interest from Atlanta, and the Braves were gone from Milwaukee after the 1965 season. They were bush league all over again, so thank God for the Packers and Vince Lom-bardi. "We really came close when the Braves left in never seeing Major League baseball again in Milwaukee," Selig said. It took some time and that old spirit Selig picked up from Perini.

Selig got a team from Seattle in town. They became the Milwaukee Brewers, harkening back to the old minor league nickname. The factors that allowed a club back into Milwaukee were born when Perini took the Braves into town in the first place. As a result, Henry Aaron got to finish his career in a Milwaukee uniform. Robin Yount went from Taft High School to shortstop in about a year. I used to sit behind him in the cheap seats when he played center field at County Stadium. Paul Molitor—the only guy besides DiMaggio who could hit without a trigger in his swing—banged his way to the Hall of Fame in Milwaukee. The 39-game hitting streak, the 13-0 start—and oh, yes—as of 2011, the Brewers won 96 games, which was not only a franchise record, but a Milwaukee record, beating the 95 wins in 1957. When Ryan Braun hit the home run in the pennant-winning game in 2011, Bob Uecker's call sounded an awful lot like Earl Gillespie's call of Aaron's home run to win the 1957 pennant. The Brewers drew three million fans in 2011 and, as in the 1950s, people from around the country wonder how the majors' smallest market does that. I can assure you, these fans are loyal. Roll out the Barrel. Some things never change. The Milwaukee Brewers got to the World Series in 1982 and lost. They have not been back since. If you ever want to get the crap kicked out of you at a pub in Milwaukee, stand up and announce you're a St. Louis Cardinals fan. Eddie Mathews will fight with you in spirit.

When the Braves won in 1957, Casey Stengel came to the Braves dressing room and congratulated Fred Haney, the little leader who was finally a big shot. Casey told him to stand on a stepstool, and the smallest manager in the big leagues was the tallest man in the room, on a pedestal at last. Haney never won the World Series again, but at least he had a major league championship ring to go along with his 1952 Pacific Coast League ring. He died in 1977, two years after his old friend, Stengel, and he left a legacy of leadership that would have made him proud. Six of his players from the 1957 Milwaukee Braves and one little brother became major league managers. Del Crandall, Red Schoendienst, Eddie Mathews, Del Rice, Joe Adcock, Chuck Tanner, and Joe Torre eventually followed in Fred's footsteps.

The party in Milwaukee roared all day and into the night, gaining steam through the hours, beer in the blood of the locals. The Braves were World Champs, and it seemed like V-J Day one more time for the parents and the start of something new for the kids. It's a safe bet that some of the kids in the conga lines did more than the bunny hop that night. They wrote slogans that became memorable one-liners to their Midwest generation, war cries such as *"Yanks are bush leaguers!" "Bushers 5, Yanks 0,"* or most pointedly, *"Bushville Wins!"*

The kids of the 1960s learned to make noise during the 1957 World Series. When the Braves returned home, 750,000 fans jammed Mitchell Field. Crowds estimated at one million overran police barricades around the city. The cops gave up, but they didn't worry. The only fire was Bushville burning, pride in the heartland, summed up by a headline in the tiny *Walworth Times*:

THEM'S OUR BOYS!
THEY GAVE THE YANKS BUSH LEAGUE TREATMENT
BRAVES 5 YANKS 0

The Braves made the cover of *Life* magazine on October 14, 1957. One fan told *Life*, "We're hicks, but we're nice hicks." At the time of this writing, Milwaukee is still waiting to throw another World Series victory party, but in the meantime, Wisconsin has kept its championship voice strong, thanks to the Green Bay Packers. The ancestral roots of the unquestionably loyal Green Bay Packers fans can be seen in the Milwaukee Braves. The Heartland community that will support players they have never met like they are members of the blood family can be seen in the story of the season Bushville won it all.

No team has ever repeated the story of the 1957 Milwaukee Braves, and few teams can claim four players like Henry Aaron, Eddie Mathews, Warren Spahn, and Lew Burdette peaking at the right time. No teammates hit more home runs together than Aaron and Mathews, 813 for those of you scoring at home. The 1957 Braves gave us Henry Aaron, of whom Warren Spahn once said, "Henry could do anything he wanted to do. If he had wanted to be a pitcher, he could have been a 20-game winner. He wanted to be a complete ballplayer, so he stole 40 bases. He wanted to outdo Mathews, so he became a home run hitter. Who ever thought he would be a home run hitter? He wanted to be the best and he had both the ability and the desire to do it. He was so great, I thought he'd hit .400 someday."

He didn't. He settled for 755 home runs, but ask him where his heart is. He never forgot what this town, team, and time meant to him. When Eddie Mathews died, Henry sent the largest bouquet in the room and never told a soul. Henry Aaron, while proud of everything he ever achieved with a baseball bat in his hands, fondly remembers where he came from. "The Milwaukee years," Henry said, "were a very beautiful time."

Hours after Game 7, legend has it that Casey Stengel paced naked in his office. People thought he was talking to himself. "That pitcher, that god-damned pitcher," he muttered over and over. "He made us look awful." Stengel had lost the World Series before, but few World Series losses haunted him like 1957, not even 1960, which got him fired. The Braves won the pennant again in 1958 with mostly the same cast of screwballs, sluggers, and beer swiggers, but this time, Mighty Casey had his revenge and was very, very polite to the Milwaukee fans in the process. He led the Yankees back from the brink of elimination. The Yankee historians don't talk about

1958 too much, because for the Yanks to cry revenge would be to remember 1957 and admit that somebody beat them in the first place. That's just not the Yankee way. "You made your moves like the master you are," Ty Cobb wrote to Casey Stengel in previously unpublished letter dated December 1958. "Hope Fred Haney will never know that, while I love him, and he broke in and played for me, I am for the league I played in."

It was Stengel's seventh World Series title to tie him with Joe McCarthy for the most pennants in Yankee history, but thanks to the Milwaukee Braves (with an assist from the '60 Pirates), he ain't alone in first place like he so desperately wanted. Perhaps he never should have muttered something about bush league . . . whether he muttered it or not, sort of like if Burdette ever threw the spitball or not.

Wait a minute! We can't end the book without finding out for sure if Burdette threw the spitball, can we? This book is published in 2012 and Burdette died in 2007, which presents an interesting problem. Some people believe the legend of the spitter has kept Burdette out of the Hall of Fame, and truth be told, some old-timers on the Veteran's Committee are probably still pissed off at Lew for being Lew. I know what Eddie Mathews would say to the veterans who have opposed his admission.

Bob Uecker, who became a Milwaukee institution as the Brewers' Hall of Fame announcer, caught Burdette when he made it to the big leagues with the Milwaukee Braves in 1962. So, Ueck, did Burdette throw the spitter?

"Oh, Burdette was a hell of a pitcher!" Uecker said. "Not only him with the spitter. They all did it. Drysdale! The worst! But those guys, they all threw it. I caught Burdette. I loaded the ball. Crandall did it. Joe Torre did it. Ask Joe Torre. Tug on the chest protector. Burdette, you'd tug on the chest protector if you wanted one loaded, just so he'd know it was coming or he would tug on his cap if he had one loaded."

Some catchers, however, will take Burdette's secret with them.

"You'd have to ask him," Joe Torre said.

He was keenly aware that Lew Burdette was not available for comment.

Del?

"I cannot say in all good conscience," Crandall said.

Lew?

Lew?

You want to get your two cents in before you crack another beer with the buddies?

"I got more pleasure out of throwing the spitball than anything else," he said in a tape-recorded 1991 interview. I'm amazed he didn't burn the guy's recorder.

But then, of course, Burdette sowed the seeds of doubt.

"Hitters are so egotistical," he said. "They all look for an excuse when they make an out." But in reality, Burdette's spitball was a very important pitch to him. He would never throw spitter after spitter, but he would save it for big situations. Warren Spahn, Burdette's roomie, admired Burdette's ability to thrive in moments like that. Spahn, won 363 games, more victories than any left-hander in major league history, but one season meant more than all of them. They were buddies until the end. Burdette and Spahn both wore hearing aids later in life, once leading Burdette to joke that it didn't matter how much shit each guy gave the other anymore. They couldn't hear it anyway, but "Hey, Asshole!" said with a warm smile wasn't very hard to lip-read. Before Spahn died in 2003, he gave his 1957 World Series ring to his son. "I wear that ring often," Greg Spahn said. "Before Dad passed, he said, 'I want you to wear this and feel good about it.'"

The other half of the Asshole Buddies, Eddie Mathews and Bob Buhl, died two days apart from each other in 2001. So that means that they had a two-year head start on Spahn and a five-year head start on Burdette. That was always the game—Eddie and Buhl took a head start in a taxi and Spahnie and Burdette had to come find them in some hole-in-the-wall bar. Burdette was last to the party. I hope they saved him one.

About a decade after the 1957 World Series, Stengel saw Spahn and Burdette late one night at a hotel bar. Burdette remembered this reunion with Stengel very well.

"Fellas," Stengel called to Spahn and Burdette.

Spahn and Burdette stopped in their tracks. They were fluent in Stengelese. They knew that Stengel calling them "fellas" and not "fellers" was Casey's highest compliment. It meant he would have loved them. It meant they could have played for him. It meant they could have been "letter mailers," for him. A letter mailer was to Stengel what an Asshole Buddy was to Milwaukee. It meant a night owl, a guy who liked to drink and have a good time. Mickey and Whitey were letters mailers, just like Spahnie, Burdette, Eddie, and Buhl, as in, "I know he ain't one to go out at three o'clock in the morning just to mail a letter."

But Casey had something very important to get off his chest before he was dead. "I want to tell you fellas something," he said. "You two are the worst two trades I ever made in my life.

"Now let's have a beer."

ACKNOWLEDGMENTS

Once, when I was about twelve years old, my mom took me to a baseball card show in Pasadena. She spotted a short elderly man with a bald head and a round tummy waiting for his taxicab. He was thirty pounds heavier than his playing weight, but she instantly recognized him. She tapped me on the shoulder and said, "That's Warren Spahn."

Wise guy that I was, I immediately said, nope, Lady, you got the wrong guy. Alas, little did I know that my mom grew up in Milwaukee during the 1950s, the heyday of what fans called "Brave Land." She walked me over and said, "Hello, Mr. Spahn," as if she had known him for years. "Hello, ma'am," he said, as if he, too, had known her for years.

Milwaukee and its fans had that connection, and as for me, it wasn't everyday that I said hello to a 363-game winner. Spahnie had a feel for kids, put me at ease, and asked me if I wanted to see his 1957 World Series ring. I sure did, so Spahnie pulled it off his finger and to my great amazement, dropped it into my palm and said, "Here you go."

So here we are, years later, and looking back, I can see the moment when this story was handed down to me. When I visited Milwaukee every summer as a kid, I once saw a Milwaukee Braves hat in someone's garage and was stunned to learn that, wait a minute, the Braves played here? And Henry Aaron played here? Huh, no kidding. You think you got the world solved when you're twelve.

I would not have been able to do this without the support and cooperation of five starters of the 1957 Milwaukee Braves, whose combined interviews with me help shape this book. My sincerest thank you to Henry

Aaron, Del Crandall, Frank Torre, Johnny Logan, and Red Schoendienst for their time and cooperation.

In particular, I'd like to thank Mr. Aaron for graciously helping me with this book and sharing with readers and fans exactly what made this town, team, and time so special. I very much would have liked to have seen you hit in the 1950s. It's the hands, the swing plane, the bat control, and the sound of contact I'd want to study most.

Special thanks also to Roland Hemond, one of my baseball mentors. Thank you to David Perini, Mr. Lou Perini's son, for sharing memories, photos, and writings, including Henry Aaron's never-before published tribute to Lou Perini. Thank you to Richard and Stuart Chapman, sportswriter Lou Chapman's sons, and Richard's wife, Nancy, for sharing Lou's photos, letters, and documents, including the never-before published letters written by Jackie Robinson and Henry Aaron. Thank you to Greg Spahn, Warren's son, for sharing his memories and a Spahnie363 beer. Thank you to Bob Uecker for a memorable interview at Dodger Stadium. Thank you to Dusty Baker—Spider and Mr. Wight would be very proud of your baseball career.

Thanks also to the following folks who helped in various ways: Ron Anderson, Jim Baggett, Adrian Burgos, Rod Nelson, Jim Sandoval, Buster Staniland, Joe Torre, George Genovese, Paul Pettit, Rick Schroeder, Jeff Flannery, Bill Deane, Jim Kaplan, Jon Eig, David Kelly, Dick Cole, Red Murff, Bob Case, Rob Goldman, Tommy Ferguson, Pat Kelly, Harry Minor, Chris Walker, Shannon O'Neill, Anne Bensson, Mark Frost, Cait Murphy, plus my all friends in baseball whose words, wisdom, and relationships are greatly valued.

Thanks to David Maraniss to Rafe Sagalyn to Pete Wolverton—this is Tinker to Evers to Chance, or actually, the Logan to Schoendienst to Torre of this book. Maraniss, I heard you wanted to grow up to be Logan, but at least I got you in the same sentence. Rafe is Red—a pro's pro, can't win without him, or as Henry Aaron said of the real Red, the missing piece to the puzzle. Pete Wolverton at Thomas Dunne Books fielded with style any balls I threw in the dirt.

To my wife Jen—hey, honey, how many of these things do you think we can pull off? Thanks for your endless hours and that rugged two-day hitch at the Library of Congress, as well as transcribing, reading, editing, and researching. My name is on it, but it's your book, too, because I'm here to say I couldn't do it without you, or as we joke around here, "Spahn and Burdette." Oh, wait, I almost forgot: love you!

Lastly, this book really belongs to my mom, Robin Kathleen Kumferman, the first of eight children, a mom to 'em all, who grew up in Milwaukee, during the good years of the Braves. She once told me that she pulled a team-photo baseball card out of the pack and, when asked on the playground what players she had, she said all of them. She wasn't lying because the whole team was on the card. That gag amused her endlessly. She encouraged me to relentlessly chase writing and baseball careers no matter who or what stood in my way. If I said to my mom, "The kid was ninety-one with late life," she not only knew what I meant, but had read so many of my scouting stories that she might ask me what kind of life, for the sheer thrill of seeing the question stun me. (For the record, sink and tail.)

I lost my mom the summer I wrote this and it hurt. She was the best mom a baseball kid could have, and before she died, she heard me read Henry Aaron hitting the home run to win the pennant.

SOURCE NOTES

PRIMARY INTERVIEWS CONDUCTED IN 2011: Henry Aaron, Del Crandall, Johnny Logan, Red Schoendienst, Frank Torre, Roland Hemond, Bob Uecker, Richard Chapman, David Perini, Greg Spahn.

PRIMARY NEWSPAPERS: *Milwaukee Journal, Milwaukee Sentinel, The New York Times, New York Post, New York Daily News, New York Herald-Tribune, New York Daily Mirror, New York World Telegraph & Sun, Sporting News, Los Angeles Times, Christian Science Monitor, The Washington Post, Hartford Courant, The Boston Globe, Chicago Tribune, Chicago Defender, Pittsburgh Courier, Mobile Advocate, Birmingham News, Atlanta Daily World, Baltimore Afro-American, Santa Barbara News-Press, Oakland Tribune, Long Beach Press-Telegram, Pittsburgh Post-Gazette,* and *Baseball Digest.*

PRIMARY ARCHIVES: The Branch Rickey Papers at the Library of Congress
The Perini Papers, National Baseball Hall of Fame
SABR interview audio files: Lew Burdette, Warren Spahn, and Joe Adcock

PRIMARY BOOKS: *Willie's Boys,* by John Klima (John Wiley, 2009)
"Deal of the Century" by John Klima, in *The Best American Sports Writing* (Houghton-Mifflin, 2007).
We Would Have Played for Nothing, by Fay Vincent (Simon & Shuster, 2008).

The 500 Home Run Club, by Bob Allen and Bill Gilbert (Sports Publishing Inc., 1999).

The Braves, The Pick and The Shovel by Al Hirsh (Waverly House, 1948).

Barnstorming to Heaven: Syd Pollock and His Great Black Teams, by Alan J. Pollock (University of Alabama Press, 2006).

Eddie Mathews and the National Pastime, by Eddie Mathews and Bob Buege (Douglas American Sports Publications, 1994).

PRIMARY WEB SITES: www.retrosheet.org
www.baseball-reference.com

INDEX